CANADA

LAKE of the WOODS

RED LAKE

MINNESOTA

RED RIVER of the NORTH

LAKE SUPERIOR

Ft. Abercrombie

GULL LAKE

MILLE LACS LAKE

Crow Wing Agency

Ft. Ripley

LAKE TRAVERSE

St. CROIX RIVER

St. Cloud

MISSISSIPPI RIVER

WISCONSIN

BIG STONE LAKE

Camp Release

Acton

C QUI PARLE

St. Paul

Ft. Snelling

MINNESOTA

Upper Agency

Ft. Ridgely

Shakopee

Red Wing

Lower Agency

RIVER

St. Peter

Faribault

New Ulm

Mankato

MISSISSIPPI RIVER

IOWA

ALSO BY SCOTT W. BERG

*Grand Avenues:*
*The Story of Pierre Charles L'Enfant,*
*the French Visionary Who Designed Washington, D.C.*

# 38 Nooses

# 38 Nooses

Lincoln, Little Crow, and
the Beginning of the Frontier's End

SCOTT W. BERG

PANTHEON BOOKS, NEW YORK

Pantheon Books and colophon are registered trademarks of Random House, Inc.

Library of Congress Cataloging-in-Publication Data

Berg, Scott W.
38 nooses : Lincoln, Little Crow, and the beginning of the frontier's end /
Scott W. Berg.
p. cm.
Includes bibliographical references and index.
ISBN 978-0-307-37724-1
1. Dakota Indians—Wars, 1862–1865. 2. Lincoln, Abraham, 1809–1865—Relations
with Dakota Indians. 3. Little Crow, d. 1863. 4. Dakota Indians—Government
relations—History—19th century. 5. Dakota Indians—Relocation. 6. Executions
and executioners—United States—History—19th century. I. Title. II. Title:
Thirty-eight nooses.
E83.86.B47 2012    973.7—dc23    2012002807

www.pantheonbooks.com

Illustrations courtesy of Library of Congress—pages 41, 141, 234, 263;
Meserve-Kunhardt Foundation—pages 61, 121; Minnesota Historical Society—
pages 5, 23, 46, 47, 49, 89, 104, 109, 117, 161, 191, 238, 241, 247, 248, 250, 281, 289; National
Archives and Records Administration—page 148; *St. Paul Pioneer Press*—page 17

Endpaper map by Paul Gormont
Jacket image: *Execution of Dakota Indians, Mankato, Minnesota, 1884,*
by J. Thullen (detail). Minnesota Historical Society.
Jacket design by Brian Barth
Book design by Soonyoung Kwon

Printed in the United States of America
First Edition

2 4 6 8 9 7 5 3 1

For Mom and Dad

# CONTENTS

# INTRODUCTION

On the bright May afternoon in 1786 when his family would be shattered and the course of his newborn country forever altered, Mordecai Lincoln was fifteen years old. The Lincolns lived on the frontier in the far western portion of Virginia, a region called Kentucky, most likely from a Wyandot or Iroquoian word meaning "land of tomorrow" or "place of meadows." They were pioneers, and like all pioneers in the Ohio River Valley during the late eighteenth century, they were lucky just to be alive. Four years earlier the Lincoln family had crossed through the Cumberland Gap, following a trail first blazed by Daniel Boone, and today Mordecai and his brothers—Josiah, thirteen, and Thomas, eight—were assisting their father as he enclosed a cornfield, working to carve out an ever-larger pocket of civilization on a parcel of land beside Long Run, a branch of a branch of a branch of the Ohio River east of the new settlement of Louisville.

As the boys helped to position the top rail of a new fence, a shot sounded. Their father tumbled to the ground and out of the woods emerged two or three Indians. Mordecai picked up his father's rifle and barked at Josiah to run as fast as he could to the community stockade called Hughes Station, fifteen minutes distant, to sound the alarm. Josiah ran and so did Mordecai, who reached the cabin his father had built just as he heard his other brother cry out. He turned to see Thomas, grasped by the hair and trousers, being carried toward the tree line. Mordecai required only a moment's look, and perhaps not even that, to know that the Indians didn't intend to kill Thomas. They intended to take him. Mordecai leveled his gun and aimed for a sun glint of metal in the late afternoon sun, a half-moon pendant dangling against the chest of his brother's would-be captor. The teenager's aim was remarkable; that, or luck was with him. The Indian went down; his companions vanished; Thomas was unhurt.

Many years later, Thomas's son Abraham, risen higher in the world than any member of the Lincoln clan could have ever dared imagine, would call this story "the legend more strongly than all others imprinted upon my mind and memory." Abraham Lincoln, namesake of his murdered grandfather, would never say much about his own early years in Kentucky, embarrassed into a lifetime of silence by his family's shiftlessness and poverty. Yet this story, of his grandfather killed by Indians, was told often enough and in enough detail that Lincoln's longtime law partner, William Herndon, collecting a book's worth of reminiscences of the late president, was able to record no fewer than six versions from four different tellers, all second- and thirdhand accounts tracing back to Thomas or Mordecai.

Like so many pieces of frontier color, the Lincolns' tale of death and attempted abduction was the story of westward expansion in miniature, tightly intertwined with breathless assumptions about the savagery of Indians and the march of civilization. For Abraham Lincoln, it was nothing less than the bedrock of the log-cabin posturing that had helped to push him toward the highest office in the land. "Owing to my father being left an orphan at the age of six years, in poverty, and in a new country," he wrote in 1848, during his single term as a United States representative, "he became a wholly uneducated man; which I suppose is the reason why I know so little of our family history." The future president rued the loss of a childhood spent on his grandfather's trim and ordered farm, and worse yet, the elder Abraham's early death represented an irrecoverable severing from the old Lincoln line and its history of military service, respectable fortune-seeking, and honorable English heritage. Writing in the third person for a campaign autobiography in 1860, framing his personal history for the American electorate, he said, "By the early death of his father and very narrow circumstances of his mother, even in childhood [Thomas was] a wandering, laboring boy," and described his own childhood, using a line from Thomas Gray's "Elegy Written in a Country Church-Yard," as " 'the short and simple annals of the poor.' " In the same document, Lincoln also presented the death of his grandfather as the wellspring of his lifelong obsession with self-instruction: "He regrets his want of education, and does what he can to supply the want."

Had Mordecai not shot so accurately, Thomas would have been carried off into a void. In Thomas's and Mordecai's tellings, the Indians emerge from that void, *are* that void. They pop out of the trees and act with the undifferentiating violence of nature, to whose embrace they return. They are without face, form, history, or agenda. No part of the story told to the future president by his father and uncle appears to have addressed why these particular Indians would have killed his grandfather and attempted to make off with Thomas. But in reality the encounter was not sudden, nor was it one-sided or unaccountable. In 1786, Kentucky was still contested territory, a frontier fringed with a fuzzy border and suffused with a moral ambiguity that would dog the continent's expansion every mile of the way. Even by the free-for-all standards of frontier settlement, Kentucky did not really belong to anyone.

The men attempting to make off with Thomas were most likely Shawnees. Occupying the land across the Ohio River near where Cincinnati would soon rise—what in the eighteenth century they called "our country"—the Shawnees were the tribe of the young Tecumseh, frontline combatants in a decades-old war, renowned among whites and other Indian tribes for their fearlessness, adaptability, resolve, and physical prowess. For many years the Shawnees had been on the move, shifting westward from river to river as they chose retrenchment and survival over a final, desperate stand that might mark the end of their independence. During the quarter century before and during the American Revolution, they had fought to keep the British and then the Americans east of the Ohio River against odds that grew by the decade, odds lengthened by the lethal combination of superior guns and epidemic diseases carried by their opponents. The Shawnees viewed themselves as a people fighting less for land or honor than for freedom, a prize for which they fought in ruthless ways, burning cabins with settlers inside, defiling dead bodies, and preferring attack by ambush whenever possible, hitting hard and backing off in a cycle designed to create maximum fear and disruption while minimizing Indian losses.

The Shawnees weren't "bloodthirsty." On the contrary, they could demonstrate many years of gift exchange, trade relationships, and personal friendships with whites to prove their amicable, if guarded, approach. But those times were past. In the 1780s, a series of murders and depredations by white militia had devastated several riverside villages and enraged many Shawnees, who responded to the loss of a young son or daughter by an old code, one that involved taking a white child in kind and raising it as their own. This, in all likelihood, was Thomas Lincoln's intended fate.

Before 1860 and his election to the presidency, Abraham Lincoln's life intersected events on the Indian frontier so seldom—just twice, in fact—that those intersections serve as a convenient pair of narrative benchmarks. The first was the death of his grandfather; the second occurred in 1832, when Lincoln, twenty-three, volunteered as a soldier during the Black Hawk War and was elected captain of his unit, his first taste of popularity at the polls. He would many years later describe his selection as "a success which gave me more pleasure than any I have had since." The Black Hawk War took the lives of seventy-seven whites and at least six hundred Sac and Fox Indians, many of them women and children who drowned or were killed in a chaotic retreat across the Mississippi River. Lincoln himself saw no battle but did come upon the mutilated corpses of white soldiers and settlers. He never wrote or spoke about these encounters, turning instead to satirical jokes about military life and tales of his wrestling prowess against more physically gifted opponents.

These yarns reached the floor of the House of Representatives in 1848, when, while making fun of the military exploits of Democratic presidential candidate Lewis Cass in the Black Hawk War, Lincoln took a poke at his own.

> It is quite certain I did not break my sword, for I had none to break; but I bent a musket pretty badly on one occasion. If General Cass went in advance of me in picking huckleberries, I guess I surpassed him in charges upon the wild onions. If he saw any live, fighting Indians, it was more than I did; but I had a good many blood struggles with the musquetoes; and, although I never fainted from loss of blood, I can truly say I was often very hungry.

During this same legislative session he would entertain reporters with similarly lighthearted stories of his early soldiering, and during his presidency he was fond of telling thrilling tales of "Indians and frontiersmen" to his sons and their playmates.

The benign folksiness of Lincoln's passing encounter with the realities of frontier war was cemented once and for all by Carl Sandburg, whose multivolume biography of Lincoln included a Parson Weems–style tale of the future president challenging his men to a fight in order to protect an old and hungry Indian who had wandered into their camp. Based on a fragmented description collected thirty-four years after the action, this has become the most famous story associating Lincoln with Indians, trotted out to emphasize his bravery and compassion.

During the 1840s and 1850s, the pathways bearing white settlers continued to wind their way westward, treaty by treaty, displaced tribe by displaced tribe. By the second year of the Civil War, one prominent arm of this migratory movement had arrived in the Northwest, not far away from where the Mississippi River began, in a raw, beautiful, brand-new state called Minnesota, a name derived from a Dakota word referring to the clarity of lake water. In August 1862, as Confederate forces moved mile by mile toward Washington, D.C., and Lincoln struggled to connect the actions of Union armies to the moral exigencies of emancipation, he would once more be forced to consider the collision of whites and Indians on the frontier. The Dakota War first came to the president's desk as one far-off manifestation of an imagined Confederate conspiracy and ended with his decision to spare the lives of 265 condemned Indians while sending 38 others to their deaths on a single scaffold in what still stands as the largest mass execution in the country's history.

The conventional narrative of United States–Indian conflict paints the Civil War as a time of suspension, an interim during which the manpower and industrial wealth of the Union had to finish subjugating the rebellious South before the federal government could return its attention to the tribes of the West. But violence between whites and a number of Indian nations was very much a part of the historical fabric of the early 1860s. By the time of the Confederate surrender at Appomattox and Lincoln's assassination in 1865, Indian wars in the Southwest had seen the Long Walk of the Navajo and the murder of friendly Cheyennes at Sand Creek, as well as the opening of extended campaigns against the Paiutes, Shoshoni, Arapaho, Apaches, and other tribes. Before any of these events, however, the Dakota uprising and Christmas executions of 1862 sparked the sequence of confrontations called the Indian Wars of the Northwest, which would culminate in such indelible moments as the Battle of Little Big Horn, the flight of

# Introduction

Chief Joseph, the killing of Crazy Horse, and the tragedy at Wounded Knee.

Just as whites discovered after battling the Shawnees in Ohio and Kentucky and the Sac and Fox in Illinois and Wisconsin, there was no final clarity to be extracted out of the potent brew of fear, danger, hopelessness, anger, and injustice that boiled over in Minnesota in 1862. There is only bravery and cowardice, kindness and hatred, forgiveness and vengeance, a story full of larger-than-life characters that begins with a predawn meeting on the prairie along the Minnesota River, where an aging village chieftain is asked to make the most difficult choice of a remarkable lifetime.

# A NOTE ABOUT NAMES

The people whites called the "Sioux" were not a single entity but rather a collection of tribes, bands, and villages loosely bound by language, custom, and kinship. In 1862, the largest major division, the Lakota, numbered over twenty thousand people and lived farthest west, up to and beyond the Missouri River, including the lands they called the *Pahá Sápa,* or the Black Hills. The Yankton and Yanktonais made up the Western Dakota and generally lived between the Missouri River and the Red River of the North, which divided the state of Minnesota from the Dakota Territory. These three are part of the multitudinous group known to white history as the Plains Indians, the buffalo-hunting tribes into which Sitting Bull, Crazy Horse, Black Elk, and Red Cloud were born.

The peoples most involved in the Dakota War, the Eastern Dakota, lived in Minnesota in a very different ecosystem made of tallgrass prairie and deciduous woodlands. Here the soil was rich and black and the waters hospitable to great quantities of fish and game. Moving roughly west to east down the length of the Minnesota River, the four major bands of Eastern Dakotas were called the Sissetons, Wahpetons, Mdewakantons, and Wahpekutes. In Eastern Dakota bands, individual villages were often known to whites by the name of their best-known and most influential residents: Wabasha's village, Shakopee's village, Little Crow's village, and so on.

The name of "Sioux" was given to the Dakota by the Ojibwe, their longtime rivals for the northern woods and waterways, before the word was co-opted by whites. While many Dakotas in the nineteenth century used the term themselves, I have given preference to the term

## A Note About Names

Dakota and the various band names (for example, Mdewakanton), reserving "Sioux" only for quoted material. I have also sometimes used "Indian" as a descriptor rather than the more accurate "Native American," "American Indian," or "First Peoples," simply because that trio of terms was not generally in use in 1862. I recognize that times and terminology have changed.

# 38 Nooses

# Chapter One

He heard them coming, more than a hundred strong, in the small hours before daybreak. The air was warm and thick over the reservation, where a series of Dakota villages were strung like beads along the government road that paralleled the southern bank of the Minnesota River. At the center of one of these villages, the one bearing his own name, the aging chief listened to the sound of gathering feet outside, listened to the call of his name and the sound of knives scraping the hide of his buffalo-skin tepee.

Like any Dakota of renown, the man who emerged from his lodge to find himself standing in the sudden heart of the Dakota world had many names. Owner of the frame house that stood nearly complete beside his tepee, at fifty-two he was still entitled to an honored position in council even if his influence had lately been on the wane. Whites had first known him as Taoyateduta, translated most often as His Red Nation; on assuming the leadership of his village he had added his father's title of Kangicistina. This meant Little Raven, a name shared by his father, grandfather, and great-grandfather, though whites and most Dakotas speaking English used Little Crow instead.

The multiplicity of names was fitting, for Little Crow seemed to have lived several lives, a cultural and historical amalgamation dressed in the collared white shirt of the white man while sporting the long hair of a Dakota warrior. A living atlas of place, change, and identity, Little Crow had seen more of America than any other person gathered in his yard this summer morning, probably more than any other Dakota alive. To the west, past the rise in the land called the Coteau des Prairies and onto the high, dry plains of the Dakota Territory, Little Crow had hunted elk and buffalo and traded whiskey and furs. To the east, in Washington, D.C., he had bargained with presidents and cabinet secretaries, and been fascinated by the urban centers and technological marvels he discovered en route.

He had survived two smallpox epidemics, played an instrumental role in negotiating treaties ceding millions of acres of Dakota homeland in exchange for annuity payments, and endured the catastrophic thinning of fox and beaver populations that left his people dependent on the United States government and its promises of gold coins and good faith. He had treated, traded, hunted, and politicked with whites, but he declined to cultivate his own farm or to forgo the use of his tepee. He had attended mission churches but had never been baptized a Christian and was a bearer of *wakan*, the Dakota medicine; as a boy he had fasted and prayed and smoked until visited by his spirit animal, the raven, after which he received an otter-skin medicine bag he would keep until the end of his life. To bear *wakan* meant a great deal that would remain forever obscure to outsiders, but at the least it made Little Crow a man of spiritual importance, a healer, a carrier of cultural knowledge, and a keeper of mysteries related to the afterlife.

Striking in appearance, grave in countenance, and famous for his physical endurance, Little Crow was also known for his "restless, unquiet disposition" and for a profligate youth that included several advantageous marriages, a lucrative time in the whiskey trade, a turn as a mercenary in support of American forces, and the frequent demonstration of his skill at cards. In 1845, at thirty-five, he had returned to the Mississippi River from his western travels to assume the chieftainship of his old village after hearing that his father, the third Little Crow and the most widely known of the Mdewakanton Dakota, had died. A small flotilla of allies and kin had followed him down the Minnesota River and onto the Mississippi, bringing him home to the village called Kaposia, which stood across the water from the new white settlement of Saint Paul. There he had found two of his half brothers waiting close to shore, armed and adamant about their own claim to

Taoyateduta, or Little Crow, 1862

the title. Crossing his hands in front of him and refusing to withdraw, Taoyateduta had sustained crippling bullet wounds that left his wrists forever gnarled and bent. His show of bravery won the day: his half brothers departed in ignominy as the new Little Crow's own fame and influence among the Dakota began to rise.

That was many years ago. All Dakotas, young and old, now lived on the far slope of catastrophic change. During Little Crow's childhood, four decades earlier, whites and Dakotas had lived in a rough equilibrium sustained by a long history of council and gift exchange, an active trade in furs, and generations of intermarriage. Then the land had been vast and the human populations far smaller, the lives of frontiersmen and Dakotas connected only weakly to major population centers in the East. Then whites had adjusted to Dakota patterns of life and customs of friendship and exchange. Now the evidence of the Dakotas' own accommodation to the white world surrounded Little Crow in the form of shorn hair, buttoned shirts, tilled fields, and the frame house beside which he and his fellow Dakotas now gathered.

But what whites hoped was happening and what was happening

were never the same thing. Many Dakotas wanted nothing to do with these ever more numerous, insistent, and unfamiliar invaders, even if that fact was wished away by the traders, missionaries, government agents, soldiers, and other whites in the region. A group of fierce young Dakota men, those who once would have been destined for honor as warriors, hunters, and tribal heads, desired a future in which the westward tide of white settlement would be reversed, in which they would take old lands by force in order to restore centuries-old hunting patterns and lifeways, reclaiming their freedom to live and move as they wished. Most of the Dakotas assembled around Little Crow's tepee were his own closest kin, warriors of the Mdewakanton band, and all were agitated and anxious, waiting to learn what would happen next. The moon was lowering toward the western horizon, a storm visible in the distance. Little Crow had been called to council countless times before, but never with so much at stake. Something was ready to flare, like a grass fire rising to catch a high, dry wind.

Four young men stepped forward to tell their story. The day before they had been hunting off the reservation in the Big Woods, a vast wedge of deciduous forest that covered the center of the state and began in the vicinity of a white settlement called Acton, eighty miles to the northeast. Unsuccessful in their pursuit of game and sharing whiskey on the road, they had stopped at a farmer's house with the intention of asking for food and drink before the journey back to the Minnesota River. One of the men found a hen's nest filled with eggs, and out of such a strange, small detail emerged a war. An argument about stealing the eggs, then an accusation of cowardice, and then a dare to shoot the white man: the particulars vary with the telling, but in the end three white men, one woman, and one fifteen-year-old girl lay dead. While the survivors had dashed off to larger settlements to raise an alarm, the four Dakotas had dashed in the other direction, driving across the prairie with a stolen team and wagon through the evening and into the night.

They had returned to their own chief, Red Middle Voice, and their own village, where Rice Creek met the Minnesota River several miles north of Little Crow's tepee. Together they moved downriver to the larger village of Little Six, the youngest of the Mdewakanton Dakota leaders, newly ascended in influence due to the recent death of his father, whose desire to accommodate white ways he had rejected out of hand. After a set of orations and resolutions, Little Six and his warriors had joined the Rice Creek men, walking and riding six more miles down the river road in the darkest hours of the night, gathering men and women from other villages along the way, and sending runners up and down the valley with the message that something enormous was happening. Soon the swelling caravan had reached and crossed the Redwood River just above its junction with the Minnesota, entering Little Crow's village even as the earliest fringe of sunlight emerged in the eastern sky.

After the four young men faced Little Crow and told their story, others spoke in turn to present a list of grievances. None of this talk was new, but the repetition held new power, here on the edge of action. Whites had not delivered treaty payments as promised, had failed to appoint honest traders, had married and abandoned Dakota wives, had raped Dakota women. And, as always, they spoke of the vanished land, the ever-tighter boundaries placed around their territory. Village leaders and others lamented how payments of annuity gold had always arrived with unyielding conditions for Indian behavior and cooperation with white authorities, how white possession of Dakota land had never come with any equivalent provisos. Forced to live under rules, customs, and habits not of their invention, they were finding that those rules had been not been written for their benefit, despite promises to the contrary. They were primed to take vengeance on a system that made them easy picking for anyone properly connected to white government, a stream of opportunists who had little personal investment in the well-being of Dakotas and who, in the words of village chief Big Eagle, "always seemed to say by their manner when they saw an Indian, 'I am much better than you.'"

This fever for retribution ran high among the members of the *tiyo-tipi*, or soldiers' lodge, a council of young men customarily organized to coordinate hunting parties but now, in this time of great pressure, often acting as an independent gathering of hard-line warriors bent on establishing and enforcing tribal traditions while rejecting all white clothes and customs. For decades, Presbyterian missionaries and other whites had observed the occasional *tiyotipi* council, but these meetings were not open to outsiders. Ever more influential among the most disgruntled and angry Dakotas and ever more independent of traditional leadership structures, the soldiers' lodges were now filling with men who felt robbed of their birthright as Dakota men and warriors, men who were ready to fight and willing to die to turn away white encroachment. The members of this newer kind of *tiyotipi* held themselves apart from all but the most fervent traditionalists and mocked their kin who wore collared shirts and took up agriculture, yet they did not view themselves as a splinter group. Their aim was not to split the Dakota into factions but rather to take an action that could unify the tribe, bringing "farmer" Dakotas, warrior Dakotas, and mixed-bloods together again as one against the pressure of outside occupation.

Little Crow listened to everything and said nothing. He understood that these young men were here not for his rifle but for his voice, that it was his life experience that made him so important to the unfolding drama. He was no longer inclined to play the warrior and knew that the hopes of these headstrong young men rested on an illusion. The waves of white settlers crashing against Dakota lands, tens of thousands arriving every year, had risen too high to turn back. Little Crow had seen the evidence firsthand on two long trips to Washington, D.C., four and eight years ago, and had said so. But he was also aware that the killings near Acton would not go unpunished. All Dakotas would be made responsible for the actions of so few. Whatever challenge to a young man's courage had been issued over a nest of eggs was magnified a hundredfold in this final council of the long night. No longer could old and new, Dakota and white, pretend to coexist.

When the arguments were complete, Little Crow faced the four young men back from Acton and scolded them for their intoxication and their impulsiveness. In the sixteen years since taking the chieftainship of his village and winning election as speaker of the Mdewakanton Dakota, Little Crow had cultivated a stubborn realpolitik as the whites came west, first by the hundreds and later by the thousands. His curiosity about white ways was keen, but his accommodations were always cautious. He was one of the first Dakota leaders to embrace government farming programs for his people, but he did not till the land himself. He had attended and left white mission schools; later, several of his children did the same. He was as likely to be described, drawn, or photographed in white dress as in warrior regalia. He had fought in the service of white soldiers but was also a leader of Dakota forays against their traditional enemies, the Ojibwe. He was one of the most influential Dakota chiefs to sign major land-cession treaties, in 1851 and 1858, but also one of the first to argue that the treaties were fraudulently kept. He had never been baptized, but the morning before this fateful council he had attended the Episcopal mission church at the Lower Agency, shaking the priest's hand after the service and chatting amiably.

Little Crow had never been loved for his compromises, but he had once been respected, and here, in the early morning, his considerable power to hold an audience reemerged. The murder of white women, he argued, would bring speedy and indiscriminate retribution down on all of the Dakota, an onslaught they wouldn't be able to withstand. The delayed annuity payments would never arrive. What was left of Dakota lands would be forfeit, and the Dakota would be pushed westward into alien places bereft of game and good soil and any connection to their ancestors' bones.

According to one account, Little Crow had his say and then "blackened his face as a sign of mourning, retired to his teepee and covered his head in sorrow." Painting one's face with charcoal was a traditional gesture of mourning in many tribes, but it seems that Little Crow was also using it to assert his command of the crowd and make a statement about the costs of an action he felt was now inevitable. For a while his old, practiced charisma held sway, until one of the enraged warriors, bolder than the rest, raised his voice in challenge.

"Taoyateduta is a coward!"

For more than two centuries Dakotas and whites had intermarried, traded, hunted together, and competed in games of chance and physical skill, ever since itinerant French traders and their employees first entered the wide, beautiful territory west of the Great Lakes in the early 1600s. Fox, beaver, elk, and buffalo had seemed innumerable and the world's demand for fur so great that trapping, hunting, and trade seemed to be a combined effort, collapsing the differences between the Dakota and their transplanted European partners. But even in the friendliest of times, the world of the Upper Mississippi River Valley had always been divided into Dakota and white realms. In many ways this division was absolute, a question not only of history and language but of separate worldviews that created two overlapping realities, side by side, their incompatibility bearing the seeds of catastrophe.

What was frontier to whites, the expanding edge of possibility, was to the Dakota just the opposite: the center of their world, growing smaller. Farms that signaled civilization to settlers were to many Dakotas, even to some who kept small acreages, a tool designed to fence them in, the symbol of a permanent halt to centuries of seasonal migration. White churches brought a message of peace but were unable to absorb other beliefs, always suspicious and dismissive of the complex polytheism of the Dakota spirit world. Whites wrote everything down, mesmerized by tables of numbers; Dakotas lived by a language of spoken tales, remembered and repeated across hundreds of years. Most of all, whites loved hierarchy, each man occupying a rung on the ladder that eventually rose to a single individual in the White House, while Dakotas operated inside a shifting, dispersed power structure that defined leadership as the ability to guide a village, band, or tribe toward consensus. Minnesota was still an infant state, only four years old but brimming over with belief in Manifest Destiny, living an irony typical of the western experience: the only true "Minnesotians" in 1862, the people who had been there first, the people whose language had given the place its name, didn't care what it was called, where it began and ended, or how it had been made a state.

For more than a year, white men had been killing other white men far to the south and east. A few Indian agency employees had offered to raise companies of Dakota soldiers for the Union army, but these offers had been quickly rejected at the state capital. The war being fought far away was not the Dakota's war, but still their interest in the great battles was intense. A few of them, including Little Crow, could read some English, and others were made aware of the fighting thanks to the "pictorial papers" that would appear on the counters at the traders' stores. Many wondered why President Lincoln had already issued three calls for volunteer soldiers and why Thomas Galbraith, the government's Indian agent for the Dakota, would recruit a company of whites and mixed-bloods he called the Renville Rangers and seek to become its captain unless a great many Minnesotans had already been killed. "The whites must be pretty hard up for men to fight the South," said Big Eagle, "or they would not come so far out on the frontier and take half-breeds or anything to help them."

If the Civil War was taking able-bodied whites and mixed-bloods away, many Dakotas were convinced that the conflict had swallowed up their money as well. Four treaties with the United States—one in 1837, two in 1851, and another in 1858—had exchanged Dakota lands for goods, services, and annual payments in gold coin from the United States Treasury. The first treaty, signed by Little Crow's father and other Dakota chiefs in Washington, D.C., had ceded Dakota lands in the Wisconsin Territory and placed his father's village and all of his fellow Dakotas west of the Mississippi River. The second and third treaties, the latter bearing Little Crow's signature on its topmost line, had limited the Dakota to a seventy-mile-long strip along the north and south banks of the upper Minnesota River, forcing thousands of Dakota families with no say in the negotiations to abandon their woodland lodges for new homes on the prairie and forever truncating their world by more than twenty million acres. The fourth treaty, in 1858, had resulted from Little Crow's own trip to meet with President James Buchanan in the U.S. capital, where he and several of his fellow chiefs agreed to the whites' demand that they give up the northern bank of the Minnesota River at a rate of thirty cents per acre, allowing the newborn state to accommodate an ever-increasing number of white settlers in search of fertile ground. At both treaty negotiations, Little Crow understood how unpopular his actions would be with many of his fellow Dakotas—he had no love for the outcomes himself—but in the end he signed out of resignation, realism, hope that the federal government might keep some of its promises, and, perhaps, a desire to maintain the only kind of influence that seemed left to a Dakota leader.

In all four cases, central conditions of the treaties had been altered, dismissed, or delayed by Congress during the ratification process; in all four cases, Little Crow and other Dakota chiefs had eventually felt it necessary to sign the amended versions or become helpless. Their only other options, it seemed, were to starve or to move many hundreds of miles farther west, where they would live hemmed in by other, unfamiliar Indian peoples. In every case, white settlers poured onto Dakota land without waiting for federal ratification of the treaties; in every case, large sums of promised gold went instead to politicians and traders, who commanded broker's fees and made sizable claims, a number of them fraudulent, on the money due to the Dakota; and in every case, shifting conditions of eligibility were placed on the payments that made it impossible for the Dakotas to exercise any remaining rights of independence. In 1857, when a renegade Wahpeton Dakota named Inkpaduta and his men, bitter over unredressed white acts of violence, had killed thirty-eight settlers near Spirit Lake, in Iowa, Mdewakantons had been ordered to give chase to their fleeing kinsmen or forfeit their annuities; one year later, the treaty of 1858 had given special privileges to Dakotas who took up farming, a stipulation that the Indian agents and other white authorities had regularly used to try to bring more resistant tribesmen into line.

In June 1862, two months before the council outside Little Crow's tepee, thousands of Dakotas had gathered for the yearly disbursement of annuity gold only to be told that the money had been delayed. A rumor had begun to flow up and down the Minnesota River Valley that the Civil War had used up all the Dakota's gold and that worthless scrip was on its way instead, a rumor lent credence by the news that other northwestern tribes had received a portion of their own yearly payments in paper. After months of hunger, owing to a cutworm infestation the previous summer and a brutal winter that covered many of their food reserves with several feet of snow, a new desperation settled in. Corn and potatoes were plentiful but not yet ripe, and with game in ever shorter supply, the result was a severely imbalanced diet that left many Dakotas malnourished, some dying, and all badly in need of the grains, beans, and meats their annuities could buy.

All through June and July, Little Crow had argued with white traders for an extension of credit and with the Indian agent for an emergency distribution of food. But now, in August, with all of the gold still undelivered, most of the traders digging in their heels, and many Dakota elders and children falling sick, he was left in a precarious position. Neither those Dakotas in favor of accommodating white notions of civilization nor those holding a hard line against white encroachment had lately found much need for Little Crow. An election just days before the early-morning council of August 18 had stripped Little Crow of his position as tribal speaker and awarded the honor to a younger man named Traveling Hail, who wore white men's clothes but was well-known as an opponent of the 1858 treaty. When Little Crow finally responded to the unnamed warrior's taunt, "Taoyateduta is a coward!," he wasn't just meeting a challenge to his bravery; he was reclaiming a long-accustomed role and realigning his personal history with that of his entire tribe.

Most of the words spoken or written by Dakotas during the events of 1862 have come down through history in the form of interviews conducted by white writers and journalists, many of them years after the fact, all imprecisely translated and subjectively edited. Only two reports of Little Crow's words in this charged moment purport to be firsthand accounts: one related by the village chief Big Eagle and the other by Little Crow's son Wowinape, who was asleep in Little Crow's tepee or in one very close by when the commotion began. Seventeen years old, one of twelve children by five wives, Wowinape was the only son to survive to his teen years and the only one of Little Crow's children with him on this morning. In an alternate timeline, Wowinape might have become the next Little Crow, but by August 1862, with the guns of whites thundering far off and the Dakota world shrinking, no one was thinking that far into the future.

Many years later, Wowinape would tell his story to a poet, lawyer, and Union army veteran named Hanford Lennox Gordon, who had conducted a set of interviews with Little Crow while living near the Dakota reservation in 1860 and 1861. Later in life Gordon became a kind of poor man's Longfellow, publishing *Legends of the Northwest, The Feast of the Virgins and Other Poems,* and *Indian Legends and Other Poems,* books containing lyric poems based on Dakota stories collected by Presbyterian missionaries. *Feast of the Virgins* and *Indian Legends* both included Wowinape's tale of this fateful morning. Little Crow's son told Gordon of how his father "sprang from his tepee, snatched the eagle-feathers from the head of his insulter and flung them on the ground." Then, "stretching himself to his full height, his eyes flashing fire, and in a voice tremulous with rage," Little Crow began to address the young men in front of him.

Ta-o-ya-te-du-ta is not a coward, and he is not a fool! When did he run away from his enemies? When did he leave his braves behind him on the war-path and turn back to his tee-pees? When he ran away from your enemies, he walked behind on your trail with his face to the Ojibways and covered your backs as a she-bear covers her cubs! Is Ta-o-ya-te-du-ta without scalps? Look at his war-feathers! Behold the scalp-locks of your enemies hanging there on his lodge-poles! Do they call him a coward? Ta-o-ya-te-du-ta is not a coward, and he is not a fool. Braves, you are like little children; you know not what you are doing.

You are full of the white man's devil-water. You are like dogs in the Hot Moon when they run mad and snap at their own shadows. We are only little herds of buffaloes left scattered; the great herds that covered the prairies are no more. See!—the white men are like the locusts when they fly so thick that the whole sky is a snowstorm. You may kill one—two—ten; yes, as many as the leaves in the forest yonder, and their brothers will not miss them. Kill one—two—ten, and ten times ten will come to kill you. Count your fingers all day long and white men with guns in their hands will come faster than you can count.

Yes; they fight among themselves—away off. Do you hear the thunder of their big guns? No; it would take you two moons to run down to where they are fighting, and all the way your path would be among white soldiers as thick as tamaracks in the swamps of the Ojibways. Yes; they fight among themselves, but if you strike at them they will all turn on you and devour you and your women and little children just as the locusts in their time fall on the trees and devour all the leaves in one day. You are fools. You cannot see the face of your chief; your eyes are full of smoke. You cannot hear his voice; your ears are full of roaring waters. Braves, you are little children—you are fools. You will die like the rabbits when the hungry wolves hunt them in the Hard Moon.

Ta-o-ya-te-du-ta is not a coward: he will die with you.

Transformed into prose poetry by Gordon in 1891 and pitched to satisfy a rising national nostalgia for the Vanishing Indian, this version of Little Crow's speech cannot be taken at face value. That isn't to say, though, that the essential facts are inaccurate. Little Crow was awakened in the early morning and did give a riveting and powerful speech, displaying the skill in public address he had established long before this day. He did ridicule the wisdom of armed warfare against whites and lash out at those who desired to hear no such reproach. And he did, ultimately, agree to go to war anyway.

In the Dakota council, with many men taking their turn to speak, Little Crow's response put him, and perhaps only him, at a midpoint between those young men of the *tiyotipi* who had entered his village set on war and a group of older village chiefs, Big Eagle among them, who argued for peace. He could elect to lead the Dakota into battle or he could step aside as the battles went on without him. They would launch their campaign for vengeance and freedom with or without his approval. Little Crow had hard-earned reasons to choose either path, accommodation or war, and he recognized that in this moment all of the Dakota people, not merely his own village and his own Mdewakanton band, must finally and forever select one road and leave the other behind.

Little Crow was not the last to speak, even if only his words would enter the historical record. Consensus, however, was not long in the making. "Soon the cry was 'Kill the whites and kill all these cuthairs who will not join us,'" said Big Eagle. "Parties formed and dashed away in the darkness to kill settlers. The women began to run bullets and the men to clean their guns." When Little Crow made his choice, it was not so much for war as for death. He, at least, felt that for the Dakota there was now little difference.

# Chapter Two

Thirty miles to the northwest and seven hours later, a white woman named Sarah Wakefield moved from room to room in her two-story brick home at the center of the Upper Agency, the northernmost of the two administrative centers run by the United States on Dakota land. Outside, her house was spare and unadorned, a match for the warehouse, agent's quarters, employee barracks, and jail spread along a windswept bluff along the government road, high above the junction of the Minnesota and Yellow Medicine rivers. Inside, the house was more city than frontier, probably the best furnished and most expensively appointed on the south side of the river. Today, every room held particular meaning as she stepped away from carpeted parlors full of black walnut and mahogany furniture, left behind wardrobes full of silk damask dresses, and abandoned hundreds of books and bound volumes of the latest magazines from the East.

Sarah's husband, John, the Upper Agency physician, appeared and asked gruffly what she was doing. "Taking a final look," she wanted to say, but, worried that she'd sound melodramatic, she made a light-hearted comment and finished stuffing a few of her and her children's things into a trunk before she went outside for a hurried and dangerous trek across the prairie.

Sarah Wakefield, date unknown

In August 1862, Sarah Wakefield was thirty-two, with little more than a year's experience of the frontier. Gregarious to strangers, prone to anxiety, and fiercely protective of her two young children, she was plain-looking and stout enough that the Dakota called her Tanka-Winohinca Waste, meaning "large good woman." The move to an Indian reservation had been her husband's choice, not hers, and she had spent the past fourteen months rattled by night noises and unsettled by the prairie's vastness while she worked gamely to achieve something resembling normality in her day-to-day affairs.

Sarah was born and raised in Rhode Island, but little is known of her time in the East other than the fact that her move to Minnesota in 1854, when she was twenty-four, occurred under some kind of dark personal cloud and coincided with the end of her speaking relationship with her mother. Within two years she had married a fellow New England transplant, a Yale-educated doctor from Connecticut named John Luman Wakefield, who had settled in southern Minnesota after five years of practice in the California goldfields, probably to be near his brother James, who was already a prominent frontier lawyer. In 1857, Sarah gave birth to a son, James; a daughter, named Lucy but called Nellie, followed in 1860, one year before their move to the Minnesota River.

The Wakefields had expected to spend one and perhaps two presidential terms at the Upper Agency, but now, in August 1862, it seemed that Sarah's time on the "Indian frontier," as whites called it, might end as abruptly as it had begun. As the sun had climbed through the morning and burned the dew off the tall bluestem grasses, reports of an Indian uprising filtered in from the villages downriver, all of them confusing, uncertain, and hard to credit. How much of this talk reached Sarah is uncertain, but she had known something unusual was afoot shortly after lunch when her husband asked George Gleason, a visiting Lower Agency clerk, to escort her away. As a pair Sarah Wakefield and Gleason were mismatched, one full of premonitions of doom and the other full of jest and bluster. "Indian scares" were a phenomenon agency employees like Gleason felt they understood and could shrug off. Indeed, they'd been through a summer of crises, all more immediate and tangible than this one, without violence from the Dakota.

None of the whites or mixed-bloods entering the Upper Agency grounds and talking of attacks against whites along the river below seemed to have reliable, concrete information. And in that absence, many at the agency took comfort in more typical and less cataclysmic possibilities. Perhaps they were only hearing the first rumblings of an Ojibwe raid near the reservation; perhaps the Yankton and Yanktonais living along the James and Missouri rivers had come to steal horses; perhaps the Upper Agency Dakota were only making noise in an attempt to hurry the late annuity payments; or perhaps, even, agents of the seceded states were in the area to stir up trouble. None of these were new threats, and today, with the community on edge and people beginning to depart in all directions, they sounded positively reassuring.

All morning Gleason told passersby that he was heading down to the Lower Agency and then eastward for a vacation, adding that the doctor's wife would be making a visit to relatives a hundred miles downriver. Sarah heard a different story. Gleason told her that their destination was actually Fort Ridgely, a small garrison of artillery and mostly untested American soldiers beyond the Lower Agency and across the river, forty miles away. This information was enough to put her into a growing state of panic. Shortly after three o'clock in the afternoon, Sarah's children were hoisted into the back seat of an open wagon, James next to her and Nellie in her lap. As Gleason climbed into the driver's seat, Sarah asked him if he carried a pistol. He told her not to worry and gave the call to start the horses moving.

. . .

Sarah Wakefield had first arrived on Dakota lands the previous summer, in 1861, as one passenger in a seven-wagon train that carried two important items destined for the Upper Agency: the medical expertise of her husband and a portion of the annuity payment for the Dakota, $75,000 in gold coins stipulated in the four treaties negotiated over the past quarter century. The distance from Shakopee, Sarah's previous home, to the Upper Minnesota River Valley was about 90 miles as the crow flies, but she had traveled for three days over 150 twisting miles on the steamboat *Jeanette Roberts* before disembarking at the Lower Agency, near the mouth of the Redwood River.

"As I landed from the steamboat, I could not help exclaiming, 'Is it here where I am to live?'" she wrote later, "for all I saw was one log hut and about six hundred filthy, nasty, greasy Indians" gathering at the Lower Agency to wait for their portion of the 1861 annuity. Soon she understood that the ferry landing along the river bottom was only a way station for her, one that gave way to high, sweeping vistas of grass and more grass as she and her party continued by wagon another thirty miles to the Upper Agency. As she headed northwest toward her new home, she worried about a bushwhack aimed at stealing the gold and remarked on the emptiness of her surroundings. "A more beautiful sight than that prairie, I have never seen," she wrote. "It seemed like a vast lake—not a tree or shrub to be seen."

Sarah and John Wakefield had not been lonely travelers headed for empty lands. A few weeks behind her own boat, the *Franklin Steele* had carried the new governor and the new Indian agent, along with an assortment of soldiers, attorneys, newspaper editors, gamblers, clergymen, and tourists from Milwaukee, Chicago, and even England. The journey was labeled a "Grand Pleasure Excursion" and promised the opportunity to see the Dakota assemble for a day of performance and ceremony. For years, traders, frontiersmen, and new settlers had come to watch the dances, singing, and speeches that highlighted a summer kinship gathering for the Dakota; beginning in the early 1850s, the annuity payment had simply been attached to those events, providing a convenient way for white authorities to bring the Dakota together for their payment and creating, at the same time, a festive occasion for adventurers and frontier aristocrats from all over.

No more illustrious visitor had ridden on the *Franklin Steele* in the

summer of 1861 than an ailing Henry David Thoreau, who had traveled fifteen hundred miles from Massachusetts with his friend Horace Mann, Jr., on what would be Thoreau's final trip away from home
before his death from tuberculosis the following spring. Thoreau, who
had nurtured a distant fascination with Indians all of his life, wrote
fancifully that "the buffalo were said to be feeding within twenty-five
or thirty miles" of the Lower Agency as a series of ceremonial councils between white authorities and Indians began on the morning of
June 26, 1861. He singled out Little Crow among the Dakota speakers for his forcefulness and charisma, but all of the chiefs, he added,
"were quite dissatisfied with the white man's treatment of them" and,
in Thoreau's view, had "the advantage in point of truth and earnestness, and therefore of eloquence." Little Crow's dissatisfaction, though,
had not dampened the festivities, which included the presentation of
two beef oxen to the Dakota, the firing of cannon salutes, songs by a
German band, and a ceremonial monkey dance created and performed
by the Dakota at the governor's formal request. All of this action,
which would be repeated by other whites and other Indians in front of
Sarah at the Upper Agency a few days later, excited and gratified the
outsiders, who could now write home with tales of their time among
the savages.

Little Crow's complaints may have been easily set aside in the bus-
tle surrounding the payment, but they were deeply felt and long in the
making. All of the week's pomp and merriment served to paper over a
pile of long-standing disputes regarding the annuity gold. The treaties
of 1837, 1851, and 1858 had reserved set sums for the Dakota in the form
of annual disbursements from the United States Treasury, which were
paid out of a dedicated fund and only after congressional approval in
the form of an annual appropriations bill. That yearly bill, debated and
signed by men who knew little of the treaty details, less of the treaty
negotiations, and nothing of the Dakota, began the process not of dis-
bursing the money to Indians but of reserving much of it for whites.

By the time the wagons arrived at the agencies, a portion of the
money had vanished, along with all clarity as to the rightful execution
of treaty provisions. Commissioner, superintendent, and Indian agent
had the authority to reroute annuity money to pay for administrative
services, construction projects, employee wages, restitution for individual depredations, or other, more creative expenditures. Any of these
men could approve the repayment of Indian debts to white agency

employees and contractors out of the annuities, who often tallied the monies due them under a system of blank vouchers—essentially signed checks with no dollar amount written in—that allowed its designees to name their price for goods and services. Unregulated and barely monitored, the validity of these set-asides and appropriations was left to the integrity of individuals who, in many cases, had taken their jobs in part because of the possibilities for financial gain.

When John Wakefield arrived at the Upper Agency in the spring of 1861 with his wife, he represented the tail end of a chain of patronage stretching up to Abraham Lincoln, whose inauguration had changed everything for the Dakota in Minnesota and the whites who surrounded them. Sarah Wakefield owed her presence on the reservation to a series of decisions triggered when Lincoln had sent "blank appointments" to the congressional delegations of the northwestern states and territories so that they might name agents to the various tribes on or adjacent to their land. Democrats had run the executive branch for the previous eight years, through the terms of Franklin Pierce and James Buchanan, but in reality the Dakota had been involved with a familiar set of agents and traders—most of them interrelated with the Indians by marriage and fatherhood—for decades. Now, with the white population booming and the Northwest gaining fast in political importance, almost everything had changed.

In one frenzied week of political dealing at the 1860 Republican convention in Chicago, lawyer and former U.S. representative Caleb Smith had received a promise of the post of secretary of the interior, while Illinois merchant William P. Dole was given a similar guarantee of the position of commissioner of Indian affairs, both in exchange for their crucial support of Lincoln's nomination. Lincoln's handlers had brokered these promises themselves, leaving Lincoln free to focus on speechifying and handshaking. Once elected and in office, Lincoln had made good on those commitments and dozens of others, discovering along the way just how much he despised the work of patronage, calling the torrent of office-seekers "a curse to this country" and taking advantage of all possible ways to shift lower-level decisions onto state governments or his cabinet appointees. The Minnesota slate was chosen by the state's congressional delegation for reasons as unconnected to the real business of Indian affairs and the real needs of Indians as Lincoln's choices of Smith and Dole had been.

The Indian superintendency of the Northern Department (encompassing Michigan, Wisconsin, Minnesota, Kansas, Nebraska, and the Dakota Territory) had gone to ambitious, hard-drinking Clark W. Thompson, a railroad speculator and close friend of Republican senator Morton Wilkinson. One level below Thompson, new Indian agents were named, and the Minnesota River post had gone to Thomas Galbraith, a lawyer, staunch Unionist, active Freemason, and loyal Republican functionary from the Wakefields' hometown of Shakopee. The superintendent and agent were entitled to enlist a new group of agency professionals that included clerks, teachers, and a physician, all "in the employ" of the agent, who became a political boss with as much control over the lives of the Dakota as the governor or Indian commissioner had over his own life.

For the Dakota, this change had created profound upheaval, as almost every tie they had to the white power structure was suddenly severed and made anew. For generations whites had grown more numerous around them and yet more distant from them. A class of men who had not so long ago come into their world as solitary entrepreneurs, demonstrating remarkable adaptability and taking great personal risks, was now too often made up of strangers lining up at a trough. What these new men shared was not knowledge of the Dakota people or Dakota customs but rather the knowledge that Indian superintendents and agents controlled a large pot of federal money. The spillover from that pot, they reasoned, might as well land in their own laps. In this era of Lincoln, a Republican who could frame an Indian's house—or teach an Indian's children, or shoe an Indian's horses—was in a far better position than a Democrat who could do the same thing.

Only the old group of traders held on at the Dakota agencies, men named Myrick, Forbes, and Roberts, among others, sole proprietors eking out a living under a system that required them to squeeze their Dakota customers ever more tightly to stay afloat. At the turn of the nineteenth century, to be a trader had meant a solitary life in a West that seemed wide open. Independent operators at first, later the employees of powerful fur companies, they were sometimes honest, sometimes designing and avaricious, but always intrepid and adventurous. Those who found the greatest success in accumulating valuable beaver furs and buffalo hides in exchange for cash or barter were those who most fully assimilated into Dakota life, living in Dakota villages, wearing Dakota clothes, learning the Dakota language, marrying into Dakota bands, and embracing Dakota traditions of reciprocal gift exchange.

Thomas Galbraith, 1861

But those times were now long past. The good furs were in ever shorter supply, replaced by muskrat pelts that sold for pennies, and a relationship that had been symbiotic, at least at its best, was now broken.

Every member of the current crop of traders among the Dakota had been appointed by a Whig or a Democrat, and all were beholden to state and federal leaders whose influence had now vanished. Most understood that their time in the field was growing shorter, well aware of the scuttlebutt that Galbraith, the new agent, would not renew their licenses for the following year. In its previous incarnation as a sparsely populated territory, Minnesota had been solidly Democratic, but the influx of new citizens, more than a hundred thousand in the previous decade, had consisted mostly of Republicans opposed to the extension of slavery into their new home and suspicious of the Democrats' anti-immigrant leanings. To the Dakota, questions of slavery and immigration and political parties were foreign concerns, but the traders' tenuous hold on their jobs brought new pressures to bear on everyone connected to the Indian agencies.

Bearing their certifications from the Office of Indian Affairs, the traders working the agency grounds had become professional creditors working to keep a system of perpetual debt in place. Their shelves laden with flour, sugar, household items, farm implements, blankets, clothing, and firearms, they offered terms that shops in Saint Paul or the other Minnesota River towns would not or could not. Managing this liberal credit was the key to their success: push too hard, and their stream of income would flow in another direction; push too little, and it would slow to a trickle. Each year, as the annuity gold was disbursed, the traders and their employees formed a ring around the newly paid Dakota, demanding money and interest due them according to figures the Dakota were often asked to take on faith. Should a Dakota refuse to pay what he was told he owed, no more credit would be extended. Should a Dakota find himself and his kin cleaned out by his previous year's obligations, he was simply granted more credit, payable out of the next year's annuities. Nothing about the process was illegal, but the perpetual spiral of debt was galling. And now, facing the possible elimination of their franchises, most of the traders would be foreclosing on all debt and demanding as much gold as they could get.

The exact mechanism of John Wakefield's appointment as Upper Agency physician at a salary of $1,000 a year remains unclear, but a trail is easy to pick out. He and Galbraith had lived in Shakopee and belonged to the same Masonic lodge. Perhaps they were good friends, or perhaps they simply moved together in the same political or professional circles; perhaps John Wakefield sought the position for a promise of ease, or perhaps he nursed a hankering for the frontier; perhaps, even, given persistent hints of marital discord before and after their time at the Indian agency, he and Sarah had gained a quiet notoriety around town as a troubled couple and needed to get away. But one thing is sure: the Wakefields were not roughing it on the reservation. Their house included a fully outfitted kitchen and storeroom full of beef, pork, codfish, mackerel, cheese and crackers, rice, butter, and eggs. At a time when Upper Agency Dakotas were hungry and demanding action from the Indian agent, the Wakefields' prosperity must have made them conspicuous.

In Shakopee, Sarah had been a doctor's wife, sister-in-law to a prominent and well-liked lawyer, but here, out on the prairie? For all her fears and racial assumptions, Sarah was inclined to be friendly and generous with the Dakota, but she still looked eastward for her cultural and material needs; she remained connected to New England through books, magazines, and expensive mail-order fashions. Not even the small group of missionaries' wives around the agencies provided Sarah with real companionship. She had never been baptized, and though she believed in God she did not find comfort in church services or churchmen. In many ways she seems to have been something of an outsider, even a wayward one. The tenor of her marriage is difficult to decipher, but all of the available evidence shows that her relationship with John up to 1862 was full of tension, including an apparent period of separation, his unilateral decision to head to the prairie, and incidents of rough, impatient treatment that may well have descended into physical abuse. Sarah was a loyal wife, but the Wakefields were not a happy couple.

When the Wakefields settled in Minnesota in the 1850s, their new hometown of Shakopee was no longer Dakota land, but it was still part of the Dakota world, a natural stop along the Minnesota River for Dakotas traveling to Saint Paul, abroad on hunting expeditions to the Big Woods, or heading out for battle against the Ojibwe. In winter, the Dakota often camped around Shakopee, which had been built on the site of a Mdewakanton village. "Not a day passed but some of the Indians were at my house," Sarah wrote, "and I had always pitied them, and given them food." In 1858, a clash between Dakota and Ojibwe warriors near the town brought several wounded Mdewakantons up to John Wakefield's door, and Sarah maintained that "they often said he saved many of their lives," creating an indebtedness she later believed saved her own life in return.

Despite her previous encounters with Dakota families, Sarah's perceptions of Indians were sometimes as reductive and bigoted as those held by her most xenophobic neighbors; her language could be insulting and ignorant, and she rarely questioned the presumed superiority of white intelligence and culture. But at other times her eyes and heart were open. She noted with anger the ongoing debasement and growing resentment among the Dakota as traders claimed tribal monies through unaccountable tallies of Indian debt. On her first Independence Day at the Upper Agency, shortly after her arrival in 1861, a stray rumor had circulated that Dakotas were coming after traders and clerks with violence in mind. The white men of the agency and their wives and children had spent the day hiding out in the jail, and the situation was eventually defused when Sarah and others performed an impromptu dance for the Dakota, took them into their homes, and served them ice cream, one of the frontier's most exotic foodstuffs.

Over the past year Sarah had seen provisions and annuity payments distributed more liberally to "farmer Indians" who agreed to cultivate the earth, dress like white people, and cut their hair, all according to the terms of the 1858 treaty, which many Dakotas had bitterly opposed. She hired Dakota wives to sew for her and wrote fondly of stopping in Dakota villages to share a pipe and join the women as they sat cooking, talking, and laughing. During Sarah's first winter on the reservation, two feet of snow fell in January and more in February, leaving few pockets of protection on the prairie and little to hunt or forage, forcing the Dakota to slaughter and share their few cattle and hogs and to travel long distances to find food and blankets, both of which were growing scarce. The hard winter had made the spring hunt a meager one, and in the summer of 1862 the Dakota, especially those of the Upper Agency bands, had turned to forage as they waited for their corn and potatoes to ripen, digging turnips, pulling tall grasses, and shooting pigeons and whatever muskrats and ducks they could find.

From her vantage point in a comfortable, well-provisioned home, Sarah had watched over the hot summer as the Dakota became more and more desperate. In early June the Sisseton and Wahpeton Dakota, the Upper Agency bands, had begun to gather, so that by July 1862 the agency grounds were crowded with more than a thousand agitated Indians. Gossip filtered in from the Indian agent and many others that the annuity gold would be arriving any day; but she also heard the unfounded though believable rumors suggesting that the money would be issued as paper currency, if it came at all. The traders, ears perked, were refusing to extend credit until they received solid assurances that the Dakota would soon have their funds. Compounding the Dakotas' anger, the brick warehouse at the Upper Agency, which occupied half of the building that also contained John Wakefield's office, was well stocked with flour, sugar, cured meats, and other provisions for the agency employees. Without a reliable assurance of payment, they had narrowed their focus to getting at that food.

On August 4, 1862, two weeks before the fateful meeting in front of Little Crow's tepee, Sarah watched hundreds of armed young Dakotas come "driving down the hill toward the Agency, dressed out very finely, and as we thought, for a dance; but we were soon convinced they meant mischief, as they surrounded the soldiers while part of them rushed up to the warehouse." Galbraith refused to open the doors. Such demonstrations had been staged before. He didn't believe the stories of starvation, and he was, besides, a man who held standard procedure in high esteem, preferring to enroll the Dakotas—counting them and verifying their identities—before issuing any goods. After Galbraith disappeared inside his office, the Dakotas came to the Wakefields' house and "rapped violently" on the door. Convinced they had come to kill her, Sarah picked up a pistol, met them in her front hall, and "inquired as calmly as I could what they wanted."

They did not want to kill her. They wanted an axe, which Sarah supplied, and soon the men began to hack at the warehouse door. The moment was thick with the threat of armed violence: a crowd of soldiers and Dakotas face-to-face, guns raised, the Indian agent out of sight and, some said, getting drunk. Galbraith's inaction meant that the task of defusing the crisis had been left to a young army lieutenant, Timothy Sheehan, who held his own quick council with Upper Agency Dakota leaders and, whether out of pragmatism, magnanimity, or a desire to play hero, opened the warehouse doors.

The confrontation had already gone well beyond the usual haranguing between Dakotas and agency employees, and Sarah and several other white women left the next morning for the Lower Agency to get out of harm's way and bring news of possible unrest to the white population there. Little Crow, meanwhile, had departed the same day from the Lower Agency in the other direction; runners and riders had brought him news of the altercation overnight. He arrived at the Upper Agency in time to find a new soldier taking command of the white forces. This was John Marsh, a veteran of the First Battle of Bull Run, who finished the job of distributing the warehouse provisions and began to talk to the Dakotas at the same time as he was placing guards around the agency. For the next two weeks, a running series of unusually charged councils and discussions took place, convened in several locations along the river valley and featuring a shifting cast, including Marsh, Sheehan, Galbraith, Little Crow, and various missionaries and traders. All of these talks centered on the growing unrest of the Dakotas who had been denied credit and were still waiting on their annuities.

Galbraith would later describe the reservation as quiet during this short period following the confrontation at the warehouse, and perhaps it was, outwardly. But the situation was full of clashing agendas, and ominous potentialities lay just beneath the surface. As a village chief and erstwhile tribal spokesman, Little Crow was speaking only for the Lower Agency Mdewakantons and their need for provisions. Marsh and Sheehan were concerned with tamping down the rising possibility of violence. Galbraith seemed to have been knocked to the sidelines;

given that he was still recruiting a company of white and mixed-blood soldiers for the Union army and still talking about becoming its captain, he may have been eyeing the end of his tenure as Indian agent and hoping that no fire lay behind all of the summer's smoke. In any case, confident that the annuity gold would soon arrive, Galbraith preferred that the traders do what they had always done and simply open one small, additional line of credit to cover the gap. The traders wanted none of Galbraith's plan. Most didn't trust the agent to renew their licenses, and their need for cash, should their remaining tenure prove short, inclined them to heed the rumor that the gold wasn't coming at all. Any interruption in the flow of annuities would mean that their last chance to profit from the Dakotas in debt to them might simply float away.

As the August heat settled in, the face-offs turned ugly. And the talk was never any uglier than when the trader Andrew Myrick was involved. Myrick and his brother Nathan had arrived on the Minnesota River a dozen years earlier and were veterans, so they thought, of the yearly routine: the Dakotas would agitate against the traders' claims on most of the annuity money, but in the end do nothing about it. Still young men, the Myricks owned stores at both agencies and employed several clerks. Their haul from the treaties and the yearly distributions had already run into the tens of thousands of dollars, and they seemed to occupy a primary position in negotiations, not least because Andrew was prone to confrontation.

At some point between August 4, when the Upper Agency Dakota attempted to break into the commodities warehouse, and August 18, when four young men told their story of killing whites near the Big Woods, Little Crow and Andrew Myrick stood face-to-face in the most heated exchange of the month. The exact location and date are difficult to pinpoint, probably on or near the Lower Agency grounds after Little Crow's return from his trip upriver. But the substance of their conversation is clear. As Thomas Galbraith, Captain Marsh, and Lieutenant Sheehan looked on, Little Crow argued that since goods had been distributed at the Upper Agency, the same thing should be done for his people to the south. His tone and words were apparently threatening enough that the mixed-blood interpreter refused to translate them, leaving the task to John P. Williamson, son of the Presbyterian missionary Thomas S. Williamson.

We have waited a long time. The money is ours, but we cannot get it. We have no food, but here are these stores filled with food. We ask that you, the agent, make some arrangement by which we can get food from the stores, or else we may take our own way to keep ourselves from starving. When men are hungry they help themselves.

Myrick responded as he often had to such sentiments: as far as he was concerned, the Indians could eat grass or their own shit. He had said so in various ways more than once in the past month, but now, following weeks of mounting unrest, the situation was far more volatile. After his words were translated, a cry went up among the Dakotas. Refused an extension of credit or provisions from the warehouse at the Lower Agency—and with the annuity gold still who knew where—the Mdewakanton Dakota, Little Crow's people, now focused on words. Myrick's statement was not one to start a war; that was far beyond the power of one white trader. But as a rallying cry, it was tailor-made. And when violence did come, there was little question as to who would become one of its first targets.

As George Gleason drove Sarah and her children south under an intense afternoon sun on the long afternoon of August 18, the government road was strangely empty of travelers. Stopping at one of the traders' stores on the way out of the Upper Agency, they had heard that Dakota warriors were killing settlers as far north as the Big Woods and as far south as the Iowa border, that Indian camps all over the Dakota reservations and in the Dakota Territory were holding councils of war, and that the Upper Agency Dakota, "her" Indians, the Wahpeton and Sisseton bands, were meeting to decide whether to join the conflict or to flee out west. Sarah had asked Gleason to turn around and go back to her house and husband, but, she wrote later, he only "made great sport of me." If the Upper Agency Dakota were agitating, he said, he would take her to the Lower Agency and recruit several hundred of the Mdewakanton and Wahpekute Dakota there, "his" Indians, to go north and fight alongside the whites.

Gleason's route, at John Wakefield's instruction, would take Sarah past Little Crow's village and into the Lower Agency, across the Minnesota River via ferry, and then eleven more miles to Fort Ridgely, the only place within eighty miles where settlers might find artillery and white soldiers. As they rode for mile after mile along the bluff, the river wound in curlicues to their left while to the right a sea of high grass filled the horizon. For long stretches their view was uninterrupted by a single tree, hill, or built structure. The third week of August was the height of the prairie's summer display, an immense quilt pattern created by pasqueflowers, golden alexander, bearded tongue, and goldenrod budding in color-rich waves. The expanse was beautiful but also so spacious as to be frightening. Sarah begged Gleason to hurry and to keep an eye out for ambush, but, she wrote later, "he would laugh, sing, shout, and when I would chide him and tell him how I felt, he would say I was nervous, and told me he would never take me anywhere again." Reaching a rise in the road they saw a "great body of smoke" rising ahead of them in the direction of the river, where the Lower Agency was situated. When Sarah asked Gleason one more time to turn back, he laughed and said, "Oh, no, it is the saw mill or the prairie on fire."

A few miles later, nearing six o'clock, their wagon approached the two-story house of Joseph and Valencia Reynolds. Here two Dakotas approached casually on foot. Sarah asked Gleason to take out his pistol, to which he answered that "they are only boys going hunting," and reined in the horses. As the two men passed by Wakefield's wagon, a shot sounded. Struck in the shoulder, Gleason twisted in his seat and fell back against Sarah, pressing one-year-old Nellie between them. Another shot, this one to his intestines, struck with enough force that Gleason was catapulted off the wagon. The Dakota who had not fired took hold of the panicked horses and spoke urgently to Sarah.

In this moment, with Gleason's blood in the wagon, on her, and on her children, Sarah was seized by terror and hope. For she recognized him. And he recognized her.

His name was Chaska, a farmer Dakota of the Mdewakanton band with cut hair and a collared shirt, who spoke broken English and who had been a familiar face among those who had camped near Sarah's hometown of Shakopee before the Wakefields' departure for the Upper Agency. Chaska hastily told her that his companion, Hapa, was a "bad man" who had been drinking and that she should not talk too much. Sprawled on the ground, Gleason called out, "O, my God, Mrs. Wakefield!" Chaska walked over to the mortally wounded man, aimed at his head, and pulled the trigger, but the hammer only snapped. Six weeks later Sarah would offer her own testimony in front of a military commission about what happened next. Hapa brushed his companion aside and shot Gleason a third and final time, then turned to level the gun at her head. It was, Sarah believed, her last moment, but Chaska knocked the firearm away from Hapa and barked out a reprimand.

The two Dakota men then argued over her fate for close to an hour while smoke continued to rise nearby, clearly the sign of something worse than a prairie fire. Chaska finally won out. Gleason's body was left to lie in the sun while Mrs. Wakefield and her children were driven back upriver, in the direction of Little Crow's village. Her captivity had begun.

# Chapter Three

Several hours before Sarah Wakefield and George Gleason left the Upper Agency, a procession of one hundred or more Dakota warriors on foot had approached the Lower Agency along the same government road. Observers reported that a man on a white horse, Little Crow or another village chief, crossed and recrossed in front of the advancing walkers. The war party, unprecedented in size for the Dakota, first arrived at the trader's grounds, a small collection of stores and houses a half mile north of the agency, and here they positioned themselves in silence, several men at the door of each building. Inside Andrew Myrick's establishment, a trader named James Lynd greeted a lone Dakota, who raised his gun and said, "Now I will kill the dog who would not give me credit." Lynd, who had unsuccessfully sought the position of Indian agent and was known for his many careless liaisons with young Dakota women, died of a single shot that also served as a signal to the other warriors to open fire. It was not yet seven o'clock.

The next target was the man hiding upstairs who made a habit of telling the Dakota to eat grass. As the Dakota prepared to burn his store, Myrick dropped out of a window onto a low roof on the north side of the building. One more leap and he was on the ground, running for the brush and the cottonwoods and the river trail beyond. When

Myrick's body was found later, within sight of his establishment, it was disfigured with multiple bullet holes, protruding arrows, and a scythe wound. One observer noted that a quantity of grass had been stuffed in his mouth. Other traders and their clerks were shot in their front halls, or in their yards, or some ways away as they tried the same dash Myrick had attempted. Half a mile down the government road was the agency proper and its larger white population, all of whom would have heard the gunfire by now, but instead of pushing on with their attack, many of the Dakota surged into the traders' stores, loading up on flour, meat, sugar, coffee, clothing, and whatever other supplies they might carry or hoist into wagons before setting fire to the buildings on the way out.

This delay was long enough that when Little Crow entered the agency grounds, most of the whites and mixed-bloods living there had begun to flee. The most obvious route of escape was the Minnesota River ferry, two hundred feet below the bluff and served by a pair of roads that made two halves of a single loop, one short and steep along the southern arc and the other longer, wider, and gradual enough to accommodate loaded wagons. A third path to the ferry existed, but dashing straight downhill through the mix of cottonwoods, grapevines, prickly ash, and gooseberry was only for the hardiest of the escapees. All routes converged in the bottomlands of the river valley, a narrow flat fringe of land dotted with small stone buildings for the blacksmith, ferry operator, and warehouse clerk. The Minnesota River bent sharply here and was perhaps fifty feet across, sometimes deep but rarely swift, a possible swim for the unencumbered. Across the river and up the valley wall, a military road ran east to Fort Ridgely.

A second avenue of escape was the government road south of the river that continued toward the large township of New Ulm thirty miles distant. Many who chose that route were cut down within a mile or two of the agency, but the ferry proved luckier, thanks to its anonymous operator, who poled back and forth for more than an hour after the first shots were heard, saving dozens of lives in the shadow of smoke, screams, and panic, until he too was finally shot dead.

Later reports, most made by disoriented whites, would not agree about all of Little Crow's actions on the afternoon of the first attack. But from the outset he had to contend with the gap between his own instructions and the wishes of the wartime *tiyotipi,* wishes that sometimes seemed to evolve minute by minute and individual by individual as the killing commenced. Whatever role he had foreseen for himself,

Little Crow was most remembered for his decisions to preserve or condemn lives. One observer heard him bark out an impatient command to kill a group of men trying to hold back the agency's horses, but amid the flash and chaos of the attack Little Crow also took pains to spare several women, including the agency's Episcopal schoolteacher, and at least three men. He ordered that the mixed-blood trader Jack Frazer, a boon companion of Little Crow's peripatetic youth, not be harmed. When Samuel Hinman, the agency's Episcopal missionary, shouted out from a doorway, desperate for an explanation, Little Crow only gave him a warning look and moved on. Philander Prescott got more than a look; the father of six mixed-blood children, all recently baptized into the Episcopal church, Prescott had lived for three decades among the Dakota as a trader and translator and was known as an honest and trustworthy kinsman. When he stepped outside to demand answers, Little Crow told him to stay in his house and show his face for no one, an order that Prescott would too soon disobey, with fatal consequences.

The next step, Little Crow knew, was to confront whatever reinforcements would soon be arriving from Fort Ridgely. And indeed, at ten o'clock that morning, John Marsh, commander of the fort and the same man who had overseen the opening of the Upper Agency warehouse at the beginning of the month, learned from a fleeing boarding-house proprietor that something horrific had erupted. Captain Marsh left a teenager in charge, gathered forty-seven men, and headed for the ferry crossing, marching at first and then riding in wagons. Along the road they met a stream of fleeing settlers and agency employees who stopped only long enough to tell confused and panicked stories of the attack on the agency. The soldiers also met up with the Episcopal missionary Samuel Hinman, now safely across the river and hurrying toward the fort, who implored Marsh not to take on the Dakota with his meager force. Marsh's men were green, without the training or experience to understand what they were facing, and their captain did them no favors by pushing on to the edge of the river valley's northern ridge, where smoke and fire were visible across the water. Descending to the ferry landing on foot, they found a scattering of bullet- and arrow-riddled bodies near the river. They also found themselves exposed to the hill behind them, the bluff ahead of them, and the thickly treed banks stretching around the bend in both directions.

As Marsh took in the carnage at the ferry crossing, a lone man with a tomahawk and a painted face called out to them from the opposite bank. This was White Dog, a "cut-hair" Dakota familiar to some of the men, who encouraged the soldiers to cross in order to hold a council. With the recent change of Indian agent, White Dog had lost the position of farmer chief and may have been nursing a grudge, but the evidence doesn't indicate whether his trap was laid willingly or under duress. Seconds later, just as the soldiers reached the water's edge, the trees all around them and across the river flashed with gunfire. Standing in rank on the northern landing, the men made easy targets for dozens of armed Dakota warriors, and thirteen of them, including the interpreter, were shot dead before they could take more than a few steps.

Marsh and the remnants of his force scrambled downstream through the undergrowth, making good progress along the bottomlands and avoiding the Dakota for a mile or two, until their cover ran out and they decided to ford the river rather than risk showing themselves in the open. A confident waterman, Marsh led the way, holding a sword and pistol over his head, but somewhere in the middle of the river he faltered. Whether from a cramp, fatigue, or a sudden swift current, he went under, never to reappear. Scrambling back up the ridge, his terrified men made their way back to Fort Ridgely, keeping an eye out for Dakotas and coming to realize that much more than a single attack on the Indian agency had taken place. As they neared their destination, they found the roads and fields thick with other fleeing whites. No one stopped to talk or turned to fight. All order was lost in the pursuit of a single objective: away, away from the advancing Indians.

When Chaska and Hapa brought Sarah Wakefield and her children back up the government road that evening, after commandeering George Gleason's wagon and leaving his body to bake on the prairie, they were not alone. Little Crow's village, once an equal among many, was now the center of the Dakota universe, receiving people like a prairie basin filling with flood rains. White women and children arrived bloodied and frightened numb, trailed by warriors bearing shotguns and tomahawks, possessive of their individual charges. Captives who entered the village in multifamily groups were soon separated and removed to different tepees. As Sarah was led into the growing mass of people, she recognized Indians she'd known in Shakopee, some that her husband had helped years earlier. Some of the Dakota women cried as they helped Sarah off the wagon.

Little Crow's house, sparsely outfitted with a table, a few chairs, a kettle, and a raised platform for sleeping, had once been a symbol of his willingness to explore white lifeways. Now it served as a command post, with as many as one hundred tepees pitched on all sides and more going up every hour, while an endless procession of warriors and captives went in and out of his front door. Almost all of those abducted were women and children. Many had seen their brothers, husbands, or fathers killed. With each set of shocked and disoriented settlers brought in, with each returning group of warriors, the agitation increased.

Amid this frenzy, Chaska began to take extraordinary steps to keep Sarah out of the hands of the most violent Dakota warriors. The first night held the greatest peril. The camp was full of returning men, many drunk, celebrating their victory and boasting of greater ones to come, dining on plundered food and all the while playing on the fears of their white captives. No protocols were in place, no allegiances clear, no guarantee of safety offered, so Chaska kept Sarah on the move, walking her in and out of the woods on the river side of the village for over an hour in the hopes of finding an out-of-the-way place to rest for the night. She had left her trunk in the wagon, and she held Nellie in her arms all the while as James walked beside her. "I kept up with him," Sarah wrote, "and tried to talk of the heavy dew which was falling, not letting him know I was frightened."

Chaska finally stopped at a tepee sheltering one German-speaking woman and a group of Dakota warriors who were going through a pile of George Gleason's things, including his clothing and watch, which was still running beneath a broken crystal. "The Indians were having great sport over his empty pockets," Sarah wrote. "He had no pistol. He had deceived me. It was not safe at any time to go without firearms, and I many times wonder why he did such an unwise thing." It seems that this stop was designed to show her off as a prisoner before spiriting her to a less conspicuous bark house, a semipermanent Mdewakanton summer lodge, where she found another German woman and a set of unexpected comforts: a well-tended fire, candles at the ready, and a bed of dried grass. Chaska instructed Sarah to stay the night there with her children, adding that she should go immediately the next morning to his mother's tent to ask for a "squaw dress."

With that, Chaska left. "No one can imagine the confusion of an Indian camp when the braves come home victorious; it is like Bedlam broken loose," Sarah wrote. "Hour after hour we sat listening to every footstep, expecting death every minute. Guns were firing in all directions, women were mourning over their dead, and the conjurors were at work over the sick and wounded, all tending to increase the confusion." Several Dakota women and children were also sleeping in the bark house. Sarah's white companion spoke little English, but she found comfort in her presence as they listened to the clamor outside, sounds that faded away only in the morning light.

The next day, Tuesday, August 19, broke bright and hot. The camp was quiet as Little Crow and most of the Dakota warriors began to file down the road to stage an attack on Fort Ridgely, eleven miles away. Sarah and several of the Dakota women with her went to find Chaska's mother, who took Sarah in for the morning hours and did as she asked, providing her a Dakota dress and braiding her hair to make her appear more "rugged." The order had gone out the night before, from Little Crow or one of his head warriors, or perhaps direct from the *tiyotipi,* that all white and mixed-blood women were to be given "squaw suits"; at the same time, the Dakota leaders had ordered that none of their own people should continue to wear white-style clothing or stay in white-style houses, Little Crow's excepted. Several Dakota women rubbed dirt into Sarah's skin and she did the same to her children, worrying all the while that James's bright blond hair would render his disguise useless.

Again her Dakota wardens kept Sarah and her children on the move in response to rumor after rumor that the warriors were coming back from the fort to kill the captives. As the heat mounted, Sarah feared sunstroke, and her mind, already agitated, began to unhinge. How far it unhinged and how far she was predisposed to erratic or melodramatic behavior is impossible to say, but among the many tales of captivity hers contains some of the most jarring and disturbing scenes, ones she would later spend much of her time trying to play down or explain away. Just as some of the Dakota women shielded white women, others took pleasure in taunting them. When an "old squaw" named Lightfoot suggested that she would be killed and her children kept for ransom, Sarah set out to murder Nellie and James rather than let that happen. "I ran to a squaw," she wrote, "begged her knife, caught up my little girl, and in a moment would have cut her throat, when a squaw said it was false."

All through the hot day flashing clouds moved down the valley from the northwest, harbinger of an angry prairie storm and another long night for Sarah and her children. Late in the afternoon, yet another stray rumor reached her ears that men were moving through the camp and killing captives. Chaska's mother quickly gathered a bag of crackers and a cup and shooed the three Wakefields into a small ravine amid the cottonwoods well below the bluff line. "It was very steep, and the banks were like the roof of a house," wrote Sarah, but the rudimentary feeling of shelter would not last. As the weather moved in, the embankment began to erode on top of the trio of hideaways, showering them with mud and water, while Sarah relied on one threadbare blanket and a small bottle of brandy in her efforts to keep her children warm.

She spent the night with one foot in a stream of rainwater, hushing her children and starting at the sound of muskrats that seemed to her wolves come to devour them. Assuming her husband dead, she turned to heaven for solace. "I never knew how to pray before," she wrote, "but I had no one to call upon but God." The following morning, Sarah waited for deliverance, fearing that daylight would betray them to any warrior who wandered nearby as she nursed Nellie, fed her children the last of the crackers, and silently painted mental panoramas of starvation or death by mosquitoes made ravenous by the rain. When Chaska's mother finally appeared many hours after sunrise, Sarah wrote, the two "laughed, cried, and, I really think I kissed her." After extracting Sarah from her contorted position and rubbing the circulation back into her limbs, Chaska's mother returned with them to her bark-skin lodge and provided coffee and painkilling medicines.

Sarah and her children were next taken north along the Minnesota River and across the Redwood River to catch up with the encampment, more than six hundred people in all, moving a step away from the population centers of Minnesota. Sarah and all of the captives understood that Little Crow was shifting his location only so that he could consolidate his people and be better positioned to launch a series of attacks on Fort Ridgely and what few settlers still huddled in the towns along the Minnesota River. The whites in camp were not to be killed yet; that much was slowly becoming clear. Sarah and the other captives knew from the start that Little Crow would be their warden and, in the end, their executioner or deliverer. Wherever Little Crow went, whatever acts of war or negotiation he might initiate, day by day and mile by mile, her fate was now bound to his.

# Chapter Four

In some other region of the West, the rangy, cleft-chinned man arriving on the scene at the commencement of the action, destined to play an outsized role in its resolution, might have been a soldier, sheriff, judge, rancher, speculator, renegade, or gambler—almost anything but a pious and proper churchman. There was something almost preposterous about the face that the Right Reverend Henry Benjamin Whipple, first Episcopal bishop of Minnesota, showed to the world: descendant of Revolutionary War veterans, relative of luminaries, friend to the great, protector of the downtrodden, indefatigable traveler, trailblazing educator, mentor, husband, and father. Tall, lean, and clean-shaven, with flowing hair and deep-set eyes, he commanded attention; a practiced orator, he always came across as the most earnest and credible man in the room. His blind spots were sizable, especially his trust in public servants to operate honestly within corrupt systems, but no one had seen violence on the horizon as clearly as he had and no man had said so so forcefully or so often. When Whipple disembarked at Saint Paul on the day after Little Crow's council and found himself in a tornado of rumor, excitement, and fear, he was perhaps the least disoriented person in the city. Almost from the moment he entered the state three years earlier, he had been waiting for something to happen and praying that it wouldn't.

The summer of 1862 had felt as ominous to Whipple as it had to Sarah Wakefield. In July, Whipple had escorted his wife and a party of four Philadelphia women, donors to his Episcopal missions, on a guided tour of the Lower Agency and Upper Agency as the Dakota began to assemble for the annuity payment. Expecting the customary round of councils and entertainments, they had found instead no gold and thousands of dissatisfied, even distraught, Dakotas. A group of accommodationist village chiefs asked the clergyman they called Straight Tongue for assurances that they would get their promised money, and from the Episcopal missionary Samuel Hinman he heard the fast-spreading story that paper currency would be substi-

Henry Benjamin Whipple, ca. 1855–65

tuted for the expected gold. "I had never seen the Indians so restless," Whipple wrote later. In mid-July he had preached a service for Timothy Sheehan's company of soldiers and was entertained at the home of Indian agent Thomas Galbraith, from whom he received a secondhand gift, the ceremonial regalia of a Western Dakota chief. All the while his unease grew. After laying the cornerstone for a mission church at the Lower Agency, Whipple had left the Dakota country "sad at heart."

At the start of August, then, as the Upper Agency Dakota began their agitation to get at the goods in the agency warehouse, Whipple was far away. After a few days spent at home in Faribault with his family, he had commenced a northward journey that took him almost the length of the state into lands where white encroachment had so far left a softer imprint. In these last years before the railroad would connect the upper Northwest to Chicago and points beyond, it was not unusual in any season or weather for someone on the prairie to encounter the bishop moving between towns and Indian villages in a sleigh or wagon behind Bashaw, his black Arabian steed. Whipple later calculated his travels with Bashaw at fifty thousand miles and was proud of his clothes' constant state of dirtiness and disrepair. He thought it important that religious men prove themselves in the field and admired preachers as much for their hardiness as for their theological wisdom or skill at public speaking.

His August travels had first taken him sixty miles by wagon to Saint Paul and then another one hundred miles up the Mississippi River to tiny Fort Ripley, tucked twenty feet above the waterline at the southernmost tip of the territory populated by the Ojibwe, traditional rivals and sometime blood enemies of the Dakota. Whipple's ultimate destination was the Ojibwe settlement on the shore of Red Lake, only sixty miles south of the Canadian border, a trip of several hundred miles that required horses, buggies, riverboats, and canoes to traverse vast systems of trails, portages, marshes, and bays. His companions included the head of the Ojibwe mission, the Reverend E. Steele Peake, as well as an Ojibwe deacon and three Ojibwe guides. "We have in the party a working church," Whipple wrote in his diary. "A bishop, a priest, two Christian Indians, one Christian white man, and the heathen to be converted."

In the late 1700s the Ojibwe had vied with the Dakota for the woods and lakes of what would become northern Minnesota, and before that the tribes had fought battles over hunting grounds and seasonal villages on the shores of the western Great Lakes, but in 1862 their peoples occupied very different worlds. Ojibwe lands were less suitable for corn and wheat and more difficult for whites to reach. Treaties in 1837, 1842, 1854, and 1855 had placed the Ojibwe on eleven reservations, and white logging operations were beginning to cut apart the northern woods, but those same agreements also contained unusual usufruct clauses that left unused lands open to the Ojibwe until such time as the president might require their surrender. In comparison to the Dakota, then, their territory still provided space for them to live in more customary ways, sustaining themselves by harvesting vast gardens of wild rice in wide freshwater bays, making maple syrup, hunting, fishing, and foraging. Most of their domain was birch and pine forest saturated with thousands of small waterways, separated from the Dakota by the Big Woods, the thick band of deciduous growth that both tribes still used as hunting grounds despite the growing white population settled there. Peake's Episcopal mission, Saint Columba, lay thirty miles up the Mississippi River from Fort Ripley, but farther up into the wilderness the residual effect of eighteenth-century French Catholic missionaries was still evident in the Ojibwe's possession of old rosary beads and pocket-sized crosses, representing what Whipple casually referred to as "the defective teaching of Rome."

All the way to Red Lake and back, as August passed Whipple had preached in lakeside Ojibwe villages when he could, but his real aim had been to perform a first reconnaissance through a region of his diocese he'd never visited, and his diary is more notable for its careful observations of the people and landscape than for any attempt to effect a Protestant awakening. In the meantime, odd portents began to accumulate. On his southward return journey, his Ojibwe guides saw marks that they determined to be Dakota tracks; wrote Whipple, "they stooped to the ground, and wherever they found traces of a footprint they carefully examined the crushed grass." The discovery of a Dakota moccasin the next day at the fresh remains of a camp put the bishop's party on high alert for the final leg of their trip, and once they'd made it back to Fort Ripley, Whipple found the Ojibwe in that place "much disturbed, showing that a storm was brewing."

He was also shown a recent letter from Little Crow to an Ojibwe chief suggesting that some kind of personal accord had been reached between Dakota and Ojibwe leaders, if not between their peoples. Another man, looking back on the events of the next six weeks, might have assigned great significance to these signs, but for the bishop they were unremarkable. For centuries the Dakota and Ojibwe had fought each other over hunting grounds and for honor, but they had also conferred on matters of trade and relations with whites, making peace and breaking peace with only glancing reference to the wishes or power of foreign governments. To most of Minnesota's residents, an Indian was an Indian was an Indian, but there were a few whites like Whipple who knew tribes, bands, and villages as individual entities. Whatever had been on Bishop Whipple's mind as he stepped onto the docks in Saint Paul after his four weeks in the northern reaches of the state, it was neither war nor alliance between the Dakota and Ojibwe. But he soon learned that the event he had so long feared and foreseen—war between whites and Indians—had finally come to pass.

The telegraph wires ran into Minnesota's capital from the east but not yet from the west, and so the news from the Lower Agency had come to Saint Paul not in one crisp flash but in a confused and disorderly tumble. Excitement filled the city all day and evening on Tuesday, August 19, just as Whipple returned from his northern journey. Tales of mayhem and murder rode in on horseback and in wagons, rushed from ear to ear in the capitol building, circulated through the streets, and soon found the editors of the *Pioneer*, the *Union*, and the *Press*, who reported what they could even if what they could report wasn't much. Behind the news came the first undeniable proof of war, a trickle of stunned settlers pouring in from the river towns to tell secondhand stories of indiscriminate murder and unspeakable mutilation, of grain destroyed and houses looted, of a valley-wide panic that seemed sure to expand to include the entire western half of the state and the Dakota Territory beyond.

As the hours and days went on, the details mounted: farmhouses burned, families wiped out, an old woman suffocated under a burning mattress, a farmer's wife and her teenage son chased into the woods and shot from behind, a baby beaten to death with a violin case, a young woman carried away on horseback to an unknown fate. In many cases, the sole survivor of a family, or even of a township, did the telling. Much of what was reported was true, much was embellished, but underneath it all lay a fear that things had gone terribly wrong:

whites always moved west; Indians never moved east. But here were the Dakota, coming *back*.

Everywhere west of the Mississippi, it seemed, the Dakota were on the move. Many whites believed that the entire Indian world had risen. Some messengers swore that columns of Indian warriors were only miles away from the state capital. Others said that the Yanktons and Yanktonais from the James and Missouri rivers and the Lakotas from the Black Hills beyond were following behind Little Crow, tens of thousands of warriors on the march with murder in their hearts. Some had heard that the Ojibwe had buried the hatchet with their ancient adversaries and were about to join the Dakota cause with an attack from the north, that the Ho-Chunks to the south were providing a third talon to the Indian claw closing on the state capital. None of these scenarios was remotely true, but the thick cloud of fear and confusion was very real.

The first official messenger to arrive in Saint Paul, a lawyer named William H. Shelley, reached the capitol and Governor Alexander Ramsey around noon on August 19 with a penciled request from the Indian agent Thomas Galbraith for two hundred armed men. Shelley had left Fort Ridgely at midnight and used up four horses and begged three carriage rides to get this far, presenting the governor with a set of eyewitness details and a crisis that represented disaster and opportunity in equal measure. His report was not the first to reach the governor, but it was the first over a recognizable signature, the one that sent Ramsey directly to Fort Snelling, the formidable stronghold perched on the first land ever transferred from the Dakota to the United States, a high, rounded cliff commanding the confluence of the Mississippi and Minnesota rivers. Built out of local limestone in the shape of a diamond, the fort had once been the Northwest Territory's northwesternmost bulwark, built in the wake of the War of 1812 to protect the interests of American fur traders, keep peace between the Dakota and Ojibwe, and establish an American military presence in the territory south of British Canada. Now its main function was to prepare men to join the Union army, and here Ramsey found the new recruits who would eventually form the Sixth Minnesota Regiment.

Nicknamed "Bluff Alec," Alexander Ramsey was a blunt, squarely built Scots-Dutchman of humble family origins, great ambition, and canny political instincts, whose career had begun as a Whig congress-

Fort Snelling and the Mississippi River, ca. 1860–69

man in his native Pennsylvania before President Zachary Taylor sent him west in 1849 to become governor of the new territory of Minnesota. Ramsey's primary goal had been to expand the region's white population as quickly as possible while enticing or forcing the Dakota and Ojibwe into treaties that would concentrate them on the smallest possible parcels of land in anticipation of the day when the territory had attracted enough white settlers to become a state. In those efforts he had been partly successful, overseeing the 1851 treaties and the removal of the Dakota from the Mississippi River Valley, but he also became the target of a congressional investigation after Democratic newspaper editors raised allegations of fraud related to his dealings with the Ojibwe. Exonerated, Ramsey spent five years as mayor of Saint Paul before being elected the state's second governor in 1860 as a newly minted Republican, taking full advantage of Minnesota's substantial support of Abraham Lincoln.

Ramsey's claim to national fame had been secured in April 1861 when, by coincidence, he'd found himself in Washington, D.C., on the day after the Confederate shelling of Fort Sumter. When Lincoln

Alexander Ramsey, ca. 1860

asked for 75,000 volunteers to mount what most assumed would be a short-lived show of military force to bring the rebellious states back into line, Ramsey had walked into the War Department building and offered a thousand-man regiment to Secretary of War Simon Cameron, an old political ally from Pennsylvania. Thus Minnesota became the first state to commit new soldiers to the war effort. The gesture had created a frenzy of volunteerism at home, and in June 1861 the recruits of the First Minnesota had steamed away down the Mississippi, destined for the railheads at La Crosse and Prairie du Chien, Wisconsin, and the battlefields of Virginia beyond. By the end of July the regiment had already distinguished itself in the Union defeat at Bull Run and was now encamped along the Maryland side of the Potomac River. Lincoln's second call for men had come to Minnesota in mid-August, a new quota amounting to 5,360 soldiers, or about six regiments, out of the nationwide total of 300,000. Companies were flowing into the fort from all over the state and being outfitted and sent away as quickly as possible, four new regiments so far and a fifth on the way. But if the reports delivered by Shelley and the other messengers were true, the arithmetic had been altered. Ramsey would now need many more armed men in his state, not fewer.

Only fifteen years earlier, the land on which Saint Paul stood had been Dakota land. Little Crow had been born in the village of Kaposia, which occupied the bottomlands of a bend in the Mississippi River ten miles below Fort Snelling and some three or four miles below the high plateau of the current capital city. In 1846 he had returned to Kaposia to seize his leadership position after his father's death, and for the next five years he presided over three hundred or more families. All of the villages of the Mdewakanton Dakota had for centuries been part of a migratory cycle; the valley of the Mississippi River was their home, each village laid out with semipermanent summer lodges—large, squat, elm-bark houses with low, gabled roofs and overhanging front porches, designed to sleep several families. From this base the warriors of the band would conduct their spring and fall hunts along the Mississippi and its navigable tributaries, especially the Minnesota and the Saint Croix, which now marked the Wisconsin border.

Few of the celebrated riverboat pilots or romanticized flatboatmen of the time knew these rivers half as well as the Dakota, for whom the waters were provider, holy place, cradle of stories, highway, and constant companion. In the treaties of 1851 the Dakota had, with great sadness, conceded the Mississippi River and its valley altogether, the first major step toward the creation of the state of Minnesota and of a safer and more permanent white pathway from the Great Lakes to the Pacific Ocean. Within days of that signing, two years before ratification in Congress and the first delivery of annuities, whites had poured into all of the Mdewakanton villages during their unoccupied seasons, a peremptory move that embittered the Dakota, who watched whites occupy their lodges during the winter, till their old fields in the summer, and peer at them with unfriendly eyes whenever they passed.

Once the Dakota had been removed, whites had few doubts about the destiny of the confluence of the Mississippi and Minnesota rivers. For Mdewakantons, this meeting of waters was a sacred site at the center of their origin stories; for whites, it was the fulcrum of all their settlement plans, providing new arrivals with steamboat landings, powerful waterfalls, and abundant and fertile farmland. By this point in American history there was a script to follow. Nothing could invalidate the promise, indeed the expectation, that Saint Paul would become the nation's next Saint Louis, Cincinnati, or even Chicago. Its newest residents were fired with entrepreneurial ambition; they possessed growing quantities of capital, labor, and civic enthusiasm to support their grand plans. In 1862 the streets were still made of dirt, and most of the houses had been thrown together in a rush, but there were

Saint Paul and the Mississippi River, 1861

also luxury hotels, pleasure steamboats, a new capitol building under way, and any number of speculators ready to take the railroad into and through Indian lands.

No city in America had grown faster than Saint Paul over the past decade, its population increasing a hundredfold to more than ten thousand people, with no end in sight. With the city situated on the higher of two broad terraces, its residents commanded a view of the Father of Waters unsurpassed along its entire length. Covered in rich black soil, close to large limestone and sandstone deposits, with bluffs punctured by several large, cool natural caves, Saint Paul was ready-made for the building trades and a thriving business in beer and produce. Already by 1862 shipping was king, as millions of dollars' worth of flour, grain, wheat, corn, and potatoes left the city's waterside landings and warehouses to float down the Mississippi. The climate was touted for its healthful, bracing air, and for many years visitors had flowed in from the South and East expecting that their various maladies might be cured by application of a dry, cold winter or a pleasant, mild summer.

Everywhere crews were at work repairing, improving, or building, and in 1860 the largest jewel of that work had been completed, a 1,800-foot trestle bridge crossing the Mississippi 82 feet above the waterline. On Wednesday, August 20, 1862, the same day that local newspapers first ran brief, alarmed stories of the events in the western part of the state, the *Daily Press* described Saint Paul as a thriving nexus of trade in agriculture, timber, and fur, "the outlet for not only all northwestern American territory, but for all northwestern British possessions." Geography was fate: "Nature has stamped upon her tablets the irrevocable destiny, and man is only working out its unanswerable truths." The city's amenities included a recently completed telegraph connection to Washington, two dozen houses of worship, a full set of thriving fraternal organizations that included the Freemasons and Odd Fellows, three newspapers, a public library, a federal fort, and, finally, an Indian frontier only two days distant that still seemed exotic enough to excite the imagination.

At the same time, for all the evidence of prosperity, there was still a hesitation to the city's progress, an inertia connected to its territorial past. In 1857, just as the question of statehood was being decided, a nationwide economic depression had fathered a calamitous series of credit busts and business failures that closed most of the city's banks, brought immigration to a temporary standstill, and contributed to a multimillion-dollar railroad bond disaster that left the treasury empty. For a decade residents had been told that rail service was just around the corner, but only in June 1862, two months before the outbreak of war against the Dakota, had the first train run over a track covering ten miles between Saint Paul and Saint Anthony, which would later be called Minneapolis. Not a mile of usable track had been laid outside of these cities, and residents who wanted to head east still had to travel two hundred miles by water to get to the La Crosse & Milwaukee line, which would get them to Chicago.

Locals seized on a rash of hotel fires, the most recent one month before the Dakota uprising, as a symbol of the backward steps that seemed to be hindering the state's big plans. Less significant, perhaps, but still deeply felt, the city lacked an identity that went beyond its role as a staging ground for westward expansion. Amid all the tumult and terror surrounding the news of violence along the Minnesota River, many citizens of the capital understood that an opportunity might be presenting itself. Little Crow was right: however few the number of Dakotas involved in the new war, all Dakotas were being blamed for it. Whatever else might result from this sudden conflict, the richest agricultural regions of the state would now need no additional pretext to become entirely white, finishing the work that Alexander Ramsey had begun as territorial governor years earlier.

Like nineteen out of twenty white Minnesotans in 1862, Henry Benjamin Whipple had been born and raised somewhere else, and he still carried sensibilities that made him a product of the East no matter how tight his embrace of the northwestern frontier. Born into a comfortable, prosperous family in Adams, New York, near Lake Ontario and the mouth of the Saint Lawrence River, his august genealogy connected him to a signer of the Declaration of Independence and to several important figures of the Civil War era, including Henry Wager Halleck, Whipple's first cousin and Abraham Lincoln's general in chief.

In his late teens Whipple had embarked for Oberlin College in Ohio, where his uncle George was a professor of mathematics, but after two years he was forced to quit his studies because of a severe bronchial problem that had dogged him through his childhood. His doctor's prescription, "activity," led young Henry first into his father's business and then into politics as a capable young campaigner for the New York Whigs. This work caught the eyes of Thurlow Weed, who would eventually become the point man for William H. Seward, Lincoln's most formidable opponent in his 1860 nomination contest, and Horatio Seymour, a leading Northern opponent of abolition who would become governor of New York and the losing candidate in the 1868 presidential election.

In 1842 Whipple married Cornelia Wright, daughter of a local lawyer and prominent Episcopalian. One year later, after his health worsened so much that throat surgery was necessary, he left for Florida on his doctor's advice, traveling without his wife or infant daughter, Lizzie, hoping to find a restorative power in the warm climate. Indeed, Saint Augustine seemed to salve Whipple's lungs, and by 1844 he had regained twelve pounds and was ready to come home, a trip he made by way of New Orleans, the Mississippi River, Saint Louis, Cincinnati, Washington, D.C., and Philadelphia. After his return to New York State, Whipple decided to enter the priesthood, encouraged by Cornelia and her brother, Benjamin, who had been baptized along with

Whipple two years earlier. He studied privately and preached for some time in Troy, near his hometown, until in 1857 he agreed to a call from the Church of the Free Communion in Chicago.

"Everyone thought it was madness," Whipple wrote in his memoirs, referring to his move to far-off Illinois with his wife and three children, but he found himself persuaded that the "great number of artisans, clerks, and railway men" in Chicago were "sheep having no shepherd" and in pressing need of his services. "So often the shadows were shifted to show that in the most brutalized lives there were traces of God's image left," he wrote, and it became his compulsion to visit those areas least frequented by men of God, where he caused a small scandal by baptizing vagrants, actresses, and even prostitutes. In some of the poorest neighborhoods of the city Whipple was struck by a powerful and lasting sense of mission. He threw himself into his calling, perusing medical textbooks in order to provide care to his most destitute charges and becoming a champion of free churches, a conviction that filled his pews and also helped him develop useful fund-raising skills. In short order he grew to love the city and his work there, so it seemed "like a clap of thunder" when in June 1859 he was named the first Episcopal bishop of Minnesota.

The distance from Chicago to Saint Paul was only four hundred miles, but socially, economically, and culturally the cities were worlds apart. To a missionary's thinking, Chicago was Sodom, a potent concentration of unrighteousness in need of God's cleansing light, while a frontier zone like Minnesota was Babylon, a polyglot and spiritually diverse mixture of Indians, Irish, Germans, Scandinavians, and easterners not so much fallen from grace as in need of a common God. "Society has not crystallized," Whipple wrote of Minnesota. "Everything is to be done—roads opened, school-houses, court-houses, and churches to be built. Old prejudices are weakened, necessity compelling activity in all secular matters, and he who would mould these restless men must be one who feels the beating of their pulses, and keeps even step with the tide of immigration."

Whipple surprised local church leaders by electing to live in Faribault, out on the prairie sixty miles south of the capital, where he could better afford a dignified house and provide himself with a more central point of departure as he traveled his new diocese behind his trusted horse, Bashaw, visiting established towns, thriving farms, and "one-roomed log huts, where my bedroom had to be improvised by partitioning one end of the room with a sheet." He found his new flock well suited to his temperament. "Many of the frontier settlers were people of refinement and culture who, in some financial panic, had lost everything and had pre-empted homes in the West, where they lived in independence, scorning to apologize to their bidden guest for their meager surroundings," he wrote. "The genuine pioneer may be a rude man, but he is seldom an infidel."

Yet "infidels" were exactly the people Whipple seems to have been seeking. From the first he found that he was as much interested in his church's fledgling mission to the Indians as in any other part of his duties. "From my childhood," he said, he had "felt a deep interest in these brown children of our Heavenly Father," and credited this interest to an old man in Adams, New York, who had delighted in telling stories about his capture by Indians as a child. But in the deeper regions of Whipple's psyche, it appears that he needed Indians as much as he presumed they needed him. "My habits of life are active," he wrote, "my preference is for missionary work such as the care of the sick and poor and the leading of the stranger to the Church." The Dakota, to Whipple, were the next challenge after the poor of upstate New York, the crackers of Florida, and the railway workers and prostitutes of Chicago. On the second page of his memoirs he told of his mother's injunction, delivered early in his childhood with her "gentle hand on my head": "My dear boy, it is always right to defend the weak and helpless."

Whipple could be as romantic as any wilderness-drunk poet about life on the frontier. "Nothing lingers longer in memory than the nights spent round the Indian camp-fire," he wrote, "in the heart of primeval nature, under the subtle influences of the ever-shining stars and the murmur of fragrant pines." His concern for Indians was founded on an intense, emotional paternalism. Despite his ever-growing sensitivity to the sophisticated patterns and traditions of Dakota life, he never stopped viewing them as pagan wards, "red children" in need of the benevolent hand of Christianity and agrarian civilization to save them from their own innocent backwardness. This view often put the bishop on the side of forces determined to push the Dakota onto farms and remove all traces of their Indianness; at the same time, it placed him in fierce opposition to anyone seeking to maltreat, swindle, or degrade the Dakota, a stance that would damn his name in the eyes of many white settlers, newspaper editors, and politicians.

Within a month of his arrival, the new bishop had visited the Reverend E. Steele Peake's Ojibwe mission church along the northern reaches of the Mississippi River and had "planted a mission" of his own among the Lower Agency Dakota to the west. He knew that to the Dakota the Episcopalians were Johnny-come-latelies, as the Presbyterians Stephen R. Riggs, Thomas S. Williamson, Samuel W. Pond, and Gideon H. Pond had been living, working, and preaching among the Eastern Dakota for decades. Most Dakotas seemed to tolerate missionaries, and some, including Little Crow, seemed to value their presence, perhaps because these were the only white people whose motives seemed to be out in the open, who were always willing to share meaningful stories, even if many of those stories were about an all-powerful God who was determined to take the place of the spirits revered by their ancestors.

Whipple was aware early on that to white settlers on the frontier he was an " 'enthusiastic tenderfoot' whose eyes had not yet been opened to the fact that there were no good Indians save dead Indians." Many of his battles would be fought against stiff resistance from his white parishioners and their fellow citizens. "Good men," he wrote, "advised me to have nothing to do with Indian Missions, on the ground that the red men were a degraded, perishing race," and soon after he began his mission work a baptism of six or seven Dakotas produced the headline AWFUL SACRILEGE—HOLIEST RITES OF THE CHURCH GIVEN TO RED-HANDED MURDERERS.

Whipple did believe that the Dakota were a degraded and endangered race, but he put the blame for their debasement on whites. A belief in the culpability of "the Indian system"—faceless, Byzantine, and long-established—would fuel the bishop's efforts on behalf of the Dakota at the same time that it kept him away from a more sophisticated assessment of the system's human architects and caretakers. Whipple's benevolence depended on his perception of the weakness, sickness, brokenness, and lostness of the "wandering Indians," a state common to all of mankind, but, in his view, magnified in the case of the Dakota. In this formulation, the only way out of lostness was Christ, and the more lost one became, the more one needed Christ. In many ways Whipple's personal brand of Episcopalianism was unusually Calvinist—he believed in the necessity of sin, suffering, and redemption—but he was decidedly un-Calvinist and unconventional in his belief that individuals of all races could take an active hand in shaping their own spiritual destiny.

As was true of many missionaries across the Northwest, including all of the competing Presbyterians in Minnesota, Whipple's pieties and paternalistic assumptions were accompanied by thorough and careful observations of Indian customs and culture. Though he didn't do it all of the time, Whipple was capable of recording the Dakota view of the world, and especially its view of whites, without criticism or amusement. He faithfully reported Dakota barbs about whites and their lack of hospitality, their mania for individual wealth, and their propensity to state something as sure when it wasn't sure rather than offering the more sensible Dakota answer, "perhaps." And more than once Whipple noted with an almost fatherly pride how the Dakota viewed the white church's focus on the afterlife as nothing more than a bribe.

Around the time of the annuity payment in 1861, a cornerstone ceremony at his new mission church had been interrupted by a scalp dance, a ritual designed to honor bravery in battle in which one woman would carry a pole bearing an enemy's skin stretched over a small hoop while other women danced and the men sang and drummed. Of the many Dakota dances, this was the most troubling to some missionaries, both for its use of human remains and for the fact that it often ended late at night and was purportedly followed by "illicit intercourse between the sexes." Through an interpreter Whipple complained to the village chief Wabasha, explaining that he had known the murdered Ojibwe man and that such a ceremony would only serve to bring forth the wrath of God. Whipple recorded Wabasha's answer precisely and without commentary: "White man go to war with his own brother; kills more men than Wabasha can count all his life. Great Spirit look down and says, 'Good white man; he has My Book; I have good home for him by and by.' Dakota has no Great Spirit's Book; he goes to war, kills one man, has a foolish scalp-dance; Great Spirit very angry. *Wabasha doesn't believe it!*"

In Chicago, Whipple had ministered to the downtrodden without asking serious questions about the origins of their condition. Not so in Minnesota, where he was soon converted to the cause of reform. "Our Indian affairs were then at their worst," he later wrote, "without government, without protection, without personal rights of property, subject to every evil influence, and the prey of covetous, dishonest white men." He began to question village chiefs about absent supplies, absent schools, and absent monies; as one Dakota elder told him, "I know that it is a long way to Washington; the cars go very fast, and perhaps the money has been jostled off and lost." Most important, given all of his other responsibilities as bishop, he found an avid apprentice and reservation preacher in the missionary Samuel Hinman, an orphan from Connecticut, who in 1862 would become the first graduate of Whipple's newly opened divinity school. Satisfied that he had left the Dakota in Hinman's caring hands, Whipple had, early in his tenure, turned his attention to Washington, D.C., and the highest office in the land.

He sent his first letter on behalf of the Dakota to President James Buchanan in April 1860, describing the Indians as "American pagans whose degradation and helplessness must appeal to every Christian heart." All his life Whipple's preferred method of persuasion was the multipoint plan, and this one contained eight "suggestions" to reform the Indian system. The central precept of his scheme was that properly behaved Dakotas should be made American citizens rather than wards of the federal government. This meant giving the United States power to administer Indian laws and consolidating far-flung bands of a given tribe on the same plot of land so that they could receive the "blessings of civilization": towns, houses, churches, and, most of all, farm allotments. Citizenship would be probationary, waiting on sustained evidence of temperance and successful husbandry. Village chiefs would retain their power as long as they played by the rules and stayed sober. What Whipple expected the president to do with his letter is unclear, but in any event Buchanan never responded, ignoring far more than just Whipple's letter as he finished out his term as a near hermit in the White House, befuddled by the approach of civil war.

After that, Whipple was silent for a time, until, in March 1861, he sent his first letter to the newly inaugurated Abraham Lincoln. "The sad condition of the Indians of this State, who are my heathen wards, compels me to address you on their behalf," he began. "I ask only justice for a wronged and neglected race." Now bearing two more years of experience with the Dakota and Ojibwe, he lambasted a system that negotiated treaties but couldn't or wouldn't enforce them and spelled out the evils of the patronage chain that awarded favored persons positions according to past political activity "without any reference to their fitness for the place." The letter contained no reference to alcohol, but otherwise his suggestions to Lincoln were the same as they'd been to

Buchanan: bring the Indians together into townships, make them citizens, provide them land and farming implements, build them schools, and spend the annuity money on necessary provisions rather than disburse it in gold.

Whipple had soon sent a reminder asking the president to read his "plea," and one week later, on March 27, 1861, Lincoln responded. "I have the honor to acknowledge the receipt of your esteemed favor of the 6th of March," he wrote, "and to state in reply that I have commended the matter of which it treats to the special attention of the Secretary of the Interior." This was no brush-off. Whipple did indeed hear from Interior Secretary Caleb Smith later in April, a letter agreeing in substance with Whipple's suggestions that kicked off a months-long correspondence that came to include Smith; Minnesota's senators, Henry Rice and Morton Wilkinson; Cyrus Aldrich, one of Minnesota's representatives in Congress; Commissioner of Indian Affairs William P. Dole; and the Dakota agent, Thomas Galbraith.

Always collegial in print, Whipple was deeply frustrated in private. All parties agreed that the Indian system was in need of repair, but all agreed that the responsibility lay at other doors than their own, and in the end nothing beyond talk was accomplished. By the spring of 1862 Whipple knew that he would be heading to New York City in October for the triannual convention of Episcopal bishops, and in his letters he made it clear that one desired outcome of all of this conversation about Indian affairs would be an audience with President Lincoln along the way. A straightforward and powerful preacher, Whipple nonetheless believed that the hearts of men were best swayed by personal appeals. When he arrived back in Saint Paul from his trip to the north country and heard about the attack on the Lower Agency and massacre in the settlements, his desire to get to Washington only increased.

For the moment, though, he had more immediate concerns. Whatever his sympathies for the Dakota, many of his white parishioners now seemed to be in mortal danger. Riding south all night, Whipple reached Faribault at the break of dawn on Wednesday, August 20. "At once," he wrote, he "sent a boy ringing a bell through the streets, with a message to the citizens to meet me in front of the hotel." There he addressed the crowd, giving what news of the attacks he could and taking the names of those who wished to fight and those who could provide horses. In short order, the Faribault company was on its way across forty miles of prairie and farmland to join the men massing at

Saint Peter, ready to steam up the Minnesota River and meet whatever Dakota force awaited them.

A few days later Whipple followed the same roads, arriving in Saint Peter to find the town "filled with refugees, many of whom were badly wounded." There he also found his friend Asa W. Daniels, the town's only doctor, former Lower Agency physician and brother of the man John Wakefield had replaced. Along with several townswomen, they helped set up the courthouse as a hospital, where Daniels set fractures and performed amputations while Whipple did the best he could with smaller wounds. His reputation as a reformer and friend of the Dakota preceded him, enough so that he had to worry about the reaction of his patients. "The gratitude of some of the sufferers not only over-paid me, but saved me from the hatred which border people felt for an Indian sympathizer," he wrote. "One German softened the hearts of her neighbors by declaring, 'Dat bishop is no pad man; he haf sewed up my wounds and made me well; he is one goot Christian man.'"

Whipple soon discovered that he had contracted an infection of the hand from hurriedly sewing and bandaging wounds in an unsani-tary environment, a discomfort that would last for many weeks and stand as his only personal injury during the Dakota War. He was not to continue doctoring settlers or gathering troops. Rather, he began to pen a plea he would call "The Duty of Citizens Concerning the Indian Massacre" with the intention of publishing his views for the people of his diocese. And he continued to lay his plans for a visit to the East, though those plans had changed materially. His design now was to lay before the president the costs of a system built on iniquity, a great moral failure that had turned into an inevitable tide of blood.

# Chapter Five

On Thursday, August 21, 1862, the news from Minnesota rode the wires thirteen hundred miles to Washington, D.C., and the telegraph room on the second floor of the War Department building, a few hundred steps across the west lawn of the White House. There it was transcribed and added to a stack of messages in the converted library facing Pennsylvania Avenue that had become a strategic crow's nest for Abraham Lincoln. The president's standard practice when awaiting bulletins from various fronts was to wear out the path to the War Department, climb the steps, and look through all of the telegrams. He would keep the messages in order until he stopped, turned to the telegraph operators, and said, "Well, boys, I am down to the raisins." Borrowed from a doctor ministering to a vomiting child, the metaphor meant that he'd reached a message he'd seen on his previous visit. More than a routine, this was Lincoln's way of wresting control of the flow of information from his generals and wiring himself directly into the mechanism of the war. Earlier in the year all of the telegraph lines in the North had been placed under the control of the War Department, and since that time keeping up with the wired messages had become an obsession.

The first telegram from Minnesota was addressed from Governor

Ramsey to Secretary of War Edwin Stanton. It began, "The Sioux Indians on our western border have risen, and are murdering men, women,
and children." A second message followed hard after, from Minnesota's
secretary of state to Stanton's assistant war secretary, C. P. Walcott: "A
most frightful insurrection of Indians has broken out along our whole
frontier. Men, women, and children are indiscriminately murdered;
evidently the result of a deep-lain plan, the attacks being simultaneous along our whole border." Other communications from the frontier
would soon follow, all elbowing for room among the business of the
Civil War. Dozens of other messages in the pile had arrived this day
from every part of the Union, almost all of them concerned with Lincoln's recent order that the states furnish 300,000 additional troops,
asking questions about transport, outfitting, pay, mustering protocols,
and timetables. There may have been no worse time during Lincoln's
presidency—or, for that matter, during the nation's history—to convey
such information with any hope of a speedy response.

Thirteen months earlier Lincoln had finished his extraordinary
first hundred days in office, shaking off the last lingering sense in the
North and South that he was a country bumpkin elevated far above
his station. He had turned the shelling of Fort Sumter into a Union
rallying cry while managing to keep the border slave states in the fold;
he had corralled, if not unified, a seemingly uncorrallable cabinet;
and he had created an army and put it into motion across the famous
"thousand-mile front" of the Civil War. These developments seemed to
be a series of small miracles. Then, in July 1861, naïve and high-spirited
Union forces had been routed at Bull Run, just thirty miles southwest
of the White House, and cold reality had set in.

Gray and frostbitten February had brought the sudden sickness
and death of his favorite son, Willie, after which First Lady Mary Todd
descended into a grief so deep and lasting that her husband feared permanent madness was finally setting in. In March the ironclads *Monitor*
and *Merrimack* had fought their famous battle in Tidewater Virginia,
resulting in a standoff that kept the Confederate navy from approaching Washington, D.C., and April had seen Ulysses S. Grant's important victory at Shiloh. A growing attachment to Tad, his youngest son,
began to mend Lincoln's heart, and as his spirits returned, so did his
energy for war: he reorganized and reassigned many of his senior generals, created new military districts, and watched with satisfaction as

Abraham Lincoln, January 1864

the Union army headed toward Richmond with 58,000 troops. Early summer was an optimistic time, even for a leader as naturally suspicious of good news as Lincoln, but it was not to last. As the summer of 1862 wore on, Union forces began to founder badly.

In June, Lincoln thought that General George B. McClellan had pinned Robert E. Lee to the ground at Richmond, but over a period of two discouraging weeks the Union forces had reversed direction, first mounting a fruitless siege and then conducting a series of retreats, a defensive strategy based on McClellan's astounding overestimations of Confederate manpower. Then, as the Northern army sat impotent on Virginia's James River, the greater portion of Lee's men headed north along a line that seemed to point straight at the White House. The failure to take Richmond or adequately cover Washington created embarrassing headlines—THE CAPITAL IN DANGER!—and had persuaded Lincoln to import yet another general from the West, John

Pope, a young, portly engineer with old family connections to President Lincoln, and give him the job of keeping the "secesh" from marching across the Potomac River and up Pennsylvania Avenue.

Pope had seen some small-scale success in early action along the Mississippi River and suffered no lack of confidence, but this didn't help him against Lee, who just two months into his command of the Army of Northern Virginia had already made every Union commander in the eastern theater look like a boy inexpertly playing a tabletop game of war. On August 19 Lincoln told his cabinet that he was now "to have a sweat of five or six days" as he waited to see if and when McClellan would coordinate with Pope to create a force of sufficient size to protect the capital and deal Lee a real blow. McClellan had finally been ordered to withdraw from the Peninsula to a position halfway up the Potomac River to Washington, and the general was following those orders, albeit with excruciating slowness.

As Ramsey's telegram arrived on August 21, in the middle of Lincoln's "sweat," generals, battles, and Indian uprisings took a back seat to a public letter written by Horace Greeley, publisher of the *New York Tribune*. It was an era of enormous power for newspaper editors, and Greeley was the most powerful of all, a man with astonishing influence and reach whose newspaper boasted the largest circulation of any in the world. Lincoln's early Whig principles had aligned with Greeley's politics—the two had briefly served together in the House of Representatives—but when Greeley supported the Democrat Stephen Douglas against Lincoln in his 1858 run for Illinois's open Senate seat, the two men had begun to walk around one another in wary, if mostly collegial, circles.

Both men were Whigs turned Republicans with modest upbringings, and both were riding out tumultuous marriages while they bent their minds to the largest and most pressing crisis in their country's history. Greeley had admired Lincoln's Cooper Union speech, both for its plain poetry and because it was delivered with such aplomb and conviction to Greeley's own people, New York's intellectual and cultural elite. Their correspondence was frequent and usually friendly. But by the time the Civil War entered its second year, Greeley's ever more vocal anti-slavery stance and Lincoln's insistence that preserving the Union was his first and only priority put them in the situation of disagreeing fundamentally about executive policy while belonging to the same party and holding many of the same principles.

Now that Lincoln's presidency had passed its first birthday and the war seemed ever more grim and intractable, Greeley had settled into a pattern of not-so-gentle prodding. What the editor wanted most of all was immediate emancipation. A proclamation to free all of the slaves was still far from an expression of the public will, nor was it Lincoln's strategy, but the president paid attention because Greeley was very smart, commanded a wide audience, and was the standard-bearer for liberal Republicans who might hold one key to increased support for the war. Entitled "Prayer for Twenty Millions," Greeley's letter had been published in New York the previous day, but only on August 21, the same day that news of the Dakota uprising in Minnesota arrived, did a copy reach Lincoln's desk. The president read the text with care. Greeley's message, as he knew before he read the first word, was anything but a "prayer." Rather, it was a 2,200-word accusation of dereliction laid at Lincoln's feet. Greeley opened by throwing down a gauntlet: "[A] great proportion of those who triumphed in our election, and of all who desire the unqualified suppression of the Rebellion now desolating our country, are sorely disappointed and deeply pained by the policy you seem to be pursuing with regard to the slaves of the Rebels."

Greeley demanded that Lincoln stiffen his spine and declare slavery to be illegal everywhere, shifting the war's focus from preservation of the Union to the cause of human freedom. The letter's third section contained the primary warrant of Greeley's argument: "We ask you to consider that Slavery is everywhere the inciting cause and sustaining base of treason." Defending the right to determine their own use of human property had been part of the Southern justification for war since before Fort Sumter, as Confederate vice president Alexander Stephens had made clear in his "Cornerstone" speech of March 1861 when he said that "the proper status of the negro in our civilization . . . was the immediate cause of the late rupture and present revolution." But at no point had Lincoln directed that any official law or policy declare the opposite principle, and so to many readers of the *Tribune,* and of the dozens of other papers in which Greeley's letter was reprinted, it seemed that a major change was now being pressed on the president.

In truth, Lincoln needed no such call to order. One month earlier, during a cabinet meeting, he had first introduced his desire to pursue emancipation in the rebellious states, and was even in uncharacteristic fashion leaking that news to influential editors as long as they agreed not to publish the information. Greeley's name was high on that list—in fact, Lincoln's courier was en route to New York when the "Prayer" was published—but the editor hadn't received his notice in time, and now the struggle to shape public perception intensified. In Lincoln's mind, Greeley's letter demanded a sure, speedy response. The president held as a matter of faith that it was always better to present unpopular positions yourself than to let others put words in your mouth. Reply he must, in the full knowledge that no response to Greeley's letter could satisfy more than a minority of Americans. In a presidency full of tightrope moments, this was one of the most precarious yet.

In 1862, the country and its leaders were facing down questions of race strictly in terms of black and white; to speak of a Lincolnian approach to Indians would be fruitless. But had Lincoln lived to see the Civil War reach its end and had to deal with its aftermath, he would have had no choice but to engage with the turmoil in Indian country. By March 1869, in fact, the building pressures would become so acute that President Ulysses S. Grant would include a substantial statement on the "Indian question" in his inaugural address, declaring that "the proper treatment of the original occupants of this land—the Indians—is one deserving of careful study," not because Grant had a personal interest in the subject but because the potential for widespread violence, even war, was becoming a national crisis as the West was overrun with white settlers and fortune-seekers who weren't waiting for federal policy to catch up with their desires.

The "Peace Policy" that grew out of this "careful study" was an aggressive federal effort to Christianize the nation's Indians—or, put another way, to pacify them—that would became a focus and ultimately a failure of Grant's presidency. Over the next three decades, the nation and the hundreds of tribes within its borders would endure an escalating spiral of conflict and violence. George Armstrong Custer's death at the Battle of Little Big Horn in 1876, the killing of Crazy Horse under cloudy circumstances in 1877, the murder of 150 Lakota Indians near Wounded Knee Creek in 1890: a line can be drawn from each of these notorious events back to the council outside Little Crow's tent on an early morning in August 1862. To examine Lincoln's role in the Dakota War is not to hold a random piece of his presidency up to the light; rather, it is to illuminate one section of a long trajectory with a very steep and bloody arc.

Many tribes, including the Dakota, referred to the president as "Great White Father" or "Great Father"—a term meant to indicate the government's obligation more than an Indian's fealty—and understood in substance if not in detail that the American government, for all its talk about the consent of the governed, had been structured from its inception such that one man often had a monarchical influence on their freedom and fortunes. George Washington had fought with and against Indians in the wilds of Pennsylvania during the French and Indian War and carried fewer fantasies about savage natures, dying races, or noble warriors than almost all of his contemporaries. In his days as a Virginia landowner and militia colonel, Washington had argued for the rights of individuals and corporations—such as the Potomac Navigation Company, of which he was a prime shareholder—to purchase land from Indian tribes without state or federal intervention. By the time he was sworn in as chief executive in 1789, though, he had reversed course to believe that Indians were autonomous peoples in sovereign nations capable of determining their own destiny. The philosophy was not as pro-Indian as it might sound: if that sovereign destiny was to sell lands to the federal government, lands the United States could then use to generate revenue, or to respond to provocation by starting wars that the whites were sure to win—thus vacating Indian lands for white settlement—so be it.

This paradox underpinned the Northwest Ordinance, crafted by the Confederation Congress in 1787 under the eye of Washington and penned by his most faithful general, Henry Knox. In the ordinance's third article Knox wrote, "The utmost good faith shall always be observed towards the Indians; their lands and property shall never be taken from them without their consent; and, in their property, rights, and liberty, they shall never be invaded or disturbed, unless in just and lawful wars authorized by Congress; but laws founded in justice and humanity, shall from time to time be made for preventing wrongs being done to them, and for preserving peace and friendship with them." Nine paragraphs earlier, however, the same document reserved to state and territorial governors the power "to lay out the parts of the district in which the Indian titles shall have been extinguished, into counties and townships." From this point forward, then, the extinguishment of "Indian titles," in one fashion or another, became the nation's primary business, one to which the United States would eventually devote hundreds of thousands of men, millions of words of legal writing, and billions of dollars.

The first federal Congress spent much of its first two sessions considering two important issues that today seem arcane. One was the authorization and placement of the "federal city" that eventually became Washington, D.C., and the other was the federalizing of Indian relations implied by the Northwest Ordinance. One sentence in the Constitution's first article had given Congress authority to "to regulate Commerce with foreign Nations, and among the several States, and with the Indian tribes," and from this seed the legislature generated a series of laws that all together became known as the Indian Trade and Intercourse Act. The language was comprehensive and unambiguous: the federal government, by way of the War Department, was responsible for establishing boundaries between Indian and white lands, for securing those boundaries against white or Indian incursions, for regulating trade across those boundaries, and for meting out punishment should whites or Indians cross those boundaries to commit theft or do violence.

In 1796, after he had made his decision not to seek a third term, Washington wrote to Cherokee leaders in Georgia, imploring them to embrace agriculture and animal husbandry and adding that "what I have recommended to you I am myself going to do. After a few moons are passed I shall leave the great town and retire to my farm. There I shall attend to the means of increasing my cattle, sheep and other useful animals; to the growing of corn, wheat, and other grain, and to the employing of women in spinning and weaving; all which I have recommended to you, that you may be as comfortable and happy as plenty of food, clothing and other good things can make you." The message was permeated with Washington's sense of foreboding that Indians who did not thus civilize themselves would be overrun by whites and cast aside by history. The man who at the same time was developing plans to free all of his slaves upon his death was aware that the treatment of Native Americans held the danger of becoming a stain on the national character and a damaging wrench in the works of nation building.

Four years later, Washington was dead and so was the vision of a powerful, benevolent federalism that he, Alexander Hamilton, and

James Madison had established at the end of the War for Independence, repudiated by the defection of Madison to the opposing camp and the election of Thomas Jefferson, under whose watch the virtuous and self-sufficient yeoman farmer, loyal to his state as much as to his country, became the emblem of the nation. Never mind that Jefferson had encountered few yeoman farmers or, for that matter, Indians. Perched at Monticello, he saw the world in an abstract mode unfathomable to George Washington, casting his mind's eye from his small mountaintop in Virginia over the eastern woodlands, past the Mississippi, and onto the grasslands beyond, a place he imagined as the perfect destination for all of the Indians who were continuing to make so much trouble about tribal lands in Georgia, Florida, the Ohio River Valley, and elsewhere. He expressed this transcontinental vision in his proposed "Indian Amendment" to the Constitution by way of an idea he called "removal," the wholesale transfer of tribes from their eastern lands to the West, which Jefferson had made unimaginably spacious in 1803 when he offered Napoléon Bonaparte $15 million for all of the French holdings in North America, finalizing the Louisiana Purchase and pushing the boundary of the United States all the way to the Rocky Mountains.

The Jeffersonian impulse to transfer the entire Indian world westward over the Mississippi would have little purchase until it found someone to do the actual work of removal, to turn Jefferson's "Indian Amendment" into government policy and dismantle the legal precedents established during Washington's administration. Andrew Jackson ascended to the presidency in 1829, and once in the White House he completed Jefferson's mission with a blunt purposefulness. A creature of will perfectly suited to an anti-aristocratic, hard-knuckle era, Jackson had killed two men in duels and was a veteran of many wars, including excursions beside and against the Creek Indians. He praised the courage of his adversaries and the resourcefulness of his allies, and considered himself a friend of the "red man," but by the end of his time in office, few Indians who crossed his path would have agreed. Jackson was not the first Indian fighter to become president, but he was the first whose raw animus toward Indians became part of his public persona. He was serious about Indian war and serious, once president, about getting Indians out of the Deep South and moving them over the Mississippi River.

Jackson's first salvo was to oversee the contentious passage, by five votes, of the Indian Removal Act of 1830, a law that denied Indians the right to claim lands as their own and removed the military protection, treaty rights, and protection from execution by fiat that had been in place since George Washington's time. Jackson wrapped this purge in a cloak of state sovereignty, denying that Indian tribes had the right to enter negotiations with the federal government as either foreign nations or, in the words of Supreme Court chief justice John Marshall, "domestic dependent nations." When three separate challenges to the removal of the Cherokee arrived at the Supreme Court, Jackson simply pulled all federal troops out of the vicinity of reservations in Georgia and set in motion a series of legal and military maneuvers that would culminate after his presidency in the Trail of Tears, the infamous forced exodus that became a death march for thousands of Cherokee Indians on their way to the Oklahoma Territory. In 1833, Jackson told Congress that Indians "have neither the intelligence, the industry, the moral habits, nor the desire of improvement which are essential to any favorable change in their condition," a sentiment that would be repeated countless times, in countless wordings, over the next three decades. The logic, that a civilized Christian nation could not leave degraded and inferior Indians free to decide their own fates, was akin to the emerging Southern rhetoric holding that immorality lay more in freeing blacks than in keeping them as slaves, the only condition in which they were naturally capable of existing.

The treatment of Indian tribes had thus far been an issue most often determined in the realms of law and policy. But in 1845, with the ruling Democratic Party clamoring for war with Mexico in order to extend the nation's reach south to the Rio Grande and west to the Pacific Ocean, a New York editor and professional visionary named John L. O'Sullivan wrote what he called the "truth at once in its neglected simplicity," grounding the expansionist urges of the United States in "our manifest destiny to overspread and possess the whole of the continent which Providence has given us for the development of the great experiment of liberty and federated self-government entrusted to us."

O'Sullivan's sentiment quickly became a kind of meeting ground for various ideologies, as political descendants of Washington, Alexander Hamilton, Jefferson, and Jackson all found in it something to like. Divisive arguments might occur as to how expansion should happen, but the reality of expansion was now cast as divinely ordained fact. No European monarch had ever made a more grandiose claim on the will of God, and the editor found a ready acolyte in President James K. Polk, a devotee of Jackson whose adoption of the phrase "manifest destiny" sealed the words inside the national vocabulary and shoved naysayers to the sidelines. "Away with all these cobweb tissues of rights of discovery, exploration, settlement, and contiguity," O'Sullivan added, giving the removal of stubborn Indian tribes a new metaphysical cast. There was the land, ready to take. Whites would work it, make it pay, make it theirs. What, they asked, could be a more self-evident good? The federalism of Washington, the anti-federalism of Jefferson, and the populism of Jackson were now subsumed by a theocratic zeal that harked back to claims made during Europe's Crusades, not the right but the holy *duty* of godly men to subjugate heathen races.

Polk also moved the offices of the commissioner of Indian affairs and its treaty-making functions from the War Department to the newly created Department of the Interior, hastening the role of presidential patronage in making treaties and operating Indian agencies by removing lifetime military men from the equation. In 1851, at the same time Little Crow and a small group of Dakota leaders were giving up the Upper Mississippi River Valley in exchange for yearly payments in gold, the first Treaty of Fort Laramie was signed after a majestic council in Wyoming involving thousands of Indians from the Lakota, Arapaho, Crow, Mandan, Hidatsa, Arikira, and other tribes. The treaty set formal tribal boundaries, promised peace, and allowed the United States to build forts in and roads through territory that encompassed twelve million acres—including the current or future sites of Denver, Kansas City, Cheyenne, Salt Lake City, Omaha, Des Moines, and Sioux Falls—in exchange for protection against encroachment by whites, permanent tribal boundaries, and $50,000 in goods each year. Whether or not the treaty was made in good faith, it would prove impossible to enforce and, like most such agreements, was altered by Congress in ratification to the dismay of the signatory Indian nations. So commenced the heyday of the "treaty era" in the West, a patchwork of overlapping agreements more immense and fraught with complication than any other foreign policy initiative before or since.

Any serious student of American history during the 1860s, a cohort that certainly included Abraham Lincoln, understood that Indians had participated in every major military conflict on North American soil: King Philip's War, the French and Indian War, the American Revolution, the War of 1812, and the Mexican-American War. The Civil War was no different. All tribes originating in the eastern theater had been removed, concentrated, or scattered before 1861, but the war was also fought along the Mississippi River, Jefferson's dividing line between white and Indian worlds. And no state was fought over more bitterly than Kansas, due to the Kansas-Nebraska Act of 1854, which had decreed that residents of these new states were entitled to make their own choice regarding the legality of slavery. Pro- and anti-slavery crusaders swarmed across the Mississippi into Kansas and began killing each other almost immediately, most notoriously in May 1856, when John Brown and his followers murdered several pro-slavery settlers near Pottawatomie Creek in Franklin County. Once war broke out across the country, the Indian tribes of the Oklahoma Territory found themselves in a geopolitical quandary: to secure Kansas and Missouri for the South, Confederate troops would need to use their lands as staging grounds, while the Union effort against the lower Mississippi River could hardly ignore them either.

Yet ignore them the Union did. A loose arrangement of reservations set aside for the tribes that had been forced out of the Southeast, including the Cherokee, Chickasaw, Choctaw, Creek, and Seminole, the Oklahoma Territory held tens of thousands of potential soldiers, many from warrior cultures, and so there is some mystery as to why it was so thoroughly disregarded by the North. Some Oklahoma Territory tribes owned slaves, it was true, but others worried about becoming slaves themselves, and in any case secession held no appeal for the Indians in the Oklahoma Territory; in a manner of speaking, they had already been forcibly seceded. Leaders and citizens of Confederate states—especially those in the Deep South—had been the busiest builders of the Trail of Tears. But in the absence of tangible support from Lincoln and the Union, some chieftains began to raise companies of men for the Confederacy, while others, choosing no side, pondered flight to Kansas or beyond. In May 1861, shortly after Fort Sumter, Lincoln's first war secretary, Simon Cameron, had decided to suspend annuity payments to the Oklahoma tribes and to remove all troops from the territory's federal forts, deeming the effort to hold the region too costly and failing to see any strategic advantage. These measures created a vacancy that the South quickly filled when Texas troops rushed north to occupy the installations and Jefferson Davis opened diplomatic negotiations with the Oklahoma tribes.

Seventy-two-year-old John Ross was Cherokee only insofar as his mother and her mother had been mixed-blood Cherokees, but still he had become principal chief of the Cherokee nation in 1828, after sixteen years as the tribe's primary delegate to Washington. A slave-owning businessman of considerable wealth with a sharp legal mind, Ross held off Congress, governors, and presidents for a decade in their efforts to push the Cherokees off their land, finally riding the Trail of Tears in 1838 and watching his wife, Quatie, become one of thousands to die along the way. The lists of friends and enemies he made inside the tribe during his fight against removal were long, and these internal frictions were only amplified by the Civil War.

Ross wanted to organize Cherokees to fight for the North and had sent messages directly to Lincoln raising the possibility of tens of thousands of Indian troops for a Union army that in the summer of 1861 numbered no more than 200,000 men. But after Cameron's abdication of the federal forts, the Confederates had organized the Oklahoma Territory into a military department under Brigadier General Albert Pike, a former schoolteacher, fur trapper, poet, newspaper correspondent, and legal scholar who aimed three regiments of Indian soldiers straight at Kansas. Still Ross had held out, declaring neutrality, but in August 1861 he'd acquiesced and joined with the Confederacy on remarkable terms: the Indians could fight under their own field officers and would be granted representation in the Confederate Congress. Though this new political clout would amount to only a single seat, the recognition was a radical step, one the Union had never so much as hinted at.

In January 1862, awakened to the potential calamity building in the Oklahoma Territory, Lincoln reversed course and decided to arm refugee Indians in Kansas and Missouri, except that one week later Edwin Stanton replaced Simon Cameron as secretary of war and Stanton didn't like the idea of Indian troops. The whipsaw back-and-forth finally ended in March, when Union forces won the Battle of Pea Ridge in northwest Arkansas, severing the Confederate supply line to the tribes of the Oklahoma Territory. When Southern troops retreated, the federal forts were quickly recaptured by relieved Northern forces, meaning that in the space of one calendar year the Cherokees had been abandoned by the Union *and* by the Confederacy.

Congress followed up the reoccupation of Indian lands by passing a set of punitive acts granting the president unilateral power to abrogate treaties with any tribe "in actual hostility to the United States." Some anti-Ross Cherokees became guerrilla fighters for the South, striking at the reoccupied federal forts in Oklahoma Territory and making excursions into Kansas, while others went about their lives with little reference to the war that was now consuming the world of black and white. Ross, for his part, was feeling his advanced age and tired of broken promises. In late August 1862, as the Dakota War erupted to the north, he set out with letters of introduction and the paper records of the Cherokee nation to seek an audience with President Lincoln. He aimed to present arguments that the United States had broken treaty promises by pulling out of the territory's forts in May, that the Cherokee had had no choice to ally with the Confederacy, and that the tribe needed considerable federal protection against the guerrilla forces and Southern sympathizers now surrounding them on all sides.

For John Ross and Henry Whipple to head to Washington at the same time was nothing more than coincidence. But if their pleas were very different in the particulars, their basic point was the same: the United States had failed in its responsibility to Indian tribes and bloodshed had been the result. They were also trying to shoehorn their concerns into a consciousness—national and personal—that was fixed elsewhere. Where did treaty relations and the evils of the Indian system fit into a world consumed by rebellion and the question of emancipation, a world in which battles were fought with 75,000 men on a side? A discussion about freeing slaves, for all its bitterness and complexity, had a clarity that arguments about Indian policy did not. The job in front of Ross, as he headed toward the White House, was to focus Lincoln's attention on the plight of the Cherokee and obtain some assurance of security in the Oklahoma Territory. The job in front of Bishop Whipple, now that the northwestern frontier had exploded, was less immediate and more ambitious. He wanted to rip down a system that had operated one way for forty years and replace it with something else entirely.

# Chapter Six

Many postwar accounts by white and mixed-blood captives would focus on Little Crow's words and actions in the first few hours after the attack on the Lower Agency, when his house became the center of the new reality on the frontier. Oratory had always been one of his gifts, the first source of his influence, and on this day he over-flowed with talk, some blustering, some calculated, and some in earnest, depending on the identity of his visitor.

His boasts seemed to shift in volume and scope according to his perception of the listener's gullibility or even of her whiteness. One white woman, Urania White, described Little Crow "walking the floor in a very haughty, dignified manner as much as to say 'I am great!'" and heard him say "after consulting with some papers, that he was going to sell the Minnesota valley to the Southern States." To the teenage bride Helen Tarble, whose family had made a farm on lands across the Minnesota in the four years since the Dakota had signed the treaty of 1858, he painted a picture of desolation, telling her that he "was determined to take back the lands of his people; that he would kill all the whites as far down the Minnesota valley as Saint Peter, and then he would take possession of all the country north and west." The state was empty of men to soldier against him, he explained to her, as "all the strong men had gone south to fight for the negroes."

He took a very different tack with mixed-blood captives and Dakota women married to white men. The young men of the wartime *tiyotipi* scorned those mixed-bloods who had adopted the manner and customs of whites, but Little Crow had come of age in another era, had made marriages across a wider spectrum of bands and villages than most Dakota men, and had spent much of his youth ranging widely with the mixed-blood hunter, warrior, and whiskey trader Jack Frazer, experiences that seem to have freed him from certain hard-line prejudices against white-Dakota liaisons and their children.

Captive Susan Brown, mixed-blood wife of the former Indian agent Joseph R. Brown, would take part in many conversations with Little Crow over the coming weeks, serving as a sounding board apart from his regular councils with his warriors and other village chiefs. On the first day of the war, Little Crow told Brown "in substance" that "his young men had started to massacre; that he at first opposed the movement with all his might, but when he saw he could not stop it he joined them in their madness against his better judgment, but now did not regret it and was never more in earnest in his life." Speaking with the mixed-blood daughter of Lawrence Taliaferro, a former Indian agent, he added that the *tiyotipi* would have gone to war with or without him: "We have begun, and must do the best we can."

Just what they had begun was an open question, for Dakotas and whites alike. In between his conversations with captives, Little Crow received reports from his head soldiers, village chiefs, and individual warriors. He learned that the ferry ambush had succeeded and probably learned that Fort Ridgely's commander had drowned. He continued to learn of killing and looting in the settlements across the river from their camp and near the white settlement of New Ulm. Little Crow's reactions, as recorded by a wide range of observers, make it clear that he had expected some Dakotas to fan out as marauders among the white farms, even if he also hoped that the young warriors would limit their killing to men and treat white women and children as captives.

Little Crow understood that some of the men had ignored this distinction and engaged in acts of unrestrained brutality, targeting whites wherever they found them, regardless of age or gender. One particularly large and fearsome warrior, named Cut Nose, seemed to have passed like a tornado through the settlements; he was credited with carrying out at least a dozen execution-style killings with the blunt end of his war club. How many of the warriors participated in this kind of violence was impossible for anyone, even Little Crow, to say. The percentage was small, at most two hundred men out of the two thousand Dakota with him, but their impact was enormous. White victims numbered in the hundreds in townships as far away as the Iowa border to the south and the edge of Ojibwe territory to the north. Some of the most vicious attacks were tightly concentrated in a narrow line along Beaver Creek, across the Minnesota River from Little Crow's village. Visible from the bluffs where their reservation lay, this was land ceded in the most recent treaty, a vista of unique sorrow for the Dakota, and the stories brought back suggested untrammeled vengeance fueled by deep rage.

Other parties, most with no more than a dozen or so men, had moved in different directions, and they now returned to Little Crow's village boasting of their success. One larger group, perhaps twenty in number, had moved down the reservation road in the direction of the larger white settlements of New Ulm and Mankato, doubling in size as it picked up other warriors along the way. Their foray began and ended in Milford, the closest white town to the reservation, where the Dakota had gained entry to homes by pretending to ask for food before killing the settlers inside and mutilating many of the bodies. No whites were spared in Milford before the Dakota looted their belongings and headed back to Little Crow's village.

Once most of the captives and warriors were back in camp, the order was issued, probably by the *tiyotipi* rather than Little Crow, that all whites, mixed-bloods, and farmer Indians up and down the river valley were to throw away their pants and don breechcloths, braid their hair, and move into Little Crow's village, where they would be required to live in tepees or summer lodges. As the raiding parties brought in more women and children hour after hour, three decisions began to press upon the Dakota: what to do with the swelling number of captives; whether to treat whites and mixed-bloods similarly; and how to best follow up the attack on the Lower Agency. Little Crow wished to push the advantage the very first afternoon, August 18, to stay on top of the white forces by moving over to Fort Ridgely before reinforcements and arms could arrive from the towns downriver, but he could see the chance was spent. The celebration was in full swing and would play out according to its own momentum.

The next morning, August 19, as Chaska's mother was making Sarah Wakefield her "squaw suit" elsewhere in the encampment, Little Crow was confronted by a group of captives who begged him to let them go unmolested to Fort Ridgely. He refused; the prisoners were far too useful as bargaining chips and as a deterrent to vigorous pursuit. Other discussions on this morning fell short of full-fledged councils, and the only consensus reached, it seems, was to send a war party in the direction of the fort and see what happened next. As for the killings in the settlements, Little Crow's position was not clear-cut. He valued the evacuation of the frontier caused by the young men, and he clearly harbored his own personal feelings of revenge, but he was wary of crossing lines drawn by Christian beliefs, which—more than traditional Dakota beliefs—held up women and children as special emblems of purity and innocence.

For the whites of Minnesota, the killings in the settlements constituted a series of out-and-out massacres. For Little Crow and especially for the members of the wartime *tiyotipi*, the perspective was different. For centuries the Dakota had fought the Ojibwe in blood conflicts and in disputes over hunting grounds, and for centuries they had seen their adversaries as unyielding. In a battle against the Ojibwe, no one was assumed to be a noncombatant; men, women, and children were expected to fight to the end, and subterfuge or surprise was often necessary to gain the upper hand. Indeed, it seems that some of the Dakota attackers viewed the passivity of their white victims as a contemptible cultural weakness, one that increased rather than lessened their anger. The preference for hand-to-hand weapons in these killings was also telling. To prefer killing with a gun was still a tactic associated with whites; to kill face-to-face, using traditional Dakota weapons, meant that coup had been counted, that the enemy had been close enough to touch. A warrior's honor and reputation were built through strength, bravery, and cunning, not superior technology. Rifles and arrows, of course, made for cleaner kills; the wounds left by war clubs and tomahawks were far more ghastly and the bodies sometimes unrecognizable, a result the Dakota warriors understood as evidence of courage and personal risk even as whites saw only an expression of barbarism and savagery.

Little Crow was older than most of the warriors with him, more attuned to white sensibilities, and weighed the actions of the wartime *tiyotipi* on a scale that was less personal or cultural and more political and strategic. "Soldiers and young men, you ought not to kill women and children," he reportedly argued. "Your conscience will reproach you for it hereafter and make you weak in battle. You were too hasty in going into the country. You should have killed only those who have been robbing us so long." As always he had a host of considerations separate from those of the *tiyotipi*, chewing on longer possibilities with one eye fixed on making a powerful presentation for potential allies and the other on future terms of peace. "Hereafter," he told his skeptical warriors, "make war after the manner of white men."

A little after nine o'clock on the morning of Tuesday, August 19, the men posted on picket duty around Fort Ridgely watched as several hundred Dakotas began to gather on a grassy rise two miles to the west, in the direction of the Minnesota River and the Lower Agency beyond. The white soldiers could see and be seen, and soon they understood that the Dakota were holding a council of some kind, presumably to prepare for an attack. Armed with long rifles and artillery, the whites enjoyed a decided advantage in firepower, but still their apprehension was high.

Fort Ridgely barely qualified as a fort, and after Captain Marsh's disastrous foray to the Lower Agency it was short most of its quota of soldiers. Perched on a high ridge north of the Minnesota River, it was the only manifestation of military power on the prairie between the Dakota reservations and the state capital. Built after the treaty of 1851, the installation had no stockade and was porously arranged around a central square visible from all directions. The fort was also surrounded by ravines and roads that provided convenient cover for advancing warriors, as well as a set of easy objectives in the stores, civilian houses, hospital, and ammunition magazines positioned along these approaches. The value of Fort Ridgely to whites lay not in its impregnability but in its location and in the weaponry it held.

For Little Crow, the fort was an important symbol and a worthy goal, but for many of the young men with him it was an immaterial distraction. In fact, what the white soldiers assumed was a war council in preparation for an attack had actually turned into an argument about the value of approaching the fort at all. A little before noon, a hundred or so Dakota warriors simply walked away from the council and disappeared over a rise in the opposite direction. What the white soldiers watching did not know was that many members of the *tiyotipi* and their allies had rejected Little Crow's advice and were bound instead for an attack on the prosperous town of New Ulm. Little Crow's numbers then dipped so low that he had no choice but to sit and watch as reinforcements marched into the fort from the east in two separate columns, companies of infantry called back in from other outposts, including the Renville Rangers, the men gathered by Indian agent Thomas Galbraith.

Little Crow rode back to his camp in a state of irritation as a great storm roiled the sky only a few miles away. Nothing had been gained and much opportunity had been lost. He was busy that night holding council with visiting chiefs in hopes of forging a military alliance with the less numerous Ho-Chunks, or Winnebagoes, who lived on a smaller reservation to the southeast, and sending new messages to Ojibwe leaders to the north for a similar purpose. This attempt to consolidate the state's three tribes was unlikely to succeed; Little Crow knew that he would have trouble convincing a majority of the Sissetons and Wahpetons to join him, and they were fellow Dakotas. Morale, it seems, was his real goal. He may also have decided that it was better to enlist older, long-established chiefs in his cause, rather than continue to rely so much on the more impulsive and independent members of the soldiers' lodge.

Indeed, close behind Little Crow in returning to camp that night were the warriors who had abandoned him for an attack on New Ulm, a foray that had not gone well: the leaderless detachment of Dakota warriors had given up when a heavy rain began to fall after two hours of sporadic, unorganized fighting. Little Crow and the other war chiefs then met more intently and made plans as a storm moved through, sitting "all night with their blankets around them until the sun was coming up in the morning." At daybreak they announced a plan to attack Fort Ridgely this day and New Ulm the next. "The young men were all anxious to go," one participant said later, "and we dressed as warriors in war paint, breech[cloth] and leggings, with a large sash around us to keep our food and ammunition in."

Later that morning Little Crow led the procession down the fort road, riding in a buggy with his son Wowinape beside him. Four hundred painted warriors followed. The Dakota surrounded the routes to the fort, all of their motion visible to the soldiers and refugees inside, and then Little Crow gave the sign for a council between Dakota warriors and white soldiers, riding a white horse back and forth. At the same time, smaller groups of warriors approached unseen from the southeast and northeast, taking advantage of the deep, thickly wooded ravines that stretched almost to the fort's central ground. Speeding uphill, the Dakota reached the icehouse, root house, and granary, found cover in woodpiles and hay, and opened fire.

After the first flash and boom sounded, all of Little Crow's plans were forgotten. "We paid no attention to the chiefs; everyone did as he pleased," said one of the advancing warriors. "We did not fight like white men with one officer; we all shot as we pleased." Little Crow was witnessing the Lower Agency attack all over again, an unorganized rush of men following whatever individual plans occurred to them, except that this time his opponent was prepared. Four cannon opened up from the top of the hill, and after another attack was repulsed, cries floated out to them from the fort: "We will fix you, you devils! You will eat your children before winter!" The mixed-bloods who had escaped in this direction, as well as those who had enlisted in the Renville Rangers and were now guarding the fort, were emboldened by the new men and the approach of darkness, and they were in a taunting mood.

Back in camp that night, lightning struck and killed an unnamed warrior. In the morning a heavy, steady rain began to fall, and so Little Crow used the day to regroup and gather men for another attack on the fort. All of this time was white time; Little Crow knew that the Dakota gained nothing by delay while his adversaries would welcome the respite. The second attack on Fort Ridgely, launched in the morning on Friday, August 22, involved twice as many men on both sides, nearly eight hundred for the Dakota, but the result was the same. Technology again won the day, as no amount of bravado or courage could fend off four artillery pieces firing six- and twelve-pound balls of iron into the sheltering outbuildings and charging lines of men. Before the day was over, three whites and at least two Dakota were dead, and Little Crow had taken his own wound, striking his head on a rock while avoiding cannon fire, leaving him concussed and incapable of riding into battle.

A few days earlier, Little Crow had told Samuel J. Brown, mixed-blood son of the former Indian agent Joseph R. Brown, that his plan was for the Ho-Chunk to sweep down the Minnesota River from Mankato, the Ojibwe down the Mississippi River, and the Lower Dakota eastward across the land between the two rivers and through the Big Woods. The three Minnesota tribes would converge at the confluence of the two rivers and make a grand charge on Fort Snelling, where, he said, they "might take a day or two to batter the walls down."

This was not a plan so much as a vision. To reach the Mississippi River, to empty Saint Paul of whites and reclaim the ground of Kaposia: that is what victory meant to Little Crow. These geographies had measureless sacred and secular meanings and were worth any fight. The options for their next target had now narrowed to a single town along the south side of the river, the first step toward Little Crow's goal. If Fort Ridgely would not fall to Little Crow, opening one route toward his old lands, New Ulm might still provide another.

Nine years earlier, in November 1853, a German newspaper in Chicago, the *Illinois Staats-Zeitung,* had published a short announcement: "The object of the German Land Company for every German laborer, popish priests and lawyers excepted, is some healthy and productive district, located on some navigable river." An immigrant looking for opportunity could have responded to any one of many such advertisements in this era, including the German Land Company's offer, which was, like most, a speculative real estate scheme offering foreign-born workers freedom of thought, movement, and economic opportunity. By 1855 eight hundred members had joined the company at a cost of between one and five dollars apiece. The routine was simple: promise a state or territorial governor eager, self-sufficient, industrious immigrants and find a navigable river that was not yet fully settled; next, work your way up that river by boat, buggy, or horseback until you found a site with enough advantages to support visions of a tidy little town and enough distance from population centers that no other company had yet put in its claim.

The German Land Company's ultimate choice lay thirty miles south of the Lower Agency, at the junction of the Minnesota and Cottonwood rivers, and seemed an ideal plot of land, rising in two broad terraces and connected by steamboat to Fort Snelling and the Mississippi River beyond. Scouting the land in the spring of 1855, the advance party had emerged into a seasonal Mdewakanton village, unoccupied but still full of summer lodges and ringed with the eight-foot-tall burial platforms of Dakota custom. This evidence of the occupancy of dozens or even hundreds of Indians had little effect on the settlers' plans. "The natural beauty of the place where the Cottonwood empties into the Minnesota worked like magic upon their tired brains and weary hearts," wrote Alexander Berghold, a Catholic priest and local historian. Rumors of rival Canadians or immigrant parties from Saint Louis created such nervousness and impatience that the advance party made a plan to stay on over the summer and winter in order to establish occupancy of the site. "They learned that the Indians would not return" until the spring, Berghold wrote, "and that they were free to occupy their comfortable palaces of bark without paying a high rent."

If there was any question in their minds that the Indians would be fine with the arrangement, it was settled when the Dakota returned before the snow fell and were outraged to find squatters on their land and in their houses. But just as territorial governor Willis Gorman was preparing to issue an official ruling on the legal boundaries of the reservation, smallpox struck the Indians and settled the issue. "What strange feelings overcame us on beholding these once noble Indian tribes," wrote one new white resident, "who, centuries ago, so hospitably received and entertained our forefathers, now roaming about like beggars in their own inheritance, and dying inch by inch amid the ruins of their former greatness!" What strange feelings, indeed. What began with a few dozen descendants of German Swabians, who honored their place of origin by naming the new settlement New Ulm, was soon augmented by a separate, much larger wave of immigrants from Chicago. Members of the *Turnverein*, or Turners, a German gymnastic society dedicated to a rationalist, anti-religious view of the world, they were particular targets of the anti-immigrant Know-Nothings and wanted a place to maintain their social and cultural insularity.

Once the new arrivals began to abandon the commandeered bark lodgings of the Dakota and build houses of their own, they found that Indians still rode through the town, sometimes begging, sometimes stopping to argue that the land was theirs, and sometimes threatening to drive away the Germans, whom they called "Dutchmen." Now and then gunshots sounded at a distance and soldiers from Fort Ridgely camped overnight. Some of the new townspeople were kind to the Dakota, sharing food, while many others openly insulted them and turned them away, mocking Indian medicines, foods, and spiritual beliefs. The Dakota, for their part, had never met any whites who were so dour, close-lipped, and willing to raise a gun at them for simply walking up to the front door.

Underlying the distrust on both sides was the fact that many of the Lower Agency Dakota, Little Crow foremost among them, believed that New Ulm was rightfully theirs. In negotiations for the treaty of

1851, Little Crow had argued unsuccessfully for including the mouth of the Cottonwood River, which later would border New Ulm on its eastern side, within the boundary of the reservation. However, in the process of ratification, Congress nullified the treaty's stipulation of a permanent reservation, leaving the Dakota along the river at the pleasure of the president, and it was this move, infuriating to the treaty signers, that also gave Little Crow the opening he desired to reaffirm his preferred boundaries. If the president's word alone gave them permission to remain, he believed, then the president's word alone could determine where they were allowed to live. During his trip to Washington in 1854, he had spoken with Indian Commissioner George Manypenny and President Franklin Pierce, unrecorded conversations that left Little Crow convinced that the site of New Ulm was part of their remaining lands.

Four years later, in 1858, Little Crow had again traveled to Washington, this time to negotiate the treaty adding to their annuities while taking away all Dakota land north of the Minnesota River. During these talks, acting Indian commissioner Charles Mix knocked down Little Crow's claims to a reservation boundary that included New Ulm, theatrically producing a copy of the 1851 treaty for a reading translated into Dakota. Mix knew well that whatever the accuracy of Little Crow's contentions that verbal promises had been made, the absence of a signed document or an official decree meant New Ulm was secure for whites. The acting commissioner then pointed out that the new Dakota reservation boundaries, like the old ones, would exist at the discretion of the president, a statement now made not as a promise but as a thinly veiled threat. In that moment, Little Crow had understood that his case that New Ulm was Dakota land was lost. In a contest pitting his word against that of the man at the top of the white ladder of power, he had no hope of prevailing. But as his words and actions would show, the wound festered.


The Dakota War produced no Ulysses S. Grant, Stonewall Jackson, or Robert E. Lee; neither did it bring forth a Tecumseh, Black Hawk, or Crazy Horse. Instead, the fiercest warriors on the Dakota side were desperate and angry young men, most anonymous to history, who saw only the near future of battle and vengeance on a people who had left them no choice but war; on the white side were equally unheralded lawyers, merchants, schoolteachers, and farmers bewildered by their losses, many of whom felt that they were now seeing the Indians for their true savage selves.

Neither did the war's battlefields approach the scale of the plains, canyons, and mountains of the West, where the Indian wars of the next three decades would rage, but the contests were no less intense or important for all of that. One hundred warriors had attacked New Ulm three days earlier with little coordination and negligible results, but as Saturday, August 23, dawned—already the sixth day of the war—both sides were better prepared. The Dakota now operated with a consensus built up in several successful war councils, while the whites of New Ulm had organized under a newly arrived Union enlistee, Charles E. Flandrau, a Faribault lawyer, member of the state supreme court, and close friend of Bishop Whipple.

Still rattled by his head wound, Little Crow was not able to ride along with his men, but his influence was visible in the feints and deceptions that preceded the main action. On the early-morning march overland toward New Ulm, the Dakota set fires to abandoned homes on the north side of the Minnesota River to convince the town's defenders that Fort Ridgely had fallen. If luck was with the attackers, the town's defenders might also believe that the main body of Dakotas was attacking from the north side of the river opposite the town. Whether or not the ruse worked, Flandrau did dispatch 75 of his 350 men to cross to the north side of the river and establish a skirmish line should their enemy arrive from that direction. The Dakota then forded the Minnesota River above New Ulm and began to gather on the prairie near the town's upper terrace in full sight of their enemy. Flandrau and his fellow defenders, some of them armed with rifles and some not, formed a concentrated line a few hundred yards outside of the town and waited, hearts racing.

Around ten o'clock the Dakota began to move forward, a loose line at first walking, then running, then sprinting across the prairie, fanning out all the while to put themselves wide of the defenders on either side. "Their advance upon the sloping prairie in the bright sunlight was a very fine spectacle," Flandrau wrote. "The savages uttered a terrific yell and came down upon us like the wind." The defenders held their line for a few moments against the whooping attackers, fired their weapons, and retreated as a group into the center of town. This sudden movement left the town's outer buildings unharmed and usable, an opportunity that was quickly seized by the Dakota, who split into small groups and occupied the abandoned stores and homes providing the best lines of fire, torching the rest in order to create billowing clouds of covering smoke.

The second Battle of New Ulm quickly became a contest to control the streets. "The fighting from both sides then became general," Flandrau wrote, "sharp and rapid, and it got to be a regular Indian skirmish, in which every man did his own work after his own fashion." Crouching in windows, around corners, behind signs, stepping out to fire and then ducking back behind shelter, the whites watched their Indian foes move with a speed and dexterity born of long hunts and many woodland skirmishes against the Ojibwe. The action came to a head close to the river when an all-out charge by the Dakota was met with a short burst of concentrated gunfire, killing many men on each side, scattering the attackers, and costing the Dakota valuable time as dusk approached. Their advance had lost them six warriors and taken fourteen white lives, but it had not taken the town. From the northern prairie across the river, Little Crow watched as darkness fell and the whites prepared to evacuate New Ulm, knowing full well that the citizens there would soon be replaced by trained and better-armed soldiery.

By now Little Crow had the knowledge, and had probably received specific intelligence, that men designated for far-off Union divisions had instead mustered downriver, ready to chase after him. War or flight, death or life, capture or escape: Little Crow saw his choices emerging clearly, if he had not seen them from the start. The next morning, leaving behind a few men to harass the city, the Dakota headed back toward their encampment. Turning captives into hostages might give Little Crow bargaining power, but all hostages could buy him was time to move and protection from indiscriminate gunfire. Little Crow's vision of rolling back the white world in one swift motion had fallen short. North and west were the only directions that mattered now. To whites, Little Crow's suppositions and plans seemed grandiose and naïve. But at other times that wide view provided him clarity. No poet, historian, or translator was on hand in this moment to record his intentions. But Little Crow's decisions suggested that he saw a space ahead where possibilities hadn't been exhausted.

Whites would read his movement as a retreat, the beginning of an end, but this was not what Little Crow believed. He saw in the short future a great push of white power descending on southwestern Minnesota and the Dakota Territory, a display that might lead to temporary defeat but that might also unite squabbling and warring tribes to the west into an allied force, forging a confederation of Indians capable of striking hard in lands they knew better than anyone. And if worse came to worst, north of the Dakota Territory lay Canada and the British, who had given Little Crow's grandfather tokens of gratitude for his support during the War of 1812 and might return the favor a half century later. A wide Indian world existed past Lac Qui Parle, Big Stone Lake, and the Red River of the North, the system of waterways that constituted most of the state's western border. Little Crow was ready to leave the home of his adult years and return to the buffalo grounds of his adolescence, a world not yet confined to reservations. He was not finished yet.

Sarah Wakefield's days would soon run together and become difficult to distinguish one from another, but for now, in this first "week of tepee life," as another white captive described it, each day had had its own identity: the day she was forced to spend with Winona, Chaska's half sister and one of Hapa's wives, who ransacked Sarah's trunk and claimed much of her clothing, dressed Sarah mockingly in tin earrings and old torn cloth, and invented rumors to frighten her; or the day Sarah was taken at sunrise to the tepee of Chaska's grandfather, Eagle Head, where she discovered many of Chaska's fellow villagers nearby, the ones so familiar to her from her day in Shakopee. And then, just a few days into her captivity, most likely on the 22nd, came a day when the threats against the whites in camp seemed so real that she agreed to leave her son, James, with a friendly Mdewakanton and dashed off with Nellie to hide in a haystack along the bottomlands until sunset. In that strange enclosure, surrounded by the footfalls of roving warriors, she had to choke her baby nearly to death to keep her from crying.

The camp was too big, widespread, and unruly to allow for close surveillance. Sarah's captivity was enforced not by ropes or guards but by the limitlessness of the prairie and the difficulty of remaining hidden in the wide-open country. Still, the Minnesota River could sometimes be forded and Fort Ridgely was only an afternoon's walk away. She knew that others had attempted to escape, and for all she knew they'd succeeded. But sheltered by Chaska and his family, separated for the moment from James and nursing Nellie, Sarah decided to stay and make herself as comfortable as possible with the situation, showing good cheer, helping her protectors sew, chop wood, and cook. She apparently offered agreement with the aims of the war, and later she would admit that she promised to kill other whites if her own safety could be guaranteed.

According to her post-captivity accounts, all of these words and actions were charades to keep her in good graces with her captors. But stories from other white women who purported to have observed Sarah in the camp would present different interpretations. The most damaging story centered on the early morning of August 24, 1862, the sixth day and first Sunday after her capture, the day after Dakota soldiers had failed to win the second Battle of New Ulm following several advances and the loss of a dozen or more men. The surviving warriors returned to the camp in an agitated and excited mood, a number of them drunk, and Chaska's mother took Sarah through the dark woods to find Chaska waiting for her in his tepee. After midnight they heard the voice of Hapa outside the door demanding that Sarah become his wife and threatening violence if Chaska did not release her to him. Sarah wrote later that Chaska now "laid down" with her for the rest of the night, a symbolic claim on her person that was the surest way to keep her away from Hapa. "My father could not have done differently, or acted more respectful or honorable," she would write later, "and if ever there was an honest, upright man, Chaska was one."

By the next day, Monday, August 25, news of Sarah's sleeping arrangements had already spread and the gossips among the white women were on high alert. The camp was in motion again, making ready to move back up the valley after the failure to take New Ulm, but still several of her fellow captives found Sarah to ask if she had indeed become Chaska's wife. Her response would dog her for the rest of her life. "I dared not contradict it, but rather encouraged everyone to believe so, for I was in fear all the while that Hapa would find out we had deceived him," she wrote. "They said they had heard I was married, and asked me if that was my husband. I replied that I supposed my husband was dead, and turned the conversation; for there were many near who could understand all we were talking about. These women went away and said I acknowledged it."

In the meantime, preparations for departure continued. Even if Chaska had become her personal guardian, Sarah Wakefield was still tied most closely to Little Crow, always his pawn or his hostage. Every one of the captives knew that in the end the train of humanity would not stop for very long at the Upper Agency or at any point on this side of the state's border. And that meant the West, not the Minnesota prairie but up the Coteau des Prairies, the great rise in the land, and onto the high and dry shortgrass plateau. If white soldiers did not come soon, the constricted land of the white-Indian frontier would give way to the eye-searing open spaces of the Dakota Territory, the Black Hills, and the lands beyond.

# Chapter Seven

L ater in the year, when decisions were made about the disposition of
lands, property, and prisoners in the wake of the Dakota War, much
would be made of the great distance between the East and the Northwest. As questions of justice, vengeance, and mercy were laid at the feet
of politicians, administrators, and lawyers in Washington, D.C., a cry
would go up along the frontier that weak-willed strangers were making
decisions about people they'd never met and places they'd never seen.
And it was true that Abraham Lincoln had never set foot in Minnesota. But the pervasive feeling of Minnesotans that they were dealing
with distant and uninformed observers was, in the end, unfounded.
The number of federal officials in Minnesota during the six weeks of
the Dakota War would come to include not only lawyers and soldiers,
but the commissioner of Indian affairs, the assistant to the secretary of
the interior, and a prominent Union major general. Each in his own
way had the ear of the president, and each would provide important
information and counsel. But no observer in Minnesota during the fall
and winter of 1862 was closer to Abraham Lincoln, personally and professionally, than his personal secretary John G. Nicolay, the dour young
German with the pronounced slouch who disembarked in Saint Paul
on August 22, just four days after the Dakota War began.

Nicolay's presence, and by extension the administration's, would come to have dramatic consequences for the Dakota and their white adversaries, but it was also entirely coincidental. Fifty miles northwest of the Upper Agency lay two picturesque bodies of water, Big Stone Lake and, to the north, Lake Traverse, between which a narrow gap of prairie marsh made a bountiful home for geese, ducks, egrets, and herons. Across this gap of land passed the continental divide, so that the waters of Big Stone Lake emptied into the Minnesota River, bound for the Gulf of Mexico, while those of Lake Traverse flowed in the other direction as the Red River of the North, heading for Lake Winnipeg and Hudson Bay, marking the border between the state of Minnesota and the Dakota Territory along the way.

The Red River's broad valley, flat as a tabletop, was the last quadrant of the state undivided into white lands and reservations, and this summer the Lincoln administration was determined to rectify the situation. As unrest among the Dakota at the Upper Agency began to boil over in early August, a group of federal officials had assembled in Saint

William P. Dole and John Nicolay in Minnesota, August 1862

Paul to head north and open negotiations with the Ojibwe bands at Pembina, an old fur-trading center on the west side of the Red River near the Canadian border. Among them were Commissioner of Indian Affairs William P. Dole, Northern Division superintendent Clark W. Thompson, several military escorts, and Nicolay.

Nicolay's daughter, Helen, wrote later that Lincoln "occasionally found it convenient to have an unprejudiced observer at some distant point" during treaty negotiations, without including any hint as to whether or how her father's traveling companions on this expedition, all members of the executive branch, had been deemed not unprejudiced. Whatever reasons existed to keep an extra pair of eyes on the treaty's progress, Nicolay was a reliable man whose loyalty to the president was as strong and impenetrable as steel. He and assistant secretary John Hay were Lincoln's most trustworthy employees, a pair of hand-picked young men who were utter opposites in temperament but who shared a partiality to backstairs gossip, a belief in their employer's superiority to every other person in the world, and a consuming love of their day-to-day work.

Nicolay had entered the future president's orbit at the age of twenty-four, in 1856, when he was a precocious young editor at the *Pike County Free Press*. Lincoln delivered a speech in Pittsfield, Illinois, in support of his Senate campaign and visited Nicolay's office, where the two struck up a conversation that would change Nicolay's life forever. Nicolay's influence exceeded his years and his short tenure on the newspaper. He had helped to create the Illinois Republican Party, grounding its platform on a hatred of slavery that nevertheless stopped short of a call for abolition. In 1857, he began clerking for Illinois secretary of state Ozias M. Hatch, and three years after that, as the Chicago presidential nominating convention approached, he published a widely read editorial comparing Lincoln with Lincoln's hero Henry Clay, an article that the future president himself may have suggested or even written. In need of a private secretary following his nomination, Lincoln had asked Hatch for a recommendation, and Nicolay's name was the only response.

An orphan who had emigrated from Germany in 1838 at the age of six, Nicolay soon came to see Lincoln as a surrogate father. The "sour and crusty" half of the Nicolay-Hay tandem, Nicolay was trim and slump-shouldered with a whopping mustache, a man whom the *Philadelphia Press* editor John Russell Young described as "scrupulous, polite, calm, obliging, with the gift of hearing other people talk." Assistant Secretary William O. Stoddard called Nicolay "a fair French and German scholar, with some ability as a writer and much natural acuteness," who "nevertheless—thanks to a dyspeptic tendency—had developed an artificial manner the reverse of 'popular,' and could say 'no' about as disagreeably as any man I ever knew." The contrast with the rakish, fraternal Hay, who loved to tell long jokes and had been named Class Poet on his graduation from Brown University, made them the capital's strangest, if most efficient, duo.

In preparation for his visit to the Northwest, Nicolay had read Edward D. Neill's *History of Minnesota* while riding the train to Chicago. A Presbyterian cleric, native Pennsylvanian, and graduate of Amherst, Neill was also an amateur historian who wrote in a sort of provincial sublime, announcing his purpose to "show where Minnesota is, its characteristics and adaptations for a dense and robust population, and then consider the past and present dwellers on the soil." Published in 1858, the year of the state's birth, the book was actually a history of the ground from which the state had emerged and a love letter to its future. Minnesota's destiny was indeed manifest, Neill believed, as was the moral superiority its natural wonders imparted upon its residents: "Grand scenery, leaping waters, and a bracing atmosphere, produce men of different cast from those who dwell where the land is on a dead level, and where the streams are all sluggards."

Presumably Nicolay was most interested in the sections regarding the Ojibwe tribe, or the Chippewa as whites called them. Much of Neill's information related to "the aborigines" came courtesy of his fellow Presbyterians Stephen R. Riggs, Samuel Pond, and Thomas S. Williamson, and was limited to the Dakota bands; unlike these men, however, Neill was full of undisguised disdain for almost all Indians. "Like all ignorant and barbarous people, they have but little reflection beyond that necessary to gratify the pleasure of revenge and of the appetite," he wrote. "While there are exceptions, the general characteristics of the Dahkotahs, and all Indians, are indolence, impurity, and indifference to the future."

In these sentiments Neill may have found a sympathetic reader. Helen Nicolay, in her biography of her father, wrote that Nicolay "entertained no sentimental illusions about the North American Indians. He had grown up too near frontier times in Illinois to regard them as other than cruel and savage enemies whose moral code (granted they had one) was different from that of whites." Perhaps Nicolay or his family had once known Indians as close-up adversaries, but the letters he exchanged with John Hay during his month away reveal two entrenched easterners' patronizing view of the frontier. "If in the wild woods you scrounge an Indian damsel," Hay wrote shortly after Nicolay's arrival, "steal her moccasins while she sleeps and bring them to me." This was typical Hay, whose contemporaneous writings sometimes made the running of the government sound like a schoolboy's lark. Nicolay, the far more serious of the two, enjoyed the banter, but he was in Minnesota for real work, hoping to help the Interior Department clean up a lingering mess without making any new ones.

In 1659 the Ojibwe had moved onto the edge of Dakota territory, along the south shore of Lake Superior, beginning many decades of tribal diplomacy and trade in furs, weapons, cooking implements, and other goods, accompanied by the occasional skirmish between hunting parties. In 1737 that skirmishing erupted into war as the Ojibwe pushed up to and across the Mississippi River, scoring the landscape with battle until the tribes settled into their eighteenth-century homes, the Ojibwe in the northern pine woods and lake districts of the Northwest Territory, the Dakota along the lower Mississippi and Minnesota River valleys and farther west, with only the hunting grounds of the Big Woods and Saint Croix River Valley remaining in dispute. Contests once fought between hundreds of warriors on a side now involved groups of five, ten, or twenty Indians raiding in competition for game, over trading rights, or in actions designed to bring a warrior honor or glory. Two might die, or twelve. The warfare was violent and quick, often performed by ambush, and sometimes women and children were the victims, snaring ever wider kinship networks in a thickly woven net of self-perpetuating feuds.

All the while the United States had increased its presence in the region, building Fort Snelling in 1819 on a small cession of Dakota land, gathering Dakota and Ojibwe leaders for a peace conference in 1825, and making a long series of separate treaties with the two tribes that, by 1862, left only the Red Lake and Red River Valley Indians on unceded lands. Like the Dakota, the Ojibwe lived in several autonomous bands and did not hold council as one people, but as one people they had ample reason to be suspicious of the motives and faith of the U.S. government. In 1850, twelve years earlier, Alexander Ramsey, then the territorial governor, had traveled north to achieve what he thought would be the accomplishment of his lifetime, bringing the Ojibwe from Michigan and Wisconsin into the Minnesota Territory and keeping them there by way of a simple ruse: Orlando Brown, commissioner of Indian affairs under Zachary Taylor, declared that the annuity payment was to be distributed in a new place—Sandy Lake, one hundred miles north of Saint Paul—so late in the autumn that the return trip to their homelands would be impossible, all to satisfy white hopes of speeding westward removal of the Ojibwe while drawing the treaty gold and its associated bounty into the Minnesota Territory, where it would benefit Minnesota's traders, contractors, and politicians.

The plan was a success, at least until news of heartbreak and destitution among the stranded Indians reached the Saint Paul newspapers. Breathless and entirely fabricated reports of cannibalism, side by side with more sober and accurate accounts of spoiled flour, rotten pork, measles, dysentery, and frostbite, generated enough attention among whites, if not anger, that the scheme collapsed. The following spring President Taylor canceled a standing removal order and allowed the eastern Ojibwe to return to their homes, ending an ordeal that left hundreds of Indians dead. Unabashed, Ramsey turned his attention to treaty-making with Little Crow and the other Dakota, whose land was far more attractive to immigrant farmers, and left the Ojibwe to a future generation of political leadership.

Now, as it turned out, "Bluff Alec" himself, returned to political prominence, was that generation of leadership. And so Nicolay and the others headed to the Northwest, hoping to sew the final loose piece of Minnesota into the white American quilt.

After arriving in Saint Paul early in August 1862—even as Henry Whipple and Sarah Wakefield were observing the unrest among the Dakota at the Upper Agency—Nicolay had written to his family that the city "seemed to him 'primitive,' and the International Hotel smelled strongly of pine and kerosene, but the week he spent there was so filled with pleasant excursions that he pronounced the region ideal for summer residence 'provided of course one has wealth and leisure.'" Here he had rendezvoused with Commissioner Dole, Superintendent Thompson, and Minnesota senator Morton Wilkinson. Together they steamed up the Mississippi to a small river town called Saint Cloud, built on old Ho-Chunk lands, where they prepared to go west, planning to follow an oxcart trail over the prairie to Fort Abercrombie on the Red River of the North, a hundred miles south of Pembina. Before their party could depart, however, they received strange, unsettling news when Ojibwe agent Lucius C. Walker ran into town in a panic, reporting that hundreds of Ojibwe warriors were gathering upriver at Gull Lake. Their purpose, according to Walker, was to attack the whites at the nearby Ojibwe agency and then move on to capture Fort Ripley just below, with Saint Cloud squarely in their sights.

Walker's most dire predictions would soon turn out to be baseless, but, as Nicolay wrote, "[t]he whole border at once took alarm. The settlers gathered up their guns and weapons, barricaded their doors and windows, and packed up their movables, to be ready to leave at a moment's warning." The next day, August 20, the news worsened when bits and pieces of talk about the attack on the Lower Agency reached Saint Cloud, prompting Nicolay's party to cancel its plans. Families sought shelter in the town's sturdiest brick buildings, and men began to throw up fences and build blockhouses. Patrols went out that night to the north and south of the town and on both sides of the Mississippi River. Meanwhile, the Ojibwe agent snapped. As Nicolay reported, Walker fled "at break-neck speed down the Mississippi, crossing and recrossing the river, and intensifying the panic by telling wild and incoherent stories that the [Ojibwe] were not only pursuing him, but attacking the settlements."

Returning to Saint Paul on August 22, Nicolay, Dole, and their companions huddled with Governor Ramsey and other state officials to repeat Walker's warnings and to hear all of the details of the Dakota War, now four days old: hundreds dead in the settlements, hundreds more taken captive, assaults on Fort Ridgely and New Ulm. What they'd been told in Saint Cloud had not been the half of it. Several companies of soldiers had been dispatched from Fort Snelling to the Minnesota River Valley, and more were gathering in the riverside towns along the way, waiting on weapons and ammunition. To the southwest lay only war against the Dakota, but the Ojibwe up north were another matter. They might or might not have been "on the warpath," as the Indian agent believed, but no concerted attacks had occurred, and there was plenty of reason to believe peace might still be possible. Nicolay would be going north to act as Lincoln's eyes and ears after all, even if the negotiations would be of a very different sort than he'd anticipated.

.  .  .

Governor Alexander Ramsey's next message to Edwin Stanton was dated 2:30 p.m. on August 25, the day the Dakota began to retreat from New Ulm along the river valley. It began with a nudge. "The Indian war is still progressing," he wrote. "The panic among the people has depopulated whole counties, and in view of this I ask that there be one month added to the several dates of your previous orders for volunteers, drafts, etc.—22d August be 22d September, 1st September be 1st October, 3d September be 3d October. In view of the distracted condition of the country, this is absolutely necessary."

The message came with a postscript written and signed by Commissioner Dole: "I have a full knowledge of all the facts, and I urge a concurrence in this request." In the federal chain of command in the midst of the Civil War, the commissioner of Indian affairs, subordinate to the secretary of the interior, ranked far below the secretary of war. Dole's urging was not likely to impress War Secretary Edwin Stanton much, and Stanton replied in the negative later that day. But no longer was Minnesota one petitioner among all of the others clamoring for attention; with Dole and Nicolay in Saint Paul, the state had a direct line to Lincoln and a way to use it. Now the executive branch was, implicitly and explicitly, speaking with itself.

They would need that direct line, because the Union's call for additional volunteers had come from the White House and thus only the president could approve an extension. Less populous than Rhode Island, Minnesota had already contributed two companies of sharpshooters, three of cavalry, two artillery batteries, and five full regiments of infantry; it was in the process of filling a sixth regiment in July when Lincoln called for 300,000 more soldiers. The state's proportional quota was 5,360 new men, or close to six more regiments, doubling the number it had already sent. In a state with no more than 200,000 people, the fraction of able-bodied young men, white and mixed-blood, was small and shrinking, so all of the patriotic machinery—bands, banners, picnics, speakers, and sermons—had begun to hum once more. Volunteerism and morale were high, but not high enough to populate the military units required for two wars.

Ramsey was not done making attention-getting requests. The next day, August 26, he wired Henry W. Halleck, Lincoln's general in chief, asking him to create a federal military department in the Northwest so that Union officers, supplies, and funds might be made available to take part in the Dakota War. Later that evening Halleck replied in one sentence that no such department was forthcoming. At ten o'clock, finally, Ramsey put Lincoln's name on a telegram, the first communication of the Dakota War addressed directly to the president. The governor's message made it plain that every word he'd sent over the past forty-eight hours had been written in conference with Dole as, presumably, Nicolay looked on. "With the concurrence of Commissioner Dole," Ramsey wrote, "I have telegraphed the Secretary of War for an extension of one month of drafting, etc. The Indian outbreak has come upon us suddenly. Half the population of the state are fugitives. It is absolutely impossible that we should proceed. The Secretary of War denies our request. I appeal to you, and ask for an immediate answer. No one not here can conceive the panic in the state."

Lincoln did not provide an immediate answer, so the next morning Nicolay finally stepped out from behind the men who outranked him and found the success none of them had managed. Later that day their peace-making party would steam back up the Mississippi River to seek terms with the Ojibwe, but at 10:30 a.m. they were handing the Saint Paul telegraph operator a message "to the President of the United States" signed by Nicolay, Dole, and Senator Wilkinson: "We are in the midst of a most terrible and exciting Indian War. Thus far the massacre of innocent white settlers has been fearful. A wild panic prevails in nearly one-half of the state. All are rushing to the frontier to defend settlers."

Ramsey had already wired Lincoln directly, and Nicolay's message contained no request and no information that hadn't already been communicated; it was intended only to get the president's notice and nothing more. Nicolay also sent a much longer telegram to Edwin Stanton.

The Indian war grows more extensive. The Sioux, numbering perhaps 2,000 warriors, are striking along a line of scattered frontier settlements of 200 miles, having already massacred several hundred whites, and the settlers of the whole border are in panic and flight, leaving their harvest to waste in the field, as I have myself seen even in neighborhoods where there is no danger. The Chippewas, a thousand warriors strong, are turbulent and threatening, and the Winnebagoes are suspected of hostile intent. The Governor is sending all available forces to the protection of the frontier, and organizing the militia, regular and irregular, to fight and restore confidence.

"As against the Sioux, it must be a war of extermination," Nicolay added. This was the first public mention of "extermination" by any government official, but as Alexander Ramsey would soon prove very fond of the word, one suspects it had been often used in private during the previous week. Given his reputation for stoicism and understatement, Nicolay's message that a major Indian war was brewing was guaranteed to raise eyebrows, along with his suggestion that Stanton accede to Ramsey's request for 1,200 cavalry, 6,000 guns, a half-million cartridges, blankets for 3,000 people, and medical supplies for three regiments.

Nicolay's telegrams finally did the trick. Lincoln's attention was, for the first time, engaged. The president's response arrived later that day and was addressed, tellingly, to the governor. "Yours received. Attend to the Indians. If the draft cannot proceed of course it will not proceed. Necessity knows no law. The Government cannot extend the time." Even after multiple readings, these sentences seemed to hold open-ended, even contradictory meanings, but Nicolay had drafted hundreds of such telegrams and notes from the president himself and he, at least, would have known how to read them. The message was stated, the understanding absorbed. They were free to hold back men in Minnesota, but not to invoke Lincoln's name in doing so. "Attend to the Indians" they would.


On Monday, August 25, the same day that Little Crow began his retreat up the Minnesota River Valley and Ramsey sent his second telegram east with Commissioner Dole's brief addendum, Horace Greeley's *New York Tribune* published two extraordinary items. Placed side by side on the front page, one would be remembered forever and the other forgotten in a matter of days. The first was the president's reply to Greeley's "Prayer of Twenty Millions." The piece had been published a few days earlier in the capital's foremost paper, the *National Intelligencer*, in the sure knowledge that Greeley would reprint it, perhaps a little quid pro quo for the original preemptory appearance of the "Prayer." Greeley didn't care, of course; he published the response happily, no doubt anticipating a bump in sales and appreciating the testament to his own national influence.

Frank, precise, and designed to please no one in particular, Lincoln's answer to Greeley's challenge has come down through history as one of his most important statements. He began with some personal needling: "If there be in [Greeley's 'Prayer'] any statements, or assumptions of fact, which I may know to be erroneous, I do not, now and here, controvert them. If there be in it any inferences which I may believe to be falsely drawn, I do not now and here, argue against them. If there be perceptible in it an impatient and dictatorial tone, I waive it in deference to an old friend, whose heart I have always supposed to be right." Then he got down to brass tacks, reminding Greeley and the nation that his loyalty lay with the Union above all else.

> If there be those who would not save the Union, unless they could at the same time save slavery, I do not agree with them. If there be those who would not save the Union unless they could at the same time destroy slavery, I do not agree with them. My paramount object in this struggle is to save the Union, and is not either to save or to destroy slavery. If I could save the Union without freeing any slave I would do it, and if I could save it by freeing all the slaves I would do it; and if I could save it by freeing some and leaving others alone I would also do that.

The third of these options was about to become government policy, sitting on his desk even now in the form of a draft of the Emancipation Proclamation, but that document had not yet been made public and Lincoln would not let Greeley and his fellow editors hound him into doing so before he was ready. The president closed his response with a small sop to abolitionists, writing that he intended "no modification of my oft-expressed personal wish that all men every where could be free," but the message had been delivered: when it came to measures as dramatic as emancipation, Lincoln would consult his own schedule and take his own counsel.

One column over from the words PRESIDENT LINCOLN'S LETTER was its companion headline, INDIAN MURDERS, below which were 540 of the strangest, least useful words Greeley ever published. Over the past week the paper had reprinted two brief early dispatches from the Dakota War, one labeled ATTACK ON THE WHITES and the second THE INDIAN TROUBLES IN MINNESOTA. Now, only six days into the conflict and with no particular intelligence in hand, the *Tribune* was ready to name its underlying cause. The first two-thirds of Greeley's editorial focused on Confederate appeals to "foreign aid" and efforts to enlist Cherokee troops in the Southern cause, efforts Greeley considered base hypocrisy in light of the fact that the South had "expelled most of those Indians from their original homes, in violation of the faith of treaties and in defiance of the earnest, protracted resistance of the loyal influences now predominant at the North." He then offered a short and reasonably accurate summary of the circumvention of treaty provisions and Supreme Court decisions that had led to the Trail of Tears, before reasoning with dubious logic that the Cherokee practice of owning slaves explained their common cause with Jefferson Davis. This primer was only a preamble, however, to Greeley's main point.

> The new out-break in the North-West has manifestly a like origin, without a like excuse. The Sioux have doubtless been stimulated if not bribed to plunder and slaughter their White neighbors by White and Red villains sent among them for this purpose by the Secessionists. These perfectly understand that the Indians will be speedily crushed and probably destroyed as tribes; but what care their seducers for that? They will have effected a temporary diversion in favor of the Confederacy, and this is all their concern. But a day of reckoning for all these iniquities is at hand.

In other words, the Dakota could not possibly have a beef of their own. Nothing could exist outside of the conflict between North and South. As argument, this was shaky; as war correspondence, a failure. As an appreciation of the dissatisfactions and debasements behind the Dakota's decision to go to war, it was wreathed in total ignorance. But as an expression of a growing national anxiety, it was spot on.

From the vantage point of officials in Washington, Alexander Ramsey's initial telegram seemed the first shudder of a tectonic event. As if they had heard a single starting bell, military and political leaders in Iowa, Wisconsin, the Dakota Territory, Wyoming, Nebraska, and Colorado began to send alarming messages to the capital portraying a sudden increase in "unrest" and "agitation" among Indian tribes. No other violence during these autumn weeks approached the scale of the Dakota War, but now almost every foray by any tribe in the West—forays that were hardly a brand-new phenomenon—was given one simple explanation.

Brigadier General James Craig, at Fort Laramie in Wyoming, began the parade on August 23 by wiring about "Indians, from Minnesota to Pike's Peak, and from Salt Lake to near Fort Kearney, committing many depredations" and adding later that he was "satisfied rebel agents have been at work among the Indians." On the 30th, Craig reported on small-scale raids by Snakes and Blackfeet and recent skirmishes with Ute Indians and concluded "that some vicious influence is at work among the Indians is proved by the fact that there never was a time in the history of the country when so many tribes distant from and hostile to each other were exhibiting hostility to the whites."

The telegrams piled up in the War Department, from military officers and Indian agents in multiple states and territories, from the governor of Iowa, and from William Jayne, once Lincoln's personal physician and now governor of the Dakota Territory, all communicating some variation of the message sent by a Colonel Patrick of Nebraska: "The hostilities are so extensive as to indicate a combination of most of the tribes, and suggest the propriety of some action by the War Department." Alexander Ramsey took to calling the Dakota hostilities a "national war," and Greeley was not the only newspaperman to agree. *Scientific American* reported that "editors in the vicinity express the opinion that this rising of the Indians is the result of rebel machinations; the Indian war being designed to keep at home a considerable portion of the military force of the frontier states."

No such "combination of most of the tribes" existed, however persistent and pernicious the belief would become. Indian alliances had been a fearsome wild card in every American war to date, and some exaggerated historical memory was at play. And the Civil War, like every other war, was conducive to conspiracies, real and imagined; as in every other war it was customary to view one's opponent as nearly omnipotent and forever scheming. But Indians and whites had struck at one another for centuries, the intensity of conflict ebbing and flowing according to the pace and push of the American frontier's advancing edge, and the Civil War era was no different. It was beyond the imagination of many that the grievances of various Indian tribes could be so similar and yet be nursed separately. What united the West, in fact, was not a confederation of Indians but rather the pervasive white fear of one.

By February of the following year the Lincoln administration would formally, if quietly, declare that the idea of a coordinated Indian offensive, planned and implemented by a network of Southern agents, was pure fantasy. Many of those most responsible for spreading the idea would issue personal mea culpas as the Union came to understand how much the South was hampered by limitations of manpower, industrial capability, and geography. But at this moment no one seemed to know how much Northern manpower would now be needed west of the Mississippi River to fight Indians, and novel solutions were in high demand.

As recently as August 23, Lincoln had refused to allow the enlistment of black troops in the Union army, at least until his Emancipation Proclamation could be announced. Two days later he changed his mind. The exact impetus for his change of mind is unknown, but August 25 was the very day that Governor Ramsey and Commissioner Dole asked for an extension of Minnesota's draft quota and the day that officials in Wyoming and Nebraska wired Washington with their fears of a Confederate-led Indian uprising. Apparently, black soldiers would be useful after all.

# Chapter Eight

Sarah Wakefield described the morning of August 26 as a "confusion of Babel" filled with instructions, rules, and warnings as two thousand Dakotas prepared to retreat from the Lower Agency with three hundred captives. "I wish it was within my power to describe that procession as it moved over the prairie," she wrote. "I think it was five miles in length and one mile wide; the teams were very close together, and of every kind of vehicle that was ever manufactured." Oxcarts, chaises, bakers' carts, peddlers' wagons, and coaches were festooned with American flags. Some of the Dakota decked themselves out for the journey in plundered dresses, bonnets, shawls, and jewelry, all forbidden to the captives but worn as trophies by their captors. Horses, dogs, and even a few cows followed along. Musical instruments sounded, many played inexpertly to hoots of laughter.

The first sight to greet the procession as it passed out of the Lower Agency and onto the reservation road in the morning was George Gleason's body, still lying where Hapa had shot him. "He was stripped of his clothing, except his shirt and drawers," Sarah wrote, "and his head had been crushed in by a stone." They slept out on the prairie that night and the next, and on August 28 they arrived at the Upper Agency, where Sarah found her house emptied of every possession except its furniture. All of the agency buildings were now occupied by Sissetons and Wahpetons who had come in for protection and what forage and supplies could still be had. Little Crow went forward and met with these Dakotas to issue an ultimatum. He was not about to stay at the agency, so close to the white settlements and whatever white forces were now coming after him, but neither would he let those forces use the Upper Agency as a base. "These houses are large and strong and must be burned," he said. "If you do not get out you will be burned with the buildings." Get out they did, hitching their wagons and riding off a few hours ahead of the main body of Little Crow's caravan.

Here Sarah wept as James was returned to her unharmed by his companions and protectors among Chaska's kin, though she didn't at first recognize her son in his Dakota dress. The boy's spirits were high, his sense of adventure kindled by living apart from schoolbooks, daily schedules, and parental strictures. As the procession prepared to move again, Sarah, who spoke better than rudimentary Dakota, was able to provide news to the other captives who crossed her path. She also admonished some of them for making such a show of their unhappiness, telling one white woman that "she took a wrong course with the Indians, that they gave her the best they had, and she must try and be patient; that her life would be in danger if she kept on complaining and threatening them." The same woman, Jannette De Camp, wife of the Lower Agency's sawmill supervisor, told Sarah that she had heard one of her captors say that he had seen John Wakefield's body, to which Sarah answered, "If that is so, I might as well pass the remainder of my days here as any place." "Here" meant "with the Indians," and it was not the last time during her captivity—or during her life—that she would make such a statement.

Her stay at the Upper Agency was short. As the procession moved away into the setting sun, Sarah watched with a sore heart as her house and the other buildings burned behind her. Little Crow kept the train moving along the south bank of the Minnesota River for another five miles until they reached the mouth of Rush Brook, a deep, picturesque creek across which lay the Hazelwood mission station, a gathering of tepees, frame houses, and farm fields on the prairie where for eight years the Presbyterian minister Stephen R. Riggs had overseen a church and school for Christian Dakotas. The Hazelwood Republic, normally home to a few hundred members of the Upper Dakota bands, was now crowded with many times that number, most of whom

Hazelwood Mission Station, ca. 1860

were fearful of Little Crow's approach and unwilling to join the war effort.

If the East held white people and white machines and white weapons, ever greater in number as one traveled toward the Atlantic Ocean, the West contained its own impediments to Little Crow's plans. The Wahpeton and Sisseton Dakota, the Upper Agency bands, were kin to the Mdewakantons and Wahpekutes by blood, marriage, language, and custom, but they were also a different people with different rhythms of living who spent much of their year out on the plains of the Dakota Territory, trading and hunting with the Yanktons and Yanktonais. In this complex world of bands and villages, understood by few white settlers or city dwellers, no overall Dakota consensus could exist. In fact, to many Dakotas living along the upper reaches of the Minnesota River, near where the state ended and the Dakota Territory began, Little Crow was no hero but a troublemaker determined to rain down misery on all of them.

That night, August 28, the Mdewakanton *tiyotipi* sent several hundred men across Rush Brook to the camp of the Sissetons and Wahpetons for the purpose of bringing them into the fold. The men surrounded the camp, riding in swift circles as they shouted, sang, fired their guns, and issued threats that the tepees of the Upper Agency Dakota would be destroyed if they did not join their Lower Agency counterparts. Dismounting, the Mdewakantons sat down to a meal and an animated conversation with their new adversaries, who called them trespassers on their land and promised to "take up arms against them and die on the spot rather than move into the camp of the insane followers of Little Crow." When the food was finished and the night growing long, the Mdewakantons got back on their horses, fired their guns into the air, promised to be back in the morning, and left. When they returned at daybreak, they found that the Upper Dakota had been busy during the night forming their own *tiyotipi,* a rival soldiers' lodge signified by a newly raised tepee, oversized and colorfully decorated, that now dominated the center of the opposing camp. The Mdewakanton warriors, who had expected no organized resistance and had been given no orders to fight a battle against other Dakotas, turned and rode away.

That afternoon, Little Crow watched as one hundred or more Sissetons and Wahpetons turned the tables, riding in and out of his own camp on horseback, their faces and bodies painted, carrying guns, bows and arrows, and knives, all the while making an ear-shattering noise of their own. The Upper Dakota were angry about the display of the night before and feared that Little Crow intended to make prisoners of any full-blooded Dakotas who opposed him. Little Crow and the men of the wartime *tiyotipi* stepped forward to meet their new adversaries and a great council began, one that would go on for several days and feature many different speakers making speeches as stirring as any the war would produce. All of the orators argued in favor of very different means to the same end. Everyone wanted a conclusion to the war, but only if it could be managed on their own terms.

The first to speak was Paul Mazakutemani, a Christian Wahpeton and an organizer of the Hazelwood Republic, who stepped up to make the Upper Dakota's demands: they wanted their kin returned to them, mixed-bloods and full-bloods, captives and warriors, and they wanted whatever plundered property belonged to them returned as well. Considered the speaker of the Upper Agency bands, Mazakutemani was every bit Little Crow's equal at holding the attention of a crowd. In his opening speech, one of great length, he went well beyond the issue of protections for his kin and decried the prosecution of the war itself.

> I want to speak now to you of what is in my own heart. Give me all these white captives. I will deliver them up to their

friends. You Dakotas are numerous—you can afford to give these captives to me, and I will go with them to the white people. Then, if you want to fight, when you see the white soldiers coming to fight, fight with them, but don't fight with women and children. Or stop fighting. The Americans are a great people. They have much lead, powder, guns, and provisions. Stop fighting, and now gather up all the captives and give them to me. No one who fights with the white people ever becomes rich, or remains two days in one place, but is always fleeing and starving.

These words were not lost on Sarah, whether she was close enough to hear them or not. Like the other captives, she knew that a "peace party" was forming, though no one yet called it by that name. She knew that many of the Dakota traveling with them had no love for what many called Little Crow's War. For those whites in Minnesota who imagined a single many-headed Dakota enemy roaming everywhere over the prairie with bloodshed in its heart—and who would continue to hold on to this vision in the days, months, and years to come—the sights and sounds of tribal wrangling would have been incomprehensible. The Dakotas opposed to the war were a heterogeneous group: old and young, men and women, Christians and non-Christians, farmers and buffalo hunters. Here above the Upper Agency, where the plains of the Dakota Territory beckoned, unusual alliances were forming as the opposition to Little Crow's aims, voiced so boldly and openly by Paul Mazakutemani, also spread from lodge to lodge in whispers.

Little Crow gauged the situation and decided that mixed-blood relations of the Sissetons and Wahpetons should be freed to join their relatives, and also that plundered property should be returned. But the white captives, he said, must remain with him. Little Crow's spokesman during the opening councils was Wakiyantoecheye, or Thunder That Paints Itself Blue, son-in-law to the powerful village leader Wabasha and a forceful speaker in his own right, who argued that the captives "should not be released, that the hostile Indians had brought trouble and suffering upon themselves, and that captives would have to stay with them and participate in their troubles and deprivations." Little Crow also abandoned his efforts to combine the two camps, now referred to as "hostile" and "friendly" to whites, into one; he recognized the obvious, that should he attempt to merge them by force, the result would be disastrous.

When Little Crow finally addressed the crowd, well into the councils, he flatly rejected any notion of surrender or parley with the whites. According to one mixed-blood observer, Little Crow finished his oration by saying that he was "the leader of those who made war on the whites; that as long as he was alive no white man should touch him; that if he should ever be taken alive, he would be made a show of before the whites; and that, if he was ever touched by a white man, it would be after he was dead."

Every day they now continued to talk in council would be a day that white forces drew nearer. Little Crow was also aware that the rival camp was setting up as a haven for hostages who might try to escape, and he was suspicious that Paul Mazakutemani and other Sisseton and Wahpeton leaders might already be sending private messages to white authorities. The time for negotiation was over, and at the end of one particularly heated debate, the young warriors of the Mdewakanton *tiyotipi* simply walked away, singing as they went.

The song was an old one, sung by Dakota warriors heading into battle against the Ojibwe, now used as the final rebuke to all of the Dakota arguing for an end to their campaign of freedom and vengeance. "Over the earth I come," they sang.

> *Over the earth I come;*
> *Over the earth I come;*
> *A soldier I come;*
> *Over the earth I am a ghost.*

Little Crow's troubles were multiplying. He now knew that he could count on no other Indians in Minnesota—not the Ojibwe, not the Ho-Chunks, not the Sissetons and Wahpetons—to join in all-out war against the whites. A growing peace party now occupied the camp not two miles away. The Dakota's ammunition was almost gone and they had no easy way to replenish it. He knew beyond any doubt that white soldiers were finally coming after him in great numbers, and more than all of this, he knew the man who rode at the head of those soldiers. As they moved into the second phase of their war, the Dakota would not be facing a white leader who was a stranger to their people and their history, or to Little Crow himself. In fact, very few generals facing off on the faraway fields of the Civil War knew each other any better than Little Crow knew Colonel Henry Hastings Sibley.

Born in Detroit in 1811, Sibley had trained for the law with an eye toward emulating the career of his father, a prominent judge, before he found his own calling in the fur trade, rising from clerk to chief purchasing agent of the American Fur Company. Once the most famous commercial enterprise west of the Alleghenies, the American Fur Company, brainchild of John Jacob Astor, had established outposts in the Northwest Territory as early as 1820, taking advantage of a near-monopoly and the worldwide mania for beaver, fox, and buffalo pelts to make Astor the country's richest man. But even as Sibley arrived in 1834 to run the Upper Mississippi district of the Western Outfit, an American Fur Company subsidiary, the fur boom was beginning to fade, a victim of aggressive competition from the Hudson Bay Company, the rapid depletion of game throughout the Northwest, and sky-high demand for plantation-produced cotton and silk.

For fourteen years, between the day he arrived and the day the Minnesota Territory was created in 1849, Sibley experienced firsthand as many aspects of Dakota life as was possible for a white man. Success in the fur trade depended on tying bonds to the Indian world via gift exchanges, displays of physical skill, earnest participation in council, and common kinship, and Sibley qualified in all respects. He befriended Little Crow's father and became a regular companion to the Mdewakantons, accompanying those warriors closer to his own age on hunting expeditions and living in the band's villages for months at a time, receiving furs in exchange for goods, weapons, and gold. In 1841, at thirty, he fathered a girl with a young Mdewakanton woman named Red Blanket Woman. Though the mother would die of unknown causes a few years later and the child, Helen, would be placed with a white foster family, in Dakota eyes Sibley had bound himself to them with the tightest possible knot.

On one of his early hunting trips to the West, Sibley had witnessed Taoyateduta, one year his junior, perform an astonishing physical feat. As Sibley and other traders pursued a great herd of elk over the plains for five days, covering 125 miles on horseback, the future Little Crow ran beside them all the while on bare feet without asking for a halt. Intoxicated by his sojourns with the Indians, Sibley published a series

Henry Hastings Sibley, 1862

of colorful frontier dispatches in *The Spirit of the Times,* a New York newsweekly for armchair sportsmen, writing under the nom de plume "Hal, a Dacotah." In 1845, when Taoyateduta's father, the third Little Crow, suffered an accidental gunshot wound, Sibley had dashed to Kaposia with a doctor from Fort Snelling, where he learned that the old man would likely die soon. That night, the trader watched as the dying chief reluctantly passed the mantle of leadership to his eldest son, one of the two half brothers who would claim the title of village leaders before Little Crow arrived. Sibley knew the rest of the story, too: how Taoyateduta stood unarmed and defiant before his siblings, who shot and crippled the younger Little Crow. He knew that the half brothers had left in disgrace, and he knew that they had soon been found dead. And he knew from the start that the new Little Crow would be intelligent, formidable, and unpredictable.

Four years later, in 1849, Sibley had become the Minnesota Territory's first delegate to Congress, where he worked closely with Governor Ramsey to "extinguish the title of Indian lands" as they built the case for statehood. His entry into politics drew a stark dividing line in his life and fundamentally changed his relationship with the Dakota. In the negotiations leading up to the treaty of 1851, Sibley emerged as the leading voice behind the traders' interests, conferring with Little Crow and other Dakota leaders to ensure that the treaty established the system of credit and debt that would escalate year by year and come to play such a major role in the outbreak in 1862.

This was accomplished partly through a "trader's paper," a second document setting aside hundreds of thousands of dollars in annuity monies for traders that many Dakota signatories were led to assume was merely a second copy of the treaty itself. The paper was a cheat, but one that some Dakota leaders with close ties to traders may have tolerated at first, failing to foresee the degree to which it would put so many of their kinsmen in arrears each year. Along the way Sibley received substantial payments out of the annuity funds, rewards running into the tens of thousands of dollars, helping to make him rich and propel him forward as a leading man in the territory. Running as a Democrat, he was elected as Minnesota's first governor in 1858; he chose not to run again in 1860 so that he might play a larger role on the national political stage.

Such was Sibley's story up to August 19, 1862, when a messenger from Alexander Ramsey, his old friend and political rival, rode up to the door of his three-story house, the first stone structure in the town of Mendota, across from Fort Snelling at the confluence of the Mississippi and Minnesota rivers. The governor considered no one else for the job, assigning Sibley the rank of colonel on the spot and asking him to take command of the hastily assembled group of impromptu militia and Union army recruits who were to head toward Fort Ridgely and quell the Indians.

Sibley took the commission and immediately stewed through a series of delays that began with the delivery of thousands of weapons mismatched with the available ammunition. Leaving Saint Peter on August 25, he had reached Fort Ridgely, only forty miles away, on August 29, eleven days after the war began and four after Little Crow began moving away westward after the attempt to take New Ulm was abandoned. There at the fort Sibley's offensive stalled again as he attended to refugees already present and those coming in, all the while working to determine Little Crow's location and waiting on supplies. Nearly half his cavalry simply went home rather than sit around any longer, and newspaper editors, settlers, and soldiers all began to question his caution and pace as attacks on the settlements continued and the fate of the captives remained unresolved.

Little Crow knew about all of these developments, thanks to the runners and riders constantly converging on his lodgings. The decision to turn and fight after the councils with Paul Mazakutemani and the other Upper Dakota may have been his or it may have been made by the wartime *tiyotipi,* but in either case he hoped that striking a quick blow would fracture Minnesota's confidence in Sibley and give the Dakota more time. Two major detachments of warriors now set out to the east from Rush Brook. One, led by one of Little Crow's head warriors and numbering three hundred men, headed down the government road along the Minnesota River, bringing along empty wagons in order to retrieve such supplies and weapons as they could from Little Crow's old village and to loot New Ulm, should they find it still abandoned. The other party, made up of Little Crow and more than a hundred warriors, moved back toward the Big Woods to ascertain the possibilities in that direction.

A day or two out, a telling exchange took place between Little Crow and his men, one that laid bare abrasions within his own circle of followers. As their party camped on the prairie, Little Crow drafted letters to Colonel Sibley and Governor Ramsey in which he boasted of the panic gripping the state and suggested a cease-fire. He would return the prisoners in exchange for a new treaty, the restoration of annuities, and a lump settlement in gold. The letters were never sent; when read aloud, they were shouted down by his warriors. This response did not bother Little Crow overmuch; such was the way of a Dakota council, and besides, he was always dipping his hand in many wells to see what he could bring up. More distressingly, though, seventy-five of Little Crow's companions rejected his plan to make a series of movements to threaten the capital and left the camp to loot and plunder at their pleasure.

As they approached the town of Hutchinson, Little Crow's party, now reduced to fewer than fifty men, came upon a company of recruits raised for the Tenth Minnesota Regiment. The skirmish cost the whites six men and the Dakota one, while Little Crow suffered only a torn coat from an enemy bullet. The Dakota took a few horses and supply-laden wagons, but they had also signaled their meager firepower and numbers to the enemy. When Little Crow followed the soldiers into Hutchinson, he found no people in sight and an impressive stockade in the center of town. Something about this fortification seems to have taken the wind out of Little Crow; surely this meant that other towns in the vicinity had done the same and would no longer be so easily frightened. After a quick attempt to set fire to the stockade, Little

Crow and most of his men abandoned their foray into the settlements and turned back in the direction of their camp along the Minnesota River, loading up their wagons with loot from the forsaken farms and buildings along the way and burning empty houses as they went.

Little Crow took no pleasure in any of this activity, disgusted that such minor mischief seemed to be all that was left to him. On or about September 6, he and his men arrived back at Rush Brook to find that Paul Mazakutemani and the members of the peace party were still camped across the creek, well aware that they had had four days to hatch their own plans. Little Crow's mood soon lifted, though, when a unexpected dispatch arrived to announce that Fort Abercrombie, the federal enclave along the Red River of the North, had been repeatedly attacked and was now under siege by a splinter group of Upper Dakota warriors allied with a few Yanktonais and Cut Heads from the Dakota Territory. Ten Indians and two soldiers had been killed so far and the garrison stood firm; still, the action represented another potential front in the war, one that might be able to draw away some of Sibley's men and, most important, encourage other western tribes to join in.

And this news was nothing compared to the information Little Crow received when the other Mdewakanton foray returned to camp, shouting excitedly and boasting of a great triumph. Moving through the settlements on the north side of the river after crossing at the Lower Agency, the warriors had come across a large contingent of Sibley's soldiers camped adjacent to a small hollow on the prairie called Birch Coulee. Captain Hiram P. Grant, along with the current and previous Indian agents, Thomas Galbraith and Joseph R. Brown, had been leading a large burial party into the fields and towns where much of the first week's killing had occurred, on the assumption that the Dakota had moved north for good. Easily surrounded and especially vulnerable from the wide depression that gave the site its name, the whites had been helpless when Dakotas had risen out of the grass on all sides in the early dawn and begun to fire. Twenty-four whites had been killed or were left dying, four dozen more were badly wounded, and hundreds of others were trapped in their ill-advised camp without food or water and surrounded by the Dakota, who backed off to a safe distance and kept the roads under watch.

The sound of so much gunfire carried clearly over the featureless grass, and that evening 240 men with artillery had set out from Fort Ridgely to see what was happening. Sibley followed with several companies, and on the morning of September 3 he arrived, unmolested by unseen Dakota, to find dead horses, dying men, and famished survivors. After ordering burials and a return to Fort Ridgely en masse, he planted a stake at the center of the field and affixed to it a cigar box with a note inside, a note he knew Dakota scouts would retrieve before heading back up the river valley: "If Little Crow has any proposition to make to me, let him send a half-breed to me, and he shall be protected in and out of camp."

Now Little Crow was back in his Rush Brook camp with Sibley's message in hand. He knew that his reply would stand as the first official exchange between war leaders and enter the record as an official statement of Dakota intent, and for this reason many interpreters were employed both in reading Sibley's note and in crafting Little Crow's answer. After council was complete and the answer prepared, two mixed-blood couriers were chosen and given a small mule and a single buggy to take south under a flag of truce. Sibley hadn't asked why the Dakota were fighting, but that was what Little Crow explained. His response referred to the governor, the Indian agent, and the insults of the traders who had been among the first to die in the attack on the Lower Agency.

> We made a treaty with the government and beg for what we do get and can't get that till our children are dying with hunger. It is the traders who commenced it. Mr. A. J. Myrick told the Indians that they would eat grass or dirt. Then Mr. Forbes told the Lower Sioux that they were not men. Then Roberts was working with his friends to defraud us out of our moneys. If the young braves have pushed the white men, I have done this myself. So I want you to let Governor Ramsey know this. I have a great many prisoners, women and children. It ain't all our fault.

Little Crow did not wait for Sibley's answer, but moved his camp away from the Rush Brook site along the river bluff, toward the village of a Sisseton chief, Red Iron, ten miles distant. Paul Mazakutemani and the others in the friendly camp followed, wary of Sibley's intentions should he come upon them and assume them to be hostile. Each removal brought the Dakota closer to the Red River of the North, which marked the state's western edge and presented a boundary that was topographical, political, and psychological. Little Crow knew that his influence was weakening, that Dakota loyalties were many-faceted, and that he needed to keep a safe distance between himself and the white forces. He may even have known that some of his own Mdewakanton people, men who had opposed the war from the start, had now taken prominent places in the peace party. Indeed, some of those men were beginning to write their own private messages to Sibley protesting their innocence, blaming Little Crow for the war, and offering to deliver up as many prisoners as they could once Sibley finally reached their camp.

As Little Crow approached Red Iron's village, a force of mounted and armed Sissetons with their chief in the lead rode down the reservation road at him, so hard and fast that the van of Little Crow's men was forced to wheel and scatter. The Sissetons did not attack; their ride was a show of defiance and independence, a warning to Little Crow and all of the Lower Dakota not to presume they could simply ride in without permission. After Red Iron and his men retreated, Little Crow gathered together his train, stopped them for the night, and sent Little Six, the young Dakota leader whose men had provided the original push for war, forward with a formal request that Red Iron join with them against the whites.

A great gathering of Dakota now formed near Red Iron's village. The factions included Little Crow's camp, home to the wartime *tiyotipi* and the white captives; the friendly camp and the leaders of the peace party; Red Iron and his warriors; and other leaders who now arrived from nearby villages, including Standing Buffalo, the most powerful and influential chief among the Upper Dakota. When the councils began, each of these groups stood at a distance apart from the others, sending forth their spokesmen and receiving reports and communications from the councils and from runners and riders throughout the region.

The talks were intense and urgent, focused on the fate of the captives, the possibility of surrender, and the likelihood that white leaders could be trusted to act in good faith. Paul Mazakutemani repeated his dismay that war had been declared without the consensus of all the Dakota bands, and then he demanded the release of the prisoners: "I want to know from you Lower Indians whether you were asleep or crazy. In fighting the whites, you are fighting the thunder and lightning. You will all be killed off. You might as well try to bail out the waters of the Mississippi as to whip them." When Mazakutemani finished, some of the Mdewakantons whooped and threatened to kill him for what they viewed as his traitorous stand, but such a threat couldn't be carried out without starting a donnybrook that would destroy all the Dakota, and the council continued.

As was his way, Little Crow waited out the various speakers. One observer recorded Little Crow's firm opposition to the demand that he open talks with Sibley. "I wish no more war," the chief said. "But if we give up all the prisoners, we must run away, or we shall all be shot. I do not justify the killing of women and children. I gave orders to kill only traders and government agents, who have cheated the Indians. But now we wish to settle the question, whether we will fight or run. We must do one or the other." Peacemaking was not a choice. If the Dakota were taken by whites, said Little Crow, they would be hanged, all of them. Die he might, but only in the fashion of a warrior.

> I tell you we must fight and perish together. A man is a fool and a coward who thinks otherwise, and who will desert his nation at such a time. Disgrace not yourselves by a surrender to those who will hang you up like dogs, but die, if die you must, with arms in your hands, like warriors and braves of the Dakota.

Standing Buffalo and Red Iron, acting from positions of advantage, listened respectfully but continued to stand aloof from the Lower Dakota. By now Little Crow knew that Sibley was finally moving, coming upriver at the head of thousands of soldiers and hoping to wipe out the Dakota warriors without harming any of their captives. At some point during the councils, a mixed-blood courier entered the camp with Sibley's terse response to Little Crow's latest message. The note contained nothing that Little Crow had not expected. "You have murdered many of our people without any sufficient cause," wrote Sibley. "Return me the prisoners under a flag of truce, and I will talk to you then like a man." Sibley also penned what he called an "open letter" to "those of the Half-Breeds and Sioux Indians who have not been Concerned in the Murders and Outrages upon the White Settlers."

> I have not come into this upper country to injure any innocent person, but to punish those who have committed the

cruel murders upon innocent men, women, and children. If, therefore, you wish to withdraw from these guilty people you must, when you see my troops approaching, take up a separate position and hoist a flag of truce and send a small party to me when I hoist a flag of truce in answer, and I will then take you under my protection.

Little Crow knew that he had become a target, and not just of white soldiers. He was well aware that someone within one of the rival Dakota camps might even now be arranging for his capture, and capture—not death in battle, which would bring only honor—was what he dreaded most. His choices, then, were to run to the West or to turn and fight. Running might give him time, but it might also allow Sibley's soldiers to keep moving on his heels while the season would still allow it. A chill was creeping into the night air, now that August was past, and Little Crow knew that no large armed force would cross onto the plains once winter began. At the very least, he needed to give Sibley's army one more reason to pause. Soon Little Crow might have to flee. But now he would fight.

John Nicolay's return trip to the Ojibwe agency at Crow Wing, ten miles above Fort Ripley, was colored from its start, on August 26, by a piece of unsettling news. Lucius Walker, the Ojibwe agent who had fled Saint Cloud in a panic one week earlier, had been found dead, his pistol next to him and a gaping gunshot wound in his side. Everywhere Walker had stopped along the Mississippi River on his dash south, it seemed, he had described an imaginary force of 250 Ojibwe warriors hard on his heels and bent on his scalp. The possibility that Walker's death, though an apparent suicide, might indeed have been the work of a small party of Ojibwe was cause for alarm, but at least now Walker's reputation among the Ojibwe as a corrupt, incompetent Indian agent would no longer hinder their negotiations.

All entreaty in the Ojibwe villages near Fort Ripley ran through one man, Bagone-glizhig, or Hole in the Day, whose life story so resembled Little Crow's that the two sometimes seemed different sides of the same coin. Both were scions in a line of consequential chiefs whose fathers had received decorations from the British during the War of 1812. Both had dabbled in Christianity without abandoning ancient systems of belief. Both had traveled to Washington to meet with presidents and other white leaders, and both had been instrumental in negotiating land-cession treaties, playing roles that had left them in ambiguous positions within their own tribes. Each had taken part in regular raids against the other's tribe, and rode with raiding and hunting parties on disputed grounds. But after rising to their leadership positions each had seen the value of regular correspondence with the other, and over the past few years they had spoken together often in Saint Paul as they found themselves more and more disillusioned with the government's broken and altered promises.

Before leaving Saint Paul to go up the Mississippi River for the second time, Nicolay wrote John Hay to say that "the muss with Hole-in-the-Day is a complicated affair, involving official frauds on the one hand and Indian depredations on the other," and adding, "I see that the rebels are almost in Washington. How does your head feel? It looks very much as if it were about as safe as my scalp." The "official frauds" involved a series of brazen embezzlements by Walker, late annuity payments, spoiled or unusable treaty goods, and the increasing coercion of mixed-blood Ojibwes into the Union army. On August 17, the day before the Dakota attack on the Lower Agency, Hole in the

Bagone-glizhig, or Hole in the Day, 1858

Day had dispatched runners to Ojibwe villages at Leech Lake, Otter Tail Lake, and Rabbit Lake, telling them, according to Nicolay's intelligence, to "kill all the whites, rob their stores and dwellings, and join him at once with their warriors at Gull Lake, some thirty miles from the Government Agency."

The order to kill whites, if indeed such an order existed, was ignored, but the few settlers in those locations—perhaps one hundred in total—found themselves plundered of their provisions and stocks, their cattle and other livestock destroyed. Some white men were taken to be held hostage at the Gull Lake negotiations. On the same day as the Dakota attack on the Lower Agency, as the number of Ojibwe warriors at the Crow Wing village grew into the hundreds, Walker had tried and failed to arrest Hole in the Day. That was when the agent had fled and eventually found Nicolay and Dole in Saint Cloud, where he delivered his prediction of statewide war and told stories of hundreds of Ojibwe warriors coming to kill him. Now Walker was dead, an interim agent in his place, and Hole in the Day was ready to treat with white officials.

When Nicolay's party reached Fort Ripley on August 29, they found that Hole in the Day had taken umbrage at the company of infantry in their wake and retreated to join the mass of Ojibwe warriors thirty miles to the north. His instructions to Commissioner Dole were to wait, and so they waited, day after day. During this interim, another letter from John Hay found Nicolay. "Where is your scalp?" it began. "If in God's good Providence your long locks adorn the lodge of an aboriginal warrior and the festive tomtom is made of your stretched hide, I will not grudge the time thus spent, for auld lang syne. In fancy's eye I often behold you the centre and ornament of a wildwood circle delighting the untutored children of the forest with Tuscan melodies, while from enraptured maidens comes the seductive invitation."

After two weeks of exasperated waiting, Dole agreed to Hole in the Day's demand that they meet not at the fort, nor at the agency, but near the Indian village at Crow Wing. At noon on September 10, 1862, almost two weeks after Nicolay had arrived, the Ojibwe approached a small dell that Hole in the Day had designated as the council ground. "They came on in irregular, straggling groups, chiefs and braves promiscuously intermingled, not following the road but the bank and beach of the river," Nicolay wrote.

It was a picturesque group. The bold, high angle of bank and point of yellow sand-beach jutting out into the bend of the stream, and the shining and rippled expanse of its waters; the swarthy figures of the savages, in their various and carelessly-graceful attitudes and costumes, clearly and sharply outlined against the dark-green background of pine foliage on the opposite side of the river, with occasional red and white blankets, making bright spots of color that lighted up the whole scene.

Dole opened the discussions by demanding the release of all white captives, following which the infantry captain assigned to guard the commissioner threatened that the Ojibwe would be "blown to hell in five minutes" should they fail to comply. Hole in the Day did not respond, other than to give a signal that brought forth one hundred additional warriors, stepping into view behind the white officials and leaving them outnumbered, subject to crossfire, and cut off from escape. Dole stepped forward to complain about the display of force but soon switched to a more conciliatory approach. As one white trader on the scene wrote, he "gave them a short nice speech telling them how glad he was to see them but I would bet he was wishing himself all the time that [he] was in his good arm chair in his office in Washington." Hole in the Day responded with disgust, telling Dole, "If you are the smartest man the Great Father has got, I pity our Great Father. You have been talking to me as if I was a child. I am not a little child."

Nicolay, who feared that "a deadly and desperate melee" was in the making, described the council that followed as "merely an hour's preliminary, pointless talk, a wordy and circumlocutory concealment of objects which would have done credit to the most bestarred and bespangled diplomats." The Ojibwe moved off, and the commissioner and his soldiers did likewise. After one more day of sluggish talks Dole decided to go back to Saint Paul and hand the job over to Governor Ramsey. Hole in the Day had no intention of joining an all-out war against the whites. Rather, two weeks of posturing had gotten the chief exactly what he did want: confirmation of his own influence and a promise that the state would attend to the grievances of the Ojibwe in order to prevent the opening of another front in their sudden war. Both sides, white and Indian, could claim success, and both sides did.

Riding the steamboat on his return to Saint Paul, Nicolay penned a final note to John Hay. "My scalp is yet safe," he wrote, "but day before yesterday it was not worth as much as it is tonight." Nicolay departed Minnesota for Washington on September 13, bearing a report for the president and a file of notes ready to turn into one of the first articles about the Dakota War to be published in a prominent eastern magazine.

The military engagement that Lincoln had so anxiously awaited during August had turned into the Second Battle of Bull Run, probably the greatest disaster of the war for the Union army. Unsupported by McClellan, General John Pope and his forces spent two weeks chasing shadows around Northern Virginia before the combined forces of Stonewall Jackson and James Longstreet sent his men scrambling back across the Potomac River, leaving the Confederates in control of all of Virginia and scuttling Lincoln's chance to announce his plans for emancipation. On September 2, the president told his cabinet that he "felt almost ready to hang himself," and while he was known to make melancholic jokes, the present circumstances leached away most of the humor. McClellan had hung Pope out to dry and deserved to be removed from command, but Lincoln had no suitable replacement in line and refused to cut "Little Mac" loose, much to the dismay of his cabinet.

It was a time of increasing division inside the White House, yet everyone could agree that the disposal of John Pope in the wake of Second Bull Run had to be handled with a great deal of sensitivity. To dismiss Pope from the service would make the administration appear incompetent for promoting him in the first place, while to leave him in charge of any forces in the East would dispirit the soldiers. There was also the matter of Pope's personal connection to the president. Born in Louisville and raised in Kaskaskia, Illinois, he was the son of Nathaniel Pope, Lincoln's favorite federal judge and the man who had admitted him to practice in Illinois's circuit court. Like his father, John was loquacious, ambitious, and prone to exaggeration, equally capable of inspiring loyalty or inviting scorn. Both were gruff, doughty men, well-read and well-educated and prone to abuse their superior knowledge in their treatment of subordinates or legal petitioners. When John graduated West Point in 1842, his final standing in the class, a respectable seventeenth out of fifty-six, nonetheless left his father dis-

John Pope, ca. 1860–70

appointed, putting a chip on the son's shoulder that took many years to fall off.

The younger Pope had been one of four men selected to accompany Mary Todd Lincoln on her pre-inaugural journey from the Midwest to Washington, D.C. Pressed into service at the start of the Civil War, Pope won a string of minor victories along the Mississippi River before using a series of newspaper interviews and letters to Lincoln to paint himself as a precocious military mind, something he decidedly wasn't. But with military talent so short in the early incarnation of the Union army and George McClellan unwilling to take the offensive, Pope had been called east to head the Army of Virginia, 75,000 men with two jobs to do: stop Robert E. Lee and drive him back to Richmond.

Pope's lasting infamy among Union forces was less a result of his defeat at Bull Run—plenty of Union generals, including McClellan, had suffered defeat—and more a by-product of his bloated, pompous style of leadership. Arriving in Virginia in early August, he had said

perhaps the most ill-advised hello in military history. "Let us understand each other," Pope wrote to his new charges. "I have come to you
from the West, where we have always seen the backs of our enemies;
from an army whose business it has been to seek the adversary and to
beat him when he was found; whose policy has been attack and not
defense." Not satisfied with insulting his men, he then insulted the
strategic acumen of their beloved former commander.

> I desire you to dismiss from your minds certain phrases, which
> I am sorry to find so much in vogue amongst you. I hear con-
> stantly of "taking strong positions and holding them," of "lines
> of retreat," and of "bases of supplies." Let us discard such ideas.
> The strongest position a soldier should desire to occupy is one
> from which he can most easily advance against the enemy. Let
> us study the probable lines of retreat of our opponents, and
> leave our own to take care of themselves. Let us look before us,
> and not behind. Success and glory are in the advance, disaster
> and shame lurk in the rear.

Pope's bombast earned him lasting scorn after he found himself out
of his depth on the fields of Northern Virginia. He had also made
Lincoln's job more difficult by ensuring that he could not be moved to
another position in the Union's eastern armies.

On September 4, Pope had arrived at the White House to lay
seven pages of complaints about his abandonment by McClellan in
front of Lincoln, who agreed with many of Pope's points but who could
also see that he had a broken, bitter man on his hands. In the end, the
Dakota War provided Lincoln with a convenient solution. Two trou-
blesome situations could now be taken care of with one order. If the
governors of the states and territories in the Northwest wanted a new
military department to deal harshly with the "Indian problem," they
would have it. Edwin Stanton's letter to Pope on September 6 oozed
insincere and unctuous regard.

> The Indian hostilities that have recently broken forth and
> are now prevailing in that department require the attention
> of some military officer of high rank, in whose ability and
> vigor the Government has confidence, and you have therefore
> been selected for this important command. You will proceed

immediately to your department, establish your headquarters at Saint Paul, Minn, and make yourself acquainted with and report to this department the actual condition of affairs, and take such prompt and vigorous measures as shall quell the hostilities and afford peace, security, and protection to the people against Indian hostilities.

The Dakota War had now been federalized, the new department placed under the command of a general who saw in his assignment only punishment and exile. As John Nicolay headed back east, John Pope was coming west, and he wasn't happy.

# Chapter Nine

All of the nineteenth-century presidents received public visitors. Few other bygone Washington customs provide a stranger spectacle for the modern imagination than that of a second-floor room crowded with common citizens waiting their turn to address the highest authority in the land, uninvited and unannounced. No matter his uncommon status as a bishop and his connections in high places, when Henry Benjamin Whipple was finally ushered inside the White House for his audience with Abraham Lincoln on Tuesday, September 16, he was still one face in a long parade seeking to somehow make a lasting impression with only a few minutes to do so. The pressing business of the Civil War and the president's general exasperation with petitioners always put visitors at a disadvantage, and this day was less opportune than most. When Governor Ramsey's first telegram had arrived four weeks earlier, Lincoln was preoccupied with looming battles and the momentous question of emancipation; today his concerns were the same, except that the battles were bigger and the question of emancipation was much closer to its flash point.

Lincoln's reassignment of Pope and reinstatement of McClellan hadn't done anything to blunt Robert E. Lee, who had pressed his advantage in the wake of Second Bull Run by leading his Army of Northern Virginia onto Union soil for the first time. Lee's aim in entering Maryland was to further demoralize his enemy and deliver a hard blow that would create enough havoc to raise the chances that the peace-inclined wing of the Democratic Party could win the 1864 elections. He also hoped that a victory would encourage European nations to formally recognize the Confederacy and force Lincoln to the bargaining table. As McClellan and his army moved in response, Lincoln's impatience mounted. Would Lee find sympathy and freely given provisions in Maryland, a border state that many had feared would secede at the start of the war? Given Little Mac's case of the "slows," would he be nimble enough to stay in front of Lee's far more mobile forces? The president no longer expected an all-out Confederate attack on Washington, but much of the capital's populace did, and that anticipation made the city giddy and anxious.

Even great luck only served to heighten Lincoln's worries. On September 13, just three days before Whipple's visit, a most extraordinary telegram from McClellan had arrived in the War Department office. "An order from General R.E. Lee," it began, "addressed to General D.H. Hill, which has accidentally come into my hands this evening—the authenticity of which is unquestionable—discloses some of the plans of the enemy, and shows most conclusively that the main rebel army is now before us." The discovery of Lee's "lost dispatch," laying out the movements and objectives of the Southern army, put the White House into an intense, expectant burn that lasted for days. Lincoln could be forgiven for assuming that McClellan now held the card to trump all others, but all the president could learn for certain was that both armies were concentrating near Sharpsburg, Maryland, just seventy miles up the road from Washington. For a week now, Lincoln had been skipping sleep and sending early-morning telegrams to McClellan importuning him to "destroy the rebel army, if possible." Every soldier in Washington who could be spared had been sent to the front, while Lincoln wrote to the governor of Pennsylvania to discuss a call-up of all able-bodied men in that state and to assure him that Philadelphia was not vulnerable to invasion.

Meanwhile, heedless of Lincoln's anxiety, his procession of visitors had continued. At nine o'clock in the morning on September 12, one day before bivouacking Union soldiers found a copy of Lee's battle plans wrapped around three cigars, Lincoln had had his first face-to-face meeting with the Cherokee leader John Ross. A veteran

Washington negotiator unintimidated by the situation, Ross made an impassioned argument that his tribe was bound to the United States by extant treaty relationships that extended back through "a long series of years" and was entitled to the promised protection of the United States "and no other sovereign whatever." The withdrawal of Union forces from Indian Territory had left the Cherokee with no choice but to negotiate with the Confederacy, Ross explained, adding that this fact had been impossible to communicate to Union leaders from a distance. Contrary to appearances, he told Lincoln, the "great mass of the Cherokee People rallied spontaneously around the authorities of the United States" whenever the smallest opportunity to do so existed. Now Ross wanted assurances of military protection and the Union's recognition of Cherokee treaty rights, and he wanted those assurances in form of a presidential proclamation.

When Ross finished, Lincoln responded without enthusiasm, saying little except to offer his thanks and ask Ross to put his complaints and requests in writing so that his concerns could be forwarded to Secretary of the Interior Caleb Smith. As Ross went back to his rented rooms to draft his letter, the president rode up the long hill of Sixteenth Street to Anderson Cottage, his borrowed summer residence at the Old Soldiers' Home three miles north of the White House, where the first family usually slept during the mosquito and rodent season. There, by candlelight, he continued work on his second draft of the preliminary Emancipation Proclamation.

Lincoln had no intention, then or in the future, of issuing a proclamation for Ross or any other dissatisfied tribal spokesman; Indian treaties were the province of Congress, the secretary of the interior, and the commissioner of Indian affairs, while military actions relative to the country's tribes belonged to the secretary of war and General in Chief Halleck. Only absolute necessity would bring about a presidential order, and at this moment Lincoln believed that enslaved Africans qualified and dispossessed Indians did not. If McClellan could win a victory in Maryland, meet and check Lee so that the Confederate army took a visible wound, the announcement that three million Southern slaves would be considered legally free on New Year's Day would go to the newspapers.

Early the next day, September 13, Lincoln's horse had thrown him as he rode down the long slope to the White House. The wrenched wrist he suffered in the fall would pain him for the next two weeks before he sought medical attention. He may have been feeling prickly later that same morning, then, as he received two pastors and two laymen from Chicago who bore a petition and a document they called an "emancipation memorial" generated during an ecumenical gathering of clergymen and citizens the previous week. Several of the attendees at this meeting of "Chicago Christians" had been old Illinois friends of the president, which may explain his willingness to receive the pastors, and also the vigor of their conversation. Lincoln had by this point of the war built up a storehouse of exasperation for people who wanted to tell him what he should do without considering what he *could* do.

"What good would a proclamation of emancipation from me do, especially as we are now situated?" he had told his guests. "I do not want to issue a document that the whole world will see must necessarily be inoperative, like the Pope's bull against the comet!" He was weary of people urging a proclamation before some Union victory put him on the advantage, but in this meeting his sharpest jab was reserved for the presumptuous invocation of God.

> I hope it will not be irreverent for me to say that if it is probable that God would reveal his will to others, on a point so connected with my duty, it might be supposed he would reveal it directly to me; for, unless I am more deceived in myself than I often am, it is my earnest desire to know the will of Providence in this matter. And if I can learn what it is I will do it!

Lincoln was not merely offering a demonstration of wit. Two weeks earlier, on the same day that he had told his cabinet that he "felt almost ready to hang himself," he had written and dated a note to himself, one that John Hay would find in his desk after his assassination. In this note, which Hay named "Meditation on the Divine Will," Lincoln had mused on God and war, probing a persistent and confounding fog in his thoughts. "God cannot be *for*, and *against* the same thing at the same time," he wrote. "In the present civil war it is quite possible that God's purpose is something different from the purpose of either party . . . I am almost ready to say this is probably true—that God wills this contest, and wills that it shall not end yet."

God was much on his mind, then. Still, of all the classes of visitors Lincoln regularly received—those seeking government posts or military promotions, foreign diplomats, inventors with technological solutions to problems pressing and trivial, wives with tales of wronged husbands—he was most wary of clergymen. He didn't like to hear preaching, especially when he was its target, and as he stood to greet Henry Whipple, three days after his argument with the Chicago Christians, he surely expected another sermon and not much more.


Henry Whipple had first visited Washington, D.C., eighteen years earlier, in April 1844, on a layover during the return trip to upstate New York after his two-year sojourn in Florida. Whipple had already navigated two disorienting changes of course in his life, from promising student to businessman to political operative, and was traveling without his wife, Cornelia, and their daughter Lizzie, born only weeks before his departure. Whipple's diary of that journey reveals precocious powers of description, as well as an ambivalence about the morality and conditions of slavery that left him sympathetic to the Democrats who argued that slaves would be better off free only when they could be shipped off as colonists of some African or South American locale or concentrated in some region of the western United States. Emancipation, in this view, could be accomplished only gradually, by an end to the purchase and importation of slaves, and never by immediate abolition. Whipple's first up-close look at slaves, in Savannah, had left him unshaken: "Every kind of labour is performed by blacks and it invariably takes half a dozen blacks to do what one white would. They seem happy and cheerful and slavery does not appear a yoke to many of them." His descriptions of plantation life might have satisfied any churchgoing slaveholder, as would have his stance that "the efforts of abolitionists at the North have only served to injure the slave and to destroy that kind & fraternal feeling which should exist between the northern and southern states."

A few days later, though, Whipple had heard accounts of the Seminole chief Osceola and his long fight against Andrew Jackson's removal policy, a litany of injustice that filled him with very different emotions. "When will the cupidity and cruelty of the white men cease?" he wrote. "Never, no never till that last lone Indian has gone to the spirit land." In 1844, he was only twenty-four and still seeing much of the world in the abstract. But the discrepancy between his sanguine view of slavery and his immediate anger at the treatment of Indians would last for most of his life, and may be explained by the fact that slaves were, by and large, Christians, while the continent's natives lived in what he called a state of "heathen neglect." His calling as he came to see it would be to bring God into rooms where God was unwanted or unheeded, wherever those rooms might be.

Whipple's sightseeing tour of Washington in 1844 had included appreciative visits to the Patent Office, the Post Office, the Treasury, the "President's House," and the Capitol, where he climbed to the top of the building's green copper dome and looked out over the landscape toward the Potomac River and the hills of Virginia beyond. Whipple had reserved his most enthusiastic praise, though, for the "wonder of wonders" he found in the Capitol's basement, a strange and delicate little machine manned by the "tall, thoughtful-faced" Samuel Morse. The country's entire telegraph network on the day of Whipple's visit consisted of twenty-two miles of wire running from the Capitol northward to the Relay House, Morse's workshop near Baltimore, but the technology seemed no less astonishing for all that. To gratify his eager visitor, the inventor tapped out a message that read "Mr. Whipple of New York is here." Moments later came the reply, traveling, as Morse told him, at 180,000 miles a second: "Tell Mr. Whipple that he is looking upon an invention which will revolutionize the commerce of the world."

The streets of the capital had been made of dirt, the private buildings clad in relentlessly uniform red brick, and the city much smaller and quieter than he'd expected. Now, eighteen years later, Washington, D.C., was a war capital, finally waking up from seven decades of fits and starts. The change in atmosphere was startling. The Capitol dome he'd climbed eighteen years earlier was gone, replaced by an ongoing construction project that would eventually give the building its high, elegant cast-iron dome; for now, the exposed and incomplete structural ribs made the building appear as if it had been rudely truncated by a giant cannonball. The National Mall featured a squared-off, half-finished obelisk that would someday be a monument to George Washington. Taverns up and down Pennsylvania Avenue buzzed every night with alcohol-fueled conversations about the doings of great armies and the men who directed them, while brothels one or two doors over did their own thriving business. The threat of Confederate attack added to the buzz, as did the certainty that Southern sympathizers were everywhere, whispering in parlors and bearing secret messages across the Potomac via the Long Bridge.

Whipple lodged at the Georgetown home of his first cousin Henry Wager Halleck, who was as haggard and worn in appearance as his cousin was straight-backed and brisk. Halleck was in his second month as Lincoln's general in chief, a job that had already come close to breaking him. "From the beginning of the Civil War he was loaded down with responsibilities which carried him to the grave," Whipple wrote many years later, and indeed, throughout the war, Halleck had written personal letters to his relative complaining of poor military strategy, creeping insubordination, outright corruption, and a debilitating lack of leadership at all levels of command below Lincoln and himself. Eight years Halleck's junior, Whipple had followed his cousin's career "intimately from boyhood," as Halleck graduated from West Point in 1839 third in his class and so distinguished himself as an engineer, military theorist, and author that he became known as "Old Brains," partly as an homage to his intelligence and partly as a comment on his sober demeanor.

After fighting in the Mexican-American War, Halleck had moved to California to become a lawyer, landowner, and railroad president. Named a general at the start of the Civil War, he had stepped in as commander of the Department of the Missouri after John Frémont had been dismissed for prematurely declaring emancipation. Early in his presidency Lincoln had read and admired Halleck's *Elements of Military Art and Science,* and in July 1862, after McClellan's failures in the Peninsular Campaign, he ordered the general to Washington to take the reins of the entire Union army. The change had been urged by several western commanders, including the ever-vocal John Pope, who called for a general in chief with the power to force coordinated action in the field and act as the military extension of Lincoln's mind. Halleck didn't want the position or the responsibility, but Lincoln needed an experienced veteran and had faith in the wisdom and independence of a man who liked to call himself "the instrument of no political faction, having no political aspirations."

The experiment was a failure from the start. Halleck's star was tarnished when he failed to force McClellan to link up with Pope's forces in time to avoid catastrophe at Second Bull Run. Now, with Pope exiled to the "Indian troubles" in the Northwest and McClellan girding for battle in Maryland, Halleck was hosting his cousin in a household full of sickness and melancholy. His wife, Elizabeth, was ill, and he was having trouble sleeping, nodding off only in the early morning or not at all. An attack of hemorrhoids that required opium suppositories often kept him prone all day and sometimes made him foggy-headed. Lincoln, who had so recently considered Halleck one of the finest military minds in the nation, soon came to refer to him as "little more . . . than a first-rate clerk," and allowed most of Halleck's responsibilities to revert to Secretary of War Edwin Stanton. Whipple, with his usual discretion, did not comment on this state of affairs even years later, pleased as he was with the access to the president and grateful for his cousin's hospitality.

If Lincoln distrusted the entreaties of churchmen, Whipple had his own ambivalent opinions of the president. After the election of 1860, as Lincoln made his slow, glad-handing tour of the states between Illinois and Washington, D.C., the bishop had written a friend to criticize the new president for "going on a tour of pleasure, cracking jokes and indulging in pleasantries when a thoughtful man would be bowed to the earth in sorrow and calmly gathering up every energy for a mighty effort to save the land from Civil War." In another private letter, he hoped for "a strong conservative element in the new administration of Mr. Lincoln" and worried that the country would suffer an irreparable fracture under Lincoln's leadership. Whipple avoided political talk in almost all social and professional spheres, but like most conservative Democrats, he was a Stephen Douglas man who had supported the Kansas-Nebraska Act and had seen no good reason to fight the war. He took offense at Lincoln's joking, folksy demeanor, at least as it was so often presented in friendly and opposition newspapers alike, and worried that the president's homespun character rendered him insufficiently serious for the job.

Still, he had praised Lincoln's first inaugural address, and during 1861 and 1862 Whipple's private recriminations had tailed off after Lincoln provided his brief but encouraging response to the bishop's query regarding the Indian system. As the war progressed, Whipple became an earnest supporter of the president's more sober and pious actions aimed at promoting national unity, starting with the call for a day of fasting and prayer in September 1861. By the time he and his cousin mounted the White House stairs in September 1862, Whipple knew that Abraham Lincoln was nothing like the hapless figure he had once seemed. He also knew that he would have only one chance to make a personal impression, but such was often the lot of a traveling missionary.

. . .

Eighteen years earlier, touring the White House, Whipple had noted that "the splendid carpet is in threads and tatters and patched in many places with other colours. The chairs are old and generally have ragged covering." He had called the building's condition "a public shame, a disgrace to the people," and not much had changed by August 1862 except for a single scandalous spending spree by Mary Todd Lincoln that had added a few splashes of luxury in the form of new carpets, draperies, and French wallpapers. The White House was still a hard-worn, lived-in place, a working residence with modest pretensions that sometimes shocked visitors, especially those from Europe, with its lack of elegance.

Lincoln's office occupied the second floor of the building, facing Pennsylvania Avenue and Lafayette Park. Visitors described it as a close, stuffy place with dark mahogany doors and wainscoting, a long table for cabinet meetings, and a worn oak desk by the window. Petitioners had to wait outside in the sizable waiting room unless they were government officials, which made Halleck's imprimatur doubly important because it also likely moved Whipple into an early-morning slot reserved for cabinet members, who were given precedence over senators, representatives, and the mass of uncredentialed citizens.

William O. Stoddard, assistant to John Nicolay and John Hay, once said of the president's towering physical presence that visitors "seemed to diminish in size in contrast with him." Yet at six foot two, only two inches shorter than Lincoln and of a similarly rangy build, Whipple may have been less likely than most to be physically cowed. And perhaps their attempt at a handshake created a moment of mutual sympathy: by an odd coincidence, both had damaged hands, Lincoln as a result of the sprain incurred in his spill three days earlier and Whipple from the infection he had received as he treated settlers in Saint Peter's makeshift hospital. Whipple also brought with him the assurance born of his place in a distinguished family and the introduction from his cousin, but most of all he brought his endless reserve of earnestness and equally endless sense of absolute rightness.

Like John Ross, Whipple came prepared and spoke quickly and to the point. Unlike Ross, though, he wasn't an official representative of any tribe or interest, not even of the Episcopal church. The bishop was not in Washington so much to talk about God as to tell Lincoln that the "Indian system" put in place during Andrew Jackson's administration thirty years earlier was more than a failure; it was a mortal sin. Nor was Whipple here to argue the military conduct of the Dakota War, of which he knew few details, or the merits of the war itself, or how those who participated in the war should or should not be punished once the war was over; rather, he was here to present the maltreatment and swindling of the Dakota Indians as an offense against "a great Christian nation."

Whipple opened with "an account of the outbreak, its causes, and the suffering and evil which had followed in its wake." His narrative of causes was built on the same practical and philosophical pillars he had outlined in his previous letters to Lincoln and other administration officials, and now he presented all of them again, along with a draft of "The Duty of Citizens Concerning the Indian Massacre," a plea for understanding and change that Whipple planned to publish in Minnesota newspapers. The core of the bishop's argument, as always, was that Indian policy should be reformed by abandoning the commitment to separate-nation status and instead making Indians citizens of the United States, following which the management of Indian affairs should be taken out of the hands of politicians and soldiers and placed in the hands of churches and other charitable organizations.

The material wasn't new, but his impression of the recipient was. Like nearly everyone who encountered Lincoln close-up, Whipple found that he had underestimated the man's ever-present air of gravity, a seriousness that almost seemed to demand relief in the form of a constant, folksy jocularity. "He was deeply moved," Whipple wrote. "He was a man of profound sympathy, but he usually relieved the strain upon his feelings by telling a story." In response to Whipple, Lincoln fell back on the same mock-epic tales of the Black Hawk War he had told as a young congressman fourteen years earlier. Then he plucked a parable clear out of the air.

"Bishop," he said, "a man thought that monkeys could pick cotton better than negroes could because they were quicker and their fingers smaller. He turned a lot of them into his cotton field, but he found that it took two overseers to watch one monkey. It needs more than one honest man to watch one Indian Agent."

Lincoln concluded their audience by handing Whipple a hand-signed note of introduction to Secretary of the Interior Caleb Smith: "Give Bishop Whipple any information he desires about Indian affairs." That, then, was that: a bent ear, an anecdote or two, a somewhat ambiguous parable, and a note. Whatever message Lincoln intended to convey, Whipple left the meeting convinced he had at least cracked the surface of the president's reserve, reporting later that his tales of Dakota woe had driven Lincoln to tears and caused him to swear allegiance to the urgency for reform.

But even if Whipple's sense of Lincoln's reaction was accurate, whatever sadness or resolve the president felt on the afternoon of September 16 was soon set aside in the face of other concerns. Lincoln spent much of the rest of his day in the telegraph room at the War Department, worrying Pennsylvania governor Andrew G. Curtin for McClellan's whereabouts before he finally came upon a dispatch from Little Mac, sent at seven o'clock that morning, telling him what he wanted, hoped, and dreaded to hear, that the two armies were now concentrated at Sharpsburg, facing each other in two massive lines and "waiting for heavy fog to rise."

# Chapter Ten

Later that same day, twelve hundred miles to the northwest, John Pope disembarked in Saint Paul to begin an assignment he found onerous and humiliating, one he hadn't asked for and didn't want. Forty years old, more rotund than ever, aged in appearance beyond his years by his fiasco in Virginia, Pope was still a vainglorious man, smitten with the language and bravado of war and convinced every bit as much as George McClellan that he knew best how to fight it. Secretary of War Stanton's letter to Pope insisting that the Dakota uprising required "some military officer of high rank, in whose ability and vigor the government has confidence" hadn't soothed the bitter general, who took exactly one afternoon to assess the situation in Minnesota and declare Armageddon. He viewed the command of the newly formed Department of the Northwest as a precipitous fall from grace and was not going to let a group of rebellious Indians slow down his quest for redemption.

Pope, who liked to title his dispatches "Headquarters in the Saddle," viewed Saint Paul—a capital city lacking a railroad connection to its own state's border—as a hinterland. But he had not always felt so. Once, in fact, he had been one of Minnesota's most enthusiastic boosters. Twelve years earlier, as an ambitious young surveyor in the Corps of Topographical Engineers, he had devoted over twenty thousand words in nine chapters to his "Report of an Exploration of the Territory of Minnesota," tasked with establishing the prospects for navigation of the Red River of the North and the feasibility of a fort at Pembina, near the Canadian border. The document was packed with distance tables, river soundings, and readings of latitude and longitude, but the bulk of the writing was made up of meticulous descriptions of the various natural wonders of the region. Pope's tone had often risen to one of infatuation: "The examination of a portion of this Territory during the past summer has convinced me that nature has been even more lavish in her gifts of soil than in her channels of communication, and has still left to the enterprise and industry of man to complete what she has so well begun."

Captain Pope had taken his job as a topographical engineer seriously, but he took even more so his duty to blaze a glorious trail for westward expansion. Describing the Minnesota River Valley and surrounding prairie, he wrote that "I can only attribute to ignorance of its great value the apathy and indifference manifested by the government in failing as yet to extinguish the title of the Indians, and to throw open to the industry of the American people a country so well adapted to their genius and their enterprise." Pope repeated this sentiment five times in the report, pointing out that since the territory's various tribes were "as yet entirely ignorant of the great value of their lands," the purchases could and should happen quickly and quietly. Already he viewed himself as a man destined to hatch and realize big plans, someone who would write his name in large characters across the national parchment. Without instructions to do so, Pope suggested the ideal borders and dimensions of a potential state with remarkable foresight, indicating the advantages of including the western shore of Lake Superior, the length of the Red River, the whole of the Minnesota River, and the falls of Saint Anthony, where Minneapolis would rise.

Now, twelve years later, his admonitions to extinguish the title of the Indians had almost been realized, Minnesota was a state dominated by waterways, and Pope was back. Soon after arriving on September 16 he went into conference with Governor Ramsey and other leaders. By 5:30 that evening, before he'd slept a single night in his rooms at the International Hotel, Pope was ready to send a wire to Halleck.

From all indications and information we are likely to have a general Indian war all along the frontier, unless immediate steps are taken to put a stop to it. I have requested the Governors of Iowa and Wisconsin not to send any troops from their States for the present without advising me about it, and have requested the Governor of Wisconsin to send forward three or four regiments now ready for service. You have no idea of the terrible destruction already done and of the panic everywhere in Wisconsin and Minnesota. Unless very prompt steps are taken these States will be half depopulated before the winter begins. Already populations have been totally abandoned with everything in them. Crops are all left standing, and the whole population fleeing to the river.

For weeks, Alexander Ramsey had been making noise about federal money and provisions, without much success, and the picture he painted for Pope was aimed in part at hurrying those resources along. Given the speed with which Pope produced the letter, in fact, Ramsey may have provided some of the text. Pope ordered the purchase of 2,500 horses for what he imagined as a great cavalry pushing thousands of mounted Dakotas across the plains, without understanding that most of the Indians were fighting on foot. Wisconsin was in no danger of "depopulating," except insofar as Pope wished to bring several brigades of that state's new recruits over to follow after the Dakota. And a full week after Hole in the Day's council with Commissioner Dole, Pope wrote without foundation that the Ojibwe "have also begun to rob and murder, and need immediate attention."

"Time is everything here," the general wrote, "and I must take unusual means to hasten matters." Presumably time was of the essence because Pope and Ramsey feared that Little Crow would take his captives out into the Dakota Territory just before winter fell, rendering a rescue expedition useless until the spring, a season that came late so far north. Pope's message to Halleck said nothing to indicate that Ramsey had already sent troops to the west, two thousand men under Sibley's command who had been tracking Little Crow for weeks now, waiting for necessary supplies and looking for their first chance to strike at the Dakota warriors without endangering the captive women and children. One week later, those white soldiers would get their chance, unconnected to anything said or done by the disgruntled general in Saint Paul. In the end, John Pope would play a minimal role in the military conduct of the Dakota War. But no one would have greater influence over its final act.

In the days following his conference with Lincoln, Whipple's destination was a Greek Revival behemoth off the beaten path, a full mile east of the White House and the adjacent Departments of War and the Treasury. First built for the Patent Office, the home of the Department of the Interior held, among other items, the paper records of the government's dealings with Indian tribes across the West. Here Whipple bent over his work for hours, intent on examining the files containing each of the four federal treaties with the Dakota, especially the 1851 agreements that had forever closed the Mississippi River Valley to them, as well as those files filled with the various claims placed on the annuity funds before and after they arrived on the reservations for payment.

In the evenings Whipple returned to Henry Halleck's house on High Street in Georgetown, where he and his cousin dined with Secretary of War Edwin Stanton and other luminaries. The night after Whipple's visit to Lincoln, all other conversation took a back seat to the news of a great and terrible battle in Maryland. For an entire day on the 16th, as Whipple importuned the president, the two armies had faced off across Antietam Creek, before joining battle early the next morning. Then, for another forty-eight hours, bulletins and rumors poured in to Lincoln, his cabinet, and Halleck, until finally they heard from McClellan himself in the form of a single curt message: "Our victory was complete—The Enemy is driven back into Virginia, [and] Maryland & Pennsylvania are now safe." Over the next few days, as news spread, Antietam became the most famous battle ever fought on American soil. Never mind that both North and South had reason to feel lucky about the outcome; never mind that McClellan had held 30,000 men in reserve without sending them into the fight; never mind that Lee's army slipped away when, at least in Lincoln's mind, one more blow might have finished him. McClellan declared the battle a complete success and as much as dared his commander in chief to disagree.

McClellan's telegram was followed by a stream of couriers and wounded soldiers who began to lay out the numbing toll: more than

3,600 dead and another 17,000 wounded, numbers that made Antietam the war's bloodiest day. Among the wounded, lying in one of the many makeshift hospitals dotting the National Road between Sharpsburg and Washington, was a brigadier general from Minnesota with the impossibly martial name of Napoleon Jackson Tecumseh Dana. No other name on the lists would have so roused Whipple; as a leading member of Minnesota's Episcopal diocese, Dana had been instrumental in securing his election as bishop and was a close friend. The news cut short Whipple's search for evidence against the Indian commissioner, agents, and traders for their malfeasance in administering the Dakota annuities. No detective and no accountant, he was still familiar enough with the history of treaty arrangements and the expectations of the Dakota to know that something wasn't adding up. But Dana now lay wounded within a day's ride, so he set aside the treaty files, for the moment, and left for the front, a man of peace on his way to get his first taste of the horrors of modern war.

Whipple was a well-traveled man of wide experience. He had worked along the poorest blocks of Chicago, witnessed scalp dances, ministered to the dying, attended slave auctions, and seen firsthand the ravages of epidemic disease. But on the farm fields surrounding Sharpsburg, Maryland, he was introduced to a completely novel scene. Whipple arrived on a warm, still Sunday, four days after the fighting, to find tens of thousands of men still cleaning up. Private James A. Wright of the First Minnesota provided an especially vivid description.

> Houses (some of them) had been shattered by shot from both sides, and the gathering crops had been burned by exploding shells. Fences had been broken down and the fields trampled by hurrying battalions until they looked as if they had been swept by a tornado. Fields of standing corn had been torn to shreds and cut away by volleys of musketry and blasts of canister until there were but few stalks left standing. The shrubs and bushes where the batteries stood when in action were leafless, scorched, blackened, and burned; fences had been demolished; the ground furrowed and the trees split, splintered, and torn by the missiles they had started on missions of destruction.

The liberty poles had been bent or torn down, the town looted of every foodstuff and item of clothing. Shattered glass was everywhere. The moaning and screams and pleadings that had hung over the field like a lingering thunderstorm had quieted. The long lines of ambulance wagons were gone, the letters of condolence and reassurance written and sent, two dozen field hospitals organized, the last pigs and chickens killed and consumed, and still the dead ruled.

"It beggars description," Whipple wrote. "It was a sickening sight—poor humanity torn, mangled, tortured, dead and to lie in a nameless grave. I never before realized what a curse had befallen our land." Oliver Wendell Holmes, Sr., who arrived the same day in search of his wounded son, a first lieutenant with the 20th Massachusetts, described the scene for readers of the *Atlantic:* "The slain of higher condition, 'embalmed' and iron-cased, were sliding off on the railways to their far homes; the dead of the rank-and-file were being gathered up and committed hastily to the earth; the gravely wounded were cared for hard by the scene of conflict, or pushed a little way along to the neighboring villages," he wrote. "The companionship of so many seemed to make a joint-stock of their suffering; it was next to impossible to individualize it, and so bring it home as one can do with a single broken limb or aching wound."

Whipple found the First Minnesota on the high ground at the very northern tip of a site that stretched along a shallow seven-mile crescent that curved jaggedly to the west. For three days they had been camping on Joseph Poffenberger's farm, making use of the still-intact barn, wagon shed, washhouse, and house that looked down the old Hagerstown road toward the North Woods, just beyond which lay a site of slaughter the men would always remember as a waking nightmare. "There was a hushed stillness which pervaded the camps," Whipple wrote. "The men had been too near heaven and hell to take their Maker's name in blasphemy."

When Whipple joined the men of the First Minnesota, as they completed their fourth day of burying the dead, doing picket duty, carrying out surveillance, picking up rifles, organizing the field, many of them greeted him as a familiar face. In May 1861, sixteen months earlier, Whipple had preached to the regiment on the parade ground at Fort Snelling as it prepared to depart, calling the occasion "one of the most solemn services of my life." Soon thereafter he'd been elected chaplain of the regiment in an "expression of loving confidence." The gesture was only that—bishops did not customarily demote themselves to chaplains—and when Whipple declined, the post had gone

Confederate dead in front of the Dunker Church, Antietam Battlefield,
September 1862

to Edward Duffield Neill, the Presbyterian minister whose history of Minnesota John Nicolay would eventually read on his way westward to negotiate with the Ojibwe.

The soldiers of the regiment had chosen as their commander Willis A. Gorman, a veteran of the Mexican War who had represented Indiana in Congress and then moved out to Minnesota, where he had succeeded Alexander Ramsey as the territory's second governor and Indian commissioner just after the treaties of 1851 were signed. It had fallen to Gorman, then, to effect the removal of the Mdewakanton villages from the Mississippi River to their new reservation. In April 1854 he had set out for Washington with Little Crow, a journey that revealed to Gorman a side of the Dakota leader that few others, white or Indian, had ever witnessed. He watched Little Crow expertly engage the credulous newspapermen in the eastern towns and also watched him marvel at the great factories and train engines of the coming revolution in industry, before the two separated in the capital to pursue their own purposes.

With the election of James Buchanan two years later, the patronage of Franklin Pierce, Gorman's fellow Mexican War campaigner, had come to an end. Freed from his executive responsibilities, Gorman practiced law and then served a second term as a member of the House, this time from Minnesota. When war erupted and Alexander Ramsey called for volunteers, the new recruits had voted for Gorman as the surest and most practiced leader available. After First Bull Run, where the Minnesotans performed admirably even if the Union army did not win a victory, Gorman had been given a field promotion, and by the time the two armies faced off at Antietam he was no longer attached to the hometown boys but was a general, in charge of the first brigade in John Sedgwick's second division of Edwin Sumner's Second Corps of the Army of the Potomac.

Gorman's second in command leaving Minnesota had been Colonel Dana, the man Whipple was coming to find, another West Pointer and veteran of the fighting in Mexico. Dana had been badly wounded in the Mexican-American War as well, lying close to death for two days before a burial detail came across his unconscious form. Various military posts sent him around the country until 1855, when he retired and became a banker and financial pillar of the Episcopal church in Minnesota. By 1858, Whipple's reputation as an innovative church leader in the rough wards of Chicago had spread northward, and when the officers of the diocese of the new state met to call a bishop, Dana's impassioned tribute had been instrumental in directing the committee's final choice. When Whipple disembarked in Saint Paul on November 12, 1859, to assume the mantle he would keep for the rest of his life, Dana was present to offer his welcome, and eighteen months later Whipple had been on hand to wish Dana godspeed on his way to the front.

The First Minnesota was the only infantry regiment from the state in the eastern theater of the war—all other Union states had donated at least two—and so its soldiers went into each battle with a singular set of colors and a particular determination to represent themselves with honor. The regiment's service before Antietam had been fairly typical: heavy fighting at First Bull Run and on the Virginia Peninsula before a winter interlude of guard duty along the Potomac River, after which they had covered Pope's retreat at Second Bull Run with only a few casualties. Still, by the time they arrived in Sharpsburg, they'd lost 80 of the 900 men they'd started with. Like Gorman and Dana, almost all the regiment's recruits had spent the bulk of their lives elsewhere, in

Maine or Illinois or Pennsylvania or even in Europe, and to a man they were fighting not just as Minnesotans. Antietam, though a thousand miles from Fort Snelling, was not a distant front in their war.

Positioned before dawn east of Antietam Creek, the First Minnesota Regiment, assigned to Gorman's brigade, had watched and listened for three hours as other Union troops fought a pitched battle one mile ahead of them. Just after nine o'clock they had been ordered into the fray at the far right of a line that included the 15th Massachusetts and two regiments from New York, the 34th and 82nd, an instruction that required all of them to cross a long open rise before moving into a cornfield thickly carpeted by the mangled, stiffening bodies of dead men and boys from Indiana. Next they had crossed the Hagerstown Pike to enter the "West Woods" just north of a small whitewashed church belonging to the Dunkers, a German sect. Dana, who had been promoted to brigadier general in February, followed directly behind Gorman in command of a line made up of regiments from Michigan, Massachusetts, and New York.

Somewhere amid the trees a set of orders had gone astray, and the far left of Gorman's line turned toward the Dunker church as the First Minnesota and the rest of the line continued to march forward. A few minutes later the brigade exited the woods on the far side to find itself boxed in by Confederate artillery in front and a mass of Confederate infantry to the left. This was every soldier's tactical nightmare, to find his company perpendicular to the enemy's front and open to "enfilading" fire that could not be returned. The First Minnesota had been saved from disaster only by its position at the end of the line away from the rebels, but the 15th Massachusetts had no such luck, and neither did Dana's line behind it.

Dana's arrival at the far edge of the West Woods surely saved lives in his former regiment, but that was cold comfort. If a commander was to lose men, this was the worst possible way, short of disease: a muddy, jumbled scrum that left him nothing to do except offer some small measure of organization to a hasty retreat. Jammed up against the disorganized remnants of Gorman's brigade, Dana discovered that he could not fire on the Confederate infantry to his left, as the 15th Massachusetts was blocking his view and acting, quite unintentionally, as human shields for the enemy. Shouting orders, trying to see through the smoke, running options through his head, Dana felt the sudden pain of a bullet wound to his left leg, a wound that would hurry Bishop Whipple north from Washington and eventually suspend Dana's service in the Union army for close to a year.

Meanwhile, the First Minnesota finally ran out of the woods on the northern edge, away from the rebels, where they met with part of the 82nd New York doing the same. The two regiments together clambered over a stone fence, turned themselves about, and made a brief stand until Union artillery came up to support them from behind and ended their activity for the day. Staggering up a short incline, they collapsed onto the earth of Joseph Poffenberger's farm. It was not yet noon. For the next eight hours the men counted their losses and followed dispatches from the southern portion of the field, where formerly unassuming features of the landscape were entering history with new names like Bloody Lane and Burnside Bridge.

All they knew for certain by the time dusk fell was that they had repulsed the Confederates. The next morning, expecting another fight, the Minnesotans found no rebels across the way and received no orders to follow Lee's retreating forces. Whether or not the soldiers believed Little Mac *should* be moving after Lee, there was a growing understanding that he *could* be doing so. The reports of their commander's cautiousness on the 17th—he had held two entire corps in reserve when their presence might very well have finished off the Army of Northern Virginia—and the palpable inaction of 18th began to turn some of the soldiers against McClellan for the first time. "When it was found that Lee had escaped," wrote Ezra A. Carman, a New Jersey officer who would become one of the battle's best-known historians, "there were those who thought that McClellan was in no wise disappointed, that it was as he wished it should be, that he was not so intent upon driving Lee into the Potomac as he was desirous to see him safely over it."

Late on Sunday afternoon, September 21, the First Minnesota took a break from its grisly work to form a hollow square around Bishop Whipple as he spoke. The regimental flag flew nearby, "pierced by the balls of half a score of battle fields." Whipple found the men far more weary and wise than the fresh recruits he'd visited at Fort Snelling the year before.

> I could not help but thank them for the bravery that had courted death so often for our sakes and ask that their faith should be that of Christian men who believed in God. They

were now hard bronzed veterans, but when they spoke to me after service of their homes I saw their hearts were tender as a woman's. I met their fellows lying wounded in farm yards, sick in hospitals but no murmur passed their lips. I could not help but ask some of them if they prayed and the answer told me that men who at other times are wayward do often pray as they stand looking into the jaws of death which at a moment may send them to heaven or hell.

The next morning, Monday, a courier rode up to Whipple and handed him a note that read, "Will you do me the favor to perform divine service in my camp this evening?" General McClellan, it seemed, was eager to see an old friend from faraway days.

McClellan's note sent the bishop on the long ride down to the general's new headquarters, well south of the battlefield and town. Few points on the site were farther apart than the farms of Joseph Poffenberger and Otho Showman, where Little Mac had moved after the battle in order to take and send messages as he coordinated the regional movements of the Union forces. Riding down the Hagerstown Pike and through Sharpsburg, where not a single building was free of damage from flames, bullets, or artillery rounds, Whipple saw enough suffering and death to fill a large city.

The bishop was only one member of a cavalcade of humanity pouring onto the streets of Sharpsburg and the surrounding battlefields. Some came in search of wounded family or friends, or of identifiable bodies to bring home, but most were curiosity seekers in awe of the destruction or souvenir hunters in search of valuable mementos. However small or ordinary, every item that might have belonged to a soldier was a target for "peeling": articles of clothing, canteens, boots, bullets, buttons, brass belt plates, unsent letters, photographs, New Testaments, hymnbooks, anything. Undertakers of diverse skill and ethical standards searched out bereaved relatives, distributed business cards, and set up embalming shops. Typhoid and smallpox began to spread in the corpse-strewn fields and into the hospitals, where doctors worked feverishly to ward off death in many different guises. Clara Barton was at work just a few hundred feet from Joseph Poffenberger's farm, tending the wounded as a member of the Ladies Aid Society, while Walt

Whitman assisted with amputations in a nearby Sanitary Commission hospital. Elsewhere on the site stood Alexander Gardner's traveling darkroom wagon; Gardner, the famous acolyte of Mathew Brady, was arranging the photographs of the dead that would soon become the most famous images of the Civil War.

The effect of all this death and destruction on Whipple was profound. In a sermon he delivered at least a dozen times between this day and the end of the conflict, he painted the Civil War as the wages of sin for the entire country, paid in blood. "The pestilence is the work of innumerable particles of poison. The storm cloud has millions of drops of dew," he said, concluding that "it is the shameless wickedness of a Christian nation which has disdained Christ its King that has brought us to the verge of ruin." Americans were "a thankless people" whose "impiety and irreligion always beget disloyalty to government and to God."

In the decades since his southern tour, he had come to call slavery a sin, but still his views had not advanced so far as to embrace abolition. Rather, he blamed slaveholders for a failure of benevolence, for their immoral neglect of the physical and spiritual well-being of their charges. The "dark sin" for him, always, was not the white man's presumption of superiority to Indians and blacks but rather the "wicked neglect and robbery of the poor whom the providence of God has made our wards." In this respect, he did not see the treatment of blacks and Indians as separate matters; rather, he yoked them together as systems in gross need of reform. The South, not through slavery but through the slave trade, had "fostered a system which destroyed the sanctity of home, which made a mock of marriage, which broke up ties of kindred which God had made holy"; at the same time, the North bore responsibility for the "inequity and fraud of an Indian system which we knew was a reproach to a Christian nation."

With more than a hundred thousand people within hailing distance, General McClellan could have called on any number of chaplains or visiting clergymen to preach a service for his entourage of officers, aides, drivers, and personal guards. But he and Whipple were connected by their shared time in Chicago and by the Church of the Holy Communion, where Whipple had presided between 1856 and 1858. The instrument of this connection had been the Illinois Central, the first land-grant railroad in the nation, created to provide the all-important link between Chicago and the Mississippi River. The project had drawn engineering and administrative talent from many different directions, especially the military, which provided Ambrose Burnside, the Mexican-American War veteran whose name now adorned the bridge on the south side of the Antietam battlefield, and McClellan, who had become the company's chief engineer on the strength of his experience assessing railroads during the 1850s for the then secretary of war, Jefferson Davis.

Prospecting for congregants among the railway workers, Whipple was advised to read about trains until he was "able to ask an engineer a question about a locomotive and he not think you a fool." This Whipple had done, noting that his ability to correctly identify a "Taunton engine with inside connections" was among the credentials that finally brought the employees of the Illinois Central to his pews. The company's executive officers, including McClellan, soon followed. Professionally, McClellan must have been happy that his employees were getting a steady dose of moral improvement, and in a time of political upheaval he must have been happy to find in Whipple a fellow Democrat and Stephen Douglas man unswayed by the growing Republican ethos in Illinois. Whipple had been in Chicago, in fact, during the Republican Convention of 1860, when he accompanied William J. McAlpine, chief engineer of the Galena railroad and a former Democratic congressman from New York, to see Douglas, who, to Whipple's surprise, praised Lincoln's speaking prowess and personal integrity.

The bishop was proud of his connections to the powerful and famous, and he was almost always credulous regarding their character and motives. After his talk with the general's staff, he retired to McClellan's tent, where, according to Whipple, the two men sat up well after midnight discussing war and God. Years later he would remember McClellan saying, "You do not know what a comfort it is in my care-worn life to have a good talk about holy things!" and "no general ever had a better regiment than the Minnesota First." The sentiments may have been predictable and generic, but Little Mac had built an entire career on his fierce loyalty to the men under his command, and he ended their visit by asking Whipple to call at the hospitals on his way to Washington. Four days later Whipple wrote to McClellan, "If it were not for wearying you I could write an hour, telling you of words of loving confidence spoken by those brave sufferers who have been with you in good and evil report."

When he arrived back briefly in Washington later in the week to

George B. McClellan, ca. 1861–63

settle Dana at a hospital before he left for New York, he found himself in the middle of a city ablaze with "the great act of the age." On Monday, September 22, the same day that Whipple visited McClellan's camp, Lincoln had announced to his cabinet that he would issue the Emancipation Proclamation the following day. All day and night on Tuesday, as Whipple made his way from McClellan's headquarters to the hospitals in Frederick, Maryland, the news had leaked into every nook of the capital. At nine o'clock in the evening a small collection of musicians had celebrated on the front lawn of the White House, while other revelers planned a parade for later in the week. Feared, scorned, embraced, loved—the proclamation entered the historical record as a war measure, its effects limited to the states in rebellion on January 1, 1863, but no one read it that way. This was a promise made by the federal government: in one hundred days, all blacks living in the Southern states would be forever free.

Horace Greeley was over the moon, walking along Broadway and beaming. Twelve Northern governors, the preoccupied Alexander Ramsey not among them, boarded a train to Washington in order to thank Lincoln in person. Radical Republicans and abolitionist editors rejoiced, while others tempered their enthusiasm. For Frederick Douglass and other black leaders, the document was far too legalistic and limited, lacking in outrage and moral clarity. For conservative Democrats the executive order meant that the presidential election of 1864, in which General McClellan would surely be their standard-bearer, was now more winnable than ever. And for a great many ordinary American citizens in the North, whose objection to slavery was in some part an objection to the presence of blacks, emancipation threatened a dismantling of the social order.

For the Dakota, though, emancipation meant nothing. It was a promise, but they had heard many promises of their own. It rendered the Civil War in a new and brighter light, but they did not benefit from the new illumination. Somewhere to the east, a parallel history was happening, but they were busy trying to ensure that their own history was not about to come to an end.

# Chapter Eleven

In the dark after-midnight hours of September 22, as Bishop Whipple sat in a tent with General McClellan and talked of God and war, Little Crow and several of his warriors stood atop a rise just south of the Upper Agency and peered into the distance. To the southeast, clearly visible across the undulating ground, they saw the fires of a military force gathered for the night around a small prairie lake along the reservation road. Colonel Sibley had finally moved north to meet the Dakota in their own territory and now the Dakota were ready to be met. In their view, the white commander seemed to have selected the site with an eye toward maximum vulnerability, and soon the news got even better, when silent scouts returned to announce that the whites were moving with no advance cavalry and had posted their pickets close in, so that approaching the camp in the night would present little difficulty.

The conflict that many whites were calling Little Crow's War was now more than a month old. The Dakota had hit hard at the Lower Agency and Birch Coulee, had twice failed to take Fort Ridgely, and had caused the evacuation of New Ulm. A few hundred men roaming across the prairie had taken as many as four hundred lives and all but emptied the state's southwestern quadrant. Still, only now were Dakota warriors and white soldiers primed to engage in something resembling a conventional battle. Scouts reported that Sibley was traveling with cannon and supplied with a lengthy wagon train, on guard but seemingly ignorant of the true extent of his danger. Little Crow was finally presented with an opportunity to "make war after the manner of white men," as he had put it, commander against commander meeting in battle between armies. If he was going to deliver the bite that would cause the white hand to pull away and give him time to maneuver or to negotiate, it needed to happen now.

The Dakota leaders knew that they could depend on two or three hundred men to fight; beyond that number, allegiances and stomach for battle were unreliable. One morning earlier, upon learning of Sibley's location, Little Crow had instructed his camp crier, Round Wind, to call out his orders: every man fit to wield a weapon must prepare to fight or be killed by the men of the wartime *tiyotipi* for not fighting. The threat was made in earnest, as was a promise: great honor awaited any warrior bringing back the white army's colors or the scalp of Colonel Sibley. All through the night and early morning, hundreds of warriors—some anxious for battle, some anxious to avoid battle—had moved out of the camp. As the war party crossed a creek, each man handed a stick to a warrior stationed by the side of the road, and in this way the force tallied its strength: 738 sticks; 738 men to face Sibley's army of more than 2,000.

Little Crow and his fellow chiefs now held council on their hilltop command post northwest of the site. They knew that the field Sibley had chosen, a few hundred yards off the government road, was not so much different than the ones at Fort Ridgely or Birch Coulee, with ample concealment available along a series of shallow hollows and creeks on three sides. Little Crow wanted to launch a raid that very night with a small force, swift and fierce, but a spirited council on the spot finally created consensus for a more traditional early-morning action. The plan was simple: when Sibley and his forces left their camp, presumably not long after dawn, their path along the government road would take them over the Yellow Medicine River, which was lined with cottonwoods and thick underbrush; here one prong of an ambush would begin, with another large group of warriors descending on the rear of the column and its supply wagons as it crossed a smaller creek running northward out of the lake. Sibley would be trapped between two watercourses with his men in a long thin line, his provisions easily targeted and his route of escape uncertain in any direction.

Moving quickly and making no noise, the Dakota set themselves in place as the moon lowered in the west, some along the river to the north, some near the creek running out of the prairie lake, others in the tall bluestem grasses along the government road. From their hiding places his warriors could hear the white soldiers talking, singing, and laughing. And when dawn came, they could see Sibley taking his time getting ready to move, oblivious to seven hundred men watching his forces and ready to attack. The sun rose in the sky, but still Sibley's men did not start, and still Little Crow waited. Today was the day. He could afford to be patient.

For weeks the leaders of the friendly Dakota had been looking for an opportunity to bring the white women and children under their protection, and now, with the Dakota warriors gone to face a formidable opponent, they had their chance. As soon as Little Crow and his force of 738 men disappeared down the road from their camp near Red Iron's village, Paul Mazakutemani and other peace party leaders crossed over to face what few hostile Dakota remained and demanded that the prisoners be released to them. Threats followed, but the scales had tipped and the white captives were allowed to go.

Once most of the captives had been transferred to the friendly camp, an armed patrol began while the women and children and older men dug deep circular trenches inside and outside of the tepees, a custom born of countless encounters with Ojibwe war parties. If the battle was lost and Little Crow or the warriors of the *tiyotipi* returned with annihilation in mind, these trenches might keep the inhabitants of the friendly camp alive when the firing began. A final contest might take place amid the Dakota as well as out on the prairie, an understanding that spread among the captives and gave them the energy to move earth with only small spades or even their hands. They had been threatened so often by Little Crow and the men of the *tiyotipi* that it had become difficult to distinguish real danger from boasting. But this moment, they could tell, was different.

For weeks Sarah Wakefield and the rest of the captives had watched as hundreds of individual agendas played out among the Dakota: those bent on killing whites, those determined to save whites, those aiding whites in order to receive more favorable treatment at the war's end, those resentful of their prisoners, and those in physical distress due to sickness or age and simply struggling along, paying little attention to the whites among them. Each captive had her own particular tormentors and protectors. How much rape occurred will never be known— after the war, many stories were told, though very few incidents were verified by individual testimony—but the perceived threat had been ever present. Now out of the confusion and fear rose a new sense of clarity built on the knowledge that white soldiers were finally nearby. The rush to enlarge the friendly camp also reunited friends and neighbors and brought news of missing husbands and children, sometimes gruesome tales of short flight and death and other times heart-lifting stories of escape.

Sarah Wakefield was not among this sudden, desperately hopeful community of friendly Dakotas and their new charges. For thirty-six days she had lived in fear for her own and her children's lives, and for thirty-six days Chaska had risked his own to keep her safe. Her hair, once auburn, was now white, and her hefty frame had shrunk by forty pounds. During and after the long retreat from New Ulm, her story continued to be one of squaws carrying her children when she tired, concealing her under blankets when violent warriors entered the camp, and making garments for her and her children so that she would not so obviously stand out. Again and again Chaska had turned away other Dakota men demanding Sarah's sexual attentions by saying that she was his wife, a claim that drew ever more vicious innuendos from other whites, who viewed her not as a resourceful and adaptable survivor but as an Indian lover enamored of her own captivity.

The series of staggered removals and stretched-out days had taken her through the Upper Agency, to the Rush Brook camp near the Hazelwood Republic, and then onward until Little Crow had halted them at a large plateau described by one captive as a "howling wilderness" twenty miles north of the Upper Agency, near Red Iron's village and the rest of the Sissetons and Wahpetons who in so many cases wanted nothing to do with the war. All the while, somewhere behind them, Sibley's column had approached at a pace Sarah found maddening. She wrote later that "the Indians made much sport of the slow movements of Sibley; said the white people did not care much about their wives and children or they would have hurried on faster." Sarah seemed not to understand or believe that the advance of white soldiers might push Little Crow or the wartime *tiyotipi* toward the desperate step of killing the captives; she expected Sibley to make battle, and finally, when the camp crier called out Little Crow's instructions that all able-bodied men must rouse themselves to fight, she understood that her wish had been granted. But as the men prepared to head off for the Upper Agency, a new set of fears emerged.

"I tried to urge Chaska not to go," she wrote, "but he said Little Crow would say I had prevented him, and that he would destroy us both." Before leaving to face Sibley's men, Chaska begged Sarah to stay with his mother and not move to the friendly camp with the other captives; he was worried that the whites and their new protectors would be destroyed should the battle go badly. That she took his advice, when almost all of the other captives were frantic to make the move, was a sure sign of the extraordinary bond that had formed between them. Sarah was left as one of only three white women in the hostile camp, by her count, another circumstance that the more vindictive of her fellow captives would eventually add to a long list of indictments against her character and conduct.

Later that day, both camps, hostile and friendly, began to hear the report of gunfire and cannonade miles away; a sound, wrote one mixed-blood captive, that was "as sweet as the chimes of wedding bells to the bride." As the battle raged, a mixed-blood courier carried a letter from Sibley into the two camps with instructions to make sure its contents were broadcast to all of the remaining Dakotas, mixed-bloods, and whites wherever they might be found.

> When you bring up the prisoners and deliver them to me under that flag of truce I will be ready to talk of peace. The bodies of the Indians that have been killed will be buried like white people and the wounded will be attended to as our own; but none will be given until the prisoners are brought in . . . A flag of truce in the day-time will always be protected in and out of my camp if one or two come with it.

Sibley sent a separate letter to peace party leaders telling them that "I have not come to make war upon those who are innocent, but upon the guilty," leaving it to the Dakota to interpret what he might mean by "innocent" and "guilty." Unbeknownst to the Dakota in the riverside camps, Sibley also sent a message farther north to the powerful village chief Standing Buffalo, assuring him that he was not aiming to make war on the Sisseton and Wahpeton, but also including a warning to "advise your bands not to mix yourselves together with the bands that have been guilty of these outrages, for I do not wish to injure any innocent person; but I intend to pursue the wicked murderers with fire and sword until I overtake them."

Early that evening the warriors began to return, one at a time or in small groups, "bearing wounded, singing the death song, and telling the tale of defeat." The lamentations of Dakota mothers and wives were loud enough to be clearly heard in the friendly camp, half a mile away. For Sarah, secured in Chaska's tepee at the edge of the hostile camp, the cacophony pressed in like a physical force. "Any one that has heard one squaw lament," she wrote, "can judge the noise of four or five hundred all crying at once." Whatever happiness she felt at the news of Sibley's victory was more than tempered by the grief of the women who had cared for her all these weeks and her fear that Little Crow and his warriors were on their way back to kill all of the captives.

Soon enough the scale of defeat was made plain. Luck had turned against the Dakota when the action opened prematurely, after a party of white soldiers foraging for potatoes had driven their wagon off the road and straight across the prairie grasses, where they nearly ran over a small detachment of Dakota scouts prone in the grass. The first gunshots roused Sibley's camp and put the initial action out of the reach of many of the warriors, especially those positioned on the northern edge of the site. Little Crow's problems also came from within. Many of the Dakota, coerced into the battle, had positioned themselves outside the main action. Some had even raised white flags. Some of those who did join in combat testified later that they fired their weapons into empty space, a contention that in many cases was surely true. Still, the fighting between whites and the core of committed Dakota warriors was fierce, and only three hours later, after a determined stand and bayonet charge by the Third Minnesota Regiment, did the Dakota break and retreat. Behind them fourteen white soldiers lay dead and mutilated, along with twenty Dakotas, whose bodies were soon scalped in retribution, much to Sibley's public indignation.

According to multiple accounts, Little Crow returned in a wrath and raised his voice to address the entire camp.

Seven hundred picked warriors whipped by cowardly whites. Better run away and scatter over the plains like buffalo and wolves. To be sure the whites had big guns and better arms than the Indians and outnumbered us four or five to one, but that is no reason we should not have whipped them, for we are brave men, while they are cowardly women. I cannot account for the defeat. It must be the work of traitors in our midst.

The Battle of Wood Lake represented the final exchange of massed gunfire in the Dakota War. The next day, Chaska reported to Sarah that Little Crow was getting ready to depart for the West and added that five mixed-bloods had been charged with taking her many miles across the prairie to Sibley's forces under a flag of truce. Sarah refused the offer, assuming that she would be killed by one of Little Crow's warriors as soon as she set foot out of the hostile camp. Two village chiefs allied to Little Crow then assured her that John Other Day, a Christian Dakota and scout for Sibley, would be coming to retrieve her himself. In the meantime, they said, they wanted her to write down an account of her treatment by Chaska and her other protectors. "I told them it was very foolish for me to write, for I could tell the people just as well as to write, and I began to be suspicious of some evil," she said later. "I was afraid they would murder us and hide our bodies, and carry our notes to the Fort." But she did write the note, though she refused to budge until the hostiles were gone.

When she understood that Chaska was right, that Little Crow was busy making preparations to leave, Sarah changed out of her Indian dress and offered tearful thanks to the Dakota women who had cared for her. Chaska's mother cursed Little Crow's name and said, "You are going back where you will have good, warm houses and plenty to eat, and we will starve on the plains this winter." Several of Sarah's protectors "cried over James and begged me leave him with them," as "he was a great favorite with the Indians all the time I was with them." Led by Chaska, she held James and one of Chaska's cousins carried Nellie as they walked over to the friendly camp, where they mounted a small hill and sat down under an American flag to watch as Little Crow's train began to depart, piece by piece. After a time, when most of the procession had disappeared over a rise to the northwest, Chaska and his cousin said good-bye and walked back down the hill toward their tepees. George Gleason's dog, another survivor, trotted beside them.

.  .  .

Cecelia Stay Campbell, daughter of the mixed-blood interpreter Antoine Campbell, later wrote an account of her father's attempt to persuade Little Crow to surrender on September 24, the final day of Sarah Wakefield's captivity. She described how her father found Little Crow inside his tepee, surrounded by a guard of his most trusted soldiers, all in battle dress and leaning on their guns as they listened in silence. The two men, old friends, sat facing each other on blankets as Little Crow announced his intentions to leave for the western plains and asked if Campbell had any final requests.

"Yes, cousin, we are most safe now," Campbell said. "General Sibley will be here soon, and I would like that you and your warriors would give yourselves up."

In response, Little Crow only laughed and said that he would consider surrender "if they would shoot me like a man, but otherwise they will never get my live body."

A morning of councils had followed, during which leaders of the *tiyotipi* argued for continuing the war and reclaiming the captives, killing any friendly Dakotas who refused to cooperate. Even now, Little Crow and the young men of the soldiers' lodge continued to operate more in parallel than in concert, acting as a kind of two-headed leadership, each taking its own counsel and issuing its own edicts. But no one in either circle believed that Sibley would honor any agreement of surrender. As Samuel J. Brown reported, "Little Crow called all his warriors together and told them to pack up and leave for the plains and save the women and children, the troops would soon be upon them and no time should be lost. 'But,' he said, 'the captives must all be killed before we leave. They seek to defy us,' he went on, 'and dug trenches while we were away.'" This was Little Crow's final threat in six weeks of threats directed at his prisoners. He had acted on none of them and would not do so now. In any event, according to Brown, the friendly Indians "simply laughed at Little Crow's bombastic talk" and dared his warriors to try to take the captives away from them.

Six weeks earlier, when four young men stood in front of his tepee and reported their act of violence in the farmsteads to the north, Little Crow had understood what war would mean. When members of the wartime *tiyotipi* and other men returned after the first attack on the Lower Agency and reported a killing spree in the settlements that had taken hundreds of white lives, including many women and children, Little Crow had understood that retribution would fall not just on the perpetrators of these acts but on all Dakotas. Yet he had continued to offer the young men his leadership, however reckless their actions and however little they heeded his instructions, for he believed that the day of reckoning was bound to arrive no matter how accommodating and pliable he might be. It had taken Little Crow most of his fifty-two years to reach the unalterable conclusion that whites would accept only one outcome: the frontier must be emptied of the Dakota, whether that meant destroying them, driving them away, or making them abandon the social, cultural, and religious customs that made them Dakota in the first place.

Exhausted from battle and council, his legendary stamina tested as rarely before, Little Crow spoke ruefully to the mixed-blood Sisseton Susan Brown, mother of Samuel J. Brown and wife of the former Indian agent Joseph R. Brown. Knowing that government soldiers would arrive from the battlefield in days, if not hours, Little Crow told her that he had decided not to follow through on his threats against the white captives in his camp, though he would bring a small number of them with him as hostages. A dispatch arrived that afternoon from Colonel Sibley demanding that Little Crow surrender the captives and promising that he would talk to the chief "like a man," but Little Crow paid it no mind. Facing his men, he made one last speech and then directed that a message be delivered to the white commander: "Sibley would like to put the rope around my neck, but he won't get the chance."

When he last looked down into the Minnesota River Valley, Little Crow saw the final forsaken homeland of his life. Whatever good-byes Little Crow did or didn't say, he knew that he left as a man hated by whites and by many Dakotas. As a young man, as Taoyateduta, he had ridden into the West within a rhythm of hunt, harvest, and hibernation. Now there was no allegiance to the seasons. He knew how different the territory up and over the Coteau des Prairies was, how cruel its cold winds could be, and how many white soldiers would follow in his wake as soon as the James and Missouri rivers opened for navigation in the spring.

His mind had already turned to stratagems involving his western kin—the Yanktons, Yanktonais, and the numerous Lakota—and the

British outposts in Canada. No longer was he thinking of reservations, of large farms tended in long rows, of white books about a white God. For centuries the Dakota had been on the move in one way or another, first arriving out of the Great Lakes regions, then settling down in the woods and valleys of the Upper Mississippi River, then concentrated on their ten-mile-wide prairie reservation. But only now, in the moment Little Crow spurred his horse, the Dakota diaspora began, one that would scatter not just the Mdewakanton and their allies but many of the Indians of the Northwest, most of whom had played no part in the Minnesota conflict. Little Crow was wise and experienced enough to understand what his present actions might mean, but exactly how and where that scattering would take place he couldn't have known. For the time being, he felt only his own motion, straight into the coming winter snows.

Sarah Wakefield assumed that the next day would mean delivery from her captivity and a full meal, a change of clothes, and a chance to wash, free of the fear and uncertainty of the past six weeks. Instead, Sibley and his men did not appear, and she spent twenty-four hours terrified that Little Crow would return to kill the captives after all. Reports trickled in that Sibley's army was sitting at the Hazelwood mission station, just ten miles away, digging sentry pits and, for whatever reason, conducting a grand dress parade. The wait, after what Sarah considered a series of unaccountable delays, ate at her and made her bitter. But if Sarah's impatience was coming to a head, Chaska's situation was far worse. All of his options now were miserable. By protecting Sarah he had made enemies; by not joining the friendly camp he had made enemies; by not going with Little Crow he had made enemies; by being Dakota he had made enemies. Still convinced that his greatest danger was that Little Crow would return to attack the friendly camp, he crossed the grassy space again and brought Sarah and her children back to his tent, as all of the Dakota dug new entrenchments.

The next day, September 26, Sibley's army finally appeared along a ridge to their north, between their tepees and the river. All morning Sarah could see them arriving in the distance, and all morning they did not approach but instead deployed howitzers and sent detachments to encircle the Dakota camps. A small group of mixed-bloods in the friendly camp did not wait, crossing over to the white soldiers' camp with a flag of truce, according to Sibley's written instructions, asking for conditions under which they could hand over the captives with their own safety assured. As they did so, an argument broke out between Chaska and Sarah. During the long uneasy night he had decided to flee, and Sarah, hearing this, urged him to stay.

Chaska knew that he could not track down and rejoin Little Crow without being fired upon as an enemy, but it might be possible for him and his family to go to the plains on their own, to find a hospitable village of Sissetons or Wahpetons, or even to go farther west and find a home among a less familiar band or tribe. He might become a refugee, but he would not be a prisoner. "He said he felt as if they would kill all the Indians," Sarah wrote, "but we told him if Sibley had promised to shake hands with all that remained and gave up their prisoners, he would do as he said." In the end she succeeded in convincing Chaska to stay. And in the end Chaska made it clear that Sarah's word, not Sibley's, was all that stood in the way of his escape out onto the plains. "If I am killed," he told her, "I will blame you for it."

At noon, finally, a squad of Sibley's men began to ride over to the Dakotas from the wide, treeless plateau, now filling with canvas tents, that someone had named Camp Release. The appearance of the blue-clad soldiers, bayonets flashing and flags aloft, accompanied by the sound of drum and fife, set off pandemonium. Samuel J. Brown described how "every man and woman in the camp, and every child old enough to toddle about, turned out with a flag of truce," a surreal scene in which every piece of white cloth that could be found was attached to "every conceivable object" as the Dakota tried to dissuade the soldiers from opening fire. "One Indian who was boiling over with loyalty and love for the white man threw a white blanket on his black horse and tied a bit of white cloth to its tail," Brown wrote, "and then that no possible doubt might be raised in his case he wrapped the American flag around his body and mounted the horse and sat upon him in full view of the troops as they passed by."

Some of the remaining captives wept, some shouted or broke out laughing, and some simply collapsed. But Sarah's mood was not joyful. "I felt feelings of anger enter my breast as I saw such an army," she wrote, "for I felt that part at least might have come to our rescue before that late hour." None of the Dakota knew from a distance what the soldiers intended, and Sibley's display of strength failed to ease their anxiety. As Sarah wrote, "The Indians became much alarmed, and drew within their tepees. We were all eager to go to them immediately, but we were told we should remain where we were until Sibley came over." A messenger crossed the short distance and announced that the white commander would follow a few hours later to speak with the remaining leaders of the Dakota.

While they waited for Sibley to enter their camp, Sarah ate the midday meal with Chaska and his mother, who seemed to bend under the weight of an evil premonition. The scene that followed was wrenching, one Sarah would remember for the rest of her life. Chaska's mother ripped her shawl in half so that Sarah might have some warmth against the cool autumn air, while Chaska prepared to turn her over to the soldiers. According to Sarah, Chaska pleaded with her as a "good woman" to "talk good to your white people, or they will kill me; you know I am a good man, and did not shoot Mr. Gleason, and I saved your life. If I had been a bad man I would have gone with those bad chiefs." Again she told him that he had nothing to fear, though other presentiments had been floating around the camp all morning. One mixed-blood witness recorded how the first group of soldiers to

Camp Release, ca. October 1862

approach "repeatedly told us we were all to be executed and the insults of the soldiers who spoke the Indian tongue seemed a convincing act that all were to be put to death immediately."

Sibley arrived in the midafternoon and ordered his men to form a hollow square, placing himself atop a wagon in the middle, surrounded by whites and Dakotas and tepees spread across a wide plateau for hundreds of feet in every direction. Speaking through an interpreter, he repeated his message of goodwill toward the leaders of the peace party and assured them that he would send men after Little Crow. In return, several of the friendly Indians spoke to condemn the war and, according to Sibley, to give him "assurance that they would not have dared to come and shake my hand if their own were stained with the blood of the whites." Next, Chaska and other Dakotas, Lower and Upper, presented 91 white and 150 mixed-blood captives, bringing them forth as individuals or in small groups so that one of Sibley's aides could write down their names. "After I was introduced to Sibley, Mr. Riggs, and others," Sarah wrote, "they requested me to point out the Indian who had saved me. [Chaska] came forward as I called his name; and when I told them how kind he had been they shook hands with him, and made quite a hero of him, for a short time." She was asked to leave the circle, apparently because Nellie was crying, and so she went inside a nearby tepee until the presentation of prisoners was finished and the time came for the white women to be taken away.

As they walked across the prairie to Camp Release, Sarah was full of frustration and fear for Chaska. Most of her fellow captives, though, were ecstatic at their release and ran across the open space, singing and shouting. Once inside Sibley's camp, the women became the object of gawking; they were given constant attention and as much food as the men could find. The night was not so festive. The long, cold nights of a Minnesota autumn had taken hold, and lacking a stove in their tent or clothing beyond their summer dresses and the occasional shawl or thin blanket, they lit small fires for warmth, huddled together in family groups, and pressed their faces to the dirt to avoid the smoke. "I was a vast deal more comfortable with the Indians in every respect," Sarah wrote, "than I was during my stay in that soldier's camp, and was treated more respectfully by those savages, than I was by those in that camp."

That same day, September 26, the *Saint Paul Daily Press* printed

a momentous announcement under the headline THE PRESIDENT'S
PROCLAMATION.

> News of the great event of the war has reached the frontier.
> The President has issued a proclamation, declaring, that on
> the first day of January, in the year of our Lord one thousand
> eight hundred and sixty-three, all persons held as slaves within
> any State, or any designated part of a State, the people whereof
> shall be in rebellion against the United States, shall be thence-
> forward and forever free, and the executive government of
> the United States, including the military and naval authority
> thereof, will recognize and maintain the freedom of such per-
> sons, or any of them, in any efforts they may make for actual
> freedom.

Abolitionist editors rejoiced, but for most citizens of the Northwest another step toward the end of slavery was an abstract development that had little effect on their daily lives. What was not abstract
was the question of what to do with the Dakota. Two weeks earlier,
Governor Ramsey had addressed the state legislature and said that "the
Sioux Indians of Minnesota must be exterminated or driven forever
beyond the borders of the state." With Sibley in possession of the captives and Little Crow far away, the process of activating both solutions
would now begin.

# Chapter Twelve

The next day, September 27, as construction began on a temporary wooden enclosure on the far side of the bluff, toward the Minnesota River, Sarah Wakefield and some of the other former captives returned to the Dakota camp to collect their things. While there she attended a Christian prayer meeting with Chaska, who was very frightened and told her that the soldiers had already begun to arrest Indians. If he was arrested, he said, he would know that she had lied about him. Stung by his words, she gave him reassurances and told him of a "long conversation with one of the officers" who had praised Chaska as a hero. As soon as she recrossed to Camp Release on the path through the grass, already well-worn from traffic back and forth, Sarah learned that she would be the first person interrogated by a court of inquiry made up of several soldiers and the Presbyterian missionary Stephen R. Riggs, who were charged with beginning the process of sorting the guilty Dakota from the innocent.

After she finished her story of Chaska's bravery and solicitude, one colonel hinted that Sarah should speak to Riggs alone, as he "thought it very strange that I had no complaints to make," probably because the officer felt she might be too proper or embarrassed to describe the sexual assaults he assumed must have occurred. The suggestion that the soldiers might not have believed her tale led Sarah to ask for Chaska, who came to her "pale and frightened," saying that "the white men were not doing as they promised, and he knew they would kill him." Apparently something said in the inquiry had changed Sarah's mind about Sibley's intentions, for she now tried to persuade Chaska to leave for the West, promising to care for his mother in his absence as she had so often cared for Sarah.

"No," answered Chaska. "I am not a coward, I am not afraid to die."

Later that night, Sarah was told by another captive that "seven of the black devils" had been arrested. She emerged from her tent to find one of the officers, Captain Hiram P. Grant, and ask him if Chaska was in the group.

"Yes," the soldier answered, "and he will swing with the rest."

Sarah responded with heat: "Captain Grant, if you hang that man I will shoot you."

She tried to take the comment back, but it was too late. There was no reason for Grant to make his reply other than to taunt Sarah, and there was no reason to taunt Sarah except that the gossip about her was already spreading. Other captive women were talking to the soldiers as well. All of Sarah's words on the long trip up the valley came back to damn her: her threats to kill her own children, her admonitions to other white women not to talk badly of their captors, her "confession" that she had been Chaska's wife, her determination to stay with the Dakota if her husband truly was dead. Colonel Sibley himself wrote to his wife that Sarah "had become so infatuated with the red skin who had taken her for his wife, although her white husband was still living at some point below, and had been in search of her, she declared that were it not for her children, she would not leave her dusky paramour," and followed with another letter reporting that Sarah "threatens that if *her* Indian, who is among those who have been seized should be hung, she will shoot those of us who have been instrumental in bringing him to the scaffold, and then go back away with the Indians. A pretty specimen of a white woman she is, truly!"

On September 28, Sibley wrote to General Pope to announce the formation of a military commission to try the Dakota and added, "If found guilty they will be immediately executed, although I am somewhat in doubt whether my authority extends quite so far. An example is, however, imperatively necessary, and I trust you will approve the act, should it happen that some real criminals have been seized and promptly disposed of." He wrote in a similar vein to a subordinate, calling the order to execute those found guilty possibly "a stretch of my authority," but maintaining that "necessity must be my justification." Sibley, at the start, was uncertain about his power to sign off on death penalties; calling courts-martial was far outside his experience, but he knew enough to understand that some post-trial review was in order. The message to Pope seems to have been an appeal to the federal commander to take over the responsibility for capital punishment and may also have been a way to appease Governor Ramsey, the settlers, and the men under his command in order to head off the immediate threat of vigilante justice.

In order to obtain information useful in the prosecution of his prisoners, Sibley directed Stephen R. Riggs, founder of the Hazelwood Republic, to gather the mixed-bloods and friendly Dakota, a group of perhaps ninety informants on whose single day of testimony many of the convictions would rest. As Riggs reported his findings, Sibley expanded his court of inquiry into a five-man military commission authorized to "try summarily the mulatto, and Indians, or mixed bloods, now prisoners, or who may be brought before them . . . and pass judgment upon them, if found guilty of murders or other outrages upon the whites, during the present state of hostilities of the Indians." The men chosen to decide the fate of more than four hundred Dakotas were all officers under Sibley's command and all had fought in battle against the Dakota over the past six weeks. The commission that was to conduct the trials of the arrested warriors consisted of officers William R. Marshall, William Crooks, Hiram S. Bailey, Rollin C. Olin, and finally Hiram P. Grant, the object of Sarah's threat just one day earlier, the man who had told her that Chaska was destined to hang. Isaac Heard, a younger soldier who had already established himself as one of the state's foremost criminal prosecutors, would act as trial recorder.

Military commissions were a form of wartime legal proceeding used when a standard court-martial or civil trial was impossible. No statute or law dictated when or how they should be used, which threw them into the realm of common law and meant that precedent ruled—except that in 1862 precedent was thin. Only sixteen years earlier, in the Mexican-American War, General Winfield Scott, frustrated that he had no way to punish an American soldier for the murder of a Mexican citizen under the Articles of War, invented a commission according to the rules of courts-martial, setting a standard still active in 1862: defendants had the right to hear charges and specifications, make pleas, and have a decision read out. All sentences were subject to the review of a "convening authority," meaning that a superior had to sign off on every judgment. How superior this superior had to be depended on the specifications laid out in the Articles of War for similar courts-martial results; some went to the commanding general, some to the judge advocate general, while capital convictions usually went to the desk of the president. No burden of proof was placed on the prosecution: as Stephen R. Riggs would say of the Dakota prisoners, the commission trusted "that the innocent could make their innocency appear." Once his commissions were established, General Scott had quickly expanded their jurisdiction to include Mexican citizens and combatants accused of offenses against whites that included theft, murder, and rape, and brought the court-martial crimes of spying and encouraging military action against Americans under the same rubric.

This was the precedent, then, that existed during the Dakota War, except that never before had a military commission been convened in a conflict between whites and Indians. Chief Justice John Marshall's 1832 definition of Indian tribes as "domestic dependent nations" was still the legal standard, but in practice that term had failed to settle any questions of the proper relationship between America and its indigenous people. What exactly it meant to try such "dependents" by a military commission was really anyone's guess, and adding to the complications, Colonel Sibley was acting under the orders of John Pope, who, as events would demonstrate, did not seem to be conversant with many of the established protocols for such tribunals. All of the difficult questions swirling around the commission would eventually be raised, some within weeks and others many years later, but in the moment there were four hundred prisoners to deal with, little food or other provisions, winter coming on, and a populace demanding vengeance.

The first trial to be held considered the case of the war's most unusual participant, an ex-slave named Joseph Godfrey who had run away from his masters and been living among the Dakota since the late 1840s. While Minnesota in 1862 was staunchly pro-Union, its abolitionism was not so pronounced, and during its territorial period, at least, Godfrey's status had not been unique. Many soldiers at Fort

Snelling had kept slaves, as had some traders, including Godfrey's first owner, a big, bellicose man named Alexis Bailly, whose wife, Lucy, had kept the household running smoothly by beating their slaves and his young mixed-blood Indian servants. And when the coffers were light, or when friends needed help, his slaves might provide a ready source of income. So it was that Godfrey had once come into the service of Henry Sibley as an errand boy, several years before he ran away and joined the Dakota.

Whether Sibley and his former hired hand reacquainted themselves before or after Godfrey's trial is unknown. In any case, there was some irony in the fact that the first man tried in the Dakota War trials was the only non-Dakota defendant, at least by blood. Two days were devoted to Godfrey, who offered detailed testimony regarding the first day's killings at Milford, setting the ground for his later appearances as a witness, when he would turn state's evidence against many of the Dakota involved. With the black man's case out of the way, the commission turned its attention to the Dakota prisoners. Twenty-nine had been taken into custody so far, but more arrests were coming. Winter was fast on its way, and there were hundreds of fates left to decide.

On the third day of trials, the commission turned to Chaska. Sarah was asked to step inside the large enclosed tent that dominated Camp Release, surrounded by soldiers and seated Dakota men awaiting their trials, as well as various mixed-blood and white witnesses. She entered and shook Chaska's hand, placed her hand over a Bible and swore to tell the truth, and thus began case number three. Using a phonetic spelling of Chaska's proper Dakota name, one member of the military commission read out the charges: "In this that the said We-chank-wash-to-don-pee, Sioux Indian, did, on or about the 18th day of August 1862, kill George H. Gleason, a white citizen of the United States, and has likewise committed sundry hostile acts against the whites between the said 18th day of August 1862, and the 28th day of September 1862."

Sarah wrote later that Chaska seemed frightened and nervous, and as he spoke little English, a mixed-blood translator named Antoine Frenier asked for the prisoner's plea. Chaska followed with a statement he had prepared, perhaps with Sarah's assistance.

I plead not guilty of murder. The other Indian shot Gleason, and as he was falling over I aimed my gun at him but did not fire. I have had a white woman in charge but I could not take as good care of her as a white man because I am an Indian. I kept her with the intention of giving her up. Don't know of any other bad act since Gleason was murdered. I moved up here with the Indians. If I had done any bad act I should have gone off.

"I have been in three battles," he added. "I have not fired at any other white man. I wanted to prevent the other Indians from shooting."

Sarah was recorded as "a witness on the part of the prosecution," though she aimed only to establish Chaska's innocence. She spoke at some length, beginning with the story of her ride with Gleason and their encounter with two Dakotas just north of the Lower Agency. She swore that Hapa had fired two shots from his shotgun while Chaska collected the horses and that whatever happened next was immaterial, as Gleason's fate was already sealed. "When Mr. Gleason was in his death agony this Indian snapped his gun at him," she said, as Heard took notes. "He afterwards told me that it was to put him out of his misery. I saw this Indian endeavor to prevent the other Indian from firing at me. He raised his gun twice to do it. He said he did not go into this thing willingly." She detailed the many protections Chaska and his mother had provided during her six weeks of captivity, the way Chaska had squired her from tepee to tepee to find safety from harassment and shelter from the cold, and how Chaska's mother had spirited her and her children to the woods to escape the imminent threat of murder. All of that time, she said, Chaska "expressed great feeling for the whites" and "had to beg victuals for me."

Angus Robertson, a captive about whom little is known, largely corroborated Sarah's reports, except that most of his testimony involved statements Chaska made in the camps. Heard's notes are thin and sketchy, recording that Robertson "heard the prisoner say before Mrs. Wakefield that he fired the second shot" and adding "he said he shot Gleason," with the last word crossed out and replaced by "didn't kill Gleason," leaving the note "He said he shot didn't kill Gleason," a statement which vaguely matched the rest of Wakefield's narrative and Chaska's testimony that he had "snapped his gun" at Gleason to deliver a mercy killing. The rest of Sarah's testimony was unequivocal: Chaska was "a very good Indian" whose "conduct has been uniformly good toward Mrs. Wakefield and her children."

Both witnesses testified that it was Hapa's shot, or shots, that killed Gleason; both said nothing about Chaska's involvement in any battles; both spoke to his efforts to protect Sarah and her children; and both held him up as a man of character and integrity. Evidence gathered by Stephen R. Riggs or another recorder from soldiers named Fowler and Coe was apparently also introduced, though that evidence was never entered into the record—nor, by the terms of the commission, given Chaska's testimony that he had pointed a gun at George Gleason and pulled the trigger, was it needed—and the two men never set foot inside the impromptu courthouse. Chaska's unrepresented "defense," such as it was, was nonetheless the most thorough and reliable of the entire set, and lasted much longer than most of the subsequent trials.

After allowing Chaska and Sarah to depart and taking a few minutes of "mature deliberation," the commission found Chaska guilty of the murder of George Gleason and of still-unspecified "sundry hostile acts against the whites." Heard's transcription ended by noting that the five interrogating officers "do therefore sentence him, the said We-chank-wash-to-don-pee, a Sioux Indian to be hung by the neck until he is dead."

At the end of the week, the first five or six of twenty-odd such days to come, sixteen trials had been completed, including those for the other five men seized with Chaska on the 26th. All but Chaska were tried for rape or for murders in the settlements. Ten were sentenced to death; six were returned to the friendly camp, which was now surrounded by soldiers and artillery. In the meantime, Pope was writing to Sibley, outlining the next step in his plan.

> The horrible massacres of women and children and the outrageous abuse of female prisoners, still alive, call for punishment beyond human power to inflict. There will be no peace in this region by virtue of treaties and Indian faith. It is my purpose utterly to exterminate the Sioux if I have the power to do so and even if it requires a campaign lasting the whole of next year. Destroy everything belonging to them and force them out to the plains, un-less, as I suggest, you can capture them. They are to be treated as maniacs or wild beasts, and by no

means as people with whom treaties or compromises can be made.

A day or two before Chaska's trial, Henry Halleck had written to Pope from Washington with the news that "Colonel Henry H. Sibley is made a brigadier-general for his judicious fight at Yellow Medicine. He should be kept in command of that column and every assistance possible sent to him." The timing of Halleck's message is revealing. Earlier that week, Pope had requested that two of his friends from former commands be promoted to brigadier generalships and sent to Minnesota. As sensible as Halleck's elevation of Sibley seemed, it also seems to have been an executive rebuff to Pope, a message that he would have to work within the confines of the existing command and not try so hard to create his own chain of military patronage. Pope took more than a week to pass on this important news to Sibley, who now became an arm of the executive branch, answerable to President Lincoln rather than to Governor Ramsey. No longer would Sibley be a Minnesotan acting for Minnesotans; now he was an agent of the Union army. With the fighting in Minnesota all but over, the distinction might have seemed academic, but Sibley's promotion would soon come to have enormous consequences.

On October 1, Sarah Wakefield and her children were put on a wagon with the rest of the captives and sent south along the government road with an armed escort, following the same path the fleeing settlers had followed on the morning of August 18, forty-three days earlier. On October 2, after passing George Gleason's grave and crossing over the Minnesota River via the Lower Agency ferry, she arrived at Fort Ridgely, where she was finally able to bathe, don clean clothes, and sleep on a mattress. The next morning, she heard James call out "There is my father!" and turned to see John walking in her direction.

"There was my husband I had mourned as dead, now living—coming toward me," she wrote. "I was happy then, and felt that I would have died then willingly, and said, 'Thy will not mine be done,' for I knew my children had a protector now."

Sarah's focus on her children's well-being in her report of this moment, rather than on her own, was hardly uncommon for a woman of the frontier era, but given the events of her life up to this point and the events to come, her choice of words may be telling. In fact, if her sentiments were accurate as reported—and there is no reason to believe they were not—this may have been the happiest moment of the rest of her married life.

On September 24, when he turned away from Camp Release to ride for the Dakota Territory, Little Crow had been part of a thousand-person train made up of members of all four Eastern Dakota bands, more than half of them Mdewakantons. But as many as seven hundred Dakotas abandoned him before he even left the state, some scattering into the West and some turning back to take advantage of the flag of truce General Sibley had offered. A few smaller parties, including that of Cut Nose, had been captured by a detachment of Sibley's soldiers. By the time he was ready to leave the state, then, Little Crow was left with two or three hundred followers, no more than a hundred of them able warriors. And among those, only a few dozen were Mdewakantons loyal to him, including four of Little Crow's wives, a few half brothers and brothers-in-law, a son-in-law, and Wowinape, his son.

During a few days' halt among the Wahpetons at Lac Qui Parle, Little Crow tried to speed things along by announcing that the main force of Sibley's army was close behind his party and bent on the annihilation of all Dakotas. His traveling party next moved some twenty miles north, to Big Stone Lake and the village of Standing Buffalo, the most powerful and influential man in the Upper Agency bands. Here he learned about the note that Sibley's mixed-blood scouts had sent to Standing Buffalo offering peace in exchange for Little Crow's capture or corpse. In council with Little Crow and the wartime *tiyotipi*, Standing Buffalo now stood firm: he would not detain Little Crow's party, but neither would he allow them passage through his territory as they moved west, nor would he join with him, supply him, or offer his voice in support. Fierce debate broke out among the Upper Agency Dakota and made for a tense visit. Little Crow's fabrication that Sibley's main force was close behind him had caused some of the Upper Agency Dakota to flee out of the state, but most of the Sissetons and Wahpetons stood with their leader, who now ordered a separate move to the northern reaches of the Dakota Territory. Standing Buffalo, who understood that he was trapped between bad choices and might never see his own village again, unless as a captive, now offered the hardest public rebuke to Little Crow since the war began.

"You have already made much trouble for my people," he told Little Crow. "Go to Canada or where you please, but go away from me and off the lands of my people."

So Little Crow went away, without resistance or support from the Upper Dakota, his mind on the hard dry plains. In a way, setting foot out of Minnesota completed his life's circle. In his early twenties he had left his home village of Kaposia, much to the disappointment of his father. He had first moved to a Wahpekute village and married a chief's daughter before leaving her for unknown reasons and traveling to join the Wahpetons on Lac Qui Parle. Here he befriended the missionary Thomas S. Williamson and his family and first indulged his keen curiosity about white culture, attending the mission school for a short time and learning some writing and arithmetic. Here he also married another daughter of another chief, then, in succession, her three sisters. During the summers he traveled westward, riding with his friend Jack Frazer and other powerful young men, trading whiskey and hunting buffalo, playing cards and befriending white traders. Then had come the news from Kaposia that his father was dead.

Now Little Crow and his own son, along with a few hundred companions and a small group of captives, would puncture the malleable membrane that existed between the prairie and the plains. Behind him he left a staggering legacy. In a century in which tens of thousands of Indians had died and would die at the hands of white soldiers and frontier settlers, while tens of thousands more succumbed to epidemic diseases, the Dakota War was one of the very few encounters between whites and Indians that had not ended in a complete rout of the latter. Operating during a slice of time when white warfare hung between ages-old chivalric ideals and the brutal realities of "total war," the Dakota had killed 93 white soldiers and between 400 and 600 white civilians while suffering only a few dozen fatalities of their own. In the aftermath of the war, those numbers would shift again as hundreds of Dakotas who had taken little or no part in the fighting found themselves starved and destitute, struggling to keep their families together and dying of disease and maltreatment, but at this moment the people of Minnesota were girding for Indian attacks the following spring and wondering just how long Little Crow's War might truly last.

The best evidence argues that Little Crow consistently resisted the killing of women and children, however frequent his bluster to the contrary. And any white opponent entering his camp at nearly any moment during the past six weeks would surely have been surprised to witness Little Crow grappling with the wartime *tiyotipi* and making concessions to the members of the peace party. But no matter: for all the white world knew, the "incarnate demon," as the missionary Gideon Pond called him, was now escaping into the West, where he might continue to haunt their most cherished dreams.

# Chapter Thirteen

Henry Whipple's September had been dominated by two extraordinary events: his audience with Abraham Lincoln and his visit to the Antietam battlefield. Neither of these, however, had been the original purpose of his journey to the East, and at the beginning of October 1862 he finally arrived in New York City for the triannual meeting of the nation's Episcopal bishops. As turbulent weather darkened the skies above Manhattan, the bishops gathered to discuss the subject of disunion within the church as well as the country. Complex and heartfelt questions of politics and preaching, of Christianity and country, were complicated by questions about the "most unhappy contest," the bitter fruit of a nation, as Whipple was wont to say, "subdued by pride and vain boasting."

The bursting metropolis that received him was not, like Washington, a bifurcated city, showing a Northern face to the world but pumping plenty of Southern blood through its veins. Rather, New York was a kaleidoscope: rich and poor, native and foreign, serious and frivolous, idealistic and conniving, peace-loving and warlike. Union and Confederate sympathies alike were expressed often and in public. Growing all the time, the city pushed northward to extend its arms around brand-new Central Park, where the luxurious estate villas of the early nineteenth century were being replaced by closely spaced brick and stone towers. The intersection called Five Points was a powder keg of conflict between Irish Catholic immigrants and American-born "natives," a patch of ground that boasted a murder rate unheard of in the nation's urban history before or since. Four thousand workers at the Navy Yard made and repaired the frigates necessary for the Union blockade of Southern ports, while the rest of the city's manufacturing apparatus worked full tilt to supply clothes, arms, tents, wagons, and a thousand other items to the war effort. And all the while Boss Tweed continued to press every corner of municipal life inside a vise grip that was making "Tammany Hall"—named after a Lenape Indian chief— a synonym for corruption, graft, and backroom patronage.

Soldiers from all of New York and New England filled Rikers Island with the barks and snaps of innumerable training drills before they marched down Broadway in smart rows to board trains destined for distant battlefields. The Italianate brownstone of the Cooper Union's Foundation Building, just east of Greenwich Village, was already a landmark thanks to Lincoln's famous speech two years earlier, and nearby on Broadway Mathew Brady's photography studio, in business for eighteen years already, displayed a simple placard out front advertising "The Dead at Antietam." This gallery, the object of much critical appreciation and morbid curiosity, attracted thousands of visitors who came to see the most arresting images many of them would ever witness, human carcasses by the score, many photographed on the two days that Bishop Whipple had been at the battlefield.

The majority of the city's working poor were Democratic and anti-Lincoln, opposed to his recent proclamation, skeptical of the war, and resistant to the president's threats of conscription should the requisite number of volunteers fail to appear. Across the East River, a "meeting of the colored people of Brooklyn" was taking place to consider Lincoln's oft-repeated proposal to settle contraband slaves in Panama, Honduras, or some other Central American locale, plans that had little appeal for the blacks of Brooklyn or of any other city in the country, whose "prevailing sentiment was against a forced emigration to any place."

Amid this storm-swept sea of humanity, twenty Episcopal bishops and various laymen and clergy from across the Union gathered at Saint John's Chapel, which faced a gated park in a neighborhood full of aristocratic mansions, midway between Broadway and the Hudson

River. The convention of bishops officially opened on October 2, when "the Secretary called for delegates from Virginia, North Carolina, South Carolina, Georgia, Florida, Alabama, Mississippi, Louisiana, Texas, Tennessee and Kansas, but from none of them was there any response." The next two days were given over to debate of a resolution calling for prayer for the return of the Southern members, "petitioning the Almighty to change their minds and restore them to the truth," a wrenching argument that became less polite when Francis Vinton, minister of New York's Trinity Church, announced that "the South has ignored the Prayer-Book, has ignored the Church, and is in rebellion to the Church." The resolution was eventually tabled by a large majority to avoid taking any "irritating action," but it laid bare important divisions between the ostensibly apolitical High Church Episcopalians and the more socially engaged Low.

Whipple did not fall neatly into either category. His desire for sectional union between North and South at the expense of the cause of abolition might have been High Church, but his muddy boots and his clamor for reform of the Indian system were decidedly Low. This was the aspect of his character most visible on the afternoon of October 5, when he delivered a sermon at Saint Thomas Church, a quarter mile up the island at the corner of Broadway and Houston Street in Greenwich Village. Still nursing his stubborn hand infection, Whipple announced that he would not be speaking on a passage from Scripture but rather that "his entire theme" would be "the condition of the Missions of the Church in the Far West." "The Far West" meant Minnesota, and "Missions" meant the Indian ministries, an undertaking, Whipple told his audience, that many of his parishioners and fellow clergy had urged him to avoid. For those assembled in the pews of Saint Thomas's he emphasized the travels, thousands of miles already by his calculation, on foot, on horseback, and by canoe, that had led him to four conclusions: "First, the American Indian is more brave, more truthful and more virtuous than any other heathen on earth; second, that he is the only heathen who believes in God, who is not an idolator; third, that he retains the old patriarchal form of government that was known in the earliest days of the race; and fourth, that it was after he came in contact with white men, and those who had acted for our government, that he first became demoralized."

Speaking to an Eastern audience that lacked immediate experience with the violence of frontier life, he laid out what he saw as the causes of the Dakota War: the treaty of 1858, which he credited partly to Little Crow's influence, that had given away 800,000 acres without consulting most of the Indians affected; the siphoning of more than $100,000 worth of annuity gold over three years' time; and most of all, he said, "the actual starving to death of the children of chiefs for absolute want, owing to this neglect; women destroyed by brutal violence, and cruel robberies committed by the whites." These, he said, "had been the dreadful causes that had led to the recent outbreaks and massacres, unparalleled in Indian annals."

The *New York Times* praised the sermon as "a valuable, eloquent and powerful discourse," and Whipple was gratified by the reaction of his audience. These were the people he could count on to donate twenty dollars, fifty, a hundred to the relief of the displaced settlers and the work of his Indian missions. Whipple's purposes on this trip, though, ran deeper. His text repeated claims and criticisms he'd made before, but in the brand-new context of a war on the frontier that was starting to gain space in Eastern newspapers, the sermon was also a rehearsal. Whipple had already made plans to deliver the same message to the people of Minnesota upon his return, and as much as he trusted in his powers of persuasion, he had no illusions about receiving a similarly enthusiastic response.

Since arriving in Minnesota in mid-September, John Pope had been agitating for the delivery of some five thousand former Union prisoners to the frontier so that they could be used to fight Indians, a plan the *Richmond Dispatch* considered to be a serious breach of the wartime protocols governing the actions of men released on parole. The *New York Times* responded to its Southern sister with a paraphrase of the editors' argument—"If our Government should send paroled prisoners of war to fight against *the Indians,* it would be guilty of a *'breach of faith'* toward the rebel Government"—and a heavy dose of sarcasm that nonetheless expressed an opinion that the people of Minnesota and some members of the executive branch were still taking very seriously.

> Are *the Indians* of the West part and parcel of the rebel Confederacy? Have the rebel authorities taken these savages into their service? Are the acts of atrocious brutality, by which those savage raids upon Western towns have been marked—

the massacre of helpless families, the tomahawking of women and children, the burning of houses, the wholesale butchery of the innocent and defenceless—are these acts done under the sanction of the Confederate Government? And does it intend to extend over them protection of its authority?

As the Episcopal bishops met in the East, out on the frontier General Sibley was writing to General Pope to inform him of the progress of the trials and to describe his own efforts to bring in more of the Dakota from upriver. At the beginning of October a large group of Mdewakantons and Wahpekutes that had broken off from Little Crow's party sent a runner south to communicate their desire to surrender and join the friendly camp, to which Sibley replied that they must send "in advance two of their principal men with a white flag" and that he would "see that no innocent person is injured who comes to me without delay." What the flag of truce and the word "innocent" meant at this moment in Sibley's mind and the minds of the Dakota was to become a point of argument, confusion, and moral ambiguity thereafter, but Sibley had no time or desire for such deliberations.

"The greater part of the men are deeply implicated in the late outrages," he wrote to Pope. Now that most of the breakaway parties from Little Crow's procession had come into Camp Release and no longer needed luring with suggestions of clemency, Sibley added, the executions of all the condemned Dakota should be swift, orderly, and very public. He then escalated his rhetoric to a pitch it rarely reached otherwise. "I have given them no assurances except that such as were innocent and the women and children should be protected," he wrote, "and I repeated to them what I had previously stated in my message to them, that if any more of their young men went off to war upon the whites I would fall upon their camp and cut them to pieces, without regard to age or sex." The language, wildly uncharacteristic of Sibley, was surely a bluff, not entirely different from Little Crow's repeated threats to kill all of his white captives. Fear was the coin of the day, spent by both sides. But it was also language that Pope and Ramsey, who so often spoke of "exterminating" the Dakota, viewed in an entirely approving light.

On October 4, the men, women, and children of eighty-six lodges returned from Little Crow's train and other points to the west, bringing the number of Dakotas and mixed-bloods at Camp Release to around twelve hundred, perhaps a quarter of them men of fighting age. Soon afterwards Sibley ordered that those Dakotas yet unarrested be moved down to the banks of the Yellow Medicine River near the Upper Agency and tasked with digging potatoes and turnips under a small guard. Sibley also began to issue a steady stream of general orders prohibiting his men from entering the Indian camps or otherwise interacting with the Dakota. He knew that many of his soldiers, especially the newly recruited enlisted men, were as inflamed against the Dakota as the most aggrieved settler. All the while Sibley received a never-ending stream of instructions from Pope, who sat ensconced at the International Hotel in Saint Paul sending frantic, sometimes maddening dispatches that seemed to have nothing to do with Sibley's reality.

For three weeks Pope had promised to send "all the men necessary" up the river valley, ordering in the meantime that Sibley should move the majority of his army out to the border of the Dakota Territory, "destroying crops and everything else belonging to the Dakota" in order to forestall the return of Little Crow with an imagined force of Plains Indians. This instruction, repeated ad nauseam, ignored the presence of hundreds, even thousands, of friendly Sisseton and Wahpeton Dakotas near the Minnesota border, as well as the approaching winter weather, the need to manage the ever-growing population at Camp Release and the Upper Agency, and the fact that Little Crow's force was by now clearly bent only on escape, with no way to make designs on Minnesotans or their property at least until the following spring. Sibley had no plan to send his main force any farther to the west, knowing that his soldiers could go only a short distance before the winter snows began to fall and forced them back into the state.

In response after response to Pope, Sibley politely outlined hindrances that worked to "embarrass the command." Even now, eight weeks after the war began, he could muster only a hundred or so mounted men, none with enough experience as cavalry to lead a cross-country expedition into hostile and unfamiliar territory. He had no ready supply of bread or meat for his soldiers and little hay for his animals. Coats and other clothing appropriate to the coming cold were in short supply, as were blankets and a sufficient quantity of bullets matched to the rifles carried by his men. Over and over Sibley expressed his concern that Pope's orders to chase after the fleeing Dakota would only put the captives with Little Crow in greater danger and result in nothing but misery for his soldiers. As for himself, Sibley wanted out. He had accepted his command and laid aside his political and business affairs at the governor's personal request, but he was feeling his age and did not believe that a more qualified federal officer could not be brought west to replace him. He had closed his first communication to Pope, in September, by writing, "I would not have been displeased to learn that you had selected as my successor in command some one of the gentlemen under your orders who has military qualifications, for to such I make little pretension," and nothing had since changed his mind.

The temperamental difference between the two commanders was pronounced. Pope was aggressive, sloppy with facts, full of braggadocio, and prone to let the emotions of his day, or even his hour, play out in every written dispatch and personal exchange. Sibley's approach to their correspondence was even-toned, patient, and forbearing, though his letters did become more insistent, sprinkled with a clenched-teeth exasperation that Pope must have noticed. Sibley was acting out of four decades' familiarity with the Dakota and viewed the actions of Little Crow and the other hostile chiefs as, in part, a personal and professional betrayal. Pope knew nothing about the Dakota and imagined them as part of one savage curtain strung across the West, with none of Sibley's understanding of cultural nuances, band and tribal differences, or individual histories.

Most of all, though, Pope was still acting out of the furious sense of injustice he had carried with him on the train to Minnesota. His letters teemed with impotent anger at finding himself in the hinterlands and out of federal favor, an anger that took the form of great proclamations of doom: the doom that had descended on whites and the doom he would visit on their Dakota malefactors. He sent his biggest and loudest bombshell of a letter, the most intemperate of an intemperate lot, on October 6, at the end of the first week of trials. Sibley, at this moment, was managing several exigencies: the progress of his military commission, the division of the Dakota into guilty and innocent, his own desire for firm retribution, and especially the logistical demands that went with the command of thousands of soldiers and the charge of thousands of Dakotas in circumstances that threatened every day to slip free of his control. In Saint Paul, where Sibley's concerns—never mind those of the Dakota—were seen at a great distance, voices were speaking over Pope's shoulder to disparage Sibley's cautious progress and to express amazement about Sibley's assurances of protection for innocent Dakotas.

Pope's letter to Sibley of October 6 began with a broadside. "I have received no dispatches from you since the meeting of the commission for trying Indians," Pope wrote, "but I consider it proper to inform you, that many persons from your camp have brought accounts very unsatisfactory of the proceedings, and which have excited the greatest indignation among the people here."

Pope was hearing from unspecified informants that Sibley had offered a flag of truce, that the friendly Dakota had been moved to the Upper Agency, that many of these friendly Dakota were still armed, and that Sibley was not, in fact, showing any signs of dashing off after Little Crow with two thousand men. These "accounts" were on the mark. But Pope didn't spend a moment wondering or inquiring why Sibley might have made these choices; rather, he told Sibley to announce a $500 reward for Little Crow, dead or alive, and added that any whites "shielding" the Dakota—whatever that word might mean—should be considered as treasonous individuals and "summarily executed." "I think still that the Indians with you should be disarmed, and brought down here," Pope wrote, "here" meaning Fort Snelling. "I will take care of them here for the winter, and put them beyond the possibility of doing mischief, execute at once any convicted of any sort of complicity in the late outrages."

Why Sibley's most recent messages, written on October 1, 3, and 5, hadn't yet reached Pope is unknown, but that very day, perhaps only an hour or two after Pope handed his own letter to a courier, they arrived. Pope read them quickly, including Sibley's uncharacteristic threat to "fall upon the [Dakota] camp and cut them to pieces, without regard to age or sex," should any further attacks occur. Here, apparently, was the firm tone and draconian attitude Pope preferred. In any case, the next afternoon Pope overturned his instructions of the previous day, writing to Sibley with orders that trials should continue and that he should "disarm, and send down to Fort Snelling, all the Indians men women and children of the Sioux tribe, upon whom you can lay your hands" in preparation for sending all of the Dakota not slated for execution "beyond the limits of the state in the spring." Three days later Pope completed his instructions to Sibley: "The whole of the Indians, men, women and children, should be brought as prisoners to the

Lower Agency where the culprits must be executed in the presence of the whole tribe."

So as to follow Pope's orders to treat all the Dakotas "as prisoners," then, Sibley directed his men to arrest more than 250 Dakota men at the Upper Agency who had not already been tried by the military commission, many of whom had been part of the friendly camp since the formation of the peace party. To separate these men from their families without causing a disturbance, Samuel J. Brown was sent into the Indian camp near the Upper Agency to tell an assembled crowd that the yearly annuity had finally come in and that the men were to gather in order to be "counted," or registered for the payment. It is a comment on the different worldviews at play, the belief still held by the friendly Dakota that any whites in power might understand their grievances and believe them innocent, that the trickery worked at all.

The playacting began around noon, probably on October 11, when the Indian agent Thomas Galbraith and a captain from Sibley's command positioned themselves at a table in front of the burned-out brick shell of the warehouse that had once housed John Wakefield's office. Whole families of Dakotas approached the table and were tallied with prop pencils on prop tablets, after which a soldier motioned each group to go to the doorway at the other end of the warehouse. Brown described the process of selection and separation.

> I would tell the men to step inside and allow the women and children to pass on to the camp, telling them, as I was instructed to do, that the men as heads of families must be counted separately, as it was thought the government would pay them extra. I would then take their guns, tomahawks, scalping knives, etc., and throw them into barrels, telling them they would be returned shortly.

Meanwhile, the arrests accelerated among the remaining Dakota near Camp Release, a succession of moments that were terrifying for his Dakota charges and troubling, if no more, to Sibley himself, who wrote to his wife that "the poor women's wailings, when separated from their husbands, fathers, and sons are piteous indeed, and I dislike to go in person to their lodges, when I have orders for their removal." He also noted that any qualms about the process were lessened by the discovery in some tents of dresses, wallets, jewelry, shoes, and other personal items from killed or captured whites. The makeshift log jail at Camp Release swelled to capacity and was placed under heavy guard as Sibley prepared to fulfill the second part of Pope's orders and move all of the Dakota down to the Lower Agency, where the trials would continue and the executions begin.

Years later a sergeant named A. P. Connolly who had been stationed at Camp Release would write that "the orders were very strict about guarding the Indians, but on the sly many acts of cruelty were indulged in by the soldiers that would hardly be warranted, for we should not for a moment forget the fact that they were our prisoners and we were not savages and should not indulge in savage propensities." And another officer, Thomas Watts, would tell a newspaper editor that some of the younger men had developed a plan to slaughter all of the Dakota under their watch: "At a given signal the guard surrounding the camp was to retire, then the battery was to shell the camp and the infantry was to do its work, and what was left, if any, the cavalry was to finish." Sibley thought such threats serious enough that he gathered his troops and threatened courts-martial, following which his officers spoke to their respective companies. "It was promised that the Indians should be court marshaled immediately," Watts wrote, "and that we should have the privilege of hanging the guilty ones." Protecting the Dakota was, their commanders urged, a way of reserving the right to kill the Dakota themselves.

On October 12, one or two days after the mass arrests at the Upper Agency, the skies opened up, leaving the procession to travel over mile after mile of slick, rutted road. Early the following morning, the Renville Rangers, the partial company of white and mixed-blood soldiers raised by Thomas Galbraith, led the great convoy away from the Upper Agency. Infantry, wagons, oxcarts, cattle, cannon, and howitzers moved through the slop as a northern winter wind descended in all its fury. Some miles behind them followed Sibley with his men and his prisoners, two dozen of them, including Chaska, already condemned to death. All told, several hundred soldiers, nearly four hundred prisoners, and twelve hundred women, children, and elderly Dakota trudged in two miserable lines toward the Lower Agency, where the skeletal forms of more burned buildings still stood open to the early-winter air, and makeshift graves dotted the earth.

# Chapter Fourteen

John Pope's messages were no less abrasive to his superiors in Washington than they were to Henry Sibley. From the start Lincoln and his military brain trust, War Secretary Edwin Stanton and General in Chief Henry Halleck, had known Pope was deeply unhappy, in spite of—or because of—the many obsequious and reassuring notes the exiled general had sent to Stanton. "I am sure you know that what I undertake I do with my whole heart," Pope had written early in his stay in Minnesota. "No considerations of any kind will affect my action in the discharge of duty." Running the Military Department of the Northwest with his "whole heart" seemed to mean, at least from Washington's point of view, issuing an endless stream of requests that stood no chance of being granted. Five hundred wagons, 2,600 men on 2,600 horses, 5,000 paroled Union prisoners, two brigadier generals of Pope's choice: all were denied to Pope, and Stanton had finally asked Halleck to "make some order defining the extent of operations to be carried on in the Northwest as an Indian campaign" and find a way to communicate that "whatever is sent to General Pope will leave a deficiency to the same extent in other branches of the service"—a polite way of reminding Pope that he was no longer the big man on the block.

In response, Pope painted a catastrophe in ever broader strokes.

"You do not seem to be aware of the extent of the Indian outbreaks," he wrote to Halleck, and then engaged in one of George McClellan's favorite tactics, overstating his opposition by a factor of at least ten, describing Little Crow's assembled forces as 2,600 mostly mounted warriors when the truth was that Sibley now reported 250 warriors "yet to be found and dealt with." Even that number was an exaggeration, but a much lesser one: the Dakota leader now traveled with little more than a hundred fighting men, most of them on foot. Pope described the Dakota and Nebraska territories as entirely depopulated and wrote that the property of 50,000 people had been abandoned when the truth was perhaps a third of that number. Even more fantastically, he repeated the claim that the Ojibwe of northern Minnesota were on the "verge of outbreak" and somehow ascertained the plans of several dozen tribes between the Mississippi River and the Rockies, warning that "the whole of the Indian tribes as far as the mountains are in motion."

Pope's reports were consistently on the mark in only one respect: the fear and chaos the Dakota had caused in the settlements southwest of Saint Paul. "You have no idea of the wide, universal, and uncontrollable panic everywhere in this country," he wrote, and to make his point, he described "children nailed alive to trees and houses, women violated and then disemboweled—everything that horrible ingenuity could devise." Much of what had been reported to Pope via messengers and newspapers was, in fact, the product of "ingenuity," but the truth was shocking enough. Over three hundred settlers were dead, many of them women and children, with hundreds of others still unaccounted for, a toll on whites exceeding that of any other Indian war in American history. Even with the threadbare economic status of many frontier farmers, the monetary losses in terms of built structures, livestock, and farm implements ran into the millions of dollars. The worst of the violence in the settlements was committed by a few hundred men at most, but they had ranged widely and at great speed, striking hard from the Iowa border up to the Big Woods. Editors vied to pass along the most lurid atrocities, almost none of which were based on firsthand reports and many of which were simply escalated retellings of a few killing scenes, but Pope made little effort to determine the truth of the situation. He seemed to revel in painting a whirlwind he could barely control.

The truth of Pope's own situation, though, was that the timing of his appointment to the Northwest had left him with little to do.

By the time his letters began to reach Sibley in the Upper Minnesota River Valley, the whirlwind was all but spent. Killings in the settlements had become sporadic and far between, and all of the shooting between soldiers and warriors had stopped, aside from the final battle at Wood Lake, which, in any event, Sibley directed on his own. Great unrealizable plans and unattainable requests aside, Pope's role as the trials began was to relieve Sibley of the responsibility for the ultimate dispensation of the Dakota, both those sentenced to death and those with no place left to go. And even that role began to recede in importance once Sibley was finally notified of his promotion to a Union generalship on October 6 and the last of the stragglers from Little Crow's breakaway party had begun to return to Camp Release and the Upper Agency.

Pope's messages to Henry Halleck, at first fairly dry and factual, soon became inaccurate, exaggerated digests of Sibley's to him. "The Sioux war may be considered at an end," he wrote in the late hours of October 9. "We have about 1,500 prisoners—men, women, and children—and many are coming every day to deliver themselves up. Many are being tried by military commission for being connected to the late horrible outrages, and will be executed." Anyone with a legal background—and Lincoln, Stanton, and Halleck all qualified—might have raised an eyebrow or two at the assumption that all of the trials would end in death sentences. At three the next afternoon, Pope sent another odd, rushed telegram to Halleck using much the same language.

> The Sioux war is at an end. All of the bands engaged in the late outrages, except 5 men, have been captured. It will be necessary to execute many of them. The settlers can all return. I have not yet heard from the expedition to the Yankton villages, but with the return of that there will not be a hostile Indian east of the Missouri. The example of hanging many of the perpetrators of the late outrages is necessary and will have a crushing effect. I shall tomorrow issue an address requesting all the frontier settlers to return to their homes.

Pope's claim that all but five of the hostile Dakota had been captured was nonsense: as was fairly well known, Little Crow was traveling west with a hundred or more warriors and was still well short of the

Missouri River. The "expedition to the Yankton villages" referred only to a small detachment of men trying to follow Little Crow's movements, but Pope began to describe an imminent battle of epic proportions in the Dakota Territory between Sibley's forces and thousands of Dakota warriors, claiming to have "no fear of the results." He also lacked a basic understanding of the "settlers" and their situations. Most of them were not prosperous farmers with hundreds of fertile acres and cash reserves; most were poor homesteaders, now left with only their oxen or horses, if that. Many were missing the heads of their households; many had seen or heard stories of their homes and barns being burned to the ground. While some were determined to reestablish their farms, many others were making plans to return to the states or even the countries from which they'd come, or planning to live with relatives in Minnesota and neighboring states for the indefinite future as they worked to piece together their shattered lives.

Finally, on October 13, for reasons lost to history, Pope's rhetoric shifted. As he indicated in a midmorning telegram to Halleck, "There is strong testimony that white men led the Indians in late outrages. Do I need further authority to execute Indians condemned by military commission?" For the first time since accepting his generalship in the Union army a year earlier, he began to question the limits of his executive authority. Perhaps a lost communication from Stanton or Halleck checked him. Perhaps some hint in one of Sibley's long letters jarred him into an understanding of the immense responsibility attached to summary executions. Perhaps he was simply protecting himself from future executive censure. Or perhaps he was influenced by information originating with the Indian agent Thomas Galbraith, who would write his own report later in the fall suggesting that traders, largely Democrats with no love for the Republicans now running the state and the country, had intentionally agitated the Dakota.

Pope would soon drop this last possibility altogether, but in questioning his authority to order executions he was finally acting judiciously. For fifty-five years, until the start of the Civil War, Article of War 65 had held sway in the matter of capital punishment via court-martial, providing that peacetime death sentences handed down by military courts required executive sanction. In writing new rules after Fort Sumter, Congress had stipulated that the president must confirm "any sentence of death, except in the cases of persons convicted in time of war of murder, rape, mutiny, desertion, or as spies." Then, in July 1862, Congress reversed course and stipulated that command-ing officers could declare punishments but that "the judgment of every court-martial shall be authenticated by the signature of the President." Precedent from other conflicts with Indian tribes was murky and inconsistent, so by putting the cases in front of a military commission Pope and Sibley had at the very least left themselves subject to review by the executive branch. In any case, it would have been strange indeed for any high-ranking officer, but especially an experienced Union gen-eral, to assume that death sentences handed down by a military com-mission should *not* be reported to the president.

In a cabinet meeting the next day, October 14, Edwin Stanton read Pope's latest dispatch from the frontier out loud; this was probably the second of the two telegrams announcing that the war had ended and that he "was anxious to execute a number" of Dakotas. That night, Sec-retary of the Navy Gideon Welles used his diary to record a personal opinion shared by many of the men in the room. "I was disgusted with the tone and opinions of the dispatch. It was not the production of a good man or a great one. The Indian outrages have, I doubt not, been great—what may have been the provocation we are not told." Just one month earlier, Lincoln had listened to Whipple's accounting of the "provocations" at the heart of the Dakota War, and it is not a leap to read Welles's words as a comment on Pope's total lack of interest in those causes.

No other documentary record of the cabinet meeting exists, but it is clear that the oral recitation of Pope's dispatch was a key moment in the story of the Dakota War. Lincoln found Pope's drumbeat for executions as dissonant as did Welles, and soon after conferring with his department heads, he made his decision. At 2:15 that same after-noon, Stanton sent a wire to Pope indicating that the cabinet meeting had taken place and that the president had instructed him "to say that he desires you to employ your force in such manner as shall maintain the peace and secure the white inhabitants from Indian aggressions, and that upon the questions of policy presented by you his instructions will be given as soon as he shall obtain information from the Indian Department which he desires."

Three days later, on October 17, Lincoln halted the pell-mell rush for vengeance. The key document has not survived, but as Pope reported to Sibley, "the President directs that no executions be made without his sanction." The outcome of the Dakota War trials would be adjudicated in Washington, D.C., not in Saint Paul. Pope's "questions of policy" were probably limited to the requirement for executive review, but Lincoln was equally interested in the legal criteria applied by the military commission and the fairness of the trials, as well as the moral and political costs of hanging hundreds of men on potentially rickety convictions. As high as the stakes were, though, this was comfortable territory for the president, whose nose for the law had been honed by eleven busy years on the Illinois circuit. He had been asked a set of very specific legal questions and would rule on those questions. Any compassion he felt for the Dakota prisoners was subsumed in his larger sense that justice might not have proceeded—or be proceeding—according to legitimate legal standards, a sense that had grown out of his deep distrust of Pope's manner and motives. In this way, and entirely ironically, Pope himself probably was as influential as anyone in bringing about Lincoln's willingness to intervene.

The word that executions had been placed on hold by the president would soon spread through Saint Paul, the state of Minnesota, and all of the Northwest with lightning speed and thunderous results. In New York, on the same day Lincoln put a halt to immediate executions, the convention of Episcopal bishops ended on a plaintive note. "To hate rebellion, so uncaused, is duty; but to hate those engaged in it was the opposite of duty," said Bishop McIlvaine of Ohio, who closed the proceedings with a prayer that "the nation and the Church might soon be united in the bonds of peace and fellowship." Before leaving the city, Whipple secured the signatures of all twenty bishops present on an "Indian statement" he hoped would prod Lincoln further on the questions he'd raised during his visit in September. In Washington and back in Minnesota, that visit had attracted notice. U.S. representative Cyrus Aldrich, reported the *St. Cloud Democrat,* was "knocked down" in a Saint Paul saloon by a former member of the First Minnesota regiment for mocking Whipple and calling him a "secessionist."

One set of battles, white against Indian, was finished for the time being. Little Crow was somewhere to the west, the threat of his return diminishing as winter came on fast. But another set of battles, white against white, was just beginning.

After six weeks of trials, the final sentence of death given to the final Dakota prisoner was announced on November 5 at the Lower Agency,

François LaBathe's Summer Kitchen, Lower Dakota Agency,
ca. November 1862

inside one of the only structures still intact, a squat, square wooden building that had once served as trader François LaBathe's summer kitchen. The tally: in fewer than thirty days spread across six weeks, 392 trials had been held, resulting in 303 sentences of death, 16 sentences of imprisonment, and 69 acquittals. The first twenty-nine trials at Camp Release, which required eight or nine days over two weeks, had at least followed the basic outline and evidentiary standards of a proper military court-martial. Then, on October 15, the pace had quickened dramatically as the commission did away with such trappings of the law as arraignments, pleas, and detailed specification of charges; now it embraced John Pope's cavalier mandate that "any sort of complicity" in the war was grounds for capital punishment. After the move to the Lower Agency, the process was further hastened to an absurd degree: most of the trials took less than ten minutes, and prisoners were sometimes brought forward in groups of six or eight, chained at the ankles.

During this last phase of the trials, in fact, a Dakota warrior was likely to be sentenced to death simply because he could not produce a witness to vouch for his conduct. The speed of the trials after October 15 was abetted by a set of simple ground rules that seemed to have no single author, though they were all guided by Pope and implemented by Sibley. None of the short war's battles—not the ambush at the Lower Agency, nor the battles at New Ulm, Birch Coulee, and Wood Lake—would be defined as an action between equal adversaries acting in a military capacity. Rather, they were to be considered capital crimes, unprovoked aggressions akin to the killings in the settlements.

Thus there was no need to ascertain which of the Dakota had visited the farms and dirt lanes along the river valley and the settlements to the north and south, bringing death to hundreds of white men, women, and children. Now, any prisoner proved to have "fired in the battles, or brought ammunition, or acted as commissary in supplying provisions to the combatants" was as deserving of a death penalty as someone who set fire to a farmhouse with a white family inside. Most crucially, the prisoners, all of whom had by this point heard Sibley's promise to punish only "murderers," were not told of this, and so may have willingly admitted firing shots at the battles of New Ulm, Birch Coulee, or Wood Lake. The ex-slave and adopted Dakota Joseph Godfrey became a kind of informal prosecutor, a role decidedly outside the bounds of a proper court-martial, not only offering evidence but dramatically cross-examining defendants, probably out of eagerness to reduce his own sentence. The information collected from the mixed-bloods and friendly Indians by the Reverend Stephen R. Riggs became ever more essential, even when it was as simple as a statement that a defendant had been seen leaving camp with a group of armed warriors in the hours before a battle. By defining the overall conflict as a war, justifying General Sibley's jurisdiction in the first place, but calling any participation in that war a capital crime, the trials allowed his commission to deliver ever more rapid summary judgments, subject to no appeal, on all of the Dakota who shuffled in and out of the tented courtroom.

Within months, an argument about the propriety and legality of Sibley's commission and Pope's standards of guilt would begin, an argument that still remains unsettled 150 years later, but out on the prairie there was no way for the Dakota to lodge a protest and no white person willing or able to stand up and slow down the process. The shift to a far more streamlined format allowed the commission to hear and decide on more than 250 cases over the last ten days of trials. No sentence was ever read out loud to the defendant, and this created great confusion among the Dakota. Some prisoners seemed to assume that the government was waiting to execute all of the arrested men together and that no one had really been acquitted; others seemed to think that the fact they had not been taken to a gallows or separated from the other prisoners immediately following their trials meant that they had been found innocent. But for all of them, the uncertainty kept them on edge and filled the camp with fear.

What was gained by conducting trials that would take anywhere from a few minutes to an hour each to decide the fates of the Dakota men rounded up on the prairie? Not justice, at least not in the legal sense of the word. And not satisfaction; as far as most of the settlers and many of the soldiers were concerned, such jurisprudence, hurried as it was, was unnecessary. "I am for shooting down the cowards as fast as they approach the camps," wrote one private, a sentiment that would continue to grow all autumn and into the winter, which crept ever closer as the prairie grasses began to frost overnight and the tents seemed made of thinner and thinner cloth.

During the latter phases of the trials, a judgment of another sort was being issued, one that said that any armed resistance to white encroachment was worthy of death. No military commission had ever before been used to try enemy combatants for firing shots on a battle-field. To set a standard that equated all acts of Dakota violence and all perpetrators, erasing distinctions between acts against civilians and acts against soldiers, was to suggest that no true conflict between the whites and the Dakota as peoples could exist. And to suggest that no true conflict existed was to suggest that every act of Dakota violence, including the pulling of a trigger in the face of firing white soldiers, was the result of cultural deficiencies and racial wickedness.

Not every white person was happy with the proceedings. After the trials were complete, John P. Williamson, son of the missionary Thomas S. Williamson, would write to his mission board in frustration and despair.

> 400 have been tried in less time than is generally taken in our courts with the trial of a single murderer. Again in very many of the cases a man's own testimony is the only evidence against him. He is first prejudiced guilty of any charge any of the Court choose to prefer against him and then if he denied he is cross

examined with all the ingenuity of a modern lawyer to see if he cannot be detected in some error of statement. Then they are not allowed any counsel. They are scarcely allowed a word of explanation themselves, and knowing nothing of the manner of conducting trials if a mistake occurs they are unable to correct it. And often not understanding the English language in which the trial is conducted, they very imperfectly understand the evidence upon which they are convicted.

Now that there would be no more Indian-chasing, the soldiers' minds turned back to the reason they'd enlisted in the first place. While the trials continued at the Lower Agency, Sibley's companies filled the empty level spaces with drills and more drills in anticipation of boarding the riverboats and trains that would finally bring them face-to-face with the rebellious "secesh." Guards made the rounds three times a night, while other soldiers combed the settlements on burial duty, still coming upon human remains from attacks that had occurred almost two months earlier. The men had split into two loose divisions, one a faction who saw their duty to protect the Dakota as part of the lawful preparation for proper executions and the other, smaller but very vocal, who saw the opportunity for mischief or individual revenge.

Since arriving at the Lower Agency to continue the trials, the soldiers had been calling their latest home Camp Sibley, but Sibley himself refused to use the term and continued to issue orders designed to keep his men away from the Dakota tepees. On October 22, he had confided to his wife, "I find the greatest difficulty in keeping the men from the Indian women when the camps are close together. I have a strong line of sentinels entirely around my camp to keep every officer and soldier from going out without my permission; but some way or other, a few of the soldiers manage to get among the *gals*." He also issued orders against taking buffalo robes from their prisoners or trading whiskey for goods and favors. For the Dakota—the innocent and the condemned—such actions were humiliation; for the soldiers involved, they were sport; for their more conscientious bunkmates and senior officers, they were a constant threat to the integrity of the command.

With all of the trials complete, Sibley ordered the implementation of Pope's newest plan, to send the convicted prisoners downriver to the regional hub of Mankato while herding the women, children, elderly, and innocent straight overland to Fort Snelling, where they would be held until the Office of Indian Affairs could decide on their final destination. Lieutenant Colonel William Marshall of the Seventh Minnesota, a banker, farmer, newspaperman, staunch Republican, and member of Sibley's trial commission, was charged with preparing 1,700 innocent Dakotas and all of their property for the trip. Aware that civilians and militia alike might be inclined to set upon the train as it traveled over the prairie, Marshall delivered a public notice to a reporter for publication in the *Saint Paul Daily Press:* "I would risk my life for the protection of these helpless beings, and would feel everlastingly disgraced if any evil befell them while in my charge. Through the PRESS, I want the settlers in the valley, on the route we pass, to know that they are not the *guilty Indians* (some 300 of whom are to be executed at South Bend) but *friendly Indians, women and children.*"

As it turned out, Marshall was not the only soldier talking to the papers. One week later, a letter to the editor written by trial recorder Isaac Heard appeared in the *Saint Paul Pioneer,* datelined "from Gen. Sibley's camp" and bearing no name. "When this outrage broke out the Indians thought they would winter their squaws near St. Paul," Heard wrote. "Their statements will prove true, but the fact will not be as agreeable to them as they supposed."

On the morning of November 6, Sibley watched as Marshall's overstuffed train crept away down the ferry road to the river crossing where Captain Marsh and his men had been ambushed on the first day of the fighting. With the families rode Marshall, the Indian agent Thomas Galbraith, the missionaries Samuel Hinman and John P. Williamson, several mixed-blood translators, and the leaders of the peace party, including Paul Mazakutemani. For whites, the journey was aimed at "housing" the Dakota noncombatants, a movement east before the inevitable move west onto some as-yet-undecided distant reservation. For the Dakota, the journey was filled only with dread and despair. For twenty-five years they had been subject to the Interior Department's fatally flawed process of treaty-making, but this was pure Jacksonian removal, the first step of a forced exodus from their last remaining lands, a dispossession that went far beyond a "relocation," a march with no ultimate destination that threatened them with death both figurative and literal.

Before dawn on November 8, back at the Lower Agency, Sibley's soldiers rose to prepare the condemned prisoners, who were placed into thirty wagons, ten to a wagon, facing each other in chained pairs with covered heads. They departed at the perfect rise of an early-winter sun, Sibley and his staff leading two regiments of infantry, behind which were the supply wagons pulled by mules and the artillery bringing up the rear. The Dakota women accompanying the train as laundresses or cooks were forced to walk. The first day took Sibley and his charges down the government road on the south side of the Minnesota River, with Fort Ridgely visible all the while on its high ridge across the valley. That night Sibley made camp across the road from a farm occupied by John Massopust, a young man who had lost his father, his two sisters, and his six-year-old cousin in the first wave of killings in August. Here, apparently, Sibley sent a courier riding off to John Pope in Saint Paul with the final list of 303 condemned prisoners under his signature.

The next day, a Sunday, the procession of prisoners again headed south toward New Ulm. This route may have been chosen in order to accommodate all of the walkers, wagons, and horses of Sibley's train, but it was provocative in the extreme. Residents and relatives were still burying bodies and cleaning up the town. Approaching the point where prairie gave way to the town's first buildings, Sibley was intercepted by two men, one the county sheriff and the other a twenty-one-year-old named Frederick Brandt, whose military dress and claim to be a major in the state militia struck Sibley as silly. Brandt stepped forward to hand the general a letter and watched as he read: "As I am told you intend to move your Indian prisoners through the town of New Ulm, I declare this an insult, and the people will resist—we are just today burying the dead, which was shot in the last engagement with the Indians and therefore better to move your prisoners out of the sight of New Ulm we don't want to be interrupted by anyone."

The letter also demanded that Sibley turn over any of the condemned Dakotas who had been implicated in either of the two attacks on New Ulm. The general was not about to release any of his prisoners to the local sheriff and his sidekick, but he did agree to move his convoy past the town via the more difficult route on its southern side, edging slowly along the top of the bluff above. On his guard now, Sibley deployed one company of about eighty men on each side of the wagon train with ball cartridges loaded in their rifles. As they passed directly above the town, they came upon a cluster of townspeople of both genders and all ages blocking the road and carrying "all conceivable weapons," including clubs, knives, stones, guns of all types, pitchforks, scythes, brooms, "aprons full of brickbats," and, according to one report, "the proverbial kettle of hot water." One of Sibley's soldiers wrote that "the first I knew, one very large German woman slipped through in front of me, and hit one of the Indians on the head with a large stone. Well, he fell backwards out of the wagon, he being shackled to another Indian that held him, so he was dragged about five rods."

The fusillade ended only after Sibley took up a rifle himself and led some of his men in a demonstration charge, bayonets forward, to scatter the attackers; he wrote later that "the presence of the women and children alone saved the male actors in this attack from being punished as they deserved by the fire of my forces." Brandt, the young man who had met him just outside of town, was arrested, along with forty or so other men. Brandt's claim that he had worked in his "utmost endeavor to prevent the attack" and his demand that the men be released to go back to burial duty met with the wrath of Sibley, who refused to comply. Sibley also sent a letter off to Governor Ramsey expressing his belief that Brandt was only claiming to be an officer in the militia, expecting that the governor, as commander in chief of the state's forces, would take some separate punitive action of his own.

That night, finally, they stopped a few miles short of Mankato, the injured Dakota riding in ambulance wagons. Work began on a wooden shed to house the prisoners, and the arrested attackers from New Ulm were set free to head back home. The spot, just west of the sharp elbow where the Minnesota River turned to the north after its 150-mile course southward from the border of the Dakota Territory, would be their home until Pope sent along directions for the executions. Someone called it Camp Lincoln, and the name stuck.

Over the previous two days, meanwhile, Sibley's message to Pope had become Pope's message to Lincoln, listing the names of the 303 Dakota sentenced to death. The president's immediate response arrived in Saint Paul by telegram on November 10 just about the same time that the condemned men were being hoisted off the wagons two by two, still paired up by their chained feet.

Your dispatch giving the names of 300 Indians condemned to death is received. Please forward as soon as possible the full and complete record of their convictions; and if the record does not fully indicate the more guilty and influential of the culprits, please have a careful statement made on these points and forwarded to me. Send all by mail.

To Abraham Lincoln the law was sacrosanct, the first religion he'd ever found, and all his life he was as sensitive to bad lawyers as a priest might be to false prophets. Now he was engaged as a lawyer, with the understanding that these sentences must become his responsibility, especially in the absence of a trustworthy and authoritative voice from the frontier. He would, over the next few weeks, become the first and only president ever to consider three hundred death sentences all at once. Later Lincoln would tell Congress that he began his review "anxious to not act with so much clemency as to encourage another outbreak on one hand, nor with so much severity as to be real cruelty on the other," firm as ever in his belief that while punishment would be necessary, punishment that failed to fit the crime was no justice at all.

The news of Lincoln's message spread through the halls of power in Saint Paul and out onto the streets of the city. Within hours, or perhaps even minutes, Pope had passed the message along to Ramsey, and from Ramsey it went to the newspapers and to many of the city's leading citizens. Both men began to compose their reactions, but Ramsey's, predictably the shorter, made it to the White House first. "I hope the execution of every Sioux Indian condemned by the military court will be at once ordered," the governor wrote. "It would be wrong upon principle and policy to refuse this. Private revenge would on all this border take the place of official judgment on these Indians."

Lincoln referred Ramsey's message to War Secretary Edwin Stanton, but not for any decision on the death sentences. He had a great deal to consider over the next three weeks, and he was not going to let himself be rushed into ordering anything "at once."

All day long on November 6 the train of Dakota families crossed the Minnesota River at the Lower Agency; the more than fifteen hundred people, with their wagons, mules, and horses, required dozens of ferry trips. The next morning Lieutenant Colonel Marshall led them up to the crest of the valley wall, across the prairie and past Fort Ridgely as they moved toward their winter quarters at Fort Snelling. With so many women, children, and elderly in the group, progress was slow. Not until November 10 did they approach the river town of Henderson, after which they would turn north toward Saint Paul. It was towns like Henderson—and Saint Peter a few miles away—that had received the greatest influx of wounded and distraught settlers during the first few days of the war, and their memories were still fresh. As it turned out, the families' ride through Henderson was as dangerous as the prisoners' had been around New Ulm. "We found the streets crowded with an angry and excited population, cursing, shouting and crying," Samuel J. Brown wrote.

> Men, women, and children, armed with guns, knives, clubs, and stones, rushed upon the Indians as the train was passing by and, before the soldiers could interfere and stop them, succeeded in pulling many of the old men and women, and even children, from the wagon by the hair of the head and beating them, and otherwise inflicting injury upon the helpless and miserable creatures.

One white woman took a nursing baby out of its mother's arms and slammed it into the ground before she was pulled away by some of Marshall's men, leaving the infant motionless and close to death. Like Sibley, Marshall had to take a personal hand in driving off the attackers, riding up to one armed townsperson and using his sword to knock the man's raised rifle away.

The procession finished moving out of the town and then stopped at a small patch of prairie by the river in order to make camp for the night. As Marshall dispatched scouting parties to find and intercept other settlers bent on violence, the Dakota went about the burial of the battered child, who had died shortly after the attack in town. The baby was "quietly laid away in the crotch of a tree" a little ways downriver in a ceremony Brown described as "perhaps the last of its kind within the limits of Minnesota; that is, the last Sioux Indian 'buried' according to one of the oldest and most cherished customs of the tribe."

Finally, on the afternoon of November 13, the Dakota families arrived at Fort Snelling. The procession stopped for one night on a rise south of the federal garrison, exposed to the full brunt of the winter winds, before Marshall moved them to the bottomlands at the confluence of the Minnesota and Mississippi rivers, with the southern wall of the fort looming one hundred feet over their heads. A soldier, Thomas Rice Stewart, described the sudden village next to the water.

> There was something about it so weird, strange, and unnatural it seemed more like a dream than reality. The many and oddly constructed tepees, some made of reeds and rushes, others of skins of animals, etc. The many camp fires, smoke from which made a cloud which hung over the camp like a pall. The barking of dogs, of which there seemed to be a goodly number. The shrill voices of the squaws as they performed their various duties. All of this combined to make it a strange scene.

Concentrated in two makeshift camps, one for the prisoners at Camp Lincoln and one for the innocent at Fort Snelling, the Dakota waited on two judgments. The first was the final removal of the families, the question of where and when their exile might begin, a decision that lay in the hands of the Department of the Interior and the commissioner of Indian affairs. The other judgment now rested in the hands of Abraham Lincoln, the man many Dakotas, even now, called Great White Father. News had already begun to spread, among whites and Indians alike, that the president himself would decide who was to live and who was to die. This was true. But first, for three weeks, the wires from Washington would go quiet.

# Chapter Fifteen

At ten o'clock on the morning of Monday, December 1, 1862, John Nicolay left the White House bearing Abraham Lincoln's second annual message to Congress. According to the protocol of the time, the president's personal secretary carried the carefully hand-copied document down Pennsylvania Avenue to the Capitol so that the clerk of Congress could read it out loud word for word in the chamber of the House of Representatives. Once the reading began, many of the congressmen paid little attention, knowing that the contents of the president's message would be reprinted in the next day's *Congressional Globe*. But even in the absence of pomp and circumstance, those contents mattered. Nicolay liked to call the annual message "a paper latch-key, opening every door," and by later standards the message was indeed rich with content, full of specific policy proposals and detailed reports from all of the executive departments.

Lincoln had used the better part of November to write the message, turning away visitors and pressing the members of his cabinet for contributions or counsel for each section of the document. Never before had a president had so much to communicate in a single message to the legislature and, by extension, to the American people. Antietam, it turned out, had been the high point of the Union autumn, and an ambiguous high point at that. Republicans had suffered wholesale losses during the November midterm elections, results that friends and foes alike viewed as a clear vote of no confidence in Lincoln's military leadership and a stinging referendum on the announcement of emancipation. The president knew that just two or three more decisive losses on the battlefields of Virginia or in the lower Mississippi Valley would force him to the bargaining table in order to consider the dismemberment of the Union.

Lincoln had finally dismissed George McClellan, whose inaction after Antietam had become ever more pronounced and debilitating. The decision solved one set of problems, allowing Lincoln to start his search for a general who would bear down on the Confederates, but it created many others. The loyalty of the rank-and-file soldiers to Little Mac, though not quite as ironclad as it had been before Antietam, was strong, and a small but noticeable number of desertions occurred. More to the point, Lincoln was well aware that McClellan, who had never met a political or military scenario he didn't think he could handle best, would most likely be his opponent in the next election, running as a conservative Democrat on a platform of peace, reconciliation, and noninterference on the question of slavery.

The president's message addressed foreign relations, the national banks, and improvements in the postal system before devoting two pages to the activities of the Department of the Interior and the Office of Indian Affairs. "The Indian tribes upon our frontiers have during the past year manifested a spirit of insubordination," the section began, "and at several points have engaged in open hostilities against the white settlements in their vicinity." Then followed a few sentences, probably with John Ross's pleas in mind, about the "recent troubles" involving the Cherokees in Kansas and the Oklahoma Territory, before the message turned its attention to events in the Northwest.

> In the month of August last the Dakota Indians in Minnesota attacked the settlements in their vicinity with extreme ferocity, killing indiscriminately men, women, and children. This attack was wholly unexpected, and therefore no means of defense had been prodded. It is estimated that not less than 800 persons were killed by the Indians, and a large amount of property was destroyed. How this outbreak was induced is not definitely known, and suspicions, which may be unjust, need not to be

stated. Information was received by the Indian Bureau from different sources about the time hostilities were commenced that a simultaneous attack was to be made upon the white settlements by all the tribes between the Mississippi River and the Rocky Mountains. The State of Minnesota has suffered great injury from this Indian war. A large portion of her territory has been depopulated, and a severe loss has been sustained by the destruction of property. The people of that State manifest much anxiety for the removal of the tribes beyond the limits of the State as a guaranty against future hostilities. The Commissioner of Indian Affairs will furnish full details. I submit for your especial consideration whether our Indian system shall not be remodeled. Many wise and good men have impressed me with the belief that this can be profitably done.

Some portion of the paragraph may have come from the pen of Interior Secretary Caleb Smith or, just as likely, Assistant Interior Secretary John Palmer Usher. But the placement of the last two sentences, along with the appearance of "I" and the phrase "especial consideration," seem to reveal that Lincoln had taken care to insert a particular thought of his own, prompted in part by Whipple's visit.

Lincoln's message then turned to the business of the Civil War and the momentous subject of emancipation, still linked in Lincoln's mind and public statements with the necessity to settle blacks in some distant locale, perhaps in Africa or the West Indies, perhaps on a reservation of their own in the American West. The reading closed with words that would be remembered as the president's most eloquent and economical statement on the subject of emancipation: "In giving freedom to the slave, we assure freedom to the free—honorable alike in what we give, and what we preserve. We shall nobly save, or meanly lose, the last best hope of earth."

The "unjust" suspicions about the Dakota War's origins that "need not be stated" were stated quite explicitly in another document written at the same time, the Annual Report of the Secretary of the Interior, completed two days before the reading of Lincoln's address and published at the same time. After a short preamble that said nothing much of use, Secretary Caleb Smith took a shortcut past any difficult thinking about the troubles in the Northwest: "The causes of the Indian hostilities in Minnesota have been a subject of much discussion. After a careful examination of all the data which the Indian bureau has been able to obtain, bearing upon the causes which produced the immediate outbreak, I am satisfied that the chief cause is to be found in the insurrection of the southern States." Smith added a note from J. R. Giddings, the American consul general to Canada, stating that the agitation among the Ojibwe was also a result of "the efforts of secession agents, operating through Canadian Indians and fur traders."

Smith's analysis derived from wishful thinking and indifference, if not laziness, and it is telling that Lincoln's own report so pointedly rejected Smith's conclusion. In his own addendum to the document, Commissioner of Indian Affairs William P. Dole, who had been among the Ojibwe just two months earlier, also saw no such convenient connections.

> It is . . . almost invariably true that the tracts of land still remaining in the possession of the Indians, small and insignificant as they are when compared with the broad domain of which they were once the undisputed masters, are the objects of the cupidity of their white neighbors; they are regarded as intruders, and are subject to wrongs, insults, and petty annoyances, which, though they may be trifling in detail, are, in the aggregate, exceeding onerous and hard to be borne.

Smith's hurried conclusion may have resulted, in part, from the fact that he had been trying to leave his job as interior secretary since March; he was tired of the administrative demands of the post, unhappy with the administration's increasing emphasis on emancipation, and pining for a district judgeship in his home state of Indiana.

The portion of the president's address dealing with the Dakota seemed to satisfy no one—especially the white settlers of Minnesota and the politicians from the Northwest who wanted to hear only that the president was committed to swift executions—but that ambiguity was part of a classic Lincolnian maneuver designed to buy time. Lincoln's collected works include only one other document written on December 1: a morning message to Judge Advocate General Joseph Holt asking a question he had kept in his pocket since November 13, when he'd first contacted Pope to say that he'd need to review the Dakota trial records.

"Three hundred Indians have been sentenced to death in Minnesota by a Military Commission, and execution awaits only my action," Lincoln wrote. "I wish your legal opinion whether if I should conclude to execute only a part of them, I must myself designate which."

Holt's reply, dated the same day, was deferential but unequivocal.

I do not understand the precise form in which the question, referred to in your note of this morning, presents itself. If it be on an application to pardon the Indians condemned, or a part of them, I am quite sure that the power cannot be delegated, and that the designation of the individuals, which its exercise involves, must necessary be made by yourself. The designation of those upon whom the sentence is to be executed, is but the exercise of the same power, being merely an approval of the sentences and refusal to pardon. I am not aware of any instance in which the delegation of this delicate and responsible trust has been attempted.

The president had expected no other answer. In legal terms, then, he could not pass the buck. The Articles of War not only demanded that he review Sibley's verdicts, but also required him to issue his own. Essentially, he was being asked to retry the cases in the distant and cool light of Washington. But in moral terms, the situation was far more fraught. Lincoln, and not any commission or jury, would have to act as savior and executioner. And in political terms, whether or not he chose to use politics as a guide to his actions, he knew that a presidential election was on the horizon. Execute all of the Dakotas and he might placate the Republican leadership and electorate of Minnesota at the cost of his legal and moral responsibilities; execute none and he might lose the state's potentially crucial electoral college votes.

He needed trustworthy men to aid him in going through the trial transcripts. And to his relief, surely, he had three close at hand, two of whom were capable lawyers and who, remarkably, had returned less than a month earlier from Minnesota and the scenes of the Dakota War. The first was John Palmer Usher, the former railroad lawyer who had been named assistant interior secretary in June, not long after Caleb Smith had made known his desire to retire to a judgeship in Indiana. From the moment he arrived in Washington, Usher had become a sort of acting head of the department, given, among other tasks, the job of coordinating communication with John Ross and the

Cherokees. Usher's performance and measured intelligence impressed Lincoln, and shortly after the October cabinet meeting at which John Pope's intemperate message was read aloud, Usher was sent west to get a firsthand look at the situation in Minnesota.

The timing of Usher's departure suggests that Lincoln was looking for an alternative to Pope's incendiary dispatches as he sought to gather information about the extent of Dakota depredations and the progress of the trials. Usher had arrived in Minnesota in late October in the company of his son Sam and of his chief clerk, George C. Whiting, the department's most capable lawyer and a prominent Washington Freemason. Unfortunately, the written record of their visit is thin, but it is known that Usher and Whiting stayed in Minnesota for several weeks in October and November, conferring with Governor Ramsey and traveling to the Minnesota River Valley to visit with General Sibley and collect a detailed report from at least one freed captive.

Now Whiting made up one-third of Lincoln's review team, along with the Interior Department lawyer Francis Ruggles; both reported directly to Usher, who presumably wrote to or met with Lincoln to provide updates on their progress. At some point on or around December 1, the president provided Whiting and Ruggles with a very specific set of instructions: they were to scour the trial transcripts with great care and identify all cases of rape, all cases involving the murder of women and children, and all cases involving the killing of unarmed men in the settlements. These sentences, in Lincoln's estimation, accorded with the purpose of a military commission and deserved speedy executions. Other instances of violence, meaning shots fired in battle against Minnesota militia or United States soldiers, did not. John Pope's criteria had been rejected, and now two lawyers in the employ of Secretary Usher bent over their work, a new kind of civilian commission in Washington acting to support or supersede the one made up of soldiers that had condemned 303 men to death in fewer than thirty days. Their findings would need Lincoln's approval, but their responsibility was profound.

For three weeks, as Lincoln had crafted his annual address and the Dakota prisoners and their guards languished at Camp Lincoln, the drumbeat for vengeance grew louder and louder. John Pope, the first to hear that the president would review the trials, had been one of the first to respond.

I desire to represent to you that the only distinction between the culprits is as to which of them murdered most people or violated most young girls. All of them are guilty of these things in more or less degree. The people of this State, most of whom had relations or connections thus barbarously murdered and brutally outraged are exasperated to the last degree, and if the guilty are not all executed I think it nearly impossible to prevent the indiscriminate massacre of all the Indians—old men, women, and children.

Pope then raised the stakes, portraying Sibley's soldiers en masse as inexperienced and unreliable, prone to disobey orders as their patience wore thin. Indians throughout the West, in the meantime, needed a demonstration of the government's resolve. "I will do the best I can," he wrote, "but fear a terrible result. Your action has been awaited with repressed impatience. I do not suggest any procedure to you, but it is certain that the criminals condemned ought in every view to be at once executed without exception. The effect of letting them off from punishment will be exceedingly bad upon all other Indians upon the frontier, as they will attribute it to fear and not to mercy."

Pope's language was absolute and inflammatory, his conclusions hasty and suspect, but his fear that some Minnesotans might resort to violence was on the mark. The frontier was boiling, and almost no one, from the governor on down, was attempting to lower the temperature. On November 12, two days after news of Lincoln's deliberations reached Saint Paul, A. J. Van Vorhes of the *Stillwater Messenger* had published an editorial, 'The Indian Imbroglio—Abraham Lincoln, Don't You Do It!' Stillwater lay on the state's eastern boundary along the Saint Croix River, where twenty years earlier Little Crow and his Mdewakanton kin had conducted their seasonal hunts. Van Vorhes was the dean of Minnesota's newspapermen, a Republican recently elected clerk of the state supreme court. In August 1862 he had joined the party traveling west to Fort Ridgely with the annuity gold, only to arrive a day too late and come under fire in both of Little Crow's assaults on the garrison. Van Vorhes's message to his readers, over two thousand words in length, filled three columns of the *Messenger*.

In the name of a thousand murdered victims on our frontier—in the name of scores of violated women and a thousand desolated farms, and hundreds of burned dwellings—in the name of rivers of scalding tears, and of suffering and anguish which can never be written up—in the name of an outraged people whose vengeance can only be satiated by the blood of their destroyers—in the name of Christianity and common humanity, we warn you PRESIDENT LINCOLN, and you, SECRETARY STANTON, never issue such an edict in the face of this people! . . . We tell you plainly and soberly [that] ten thousand men can be found who will dedicate their hopes, their fortunes, and if need be their lives, to the extermination of that race. The war against the rebellion will pale in the presence of the intensity of the war against the savages. "NO PEACE!—DEATH TO THE BARBARIANS!" is the sentiment of our people.

As vitriolic as his prose made him out to be, though, Van Vorhes was no match for the editor of the *St. Cloud Democrat*. Jane Grey Swisshelm was a most singular figure on the nineteenth-century newspaper scene, a divorced woman living with her daughter and running a fiercely abolitionist newspaper in the middle of firmly Unionist country. The title of her newspaper was not only a misnomer, it was a taunt to the largely Democratic community of Saint Cloud, which found the "bustling little woman" from Pennsylvania so threatening that her printing presses had been stolen and dumped in the Mississippi River. Raised as a Covenanter Presbyterian, an insular sect with a Calvinist core, Swisshelm had made a break from the rigidity of her upbringing; at the same time, she still saw in every conflict a clear and inarguable division between good and evil. In the case of slavery, the South was full of malefactors whose sin could not be redeemed in the temporal world. In the case of the Dakota War, she was firmly on the side of the whites.

In this she was the opposite of Henry Whipple. She too believed that an essential difference between blacks and Indians was found in their spiritual nature, but where Whipple saw the Dakota as lost souls in need of shepherding, Swisshelm saw them as devils in human form who existed beyond the horizon of help or mercy. At first, like so many other whites, she had blamed the attacks on Confederate agitators, but by early September she had decided that it would be easier to simply equate the two than to seek proof that they were acting in league. "The Indian and the Slaveholder have been the aristocrats of American society," she had written early in the conflict. "They have been fostered and fed and kept in idleness like a den of rattlesnakes and cage of pet panthers until grown strong and insolent they have simultaneously broken loose to sting and tear those who have fed and fondled them."

By October 2 she had reversed her position on the question of "secessionist agents," writing—probably in a rebuff to the news of Whipple's visit to Washington—that anyone "who attempts to screen these monsters by throwing the blame of their crimes on the white men, is a dangerous messenger to send East." Later in October she had opined that "a Sioux has just as much right to life as a hyena, and he who would spare them is an enemy to his race." But only in mid-November, after news spread of Lincoln's decision to review the trial records, did she finally cut loose.

> It rests upon the people who do not expect to make money by the Red Fiends to arm themselves and see to it that every Sioux found on our soil gets a permanent homestead 6 ft. by 2. Shoot the hyenas and ask no odds of any man. But we do not know a Minnesotian who is not sworn to this. Exterminate the wild beasts, and make peace with the devil and all his host sooner than with these red-jawed tigers whose fangs are dripping with the blood of the innocents! Get ready, and as soon as these convicted murderers are turned loose, shoot them and be sure they are shot dead, *dead,* DEAD, DEAD! If they have any souls the Lord can have mercy on them if he pleases! But that is His business. Ours is to kill the lazy vermin and make sure of killing them.

As editors and letter writers competed to see who could raise the shrillest cry for "extermination" or "private revenge," Bishop Whipple had begun his own campaign designed to counteract the din. On November 8, while staying in Philadelphia on his return trip from New York, he had written Governor Ramsey to report on funds he had raised in the East for the war's white survivors before turning to the topic of culpability: "We leave them really without any government—then after nurturing every mad passion, standing unconcerned to witness Indian wars with each other, looking on their deeds of blood, and permitting every evil influence to degrade them, we turn them over to be robbed and plundered and at last wonder we have reaped what we sowed." His next letter went to Senator Henry Rice, who as a Democrat was the odd man out in Minnesota's congressional delegation. Whipple knew well that Rice was a former fur trader and treaty negotiator in Ojibwe territory, a man who shared his own political leanings.

"We cannot hang men by hundreds," Whipple wrote. "Upon our own premises we have no right to do so. We claim that they are an independent nation and as such they are prisoners of war. The leaders must be punished but we cannot afford by any wanton cruelty to purchase a long Indian war—nor by injustice in other matters purchase the anger of God." Setting aside the question of God's anger, this was a complete reversal of the popular argument that *not* executing all of the prisoners was a show of weakness that would only lead to more depredations, more massacres, more vigilante justice, and, sooner or later, a full-scale national war.

Rice's reply to Whipple was the latest in a very long line of non-replies, although it was far more immediate and personal than most. Whereas men like Galbraith, Ramsey, and even Sibley were likely to stick to well-rehearsed expressions of generic concern, Rice offered a glimpse of personal sympathy, no doubt one that grew out of his own sense of powerlessness as a member of the opposition party. Rice did not agree with Whipple's opposition to wholesale executions, though, or with the bishop's contention that most of the Dakota should have been treated as prisoners of war, and in explaining his view Rice was transported by his anger. "When I know that they opened the throbbing womb of the mother and tore therefrom the unborn infant and dashed its brains against the dead mother's head—when I know that the squaws held the young helpless white girl until savages gratified their beastly passions until life relieved the victim—when I know that infants were nailed to trees alive there left to die in sight of their captive mothers—would I spare them? NO never!"

Rice concluded by saying, "When I sat down to write, I only intended to acknowledge the receipt of your note and to give you assurances of my cordial cooperation, but as my mind became fixed on the subject—my hand penned the running thoughts—Crude as they are I sent them to you." Whatever Rice's personal feelings, though, he followed through with his promise to hold an interview with Lincoln regarding Whipple's concerns and to lay before the president the statement written and signed in mid-October by the collected Episcopal bishops in New York. Rice's subsequent report of the visit was hopeful and discouraging in equal measure: he seemed to have nudged Lincoln into placing Whipple's desire for reform into the annual message, but he also predicted a backlash from Senator Wilkinson and other Minnesota politicians.

On December 3, during the same week that Lincoln's annual message was read out in Congress, Whipple took his case to the people of Minnesota for the first time, publishing "The Duty of Citizens Concerning the Indian Massacre" in his hometown paper, the *Faribault Central Republican*. "Who is guilty of the causes which desolated our border?" he asked. "At whose door is the blood of these innocent victims?" By framing these provocative questions at all—for in the minds of most Minnesotans responsibility began and ended with the Dakota—he knew that he was calling down hatred on himself. "No wonder that deep indignation has been aroused and that our people cry vengeance," he wrote. "But if that vengeance is to be more than a savage thirst for blood, we must examine the causes which have brought this bloodshed, that our condemnation must fall on the guilty. No outbursts of passion, no temporary expediency, no deed of revenge can excuse us from the stern duties which such days of sorrow thrust upon us."

Whipple was not arguing that all of the executions be commuted, just that the number be reduced in the understanding that most Dakotas had been treated infamously by whites and by their own war leaders alike. In his editorial, Whipple brought forth the fruit of what little investigation he'd been able to conduct at the Department of the Interior, presenting his own summary of annuity money that had failed to reach the Dakota. His precise numbers had no hope of accuracy, given his rushed trip through what were surely unreliable files, but the enormous tallies of vanishing funds were a fact not usually broadcast in public. The full and timely delivery of the gold was, Whipple wrote, "a sacred trust confided to us by helpless men," a trust that had been irreparably broken.

Most of his readers didn't understand or care about the annuity money, though, and were far more sensitive to the bishop's admonition to temper their enthusiasm for hangings. "While we execute justice, our consciousness of wrong should lead us to the strictest scrutiny, lest we punish the innocent," he wrote. "Punishment loses its lesson when it is the vengeance of a mob. The mistaken cry, 'Take law into our own hands!' is the essence of rebellion itself." The word "rebellion" was not an arbitrary choice; connected as it was so closely to the cause of

Southern secession, it underlined Whipple's determination to throw ice water in the face of his fellow Minnesotans.

The next day, December 4, Whipple capped his monthlong outpouring of prose with two letters to Washington. The first went to Lincoln. "With all my heart I thank you for your recommendation to have our whole Indian system reformed," he wrote, referring to Lincoln's few sentences on the matter in the annual address to Congress. "It is a stupendous piece of wickedness and as we fear God ought to be changed." He also wrote to Henry Halleck on the same day, asking his cousin to help him keep up the pressure on Lincoln in support of one of Whipple's key tenets in "The Duty of Citizens Concerning the Indian Massacre": the creation of an independent commission to oversee Indian affairs, a nonpartisan group made up of clergy and citizens empowered to initiate change and given the tools to investigate malfeasance. "This Indian system is a sink of inequity," he wrote. "The President has recommended reform. You have his ear. Do, for the sake of these poor victims of a nation's wrong, ask him to put on it something better than politicians."

To both letters he attached a "discussion of the causes of the war," probably copies of his recent editorial. He knew he was trying to get the attention of some very distracted people who were making some very important decisions. This was Whipple's way, singing the same song over and over until the melody stuck.


As Minnesota's discourse boiled over and Lincoln's subordinates in the Department of the Interior began to pore over the trial records, Camp Lincoln was on high alert with the expectation of an attack on the Dakota prisoners. At the center of the storm was Colonel Stephen Miller, once a lieutenant colonel in the First Minnesota, who had political aspirations as a Republican and who had been called back to Minnesota from Maryland by Sibley to take charge of the Seventh Regiment and then given command of the condemned prisoners. Like William Marshall, the man who had brought the Dakota women and children to Fort Snelling, Miller was a conscientious soldier who believed in duty above all and vowed to protect the prisoners with his life and the lives of his men, while wishing that Sibley had left him with more resources to do so.

Miller was handed the reins of guardianship at Camp Lincoln on

November 15, and by the end of the next day he had held a long conversation with the head of a Wisconsin regiment who passed along whispers of "an extensive secret organization" that had collected men from every rank on the social and economic ladder, as well as many of the regular soldiers and some militia. This shadowy group would be waiting carefully for Lincoln's final judgment, and should that judgment land in favor of clemency for the condemned Dakota, Miller was told, there would be trouble: at the least, an attempt to harass the prisoners wherever they went within the state, and at the most, lynchings or midnight murders. Miller wrote a respectful warning to Sibley that should one of these rumored attacks occur, it would be "a matter of deep regret that a sufficient force was not left here to protect the prisoners, or that they were not taken with the troops to Fort Snelling or some other place of security." He added that the sheriff of Blue Earth County "was very busy exciting the citizens upon this subject" and that he had heard many reports of citizen clubs ready to launch their own attacks against the condemned prisoners.

In a subsequent letter to Sibley, Miller noted "a firm and almost universal determination on the part of the citizens to execute the Indians by violence, should the Government much longer postpone it." By "the Government," of course, he meant Abraham Lincoln. Many of his men, he told Sibley, "participate in this feeling and determination," but he reiterated his resolve to protect his charges, even if it meant using force on American citizens or on his own soldiers.

Half a foot of snow fell during the week bridging November and December, and on December 3 the prisoners attempted to set fire to the straw beds in their wooden shed, hoping to relieve their frostbitten extremities. The next evening Colonel Miller received multiple reports, by letter and by word of mouth, informing him that citizens from New Ulm, Saint Peter, Traverse des Sioux, and other river towns were converging on Mankato and filling its taverns. Well aware that he might be facing a thousand or more drunk, angry, and armed citizens, Miller called for reinforcements from the very same towns that had produced those angry citizens and worried about how his own men would respond if asked to raise their rifles against an advancing mob. Two reliable dispatches told him that an attack was scheduled to happen before midnight, and so it was a relief in the early hours after dark when his forces were augmented by several companies of cavalry, their horses foaming from the hard, cold night ride. Now he commanded five hundred men, though he had no idea how many could reasonably be induced to exert themselves protecting the prisoners. With some kind of action imminent, Miller took a hard line, promising to shoot any soldier who disobeyed orders to drive away armed citizens.

As eleven o'clock approached, Miller placed his men below the road just north of Camp Lincoln and out of sight of lanterns or torches. When the sound of many footsteps approached, he rode forward into the night, alone.

"Who comes there?" he said.

"We have come to take the Indians and kill them," came a voice out of the dark.

"Well," Miller answered, "you will do nothing of the kind."

At a signal, the recently arrived cavalry emerged out of the darkness behind the mob, cutting off their escape and rendering them vulnerable from all directions. The attack squelched, Miller told the mass of citizens to go home, but not before he arrested the men at their head. That night Miller left his newest prisoners beside a bonfire in sub-zero winds to ponder their actions. The next morning, after extracting oaths of good behavior, he let the men return to their homes, but not before some of them told him without embarrassment that two thousand more vigilantes would soon be heading Miller's way from New Ulm with the identical purpose of setting on the imprisoned Dakota. According to Miller's informants, the man at the head of this second, larger group was none other than General Sibley's recent adversary, the twenty-one-year-old self-proclaimed militia major Frederick Brandt.

Miller reported this news to Sibley and threatened to make Brandt a prisoner should he make it as far as South Bend, a sentiment he knew Sibley would share. In fact, two days after the previous incident, Sibley had written to John Pope asking that Governor Ramsey officially investigate Brandt and strip him of any actual or presumed rank in the state militia. Pope had forwarded the letter to Ramsey, endorsing Sibley's request for "immediate action," which eliminated the possibility that the governor—who had already written Lincoln on November 10 talking darkly of possible acts of "private revenge"—was not aware of Brandt's actions and Sibley's desire to get him out of the way. But here, now, was new information that Brandt was still at the head of a mob, still calling himself a member of the militia, and still bent on taking the Dakota prisoners away from Sibley's troops.

This second procession of armed citizens never approached Camp

Lincoln, probably tipped off that the first group had been intercepted and that Miller's soldiers were aware of them and unwilling to let them pass. Sibley's hackles were up, however, and there was no need to wait for support from Pope or any other higher-up now that he was a federal officer with the authority of the federal government resting in his own hands. After receiving Miller's report, he pulled rank on the governor, sending him an irritated letter dated "half past two A.M." on December 6. In case Ramsey missed his point, he referred to his new federal status three times in three sentences.

> Much as I should deplore any collision between the United States forces and the citizens of the state, I deem it my duty to state to you, that any degree of force requisite to resist the unlawful attempt referred to, will be resorted to by the United States troops under my command. Other consequences must rest upon those who persist in endeavors to accomplish what can only be done by an open defiance of the authority of the government of the United States.

Another implication was clear: should Brandt succeed in harming any of the prisoners, the federal government would take notice of the fact that Brandt had been brought to Ramsey's attention weeks before his semi-coordinated lynching attempt.

The governor quickly backtracked by delivering a message straight to the offices of the *Saint Paul Daily Press,* which printed it the next day under the headline PROCLAMATION TO THE PEOPLE OF MINNESOTA:

> Death, indeed, is the least atonement which these savage miscreants can make for their dreadful crimes. But the greater the crime the greater the need that its punishment should carry with it the weight and sanction of public authority. It is not the blind fury of a mob to which Providence has entrusted the sword of public justice. The lawless violence which would anticipate the course of legal procedure by the massacre of these helpless prisoners in defiance of the authorities would deprive their punishment of all its legitimate effect.

Ramsey added that "our people indeed have had just reason to complain, of the tardiness of executive action in the premises, but they ought to find some reason for forbearance in the absorbing cares which weigh upon the President." The governor also sent the newspaper a copy of Sibley's early-morning message, and this too was published, though with all references to Major Frederick Brandt expunged.

Meanwhile, Colonel Miller finally moved the condemned Indians into the heart of Mankato. As the *Saint Paul Union* described it, the procession moved through town on December 5 with a "cavalry battalion in front; next, the commandant of the post; next, the field piece, then the long array of blanketed red devils, mostly on foot, chained two and two, by the feet—chains rattling—a close file of infantry on each side, bayonets bright, and cavalry in the rear." Once the prisoners were sequestered inside yet another newly constructed log prison, a further report arrived saying that a contingent of New Ulmers and others at least a thousand strong was on its way, Major Brandt once again in the lead. This time, Miller skipped the diplomacy, threatening to ship Brandt to Saint Paul in chains and adding that "if he resists unless forbidden by General Sibley I shall kill him upon the spot." The report proved false, and in the event, as Miller told Sibley, the "best citizens of this town" had given solemn assurance that they would not let a mob disrupt the orderly dispensation of justice—unless, they added, "the President should pardon or attempt to release the prisoners."

By allowing Miller's soldiers and their prisoners free passage into the heart of their town, the citizens of Mankato were staking their claim to whatever hangings did occur. The Dakota were welcome to march into town, in other words, as long as none of them ever marched out. Many of the citizens of New Ulm, by contrast, were far less satisfied with the turn of events and wanted some blood to call their own. Not without cause, they viewed themselves and not Mankatoans as the primary victims of the past eighteen weeks, and they were none too happy to be thwarted in their efforts to exact some punishment with their own hands.

In the meantime, 303 condemned men sat in their wooden prison, awaiting the word of the president. In early December, the *Mankato Record* reprinted a Tennyson parody, first published in the *Saint Paul Union*, called the "Charge of the Hemp Brigade."

> *Hemp on the throat of them,*
> *Hemp round the neck of them,*

*Hemp under ears of them*
    *Twisting and choking;*
*Stormed at with shout and yell,*
*Grandly they'll hang and well,*
*Until the jaws of Death,*
*Until the mouths of Hell*
    *Takes the three hundred.*

*Theirs not to make reply,*
*Theirs not to reason why,*
*Theirs but to hang and die,*
*Into the valley of Death*
    *Send the three hundred.*

*Hemp on the throat of them,*
*Hemp round the neck of them,*
*Hemp under the chin of them*
    *Twisting and choking.*
*Stormed at with shout and yell,*
*Where wives and children fell;*
*They that had killed so well,*
*Come to the jaws of Death,*
*Come to the mouth of Hell,*
*All that is left of them,*
    *Left of three hundred.*

*When can their mem'ry fade?*
*O! the sad deaths they made!*
    *All the State mourned,*
*Weep for the deaths they made;*
*But give to the Hemp Brigade,*
    *The Devilish three hundred!*

According to Secretary of the Navy Gideon Welles, President Lincoln had already made his decision to spare most of the condemned Dakotas by the time of the regular cabinet meeting on December 4. "The Members of Congress from Minnesota are urging the President vehemently to give his assent to the execution of the three hundred Indian captives, but they will not succeed," Welles wrote in his diary. "When the intelligent Representatives of a State can deliberately besiege the Government to take the lives of these ignorant barbarians by wholesale, after they have surrendered themselves prisoners, it would [seem] the sentiments of the Representatives were but slightly removed from the barbarians whom they would execute. The Minnesotians are greatly exasperated and threaten the Administration if it shows clemency."

Welles's description makes clear that just as John Pope's intemperate letters had been instrumental in causing Lincoln to hold off on approving early executions, so too did the rhetoric of Minnesota's congressional delegation make the president resist rubber-stamping the conclusions of Sibley's five-man military commission. Lincoln was feeling his way toward an understanding of the problem, of its full scope and nature, but whatever inadequacy he felt was likely eased by his knowledge that at least one of the men going through the trial transcripts, as well as the assistant interior secretary, had so recently been in Minnesota. John Palmer Usher and George C. Whiting had spoken with Sibley in the Minnesota River Valley, had met with released captives and perhaps seen the prisoners firsthand, had listened to Alexander Ramsey's descriptions of events, and had read the cries for summary executions in the local newspapers. Now Whiting and Francis Ruggles were moving through the transcripts, taking careful notes, comparing the trials, and considering the reliability of each piece of testimony.

The most visible "exasperated Minnesotians" were three of Lincoln's fellow Republicans, Congressmen Cyrus Aldrich and William Windom and U.S. Senator Morton S. Wilkinson, a tall, serious Michigander by birth who bore more than a passing resemblance to Bishop Whipple and who for most of the war had been a vocal supporter of the president, often rebutting conservative Democrats in debate and carrying the flags of union and abolition in his own speeches. On December 5, the day after Lincoln tipped his hand to his cabinet, Wilkinson rose in Congress to present a petition from the citizens of Saint Paul asking for the immediate and simultaneous execution of all 303 convicted men, after which he presented a resolution prepared in conference with Aldrich, Windom, and Alexander Ramsey: "Resolved, That the President be requested, if not incompatible with the public interest, to furnish the Senate with all the information in his possession touching the late Indian barbarities in the State of Minnesota, and also the evidence in his possession upon which some of the principal actors and headmen were tried and condemned to death."

The resolution may have been a preemptory gambit to bring Lincoln's private deliberations out into the open, or it may simply have been a way to distance the Minnesota contingent from Lincoln's decision should he come down on the side of clemency. Wilkinson followed with a floor speech that cut much closer to bone, complaining of "a general sympathy expressed on behalf of the Indians who have recently committed barbarities in Minnesota" and referring to recent visitors to Lincoln requesting clemency, visitors he was well aware had included Bishop Whipple. If the president was indecisive, Wilkinson continued, he wanted "the people of the eastern country to know what are the barbarities which have been committed."

Most of the rest of his oration was filled with renderings of several of those "barbarities" in florid, gruesome detail, ending with a description of a married couple found by the road, the man headless and slashed from neck to toe, the woman "completely ripped open with a knife." Some of his reports were drawn from true stories, some not, but few applied to the majority of the convicted Dakotas, many of whom had been condemned simply for firing a shot at a battle. General Sibley, Wilkinson said, "ought to have killed every one of the Indians as he came to them," and then he hinted that Sibley's time as a trader among the Dakota might have blunted his ardor for immediate executions.

In conclusion, Wilkinson raised the specter of guilty Dakotas "turned loose among our people" and joined the long list of politicians, soldiers, newspaper editors, and common citizens darkly hinting that any vigilante justice that might follow an announcement of clemency would be blood on Lincoln's hands. "If this Government will not protect them," Wilkinson concluded, the fire in his voice filling the Senate chambers, "they will protect themselves. It is human nature, and I could not stop it if I wished to do so."

That same afternoon, the president sat at his desk and addressed an extraordinary document to Henry Sibley. In his deliberate hand, Lincoln wrote:

Ordered that of the Indians and Half-breeds sentenced to be hanged by the Military Commission of Colonel Brooks, Lt.

Colonel Marshall, Captain Grant, Captain Bailey, and Lieutenant Olin, and lately sitting in Minnesota, you cause to be
executed on Friday the nineteenth day of December, instant,
the following names, to wit.

He then transcribed the names of thirty-nine Dakotas to be hanged,
taking pains to spell their Dakota names correctly according to the trial
transcripts, each name placed within quotation marks and followed by
a trial number and the words "by the record." He finished by telling
Sibley that "the other condemned prisoners you will hold subject to
further orders, taking care that they neither escape, nor are subjected
to any unlawful violence."

Earlier that same day George C. Whiting and Francis Ruggles
had finished their scrutiny of the trial results, work they had treated
with the utmost seriousness, as shown by their careful trial summa-
ries, as well as their numerous pencil notes and cross-references on the
transcripts. Out of the nearly four hundred defendants, only two had
been "proved guilty of violating females," and these they put near the
top of their list, presumably at Lincoln's behest, underlining the word
"ravished" for special emphasis. Their quest to find those "proven to
have participated in massacres, as distinguished from participation in
battles" had eliminated 264 convictions. The recommendations spoke
loudly in opposition to Pope's flimsy standard of culpability—"any sort
of complicity"—but at the same time they forcefully supported the
jurisdiction of the military commission as constructed by Sibley. These
decisions would be debated, then and into the future, both by those
disappointed with Lincoln's clemency and by those who held all the
trials to be an unsupportable farce. But in this moment, his hand penning the doom of 39 men and saving the lives of 264 others, Lincoln
was satisfied that a miscarriage of justice had been avoided and that his
final decisions—to continue with some of the executions and halt the
rest—were careful, clear, and just.

Only in one instance, that of Joseph Godfrey, the ex-slave whose
case had taken up the first two days of trials, had Lincoln been asked
to weigh the sentence on his own, as this was the only verdict on which
Sibley, who favored execution, and his commission, who had used
Godfrey as its key informant, disagreed. Lincoln, looking for reasons
to lower the number of executions without arbitrarily violating his own
criteria, commuted Godfrey's sentence to ten years because he had

turned state's evidence. That judgment made, the list was done. Lincoln finished writing the names and then, that same day, called John Nicolay into his office and asked him to copy the message and to send that copy to Sibley by special messenger.

"We-chank-wash-to-don-pee"—Chaska, Sarah Wakefield's protector—was not on the list. It seemed that he would not be hanged after all.

One week later the president received news of a crushing blow at Fredericksburg, Virginia, where bluecoats under the command of General Ambrose Burnside, his handpicked successor to George McClellan, had made fourteen separate uphill charges toward a low stone wall behind which Confederate riflemen fired and reloaded again and again until the field was a mass of Union dead, more than a thousand in all. The defeat was another disaster, not least because Halleck and the members of Lincoln's cabinet had been instrumental in guiding Burnside to the Rappahannock River crossing in Fredericksburg with visions of a quick, bloodless crossing and a triumphant advance on Richmond. "If there is a worse place than hell I am in it," Lincoln lamented, and asked Andrew G. Curtin, governor of Pennsylvania, "What has God put me in this place for?"

The Civil War, already unimaginably bloody, would have to escalate. A swift resolution in the form of a single decisive battle was a hope of the past. Now the contest would become a game of numbers, what Lincoln called the "awful arithmetic" involved in sending ever more men, spending ever more money, and building ever more machines to smother the South into defeat. The victory at Antietam had given him the space necessary to issue the Emancipation Proclamation, but no one knew what New Year's Day would bring. Confronted with the tragic debris of the Dakota War, he had ordered that some men should live and some should die and he had planted a small seed of systemic reform, but in the wake of Burnside's performance at Fredericksburg, the concerns of the northwestern frontier quickly receded into the distance.

"No man on Earth hated blood as Lincoln did," wrote David R. Locke, editor of the *Toledo Blade* and a famous Civil War humorist much quoted by the president, "and he seized eagerly on any excuse to pardon a man when the charge could possibly justify it. The generals always wanted an execution carried out before it could possibly be brought before the President." More than sixteen hundred court-martial convictions came across his desk during the war, and Lincoln exasperated many of the governmental and military leaders closest to him by taking them so seriously, applying his signature mix of compassion, logic, and legal acumen. "If a man had more than one life, I think a little hanging might not hurt this one," Lincoln said, "but after he is once dead we cannot bring him back, no matter how sorry we may be."

In the case of Minnesota's Dakota Indians, just as in his dealings with recalcitrant or mutinous white soldiers, Lincoln was perfectly willing to sanction executions where he felt reasonable moral standards had been violated and reasonable legal standards, according to the strictures of the day, upheld. On the question of war and emancipation, Lincoln lost sleep, but not so on the many death sentences he confirmed or commuted. Just as the president was famous for his willingness to reconsider capital convictions, he was also well-known for his reluctance to discuss such cases once they had been settled. The historical evidence suggests that once he handed the "black list" of thirty-nine names to John Nicolay, Lincoln was done with the Dakota War. But the Dakota War was not done with him.

# Chapter Sixteen

By Christmas Eve, the slashing winter weather of early December had given way to blue skies and unseasonably mild air, turning snowfall to slush and turning all roadways to mud, but still Mankato kept filling with people. Hundreds rode in, hour by hour, crowding into every available corner and cranny as they waited to witness the event of the century. Christmas on the northern prairies centered on private rituals: a fresh coat of paint for the walls, the careful construction of paper ornaments, tables laden with meats, sausages, home-brewed ale, dried apples, creamed porridge, breads and cakes. In these pioneer days, before a single church had been finished in town, religious observances usually happened at home, with a reading of the nativity scene and the singing of a few hymns and folk songs. But this year, all traditions were disrupted or placed on hold. The execution of thirty-nine Dakota Indians was set for ten o'clock on the morning after Christmas.

Perched just above the sharp, twisting bend where the Minnesota River made its turn toward Saint Paul, Mankato was the most common stopover between the state capital and the southwestern quarter of the state. Every guest chamber was full, or overfull, and so too were many of the private homes that had welcomed relatives or rented out beds. Those visitors too late to find lodgings had gone back downriver or across the prairie to towns close enough to allow them to make a short return ride on the 26th. Many camped in tents or slept in their wagons. More than a thousand soldiers were already present, charged with watching for signs of trouble. Eager spectators were staking claims on rooftops and balconies and windows, in the streets and up on the bluff overlooking town, on the sandbar in the river and even along the opposite shore. Only one criterion served to recommend a vantage point: an unobstructed view of the giant gallows nearing completion on a clear, grassy table of ground in the town's lower plateau, between Front Street and the river landings.

Thirty miles apart, similar in layout and parallel in history, the settlements of New Ulm and Mankato were still so different that they serve as object lessons in two principal threads of American town-making. New Ulm exemplified the utopian urge in western settlement, the idea that an insular group of people could find a refuge away from the corrupting pressure of large cities in order to exercise whatever ideas of society, religion, or politics they held most dear. The Turnerians of New Ulm were, to many other settlers, an odd, suspicious bunch, often referred to as a "colony" and distrusted for rationalist views that disregarded the Sabbath and kept to a social calendar built around exercise sessions at the town's Turnhalle, which also hosted plays, concerts, lectures, and dancing exhibitions. For more than a few locals, looking in from the outside, the activities of the Turnerians seemed too separate for comfort, too removed from mainstream practices to be considered fully American.

Mankato modeled a different sort of freedom. The birth of Mankato, like that of most other Minnesota towns west of the Mississippi River, had been enabled by the treaties of 1851, which moved the Dakota off six million acres of tribal lands and placed them along the Minnesota River. With those treaties, tens of thousands of plots of dark, rich alluvial soil were made available for white homesteaders and speculators. In 1852, one year before the Chicago Land Company sent an exploratory party north to the New Ulm site, brothers-in-law Henry Jackson and Parsons King Johnson had ridden beside the Minnesota River to its southernmost point, where they found a Mdewakanton Dakota leader named Sleepy Eye who was willing to accept food and supplies in exchange for a place to rest and information about the landscape. According to the story Jackson and Johnson told, Chief Sleepy Eye guided them to a spot above the high-water mark just a few hundred yards east of the mouth of a tributary of the Minnesota River the Dakota called *Makato Osa Watapa,* or "the river where blue earth is gathered." Less than six months later the brothers-in-law were in business as the Mankato Townsite Company, bringing people and supplies by steamboat to establish a foothold before other Indians or other white speculators could intervene.

If indeed Sleepy Eye recommended the spot, he had done well for Jackson and Johnson. Ideally situated a full day's stagecoach ride away from Saint Paul and usually open to steamboats two or three weeks longer than New Ulm, Mankato boomed. Within ten years, as the white population of Minnesota Territory rose from 10,000 people to over 100,000, Mankato grew to encompass a major steamboat landing, a log schoolhouse accommodating more than a hundred students, a nondenominational private school, and growing communities of Methodists, Baptists, Presbyterians, Episcopalians, and Catholics. The all-comers impulse put the town into competition with similar settlements along the river—Saint Peter, Shakopee, Henderson, Le Sueur—all of which were working without rest to attract more settlers, business dollars, and steamboat traffic. At the same time, the river valley citizens came to act and think as one community, bonded by family ties, social events, churches, and mercantile relationships. Those bonds were especially tight today; today more than any other day in their short history the whites thought of themselves *as* whites, as one people with one common purpose.

Crews of soldiers and carpenters would continue to work through the evening and all of Christmas Day to make the scaffold ready, but already the structure was transfixing, a towering instrument of death built so sturdily that it might, in the words of one reporter, "serve well for future occasions of a like character." Twenty-four feet square, it was wider than many of the town's houses. Built to accommodate forty nooses, ten to a side, the entire structure was supported by eight equally spaced oak posts fourteen feet high and a foot square. Each of the top rails was notched ten times on its outer edge so that ropes could be draped over and fastened tight without fear of fraying and snapping under the weight of the condemned men. The giant platform on which the thirty-nine prisoners would stand was built so that it could drop straight down underneath the prisoners, as one piece, at the cutting of a central rope.

Even at this unheard-of scale, though, some expressed disappointment with its dimensions. A reporter for the *Saint Paul Press* lamented that the apparatus could have been much larger "had the President been less squeamish, and even then justice would have been defrauded of its dues." The hanging, originally scheduled for the 19th, had been postponed for one week due in part to Colonel Miller's inability to find four hundred feet of properly thick rope in town. Residents and visitors wandered by and stopped to watch the work in progress, chatting with the soldiers and marveling at the size of the structure. One man asked to be allowed to drive a single nail "in a place where it would be of service." Handed a hammer, "the man drove the nail home, into a plank of the platform, thanked the soldier, said he was satisfied, and left."

Closer to the river and in full view of the gallows stood a heavily guarded wooden enclosure containing the 264 Dakotas whose sentences had been stayed by the president, men whom whites despised all the more for being allowed to live. Many white observers reported their satisfaction that the gaps between logs in the prison wall were wide enough to allow an edifying view of the event. Meanwhile, "the thirty-nine," as most whites now called those Dakotas selected by Lincoln for death, had been separated from their fellow prisoners and moved to the back room on the ground floor of a three-story stone warehouse adjacent to the stockade, whose waterside door faced the scaffold across a small lawn. Whispering spectators watched various men and women enter and leave the building—soldiers, clergy, and reporters, as well as wives and sisters bearing food—and surely they imagined the scene inside. At ten o'clock on the morning after Christmas, the condemned would emerge to mount the scaffold and then, in the words of one newspaper, "the slash of a sword, or the stroke of an axe, upon [the] rope, will drop the platform, and launch 39 horrible murderers into Eternity."

On Monday, two days before Christmas Eve, several of the town's leading citizens had approached Colonel Miller to request that the armed men filling Mankato be put to use keeping order and squelching dark plans of "private revenge." Rumors moving along the river valley suggested that secret societies were forming. The governor was still writing to Pope and Lincoln about the threat of "designing combinations" of men and women. And without a doubt some of the whispers were true: in back rooms and private parlors, in barns and even in sheriffs' offices, conspiratorial ideas were being voiced, violent possibilities raised. During this Christmas week, members of some of those impromptu groups were surely in town, measuring their courage as they eyed the fenced enclosure holding the reprieved men. The most dire scenario in the eyes of Mankatoans was that of a drunken mob attacking the jail or, even worse, rushing the scaffold before the platform dropped. Colonel Miller, whose chief strength seemed to be that he took all possibilities seriously, issued his twenty-first general order, a seven-part declaration built around item number four, which decreed that "the sale, tender, gift or use of all intoxicating liquors . . . by soldiers, sojourners, or citizens, is entirely prohibited until Saturday evening, the 27th instant, at eleven o'clock."

If Miller had his way—and more than a thousand armed men all but guaranteed he would—no one would be drunk the night before the executions, the morning of the executions, or the evening after the executions. The occasion would be sober, without lubricant beforehand or revelry afterwards, and it would not be hijacked by out-of-towners with their jealous designs.

As the level of expectation rose along with the gallows, a much more private set of scenes unfolded in the unadorned ground-floor warehouse room where the thirty-nine waited, ankle irons chained to the floor, as the hour of their doom crept closer. A few were dressed in trousers and collared shirts, but most wore leggings and draped blankets over their shoulders. They had known of their ultimate fate only since Monday, when a company of soldiers had entered their log stockade at the heels of former Indian agent Joseph R. Brown, who gathered the 303 convicted men together to read out thirty-nine names. After answering, some with a grunt and some by saying "Ho," each man was told to step forward so that he could be separated from his partner in chains.

At least one of the men who stepped forward, however, had done so as the result of an entirely preventable mistake. When Brown read out "Chas-kay-don," he should have been presented with a reason to take special care. At least three men of the 303 in the enclosure, and probably more, answered to the name "Chaska," which simply means "firstborn, if a male" in Dakota, and the three known examples present on that fateful day were in very different straits. Only one, Chaskaydon, was on the "black list," condemned for killing and cutting open a pregnant woman in the settlements. Another Chaska, a Christian Dakota who also called himself Robert Hopkins and had been convicted of taking part in several battles, but not of murder or rape, had been singled out in a note from President Lincoln, following direct appeals from the missionaries Samuel R. Riggs and Thomas Williamson, vouching for his character and pointing out his efforts to save whites in the first days of the war.

The third Chaska, Sarah Wakefield's protector, was also not on the list of the thirty-nine forwarded from Washington. But when the men were removed to their final prison room next door, there he was, marked for death, while the condemned Chaskaydon remained behind, with no inkling as yet of what a momentous turn his life had taken. No record exists to answer a set of crucial questions: Did Brown, or another officer, call out the name, after which Chaska stepped forward? Or did someone point at Chaska? Is it possible that he momentarily assumed that he was being separated out for further questioning or even to be set free? The question is unanswerable; in any case, Chaska did step forward. In that single awful moment his fate was sealed, though still he did not know it.

The soldiers who escorted the thirty-nine men out of their fenced enclosure began to taunt them, apparently against orders, saying that they were to be executed. Some of the soldiers had been doing this kind of thing for weeks now, ever since the formation of Camp Release, but Chaska and his companions knew they had reason to pay special attention. After they were moved into the warehouse, they were made to wait until midafternoon, when Colonel Miller and several of the men on his staff arrived with a small group of townspeople in tow. With them was the Presbyterian minister Stephen R. Riggs, the man who had collected much of the evidence against them. Colonel Miller read from a paper to Riggs so that the missionary could translate.

> Tell these thirty-nine condemned men that the commanding officer of this place has called to speak to them upon a very serious subject. Their great Father at Washington, after carefully reading what the witnesses testified to in their several trials, has come to the conclusion that they have each been guilty of wantonly and wickedly murdering his white children. And for this reason he has directed that they each be hanged by the neck until they are dead, on next Friday, and that order will be carried into effect on that day, at ten o'clock in the forenoon.

This was the first official reading of their sentence, the first moment since their arrests north of the Upper Agency that any of the Dakota knew for certain they had been marked for death. Most of the men, it was reported, received the news "very coolly." Miller had more to say. The prisoners were sinners whose only hope of redemption was through God, and as such each prisoner was "privileged to designate the minister of his choice," which in the translation may have come across as a requirement as much as an offer. It is unclear if any of the prisoners chose, or were allowed to choose, to have no spiritual adviser. Twenty-four of the condemned chose Father Augustin Ravoux, now fifty-seven, who had come to the Minnesota Territory from France twenty-one years earlier to become the only Catholic priest among the Dakota. Riggs apparently removed himself from consideration, so twelve more were attached to Thomas S. Williamson. These clergy, plus at least three newspaper reporters, two from the Mankato papers and one from Saint Paul, would become constant presences in the room during the week, along with the soldiers guarding them and the women, often kin, who prepared their food.

On Tuesday morning, the day after their separation from the other condemned men, Riggs had returned to their cell to collect statements that were widely published as "confessions," a term probably used in a religious sense. A few of the men were demonstrative, imploring Riggs's help, but, he wrote, they "were immediately checked by the others, and told that they were all dead men and there was no reason they should not tell the truth." "The truth," as it turned out, wore thirty-nine different guises and in every case contradicted the testimony of Joseph Godfrey and the witnesses collected by Riggs and the members of Sibley's military commission. Some of the stories seemed too convenient to be believed, while others displayed logic that was more difficult to disregard. One prisoner said that his only crime was to resist the release of the captives to the peace party of Dakotas. One said that he had fired only at whites who were already dead. One said he had armed to fight Ojibwes, not whites. One pointed out that "if he believed he had killed a white man he would have fled with Little Crow." Some complained about the unfairness of the trials and the lack of representation, and many blamed Little Crow or other leaders for forcing or coercing them into fighting.

White Dog, the man who had met Captain Marsh at the ferry

and called the soldiers across the river before many of them were shot dead, complained "bitterly that he did not have a chance to tell the things as they were; that he could not have an opportunity of rebutting the false testimony brought against him." He added that he and his Dakota brethren "have done great wrongs to the white people, and do not refuse to die, but they think it hard that they did not have a fairer trial. They want the President to know this."

One older man named Tatemina, or Round Wind, who had been Little Crow's camp crier and was described by Riggs as "the only one of the thirty-nine who has been at all in the habit of attending Protestant worship," told his interrogator that "he was condemned on the testimony of two German boys, who said they saw him kill their mother. The old man denies the charge—says he was not across the river at that time." Some dictated messages for Riggs to translate, others handed him letters they had written themselves. One prisoner, Thunder That Paints Itself Blue, who had been convicted of arguing to kill white captives, wrote a bitter note to his father-in-law, the village chief Wabasha.

> You have deceived me. You told me that if we followed the advice of General Sibley, and give ourselves up to the whites, all would be well—no innocent man would be injured. I have not killed, wounded, or injured a white man, or any white persons. I have not participated in the plunder of their property; and yet today, I am set apart for execution and must die in a few days, while men who are guilty will remain in prison.

When it was Chaska's turn, he told Riggs that though he had headed to the Lower Agency on the first day of the killings, he and Hapa were instead sent away to check on a report that a white man was on the road. "Then came along Mr. Gleason and Mrs. Wakefield," Chaska continued. "His friend shot Mr. Gleason and he attempted to fire on him, but his gun did not go off. He saved Mrs. Wakefield and the children, and now he dies while she lives."

This bitter defense was Chaska's final recorded statement. His deeds and words, for most of his life unnoticed by whites, had now in one six-week span been remembered, recorded, and passed along by Sarah Wakefield, by the trial recorder Isaac Heard, and finally by the Reverend Stephen R. Riggs. Chaska could have, and might have, protested the misunderstanding that had put him in the cell, but this is unlikely; to beg for mercy was not the way of a Dakota warrior, and to argue for another man's doom in order to save oneself was considered the act of a coward. The point, in any event, was moot, for Chaska was never told that Abraham Lincoln had lifted his sentence.

That night the prisoners sent a request to Colonel Miller that he allow them to perform an important ceremony, and at nine o'clock, just as darkness fell, the thirty-nine "extemporized a dance with a wild Indian song." The guards, fearful that the condemned were creating a cover or somehow seeking to communicate with the men imprisoned outside, then took the final step of fastening their ankle irons to the floor so that their physical freedom, taken away in increments small and large for so long, was finally reduced to its practical minimum. It was in this state that the prisoners received their kin from among the reprieved men, who were allowed inside on Christmas Eve in twos and threes to say their final good-byes.

"Several of the prisoners were completely overcome during the leave taking, and were compelled to abandon conversation," wrote one of the reporters, who noted that others "affected to disregard the dangers of their position, and laughed and joked apparently as unconcerned as if they were sitting around a camp fire in perfect freedom."

Riggs wrote later that many of the men spoke messages to be passed along to wives and children at Fort Snelling, but they must have understood that those messages might never arrive. How would such words of comfort, advice, or courage travel? When and where would kin be reunited? It was clear to all of the Dakota now that a terrible dispersal had begun, one that had already rent individual villages and families into separate pockets seeking survival. Fifteen hundred Dakotas, mostly women, children, and the elderly, were being held in the camp at Fort Snelling; a few hundred were still with Little Crow, moving to the northwest; untold numbers had joined Sisseton and Wahpeton kin in whatever scattered movements those bands were making across the Dakota Territory; and the rest were here, in Mankato. Thirty-nine were slated to depart on a celestial path they expected would lead to the country of spirits, a land populated by their ancestors; the others knew only that the journeys to come would be long, arduous, and no less mysterious.

Ravoux and Williamson were behaving as any clergyman attached to any military unit in the Civil War would have acted. In this way, and perhaps only in this way, whites thought of Indians and themselves as mostly the same. If Union chaplains felt bound to aid mortally wounded slaves or Confederate soldiers, helping them to prepare for imminent death, so too did the Minnesota missionaries believe in their powerful obligation to send the Dakota off to a better place. Indeed, much ink would be devoted to reports of the successful conversions of the prisoners, but again the evidence of Riggs's translations said otherwise.

Round Wind, the old camp crier, asked that his kin be informed that "I have every hope of going to the Great Spirit, where I shall always be happy." Several of the prisoners expressed similar sentiments, but Round Wind's words ring loudest in the record, because that night a most extraordinary scene occurred when Colonel Miller came to separate him from the others and return him to the log enclosure outside. Whether or not the other prisoners were told of the reason for his departure, Round Wind's contention that he had been nowhere near the site of his supposed crimes had been vocally supported by the missionary Thomas S. Williamson, and earlier that day a telegram had arrived from the president granting his stay. Lincoln and his lawyers still seemed inclined to shrink the number of executions, provided that they could point to a reputable voice of supplication, so Round Wind's final travels, wherever they might lead, would not begin yet. Thirty-nine were now thirty-eight.

At sunup on the morning after Christmas, the small party of reporters was allowed inside for the last time. Wrote one, "The doomed men wished it to be known among their friends, and particularly their wives and children, how cheerful and happy they all had died, exhibiting no fear of this dread event. To us it appeared not as an evidence of Christian faith, but a steadfast adherence to their heathen superstitions." And indeed it became clear that, despite several baptisms and professions of faith, most of the thirty-eight would seek to meet death in the manner of Dakota warriors. When white soldiers followed the reporters into the makeshift cell, they found that most of the prisoners had painted their faces and were laughing off their fate, asking the troops what had taken them so long and why things weren't moving along more quickly.

"All at once" they began a death song, "wonderfully exciting" to the whites, a deep, dissonant singing and chanting that would continue on and off for the next several hours as one by one their chains were stricken away and their arms pinioned, elbows tied behind and wrists in front. As the hour of their execution approached, White Dog said his last piece, again blaming Little Crow and the leaders of the Mdewakanton *tiyotipi* for dragging them into the war. Father Ravoux led them in a final prayer session, and the prisoners were fitted with long eyeless caps made of white muslin. For the Dakota this was an immense indignity, the sign of a bad death; they would meet their fate with heads hooded, in the dark. "Chains and cords had not moved them," wrote one reporter, "but this covering of the head with a white cap was humiliating."

Just before ten o'clock all of their irons were knocked off and their legs given back to them for the first time in many weeks. Soon they were led out the door, arms bound, and across the lawn. They could see the rows of spectators stir and hear the sudden shift in sound as they stepped into the winter sunlight. Aware of the intense attention, they made exaggerated signs of their unconcern, "crowding and jostling each other to be ahead, just like a lot of hungry boarders rushing to dinner in a hotel." Delivered to the officer of the day at the foot of the gallows, they began another death song. Again they shoved at each other as they climbed the steep steps, and then they were maneuvered into position. Up the hill, they could see prairie; downslope, the Minnesota River; all around them, the encroaching whites who had closed off so many Dakota lifeways forever. For only a few moments, they could see the full extent of the crowd, five thousand people in all, what must have seemed the entire white world on hand to see them off.

Rough hands now slid thirty-eight separate ropes over their heads to rest heavily on their shoulders. Their caps were rolled down over their faces, and one by one they lost sight of the world. All of existence became their own singing and the sounds of the murmuring crowd. A commotion erupted to one side as one of the prisoners improvised a vulgar ditty naming the location of a decapitated body, and then a collective gasp sounded as another of their number managed to drop his pants and undulate his naked lower half at the whites. A small struggle ensued as the man's leggings were hoisted up, and then it was time.

Sixteen minutes had elapsed since the prisoners had emerged into the unusually mild winter air. In the hush, a sharp spoken order was given, followed by the sound of three deliberate drumbeats.

In the moment that Chaska "passed into eternity," Sarah Wakefield was two hundred miles to the east, in Red Wing, a Mississippi River

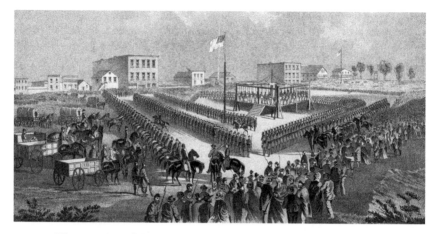

The execution of thirty-eight Dakota Indians at Mankato, Minnesota,
December 26, 1862

town along the Wisconsin border named after a Dakota chief who had
decades earlier vied with Little Crow's father as the most influential
leader in the Mdewakanton world. For eight weeks after her release,
she and John had lived in their old house in Shakopee, but for reasons unknown she had left her husband in early December and taken
her children with her across the state. She would soon return to him,
and perhaps the temporary removal was unrelated to her traumas of
autumn, but the timing suggests deeper and more lasting stresses at
play.

Soon after arriving in Red Wing she had opened a local paper and
read the "black list" of thirty-nine men slated for execution. There she
had seen the name of Chaskaydon, who was described as having been
"convicted of shooting and cutting open a woman who was with child."
Knowing well that the name was as common among Dakota men as
her husband's was among whites, and knowing that her Chaska had
not been tried, much less convicted, for any such crimes, she "felt it was
all right with him" and pushed the execution away from her thoughts
as best she could. That episode in her life, she felt, was behind her.
Chaska had received a reprieve, and whatever hard lash her conscience
may have felt for discouraging his escape to the West, she knew that at
least she would not have his hanging on her hands.

John Pope, in the meantime, had been in his new headquarters
in Milwaukee since November, planning a spring offensive against

Little Crow and whatever allies he might have found, a force that in Pope's imagination amounted to many thousands of mounted men, fierce Plains warriors all. More important to Pope, though, was his new location so much closer to Illinois, his home state and the place where his political and social connections were still tightest. There he could mount a concentrated political campaign aimed at achieving his return to active duty against the South.

Governor Ramsey was in Saint Paul, and Henry Sibley was upriver, in Mendota, having assumed command of the newly fashioned "Minnesota district" of Pope's military department. For the first time since August, Sibley was finally free of the responsibility of prosecuting the Dakota War, and he was looking forward to a winter spent putting his political and business affairs back in order. He knew that he might be leading Pope's columns of men into the Dakota Territory the following spring, but that action was months away and making few demands on his time here at Christmas. His home life was far more amenable now that he had acceded to his wife's request to make a new home in Saint Paul after the new year, a move from the former trading center of the Minnesota Territory to the current capital of the state that would symbolize the completion of Sibley's own personal evolution.

Jane Grey Swisshelm, the firebrand editor of the *St. Cloud Democrat,* might well have traveled to Mankato to provide a firsthand report of the executions but for the request of an unnamed state official that she "go East, try to counteract the vicious public sentiment, and aid our Congressional delegation in their effort to induce the Administration either to hang the Sioux murderers, or hold them as hostages during the war." She had accepted the invitation without hesitation, disgusted that the "Eastern people" had "endorsed the massacre and condemned the victims as sinners who deserved their fate." As the drum sounded in Mankato, she was in Saint Cloud, transferring ownership of her newspaper to a subordinate and hurriedly packing for a move she had already decided would be permanent. Once she had deposited her daughter with her ex-husband's family in Pennsylvania and settled in the national capital, she planned to use her fame and high connections to see Abraham Lincoln herself so that she might talk him into speedily reinstating the executions of the remaining 264 condemned Dakotas.

As for the president, on Christmas Eve he had had a long talk in the evening with Massachusetts senator Charles Sumner about the implementation of the Emancipation Proclamation, due to take effect in seven days. On Christmas Day he and Mary Todd Lincoln had spent the afternoon making the rounds of Washington's military hospitals to greet and thank wounded soldiers before they went home for a subdued Christmas night, their first without son Willie, who had died in February. The next day, as his execution order was carried out in Minnesota, the second floor of the White House was engaged in business as usual, the president's mind on matters much closer to home. Most of the usual Friday cabinet meeting was devoted to hashing out the creation of West Virginia, with Lincoln's closest advisers split three against three regarding the desirability and constitutionality of doing so.

Alone among Minnesota's most prominent citizens, Henry Whipple intended to attend the hangings. But like many others, he had fallen victim to the unusual warmth of the season, setting out to cross the farmlands between Faribault and Mankato in the days before Christmas only to find himself stuck in the mud with a broken-down wagon and no way to make repairs in short order. But he, too, had left the condemned behind. Already he was pondering a way that he might shelter the Dakota most committed to Episcopalianism, those he had baptized before the late war and those who had acted against Little Crow and in the interest of the white and mixed-blood prisoners. The forces massed against him were powerful and many-headed: measures were moving through the state legislature to put a bounty on any Dakota scalp brought back to the capital, while the national government considered the question of the Dakota lands and annuities covered by the treaty of 1858. Even now, Minnesotans' thirst for revenge was settling into the understanding that the state was now theirs, that the need to coexist with the Dakota had been replaced by the need to keep the Dakota out.

The disposition of Indian lands—the "extinguishing of title," as the phrase went—had been the first priority of every leader the territory and state had known. Now, with one mass execution, however paltry and insufficient in the minds of so many, complex treaty questions and expensive efforts to civilize the Dakota could be cast aside. In the eyes of many citizens, this new state of affairs—whatever white and Indian blood had been spilled to bring it about—made for a just and logical conclusion. In the white towns of western Minnesota, shattered families who were faced with forever altered lives and pain that would not end found nothing but bitter consolation, but in the halls of two capitol buildings, one in Washington and one in Saint Paul, many politicians found a yearned-for objective realized more quickly than they had hoped. To many Dakota, on the other hand, it seemed that the story of the past twenty-five years, since the treaty of 1837, had been a single extended provocation designed to goad them into a war that would only accomplish their banishment and destruction.

No one doubted that the monetary burden of the war to Minnesota would be quickly ameliorated. The reservations were federal creations, the treaties were federal documents, and so reparations would be paid by the federal government. The annuity monies once destined for Dakotas and the white traders among them would now belong to the government and could be used wherever the government might need the money most. The reservation land south of the Minnesota River could now be held as federal land for settlers under the Homestead Act passed earlier that year: New Ulm would soon be rebuilt, white towns called Redwood Falls and Granite Falls would soon grow on the former reservation, and white farms would soon emerge on or near all of the former Dakota village sites along the river. Warehouses and levees in Saint Paul and throughout the river valleys prepared for the increase in shipping of every manner of provision. Boom times were coming.

The state's animus toward Lincoln cooled quickly. The president had, in the end, forcefully upheld some executions. And even as he had called off others, he had agreed to hold off on the final disposition of the reprieved men rather than issue any blanket pardons. "I could not afford to hang men for votes," Lincoln would later say to Ramsey, but in political terms the opposite was also true: he could not afford to free all of the Dakota. The 264 men had received a stay of execution, not pardons, with the promise of future dispensation that could mean freedom, extended incarceration, or even hangings—and for most Minnesotans, it seems, that was enough. Perhaps the opportunity to vote against the president's party in November had also dampened some of their fire.

Things were moving quickly in Washington: General Sibley's suggestion that $2 million might be a satisfactory federal contribution to the state's recovery effort had eventually resulted in the introduction of a bill setting aside three-quarters of that amount for reparations— a total that nearly matched the entire annuity negotiated in the treaties of 1858—while Secretary of the Interior Caleb Smith had already agreed to the complete expulsion of the Dakota and the Ho-Chunk tribes, emptying the fertile southern half of the state of Indians. In the days immediately following the hanging, the messages were succinct: Sibley could telegraph Lincoln that "everything went off quietly" and Senator Wilkinson could assure Governor Ramsey that "our Indian matters look well." As far as the Dakota were concerned, of course, there *were* no more "Indian matters" in the lands they had called home for two centuries. But that was, at least in part, Wilkinson's point.

Considering all of the prominent Minnesotans absent from the hanging—General Sibley, Governor Ramsey, and Bishop Whipple, most notably—it is remarkable that somewhere amid the thousands of spectators stood a man whose name would one day far exceed theirs in national and international renown. In fact, when William W. Mayo set out from Le Sueur for Mankato sometime during Christmas week to watch thirty-nine Dakota Indians meet their death, he left two young boys at home, Will and Charlie, who would one day become the most famous siblings in the medical world. Mayo, who had played a small but valorous role in the recent war, sought no special personal closure or satisfaction in the Christmas executions. Rather, it was the educa-

William W. Mayo, ca. 1868

tion of his children in the structure and construction of the human body that brought him to the hanging—that, and the fact that he had been in the Minnesota territory long enough to form a small personal connection with at least one of the condemned men.

An emigrant from England, son of a ship captain and relative of several famous doctors, schooled in medicine and chemistry at Manchester and Glasgow, Mayo had come to America in 1845; he found work as a pharmacist in New York's already notorious Bellevue Hospital and then in Buffalo before finishing his schooling at Indiana Medical College. Married shortly thereafter, he made another stop in Saint Louis before settling for good in the Minnesota Territory in 1854, where, he wrote, "I was perfectly charmed with the new country and I was anxious to see it in all its wild beauty and to tread where the foot of man had never trod before, unless it be that of the Indian." He first considered setting up shop in the northeastern tip of the future state, in Ojibwe territory, but finally settled on a farm near Le Sueur, then in the town itself, where he had slowly built his practice while he ran the town's ferry across the Minnesota River and published its Democratic newspaper for extra income.

After the news of Fort Sumter, Mayo had lobbied loudly to become surgeon of the Third Minnesota Regiment, destined for duty in Kentucky before returning to take a major role in the action at Wood Lake; rebuffed, he continued his family practice and became an examining physician for new recruits instead, preparing lists of the "halt, lame, and blind" in the county and assisting in recruitment efforts when Lincoln's call for 300,000 went out after Second Bull Run. When news reached Le Sueur on the morning of August 19, 1862, that the Dakota were attacking traders and settlers, he set out for New Ulm and arrived one day later to find the town full of dead and wounded from the first, aborted battle, its citizens in a panic at the prospect of another, more substantial attack. Setting up shop in a hotel named the Dacotah House, he had spent the second day of battle performing amputations and other surgeries, stepping outside in one instance to shake his surgical knife in disgust at a pair of citizen-soldiers running away from the action. That had been the extent of his involvement in the war, until the place and date of execution was published in his hometown newspaper.

At the cutting of the central rope, a loud cheer had gone up from the crowd surrounding Dr. Mayo, who watched most of the hooded men kick and struggle for several minutes; the ropes had apparently not been long enough to snap their necks cleanly and so suffocation had done the killing work instead. Twenty minutes after the platform fell away, finally, the bodies were examined and all life "pronounced extinct." The corpses were then cut down, placed in four army wagons, and driven downriver a short distance to a long, shallow, unmarked grave located amid a copse of swamp willows by the water. Thirty-eight bodies were thrown into the pit one by one, after which they were roughly positioned in two rows, feet to feet and heads outward, covered with blankets, and buried under a loose pile of sand.

Such a grave was designed to be anonymous and, given the floods that would inevitably disturb the bones, quite temporary. But no waters would ever wash these men away. Most of the thirty-eight stayed in their resting place only until dark fell, when Mayo and a group of his fellow local doctors, at least a half dozen in number, arrived with spades and wagons, hoping to grab their prizes before a gang of less academically minded men following close behind beat them to it. Stealing the corpses of the indigent, criminal, and unmourned was a habit of doctors across the world during the nineteenth century, and Mayo's local prominence may have given him first choice of the cadavers. The body he chose was, he believed, that of Cut Nose, the most feared of all the combatants, convicted of participating in the murders of two men, four women, and eleven children in the settlements on the first day of the war. According to Mayo, the infamous Dakota was easily identified by an old gash to his face once the sand, blankets, and caps were removed.

The Indian's size may have mattered to Mayo; probably the tallest and largest man among the condemned, Cut Nose was an imposing physical specimen. But Mayo had also known him, if only in passing, thanks to a random encounter early in his days of making the rounds near Le Sueur, when Cut Nose and two other warriors, all described by Mayo as drunk, had emerged from beside the road for a discussion about the doctor's fine horse. Mayo, fearful that his mount was about to be stolen from him, charged at the Indians, turned, and rode off. Cut Nose was the symbol of massacre for many whites, a man who killed with a unique fury and was the central character in any number of credible and not-so-credible stories of babies nailed to trees, pregnant women clubbed to death, or young boys chased down and scalped in the fields.

Once Mayo and the other doctors had departed the gravesite, most

Cut Nose, 1862

of the remaining corpses were divvied up by other hunters after other prey. John F. Meagher, an Irish immigrant who owned a metalsmith's shop on Front Street, left much less of an impression on history than Mayo, but he, too, had a connection to the dead and wished to fulfill a particular purpose. As Meagher later wrote, he accompanied the doctors with a team and wagon for the purposes of making "sure that all who were executed were good Indians," a play on the oft-repeated saw about the only good Indians being dead Indians. As the bodies were removed, he found what he was looking for. "Among those resurrected was Chaska Don," wrote Meagher. "We all felt keenly the injury he had done in murdering our old friend Gleason, in cold blood. I cut off the rope that bound his hands and feet, and cut off one brade of his hair with the intention of sending them to Gleason's relatives should I hear of there whereabouts."

By the time Mayo, Meagher, and the others had gone, only a few of the bodies remained, Chaska's perhaps among them. But when spring came, those too would be impossible to find, as would the grave itself.

The erasure would be complete. The gallows, too, would be no more, despite the desire of some to save the structure for future executions. An auction was held, and piece by piece it was carried off to become emblems of satisfaction, markers of grief, totems of revenge, family keepsakes to be handed down from generation to generation. Still, if another such device was required—and many hoped fervently that one would be—they now knew that killing forty men in a single moment was not so difficult a task as it might have first appeared.

# Chapter Seventeen

As thirty-eight of his kinsmen mounted the scaffold in Mankato, Little Crow was six hundred miles away, having traveled several times that distance since late September, his circuitous route reported breathlessly by Minnesota newspapers that were never quite sure where he was. His new home was a gathering place for many Indian tribes, a body of water that whites called Devils Lake, a mistranslation of the Dakota name *Mdewakan*, meaning, roughly, Mysterious Lake. But both monikers seemed a snug fit. Seventy miles south of the Canadian border in the northeastern quadrant of the Dakota Territory, Mdewakan was a place of legend among the Dakota, who told stories of giant whirlpools that pulled men under the water, of never-ending floods that spread to cover the entire world, and of a hideous and ancient monster who had come to this spot through an underground river.

A white traveler might concur with the description of John Charles Frémont, the Union general, who had once called Devils Lake "a beautiful sheet of water, the shores being broken into pleasing irregularities by promontories and many islands." But that was the lake viewed only in one moment. One needed to watch the water over time to stand in awe of its strange and singular behavior. No river or stream flowed into or out of Devils Lake, making it a rare American example of a "closed-basin" lake, a broad bowl sunk into the northernmost Great Plains whose waters did not simply rise and lower with the rains; rather, it filled and emptied, all of its water unfit to drink, brackish and full of minerals. From century to century the surface level of the lake might change by forty feet or more; in the memory of their grandfathers it had been nearly dry, but now, in early 1863, the water was near its utmost height and mostly frozen, spreading its irregular bays and fingers across more than 200,000 acres of land and threatening to overspill its highest, outermost banks.

Many spirits resided here. And as the new year began and the spring thaw slowly approached, so did many thousands of Indians. Little Crow had arrived in December to join a great gathering of tribes, but whatever reports to the contrary might have been reaching white ears, this was no unified gathering of armies on the plains. Rather, it was a collection of smaller winter villages spread out in defensible positions among the fingers of land created by the lake's many bays, of camps along the Sheyenne River to the south or on the banks of a series of smaller freshwater lakes to the north, where Little Crow and his followers were now staying. From the east came the Upper Agency Dakota, the Sissetons and Wahpetons; from the north arrived bands of Ojibwe and Red River Métis, those descendants of French traders who, unlike the Dakota mixed-bloods, had kept themselves and their culture separate from whites and Indians alike; and from the west came Lakotas, Yanktons, and Yanktonais, even some Mandans and Hidatsa and Arikira from the upper Missouri River. The eight thousand or more Indians gathered on the northern plains were in no sense one people and shared no common agenda, but their concentration did give Little Crow a final opportunity to nurture a frayed and fast-fading dream of forming a confederacy bent on returning to Minnesota and teaching Sibley and his army the full meaning of Dakota war.

In August, Little Crow had talked eloquently of dying with his warriors, but he hadn't said anything about when or how that might happen. Early in the war, probably at some point soon after he'd begun the westward retreat from New Ulm, he had made the decision that, should he fail to accomplish his goals in the Dakota Territory, he would head north toward Canada and the British presence there. In his childhood Little Crow had heard stories of his grandfather's participation on the side of Britain in the War of 1812, an alliance marked by many war councils, promises of fealty, gift exchanges, and side-by-side fighting, including a siege of Fort Meigs and a futile assault on Fort Stephenson, both near the westernmost tip of Lake Erie. His grandfather's allies during those battles had included Tecumseh, who would perish later in the war, shot during the Battle of the Thames. There was something of the legendary Shawnee leader in Little Crow's endgame strategy: his first hope, however inchoate, was to unite his people into one great force, enlisting the Dakota of the plains, the horse riders and buffalo hunters, into the war that many whites had now named after him, so that he might create such trouble for Washington that an advantageous peace might be made. All the while he would keep one part of his mind on the 49th parallel, the line across which lay Canada and the possibility of arms and refuge.

After an initial stop at Devils Lake in October, Little Crow had traveled hundreds of miles across the plains to the Missouri River, where he discovered six hundred lodges full of Yanktons and Yanktonais, his Western Dakota kin, raising his first hope that he might find willing warriors to follow him back into battle. In early December the Indian agent to the Yankton tribes had written to Washington to say that Little Crow and as many as a thousand Dakota warriors were "now on the Missouri River, above Fort Pierre, preparing for an early spring campaign against the whites. They are murdering all the whites in that region." The second sentence was false, though scattered killings had taken place, but the first sentence was true, even though the count of fighting men was probably exaggerated. For a time it seemed Little Crow's councils might bear fruit, but negotiations broke down close to Christmas, when the Yanktons and Yanktonais prepared to move their encampment and sent men to guard their traders at Fort Pierre without making the smallest commitment to the cause of war.

This had left Little Crow little choice but to move well north along the Missouri River toward the region called the Painted Woods, where he might recruit the Mandan, Hidasta, and Arikira peoples who made their winter lodges there. Little Crow and his advance warriors made signs of peace as they approached, but the Mandans only shot at them and Arikiras made ready to surround them. News of Little Crow's mission and the danger it would pose to those appearing friendly to his cause had apparently preceded him. Here, in the open spaces of the Dakota Territory, where tillable farmland was in shorter supply and the discovery of gold and other precious ores was yet to come, the Dakota still greatly outnumbered white settlers and had not yet felt the full military and commercial force of the United States. Little Crow, a man who seemed to many of them bent on bringing down that might on the heads of all of the western Indians, was as much a threat to their way of life as any far-off federal government.

His options growing short, Little Crow knew that shelter and provision for the winter would soon become more important than forming an army, and so he headed back to Devils Lake. Here he crossed paths with Standing Buffalo once more and discovered that their plans seemed to be converging even if their goals remained far apart. In late December, Standing Buffalo had left with a delegation of Upper Dakota Indians to move north up the oxcart trails paralleling the Red River and into Canada, where there were many métis and few white soldiers, in order to look for a place of peace away from the carnage. Little Crow did not go, but he watched carefully. If Standing Buffalo received encouragement, or even simply a cordial welcome, he might have one more card to play.

As Little Crow roamed farther and farther north, ever more distant from the old places of his people, 1,600 of his fellow Dakotas were living under the eye of white soldiers not five miles from where the bark lodges in his former village of Kaposia had once stood. No feature of the landscape was more important to the Eastern Dakota than the confluence of rivers, and no confluence was more important to Little Crow's band, the Mdewakanton, than that of the Minnesota and Mississippi. Long a vital nexus tied to trade, hunting, shelter, travel, and the spirit world, it was now a prison, center of a deep spiritual dislocation and despair that no white could fully understand.

Surrounded by a twelve-foot-high fence, their tepees arranged across three acres in precise rows "with streets, alleys, and public square," they now lived their days in stasis. Abutting the river on "a low flat place in parts of which the water still stands," the captives had endured the harsh, changeable winter as best they could, but their spirits remained low. As one mixed-blood wrote, "We had no land, no homes, no means of support and the outlook was most dreary and discouraging."

A teenage Wisconsin private named Chauncey Cooke left a written record of his first tour of infantry duty in a series of lengthy, preco-

Fort Snelling Internment Camp, ca. 1862–63

cious letters to his mother that he later edited for publication. In one, he described the scene at Fort Snelling: "Papooses are running about in the snow barefoot and the old Indians wear thin buckskin moccasins and no stockings. Their ponies are poor and their dogs are starved." Cooke also engaged in what was apparently a common pastime of visitors and soldiers alike by, in the words of one visiting pastor, "lifting up the little doors and looking in without saying as much as by your leave." More attuned to the helplessness and degradation of the captives than most whites, Cooke noted the "angry eyes" that met him in return. "Nearly all of them were alike," he wrote. "Mothers with babies at their breasts, grandmothers and grandsires sat about smouldering fires in the center of the tepee, smoking their long stemmed pipes, and muttering their plaints in the soft guttural tones of the Sioux."

Cooke was not the only white person peering into the Dakota tepees. Beginning on the first day of their arrival, the destitute families became curios for politicians, reporters, and men bearing cameras. Very few photographs remain from the war itself, but these 1,600 Dakotas represented no danger to whites and were now close enough to the ever more numerous studios in Saint Paul that a windfall could be had. No Mathew Brady or Alexander Gardner had roamed the battlefields of Minnesota, but still "The Dead of Antietam" found an analogue in

Dakota women at Fort Snelling Internment Camp, ca. 1862–63

many dozens of portraits and commemorative postcards of the captive families held at Fort Snelling. For the first time, a rich visual record emerged. The bluff one hundred feet above the camp provided a dramatic view of the tepees, highlighting their arrangement in tightly packed straight lines and providing an unsettling contrast to the circular layout of a traditional Dakota village. But it was the photos of individual Dakotas that sold best, images that banked on all of the usual associations with Indians: nobility, savagery, primitiveness, and most especially tragedy. Indians captivated the white imagination precisely because they seemed to be vanishing.

Of the true lives of their subjects the photographers knew nothing, and the photos did little to reveal individual personalities. Still, if the pictures were intrusive and patronizing, they were also mesmerizing. The stock shot captured a woman seated outside her tepee, staring forward without expression; only beneath flat eyes did something seem to stir at a great remove from the man behind the camera. These images were mailed all over the United States and even overseas. Some also found their way into the hands of the captive Indians at Mankato, traveling with letters that were first censored by Major Joseph R. Brown and other representatives of the government.

The list of people, land, objects, and freedoms that been taken away from the Dakota families was long. Their wagons, yokes, and harnesses were now lost or had been confiscated, while all of their horses, oxen, cows, and mules had died, vanished, or been sold to pay for their upkeep. To make them winter on an open flat protected only by a two-inch-thick wooden fence was, in their eyes, insanity; as the missionary John P. Williamson had written in mid-November, "They would like to have some place in the woods a few miles off and as they are here I think it would be the best they could do for them. It is going to be a hard time for the Christian Indians. Temptation comes in like a flood. If their enemies cannot destroy them by the sword they will destroy them by corruption."

On November 19, before the enclosure was completed, the *Saint Paul Pioneer* reported that "an Indian squaw" had been killed and added, "we doubt not but there will be many such accidents if Abraham don't consent to let them hang." A fusillade of dueling articles had then appeared doubting the charge or demanding an investigation and punishment, until a letter published three days later in the *Saint Paul Daily Union* seemed to have settled on an agreed-upon version: "The truth of the matter appears to be, that the squaws have been in a habit of gathering wood for their campfires and one of them, thus engaged, having wandered some little distance from the encampment, was seized by a number of soldiers and brutally outraged."

Another series of general orders, almost identical to those issued by Sibley and Marshall on the marches of early November, had threatened court-martial and execution should such incidents recur, but the camp was too large to create any confidence in their enforcement. In the end, the threat of disease did more than anything else to keep renegade soldiers and parasitic civilians away. The measles raged up and down the rivers that winter, along with diphtheria and typhoid, all of which made their way into the camp in short order. As Stephen R. Riggs wrote in mid-December, "Since the Dakota camp has been placed at Fort Snelling, quite a number have died of measles and other diseases. I learn that their buried dead have, in several instances, been taken up and mutilated. They are now keeping their dead or burying them in their tepees." Henry Whipple wrote to his wife, Cornelia, predicting that as many as three hundred Indians would die before the warmer months, and shortly thereafter Riggs reported that "the crying hardly ever stops" and that "from five to ten die daily."

The day of the hangings brought the camp low, the embers of white retribution stoked by a small, vocal number of soldiers who, as always, made it their purpose to make the prisoners aware of outside events they might find distressing. The Dakota families took little solace in Lincoln's intervention, not with thirty-eight dead and the final disposition of the reprieved men still as mysterious as their own. "The ever-present query was, 'What will become of us, and especially of the men?'" wrote John P. Williamson, the missionary's son. "With inquisitive eyes they were always watching the soldiers and other whites who visited them, for an answer, but the curses and threats they received were little understood, except that they meant no good. With what imploring looks have we been besought to tell them their fate."

Williamson and Samuel Hinman, Bishop Whipple's protégé, had traveled every step of the way with the captive families and now lived among the Dakota in their encampment. After the executions they were joined for many days at Fort Snelling by Father Ravoux, Stephen

Bishop Whipple confirming Dakota Indians,
Fort Snelling Internment Camp, April 1863

R. Riggs, and the old Presbyterian missionaries Samuel and Gideon Pond, along with various clergy from Saint Paul. Daily services were held by each of the various denominations, wrote Whipple, noting that the prisoners who attended "were subdued, and felt very sore because their chiefs and medicine-men had misled them in their prophecies of a successful war."

The bishop visited once a week, performing baptisms and confirmations, accepting surrendered charms and medicine bags, and conferring with the other religious men on the site. Noting a set of stitches in Samuel Hinman's scalp, Whipple extracted the story from him: one night after dark "some white roughs from St. Paul" had forced their way into the camp and assaulted Hinman, who was left bleeding and unconscious but not bowed. "Those who live much with the Indians," wrote Whipple, referring to Hinman's stoic acceptance of his scar, "seem to imbibe their spirit of fortitude and apparent indifference to suffering."

Whipple now began to concoct a plan to shelter those former members of the peace party who wished to stay in the state and become Episcopalians. At the same time, he wrote perhaps his most pointed and personal letter of the war, having heard, accurately, that Henry Sibley was seeking the go-ahead to execute fifty of the reprieved prisoners still held in Mankato and place the remainder in prison for life. On March 7, Whipple wrote to the general, saying he was "sure that our friendship will be a sufficient apology for addressing you upon the subject of the Indian prisoners at Mankato." Then he continued in an entirely atypical vein, calling Sibley to personal account.

> Your official report to Gen. Pope states explicitly that these men came to you under a flag of truce. Captives have declared the same to me . . . Officers have told me privately that the trial was conducted with such haste as to forbid all justice. I have even been informed by one high in command that of those executed there was one innocent man. The civilized world cannot justify the trial by military commission of men who voluntarily came in under a flag of truce . . . I have hitherto refrained from saying one word to any public officer. May I not ask you to look at this subject again in this view of the matter. I believe you will change your views.

The request was remarkable: he was asking Sibley to examine his own conscience, to consider the moral propriety of disregarding the flag of truce the general himself had encouraged and the results of trials that the general himself had ordered, organized, and overseen.

This may have been the only such letter Sibley ever received in the course of his career, and he replied with heat. "There were no such flags, strictly speaking, used," he wrote, the "strictly speaking" adding a touch of hair-splitting that belied his seeming assurance. He employed no such legalese, however, in explaining his stance toward the captured and surrendered Dakota. "If I had not received the President's orders to the contrary," Sibley wrote, "I should have executed these Indians as fast as convicted."

None of the hardships of Sarah Wakefield's captivity—the initial burst of terror, the endless nights full of fear, the insults of drunken Indian warriors, the uncertainty of her fate—were as harrowing for her as the first few months of her freedom. The "trouble" about which she wrote so frequently and in such broad strokes seems to have been less social than moral, some notorious event in her past or tendency in her present that caused the church to keep her at arm's length and forced her personal relationship to God out of the usual channels. And now she was also trying to make sense of Chaska's death, an event that seems to have haunted her every day.

At some point after her move to Red Wing and in the new year, she had picked up a newspaper and found there the reprinted "confessions" gathered by the Reverend Stephen R. Riggs. Reaching the transcription of Chaska's interview, she saw her own name printed twice, as if to make sure she could make no mistake in her reading: "Then came along Mr. Gleason and Mrs. Wakefield. His friend shot Mr. Gleason and he attempted to fire on him, but his gun did not go off. He saved Mrs. Wakefield and the children, and now he dies while she lives."

Guilt lashed her, and over one forty-eight-hour period in March, she wrote two unnerving letters that demonstrated her precarious state of mind. The first, on the 22nd, went to Riggs, expressing her anger over Chaska's mistaken hanging and demanding an explanation. "I understand that Chaska's mother hung herself the day he was executed," she began. That piece of information, wherever she'd heard it, was incorrect, but her tone was set and she went on, one sentence after another, in rushed and rattled prose such as she never wrote in any other surviving private or public document.

> I would be pleased to learn the particulars also in what way and by whom the mistake was made whereby an innocent man was hanged. I did not fully understand the day you was here, as I am about publishing a narrative of my life among the Indians every thing of any moment is of course necessary that is any way connected with that family names of course I care not to bring in to print but every occurrence I shall want to give to the public.

Here is the first suggestion that the narrative she would soon publish, a book that would become one of the most widely known accounts of the war, may have been born at least in part out of her dismay at Chaska's fate and her desire to create a public argument for his innocence, tied always to her need to defend herself against the charge that she had become his lover. The next day, on March 23, she poured even more of her bewilderment and grief into a letter to Abraham Lincoln. By this point the president had heard about his handling of the Dakota War from bishops, missionaries, state and national legislators, newspaper editors, citizens' assemblies, and, indirectly, the Minnesota voters who had helped to reduce the size of the Republican majority in Congress in November. But no one else had written to him as Sarah did now, outlining an acknowledged case of mistaken identity that she viewed as entirely intentional.

"I will introduce myself to your notice as one of the Prisoners in the late Indian War in Minnesota," she began, and then told Lincoln of her capture, Chaska's role in her deliverance, his arrest and trial, his commutation, and the "sad mistake in the number, whereby Chaskadan who saved me and my little family was executed in place of the guilty man this man is now at Mankato living, while a good honest man lies sleeping in death." Next she turned to a matter that Lincoln couldn't possibly be expected to adjudicate.

> I am extremely sorry this thing happened as it injures me greatly in the community that I live. I exerted myself very much to save him and many have been so ungenerous as to

say I was in love with him that I was his wife &c, all of which is absolutely false. He always treated me like a brother and as such I respect his memory and curse his slanderers.

The blame, Sarah wrote, belonged to "a certain Officer at Mankato who has many children in the Dakota tribe," a statement that could only refer to Joseph R. Brown, the former Indian agent known for his lifelong pursuit of Indian women, the same man who had come to the prisoners' enclosure to read out the names of the thirty-nine. She referred vaguely to a "promise" made to her at the trial—an odd contention given the finding of guilt and the sentence of death—and described how she discovered the mistake via Riggs's translations of the prisoners' final "confessions." Then she made a plea that Lincoln might make things right—"it would be extremely gratifying to me to have these heedless persons brought to justice"—but only in passing, as the real point of her letter seemed to be something much more personal.

I am abased already by the world as I am a Friend of the Indi- ans. This family I had known for 8 years and they were Farmers and doing well. Now this poor old Mother is left destitute, and broken hearted, for she has feeling if she is an Indian, surely we are Brothers all made by one God? we will all meet some day, and why not treat them as such here. I beg pardon for troubling you but there is much said in reference to his Execu- tion. The world says he was not convicted of Murder then why was he Hanged? Then they draw their own conclusions: if this could be explained to the world a great stain would be lifted from my name. God knows I suffered enough with the Indians without suffering more now by white brethren & sisters.

Lincoln received thousands of letters every year from private citi- zens seeking office, proposing policy, praising or condemning the con- duct of the Civil War, selling goods or services, or outlining personal grievances. A high proportion of these supplicants or critics began their letters by begging the president's forgiveness for intruding on him "amidst his multitude of cares," or some other such phrase. John Nicolay, John Hay, and various assistant secretaries handled most of this mail and forwarded what seemed important. The president's per- sonal history, melancholy countenance, and well-earned reputation for compassion made him a tabula rasa upon which people wrote their dreams, hopes, anxieties, and terrors, whether or not he was able to respond. Bishop Whipple had shaken Lincoln's hand, while Sarah Wakefield's message seems to have disappeared into a great whirlpool of anonymity. But both were saying the same thing in their appeals for a more humane consideration of the plight of the Dakota.

"God and you Sir," Sarah closed, "protect and save them as a people."

# Chapter Eighteen

The shelling and evacuation of Fort Sumter had taken place only twenty-one months earlier, but by the time 1863 arrived the Civil War seemed to have lasted an eternity. Time now sat as heavy on Abraham Lincoln as any of his other cares; on many days, the future seemed to hold only a slow, endless journey down an ever-widening river of blood. Battle along the lower Mississippi River had turned against the Union. The despondency left in the wake of Fredericksburg refused to abate, and by the end of 1862 haggard Ambrose Burnside had been shuffled off to Ohio after fewer than three months in command and replaced with Fighting Joe Hooker, a career federal officer who was handsome, brash, self-assured, and prone to expressing his distrust of civilian control of military affairs. It was a sign of how farcical and disheartening Lincoln's search for a ranking field general had become that his letter to Hooker announcing the appointment also included a warning about the evils of military dictatorships.

The president spent New Year's morning wrapping up his final changes to the text of the Emancipation Proclamation. He had hoped to print and issue the official proclamation by noon, but a single error in wording had created a three-hour delay, a hiccup in the flow of history that Lincoln filled by walking downstairs at eleven o'clock to greet the crowd at the annual White House levee. He found the East Room full of diplomats, Supreme Court justices, cabinet members, generals, veterans of the War of 1812, and the general public, who had begun lining up hours earlier. Three hours of vigorous greetings left his hand trembling and so weak that he'd had to pause for several moments before putting his signature to the final, corrected text of the proclamation. With one painstaking pen stroke, more than three million slaves were made free, a moment that had little immediate effect but filled the air like a sudden change of climate. The prosecution of the war went on much the same, but the stakes were utterly transformed: a Union victory would now mean a country whole *and* without slavery. Union soldiers were now fighting not to restore the same country they had lived in before but to institute an entirely new one.

And what would happen to the freed slaves? Lincoln continued to occupy himself with the question of where they might most magnanimously be encouraged to go. His hopes for a colony in Panama all but dashed, he now explored possibilities in Africa, South America, and Canada, and even began to listen to suggestions that the freed slaves be concentrated in some western territory. Not on reservations, exactly; not removed, exactly. John Nicolay spent part of his New Year's Day finishing an editorial that would be published on January 2 in the *Daily Morning Chronicle,* in which he maintained that one of the proclamation's great achievements would be the permanent separation of black and white.

> The two races cannot live together under the contingencies of future growth and expansion. The white man is the child of the snow, the black man is the child of the sun. One finds his natural and congenial home in the North, the other in the South. The accidents of destiny may confuse and change their abiding place for a time, but the same destiny is in its grander operations always true to nature, and will in due time lead each to his land of promise. We can hardly be mistaken in predicting that the United States are to be the theater of the white man's achievements for some centuries to come; and we may as confidently hope that a great and useful future may be wrought out by the black race in the equatorial regions of Central and South America.

In a roundabout way, the Emancipation Proclamation also helped to herald a sea change in the Lincoln administration's handling of Indian affairs, when Interior Secretary Caleb Smith resigned his post just before the new year, in part because of his firm opposition to emancipation. One thing above all recommended John Palmer Usher, the new secretary, over Smith: he seemed to want the job. One of his first steps was to answer Minnesota senator Wilkinson's resolution asking that Lincoln and his administration supply "the information in his possession touching the late Indian barbarities in the State of Minnesota, and also the evidence in his possession upon which some of the principal actors and headmen were tried and condemned to death."

Following Smith's departure, Usher finally received an official report from the Indian agent Thomas Galbraith. Galbraith's report was sent eastward on February 7, later than Usher would have liked, and the agent had taken extra care in constructing his chronology of events, arranged so as to downplay his absences, his abdication of authority, and the extent of that summer's unrest among the Dakota. Attached to Usher's report and running for thirty-one pages, the letter stated, in a vintage Jacksonian phrasing, that the "radical moving cause of the outbreak" was "the ingrained and fixed hostility of the savage barbarian to reform, change, and civilization." Galbraith also included his contention that certain white agitators had fanned the flames of war: "That there was any *direct* interference by rebel emissaries with the annuity Indians I do not have evidence sufficient to assert with any degree of certainty," Galbraith wrote, "yet I am clearly of the opinion that rebel sympathizers did all in their power to create dissatisfaction among the Indians in my agency, and I firmly believe that time will bring out in full relief this fact not only, but more—much more. Let us wait and see; 'sufficient unto the day is the evil thereof.'"

He was willing to blame the traders for the war, in other words, but not yet in public, not until, perhaps, they were delicensed. Galbraith had no doubt that Myrick and the other traders had been "agitating" the Dakota to serve their own interests, encouraging them to distrust the government's ability to provide the annuities and continue to depend primarily on credit from the traders. "Rebel sympathizers," in any event, did not mean Southern spies or out-and-out traitors: it simply meant Democrats who bore no love for a war that threatened to take away money from the Dakota, money they viewed in many cases as rightfully theirs. It did not help the traders any more than it helped the Dakota that Galbraith, a Republican functionary, had spent all summer playing soldier, raising the Renville Rangers and exhibiting every sign than he was not long for his own job on the reservation. Galbraith's contentions that the traders had been "tampering with the Indians and exciting their apprehensions and distrust against the government" may have been correct. But the notion that responsibility for the outbreak belonged more to the traders than to the Indian agent charged with the care and protection of the Dakota bordered on ludicrous.

Usher understood this. He was no distant assessor. He had been in Minnesota in the immediate aftermath of the war and had conferred with many people in positions not so different from Galbraith's, including their mutual friend Alexander Ramsey. Still, his own conclusions were much less assured. "As to the real cause of the recent Sioux outbreak," he began, "it is difficult, if not wholly impossible, at the present time, to determine with that degree of certainty which the character and magnitude of its results demands. Conflicting opinions have been expressed, even by those who had enjoyed the best opportunities for an intelligent and correct judgment." The document went on with an almost meticulous evenhandedness, acknowledging Dakota dissatisfaction with treaties—the "misunderstandings" in treaty provisions, the confusions caused by overlapping treaties, and even the white fraud that had followed behind the treaties in the form of unnamed "unscrupulous and designing persons whose cupidity is ministered to by misrepresentations and intrigue," all complaints that Little Crow and most other Dakota leaders would have made themselves.

Usher took at face value Galbraith's contention that "the most ample arrangements" had been made for the Dakota's "civilization and material advancement," a statement that was true, at least as far as the agent's promotion of agricultural husbandry and support of the "farmer Indians" might demonstrate. Galbraith's accompanying claim—that the Dakota's "general and cordial co-operation with him afforded reasonable assurance of eminent success, and rendered their future prospects bright & cheering"—was more difficult to believe, but Usher let it pass. In this manner, long stretches of Usher's report became a gloss on Galbraith's, alternately supporting and distancing itself from the agent's explanations. The secretary's conclusion hinted at a deeper understanding of the forces at play, but ultimately he could not break free of the standard supposition of the Indian's savage inferiority that prevented any real insight.

> From all the inquiry and examination I have been able to make, I am inclined to the opinion that the Sioux outbreak was chiefly caused by the unfortunate affair, in which a few dissolute and reckless young men of the tribe become involved at Acton, through the influence of intoxicating liquor —that fruitful source of embarrassment in the management of our Indian relations, and of loss to the Indians and to the white settlers in their vicinity. This occurrence happened at a time when the minds of the Indians had become restless and agitated by accounts, incautiously or maliciously communicated to them, of the bloody conflict in which the army of the United States had become engaged, and when they had become distrustful and uneasy because of the delay which had occurred in the payment of their annuities,—the reason for which had been misrepresented to them, as is alleged, by evil disposed persons who taught them to believe that the Government had been broken up, and they left to take care of themselves as best they could. Exasperations thus produced, added to their long felt dissatisfaction at having parted with their lands, no doubt led them to attempt to re-possess themselves of their former hunting grounds,—now become fruitful fields in the hands of the industrious whites,—and to wreak, with their accustomed ferocity, vengeance upon all the defenseless inhabitants within their reach, for their imaginary wrongs.

Usher dismissed the idea that Confederate agitators had been behind the outbreak while fully supporting Galbraith's notion that some whites—the traders and their employees—had been whispering in Dakota ears. But Usher also included a rebuke of Galbraith's ill-timed decision to abandon his responsibilities as he formed the Renville Rangers.

> I cannot but regret, however, the misdirected zeal and patriotism which induced the Agent to leave his post at so critical a moment, nor escape the painful conviction that his contin-

ued presence there might possibly have been the means of averting the terrible calamity which so [soon] succeeded his departure . . . the fact that the Agent—the only officer of the Government to whom they looked for the payment of their anxiously expected annuities, and for counsel and guidance in trouble—had taken many of the employees and most of the able-bodied white men in the neighborhood, and left the Indian country, was not well calculated to remove from their minds the impression that they had been abandoned by the Government.

Finally, the new interior secretary put to rest the notion, still receiving attention in Minnesota, that the Ojibwe and Dakota had entered into a bona fide military pact. He briefly recounted how the death of Indian agent Lucius Walker had tamped down what apparently was a growing personal animus between Walker and the Ojibwe chief Hole in the Day, a conclusion that demonstrated a sophisticated understanding of the situation and leads one to assume he had conferred with John Nicolay or William P. Dole before writing his report. In total, Usher's document was a remarkably clear-eyed refutation of much of the prevailing wisdom that held all Dakota Indians wholly to blame for the events of 1862 in Minnesota. Perhaps it gave too much play to Galbraith's contentions of the traders' agitation, especially since it was clear that Galbraith had ample reason to cover his tracks, but of the hundreds of official communications generated during the war, Usher's was one of the most temperate. In any event, whatever the document's strengths and shortcomings, Usher's words would stand as the Lincoln administration's—and so Lincoln's—final official statement on the subject.

The Christmas executions did not sit heavily on the president. Wholesale vengeance had been averted. The expectation of the swift disposition of monetary reparations and Indian lands to Minnesotans had clearly mollified important political supporters. In the Mississippi Valley, the specter of Cherokee regiments fighting for the South had instead turned into the reality of thousands of Cherokee refugees who had been driven out of the Indian Territory and were now living in Kansas. John Ross was with his family in Philadelphia, and while Cherokee general Stand Watie continued to make incursions onto Union lands, these represented regional annoyances and not a national military crisis. In the Southwest, after years of armed conflict between whites and Indians, Kit Carson had emerged as the Union's point man in the fight to bring the Navajo to heel and force them onto reservations. On the ground in New Mexico, the conflict was every bit as stubborn, bloody, and tragic as that in Minnesota, but the view from Washington was different. Lincoln and his cabinet knew that the Southwest would not become another theater of the Civil War, that the Confederates had been driven out of the region and would not be returning. The administration's Indian matters did indeed "seem well."

With the executions out of the way, the executive branch could resume, at least outwardly, its more customary ceremonial relationship to the Indian frontier. On March 27, 1863, Lincoln received a resplendent delegation of tribal chieftains from the Cheyenne, Arapaho, Comanche, Apache, and other western tribes. No record remains to say if they had been summoned or had asked to make the long journey east for an audience with the Great White Father, but such gatherings often did not have any official purpose other than to air general grievances. No treaty with these tribes was under immediate consideration, no outright war under way, and the air of the audience was that of a levee, with all the requisite pageantry, regalia, and affirmations of friendship.

Arrayed in a row, fourteen Indians sat in front of a crowd of luminaries including Secretaries Seward, Chase, and Welles, New York attorney general Daniel S. Dickinson, Lincoln's personal physician Anson G. Henry, and various reporters, dignitaries, and society women. Altogether the assemblage represented a more powerful version of the visitors who had stepped off steamboats to witness the annuity payments along the Minnesota River; gawking at Indians was apparently a pastime that cut across boundaries of class and influence.

John Nicolay did his officious best to keep the whispering onlookers quiet as they waited for Lincoln to arrive. As for the guests, an anonymous writer for the *Daily Morning Chronicle*—probably Nicolay himself—described "the hard and cruel lines in their faces which we might expect in savages; but they were evidently men of intelligence and force of character." The same reporter described how the president stepped into the circle at 11:30 and shook each chief's hand as Commissioner Dole stood by, introducing each by name, after which Lincoln listened to unrecorded speeches by the Cheyenne chief Lean

Indian delegation to the White House, March 1863

Bear and the Arapaho chief Spotted Wolf. When it was his turn, the president spoke through a translator, addressing the Indian audience in front of him but also well aware of the whites in the crowd and the reading public beyond.

"You have all spoken of the strange sights you see here, among your pale-faced brethren, the very great number of people you see; the big wigwams; the difference between our people and your own," he began, and then turned to scientific matters. "We pale-faced people think that this world is a great, round ball," he said, and at this cue a globe was brought into the room. The president then called on Dr. Henry, whom he called "Professor," to "explain to you our notions about this great ball, and show you where you live."

Henry stepped forward and obliged his friend with a tutorial, no doubt accompanied by many exaggerated gestures, explaining the formation of the earth, the relative quantities of land and water, and the names and locations of the United States' foreign trading partners. The lesson complete, Lincoln took the floor once again.

There is a great difference between this pale-faced people and their red brethren, both as to numbers and the way in which they live. We know not whether your own situation is best for your race, but this is what has made the difference in our way of living. The pale faced people are numerous and prosperous because they cultivate the earth, produce bread, and depend upon the products of the earth rather than wild game for a subsistence. This is the chief reason of the difference, but there is another. Although we are now engaged in a great war between one another, we are not, as a race, so much disposed to fight and kill one another as our red brethren.

What the delegation of western chiefs made of this very curious contention is unknown. The *Daily Morning Chronicle* reported only that " 'Ugh' [and] 'Aha' sounded along the line as the interpreter proceeded." Lincoln then offered some unsolicited advice that harked back to George Washington's plea to the Cherokees: "I can see no way in which your race is to become as numerous and prosperous as the white race except by living as they do, by the cultivation of the earth." The United States desired peace with all Indians, he added, and then, beginning to close the audience, offered the most roundabout of apologies. "We make treaties with you, and will try to observe them; and if our children should sometimes behave badly, and violate these treaties it is against our wish. You know it is not always possible for any father to have his children do precisely as he wishes them to do."

The president and the original inhabitants of the country over which he presided had always known one another at a great distance. What evidence exists does suggest that Lincoln believed in the necessity of reform and was prepared to make such efforts more than a minimal part of his postwar policy. And reform would come, without Lincoln, in the form of parochial schools that taught Indian children to hold their own culture in contempt and land-allotment plans that emphasized individual ownership of property and slowly dissolved reservations from within. Perhaps Lincoln's considerable compassion might have blunted the effects of such measures; or perhaps, in the most optimistic scenario, he might have guided peacetime policies to more humane destinations. But now, confronted with "bad behavior" on all sides, white and Indian, the allegory he put before the western chiefs traveled in only one direction. Forgive us, he was saying, for our hearts are in the right place, whatever the less scrupulous among us might do to make you doubt the contention. If the same logic had been applied to the Dakota, it would have demanded that the United States absolve those thousands of Indians opposed to the war for the actions of the few hundred warriors most involved. That such a declaration lay beyond the reach of an extraordinary president who was occupied with a crushing multitude of cares, not least the emancipation of African slaves and the preservation of the union, may be understood. But it is no less a tragedy for all of that.

# Chapter Nineteen

What Little Crow began as a desperate gambit against Americans in August, had now, by the end of May 1863, become a game of wary diplomacy with the British. Shunned by every tribe and leader he'd encountered in the Dakota Territory, Little Crow moved his camp to the Hudson Bay Company post near Pembina, the old trading town where the Red River of the North flowed across the national boundary. Here, even as the snows began to melt, his welcome grew colder: the métis told him, falsely, that Sibley's spring offensive had already commenced, while the northernmost Ojibwe, who just wanted him to go away, sent one of their leaders to council draped in the American flag. Little Crow now played his last card, adopting the Union Jack as his tribal ensign and continuing on into Canadian territory with the intention of asking British officials to grant the fleeing Dakota a new and permanent homeland beyond the reach of American rifles.

On May 27, Little Crow and a few dozen loyal Mdewakanton warriors and women paraded through the gates of Fort Garry in high style. The garrison, built by the Hudson Bay Company in 1822, was as formidable as Fort Snelling and situated in similar fashion at the confluence of two major trade routes, the Red and the Assiniboine rivers. Little Crow dressed in his finest for the occasion, bedecked in "a black coat with velvet collar, a breechcloth of blue broadcloth, and deerskin leggings," while the women in his party sported parasols and wore dresses taken from their former captives. Despite the show of buoyancy, Little Crow also seemed to observers to be bearing a great weight, worn down by the "heavy price on his head," his "thin and cadaverous" features betraying the anxiety brought on by his failure to form a new Indian confederacy.

Over three days Little Crow worked to bring his powers of persuasion to bear on yet another man who wanted nothing to do with him. Governor Alexander Grant Dallas oversaw Rupert's Land, a position that ostensibly made him master of more than a million and a half square miles of Hudson Bay Company holdings in Canada; but the truth was that Dallas commanded few soldiers, administered few established communities, held sway with few of the indigenous tribes, and found his hands tied in any event by brutal weather from October to April of each year. Given a force of sufficient size, Dallas would surely have chased the Dakota back across the border, but as it was, he listened respectfully to Little Crow's entreaties. Seeing that his proposal for a tribal homeland in Canada had little chance of success, Little Crow swore everlasting enmity to the Americans and offered peace and friendship to Dallas, referring to the old agreements between his grandfather and the British government during the War of 1812 and making a formal display of tokens from that alliance. He also repeated words passed down through his father, a British pledge that "the folds of the red flag of the north would wrap around them and preserve them from their enemies."

For an Indian chief, such a promise bore considerable weight. The Dakota understanding of time often presented whites with a confounding lack of linearity; for Governor Dallas, fifty years was a long, long time, but in Little Crow's mind, any pact made by his grandfather was as present as the early-summer sun now thawing the Red River. The picture he painted for Dallas was one of the American government defaulting on its claims and hunting the Dakota like animals. Bringing all of his oratorical skill to bear, he asked for provisions and permission to hunt for game along the Red River north of the American border. As he spoke, Little Crow skipped past the unfortunate truth that the British had treated the Dakota no better at the end of the War of 1812 than the Americans were treating them now. In 1816, after British commanders had deserted their Indian allies, offering only blankets and knives as thanks for their spilled blood, Little Crow's grandfather had traveled more than a thousand miles to Lake Huron so that he might stand in council to deliver a stinging censure of his erstwhile allies.

> After we have fought for you, endured many hardships, lost some of our people and awakened the vengeance of our powerful neighbors, you make a peace for yourself and leave us to obtain such terms as we can! You no longer need our services, and offer us these goods to pay for having deserted us. But no! We will not take them; we hold them and yourselves in equal contempt.

"Such terms" as the Mdewakanton obtained in the wake of the British withdrawal had included the first American stronghold in the region, Fort Snelling, which began to take shape in 1819, heralding the treaty era that would begin to end with Little Crow's early-morning council forty-three years later.

Governor Dallas and other Canadian officials responded to Little Crow's requests by making clear their desire that the Dakota warriors exit the country, and so in a second interview Little Crow said that should he be forced to return to the United States, he would fight to the last man in the "war of extermination" that whites were planning, with the implication that it was within the power and to the advantage of Canadian authorities to broker a peace with General Sibley. This proposal seemed to give Dallas the out he needed and allowed him to punctuate the talks with vague assurances that he would "endeavor to bring their grievances to the notice of the American government, with a view of establishing a better understanding in the future."

For Little Crow, this was only the toothless language typical of treaties, and he left his last council with Governor Dallas on May 29 knowing that it was also his last day of leadership among the Dakota people. Taking advantage of the scarcity of white settlements and the open spaces of Rupert's Land, most of the Dakota in the region, numbering as many as a thousand Mdewakantons, Wahpekutes, Sissetons, and Wahpetons, remained north of the border, and there many would live out the rest of their lives, creating villages and communities that still exist today. Little Crow returned to the United States at the beginning of June 1863 with only eighteen men, including his son, aware that he had become, in the end, no one's spokesman or chief. Blamed in advance by whites and many Indians for whatever disasters might follow the Dakota uprising, he now moved with a core of very few warriors able to travel at great speeds, surely bringing to mind his earliest elk and buffalo hunts in the West and his once-frequent excursions against the Ojibwe over disputed hunting grounds in the Minnesota Territory.

In early June he managed to plant a message in the Saint Paul newspapers telling Pope and Sibley to "look for him" at the old Lower Agency site along the Minnesota River. Little Crow's plans excited great curiosity and wide conjecture, a fire he stoked by telling traders, agents, reporters, and mixed-bloods in the Dakota Territory that he planned to steal enough horses to seat an army, that he planned to kill whites until he was killed, that he was on his way to retrieve a cache of buried treasure and then ride for the Black Hills. By this time, he was fully aware that General Sibley was preparing an army to hunt him down, and the statements read like a smoke screen and a provocation. But whatever the reason—whether to die, or to kill, or simply to once more dip his hand into familiar waters—Little Crow was indeed heading home.

Sarah Wakefield's plea to Abraham Lincoln seems to have been the final step she took through official channels to remedy the mistake made in executing Chaska. Sarah's daughter, Nellie, would eventually burn Sarah's letters, meaning that only a few highly charged documents serve to record the aftermath of her captivity. As Little Crow made plans to visit Fort Garry for his final parley, Sarah was at work on three pieces of writing that, all together, provide an extraordinary picture of a soul in turmoil. The first was the book-length narrative called *Six Weeks in the Sioux Tepees,* in which she would provide a chronological account of her captivity and a fierce defense of Chaska's conduct. The second and third documents were a pair of letters written to the missionary Stephen R. Riggs, expressing sentiments startling for the nakedness of their heartache, desperation, and anger.

This second round of communications with Riggs began on April 9, 1863, with a bolt from the blue. "I have determined if I can procure a situation of some kind to accompany the Indians," she wrote. "I care not for any remuneration all I wish is to make myself useful: I need employment so I will not have as much time to think as I now have: if I could get interested in some way I would be much happier now I am alone without Friends or Relatives." Sarah was surely talking about the plans to ship the captive families at Fort Snelling off to a reservation in Nebraska or the Dakota Territory, but what "situation" she imagined herself occupying is not clear. What she did make clear was the fact that John Wakefield, her husband, concurred in the plan and had been the one to suggest that she write to Riggs to sound out the possibilities.

In the end, Sarah did not go with the exiled Dakota. She would live in Minnesota another thirty-three years, but now, in April 1863, she saw no future for herself in her old community. "I could willingly devote the few remaining years of an unhappy life to the Indians for what they done for me while with them," she confided, adding that "I have not one friend to consult with or go to now I am in trouble." She mourned her late father, whose death had robbed her of a place "that would seem like home," and confessed her permanent estrangement from her mother. Both of her parents have so far escaped the historical record, as has the nature of Sarah's post–Dakota War separation from her husband, the second such schism of their married life. John Wakefield was a drinker, and there is reason to believe he sometimes abused her, but that is only informed conjecture. What is not conjecture is her declaration to Riggs that life with the Dakota was preferable to life anywhere else.

Her next letter to Riggs, written sixteen days later, addressed the subject of God. Her opening query was, to say the least, uncharacteristic of most letters written to clergy in the mid-nineteenth century: "Did Jesus Christ come into this world to save sinners?" she began. Her despair was helping to drive an anxious investigation into her proper relationship to the divine, an impulse that seems to have flowered during her time among the Dakota. Sarah was no theologian—she was simply a woman living within an intensely religious society, trying to make all of the pieces fit—but still she was able to issue a series of pointed challenges to Christian orthodoxy. Again she made an oblique reference to "the trouble I had few years since in Shakopee," trouble that she said caused the "Gods church" there to refuse her children baptism. Whatever the "trouble" was, it had been enough to damage her reputation but not enough to permanently end her marriage or drive her out of the town for good. Now she was readjusting her relationships to everything and everyone, and God was no exception.

I always attended church and never forgot that there was a God and have tried to go to Him in my many hours of afflictions of different kind. I have had sorrows and troubles enough before this last to drive a woman wild but I have asked God to help me bear them in secret for rather than have them known, I would have suffered death first: When I was taken by the Indians I thought my cup was at last filled to overflowing, and I thought that all my prayers and tears were thrown away that God had forsaken me.

Sarah's temporary move to Red Wing after the war seems to have been designed in part to have her children baptized in the Episcopal church there. At the same time, her effort to be baptized herself at Christ Episcopal Church in Saint Paul, the largest congregation in Bishop Whipple's diocese, was rebuffed, much to her dismay. "This course of conduct by God's ministers serves to harden my heart against all mankind," Sarah told Riggs, "[and] I often wish I was in a wilderness away from all human creatures."

The next portion of the letter alternately praised and rebuked her husband, who, she wrote, "blames me very much for my talking so much at Camp Release and does not have the pity for me that he would have otherwise. He says I have brought my trouble upon myself and now I must bear it." Another wedge had been driven into her marriage and her life in society by her friendship with Chaska, whose execution had delivered the final blow to her reputation by seeming to place her in sympathy, if not in league, with one of the few Dakota Abraham Lincoln deemed foul enough to die for his crimes against the white world. Her husband, she wrote, hurrying her thoughts along, "cannot realize how a woman could try to save an Indian who had her a captive he thinks he would have killed himself before he would remained there in a tipi, but he little knows a mother's feelings that Indian saved my children and what mother could forget it and not only my children lives were spared but I was saved from dishonor, but my anxiety to save him just cursed me and killed the man."

This letter shows Sarah working to tie together two warring halves of herself: her faith in a personal, forgiving God and her anger at the injustice of her treatment at the hands of whites after her captivity was over, all in the shadow of a husband who seemed to be ashamed of her. The letter went a step further, surely startling Riggs whether it aimed to or not: "If I could have done it I would have released every one of them: I never shall feel as if the Indians were the guilty party. I know they done wrong but white men in the same situation as they were last summer would have done much worse." She closed by drawing a poignant connection between herself and another aggrieved woman before considering the question that lay at the heart of her letter.

> I wish when you see Chaska's mother that you would explain to her how her son was executed I can see her sorrowful face in my dreams as I saw her last sitting on the bank of the Yellow Medicine River all alone such a moan as escaped from her was heart rending I hear it now and it seems to be continually sounding in my ears: for she blamed me as I do myself for not letting him go with Little Crow. I over persuaded him to remain and I feel as if I was his murderer. I hope you will pray for me that I may be able at last to reach heaven.

One April day in 1863, a small group of the Dakota families held at Fort Snelling was fishing along the riverbank when they spotted a steamer more than a mile upriver and moving slowly in their direction, working its way through the final channel of the Minnesota before breaking into the deeper waters of the Mississippi. Even from this distance, the Dakota could see that the deck of the *Favorite* was crowded with men draped in a shade of red particular to their history, the berry dye used for their winter blankets. In an instant they knew that these were the reprieved prisoners from Mankato: friends, fathers, brothers, husbands, and sons they had not seen for seven months.

It was a simple matter to spread the news via a chain of shouts and fluttered blankets, and before long well over a thousand Dakotas rushed to the water's edge, frantic with anticipation and fear. Would the steamer stop beside the encampment for an exchange of greetings? A visit? Were these men, hope against hope, being brought to join them? Or were they on their way to meet the same fate as their thirty-eight brethren? Whatever the case, something had finally been set in motion. Under other circumstances, that something would surely have bred only fear and suspicion in the camp, but such thoughts were now set aside. A line of soldiers, nearly one hundred in all, stood between them and the water. Behind the soldiers the steamboat was close enough that they could see their men, still wearing their paired shackles, still prisoners.

After the boat's ramp was lowered, many Dakota men walked onto the shore, but not nearly enough. These were the 48 acquitted men who had been brought along to Mankato, now joyfully reunited with their closest kin, while more than 260 others, the men who had been spared hanging, remained rooted to the steamer deck. Soon the ramp was raised again and the steamer made to move out into the center of the current. All of the Dakota families had learned that freedom and innocence were relative terms, but this was a new pain: if the rest of the men were not to stay at Fort Snelling—which was, after all, only another kind of imprisonment—they must be marked for something even worse. And the only thing worse, they believed, was to be hanged after all. A writer for the *Davenport Democrat* reported the reaction of the distraught families in purple, patronizing prose that nonetheless managed to catch the scene's essential awfulness.

> As the boat moved off with all their wild hearts held dear, snatching them again from the arms already outstretched in joyful welcome, to take them to a horrible death, the whole vast crowd of savage forms writhed in the agony of disappointment, and a wail of grief went up from hundreds of shrill, wild voices which it was heart-rending to hear. The poor creatures flung themselves on the ground, and pulled their hair, and beat their breasts with the anguish of the sudden revulsion from hope to despair. If they might only speak to their beloved ones! But no; sternly and exorably as Fate, the boat moved on and their last hope fades away as it disappears in the distance.

The colonel in command of the Fort Snelling encampment, William Crooks, another member of Sibley's trial commission, hurried to hold council with the Dakota families and explain that their men were not to be hanged but rather brought down the Mississippi to an enclosure not unlike their own near the Iowa border. "This assurance calmed them somewhat," reported the *Davenport Democrat*, "but the air was still filled with their lamentations as if they mourned the dead."

Just a few days later, the Dakota at Fort Snelling learned from Colonel Crooks that it would soon be their turn to board a boat and enter into a mysterious future of their own. The restrictions on movement in and out of camp that had been relaxed after the first few weeks of their imprisonment were now reinstated; no one was to leave the enclosure, and the nightly guard was stepped up. Not all of the Dakota would be going downriver. Most of the leaders of the peace party and their families were already stationed up on the prairie, preparing to act as scouts for Sibley's punitive expeditions into the Dakota Territory; whether this was for some reward or in response to some coercion is unknown. The rest of the Dakota went about finishing the job of striking their lodges and packing their things inside the rolled tepees so that they could be strapped onto their backs.

On May 4, beneath threatening skies, 711 Dakotas, mostly women and children, were herded aboard the *Davenport*, a midsize steamer designed to comfortably carry half that number. A few whites rode along, including a company of soldiers and the missionaries John P. Williamson, a Presbyterian, and Samuel Hinman, Whipple's unflagging protégé, who had made the choice to accompany the captives to their new home and set up an Episcopal mission there. Williamson and Hinman must have been told of the government's plan for a new reservation, and so the captives may have learned that they would travel down the Mississippi past the boat's namesake town, where the reprieved prisoners were now being held, then on to Saint Louis and up the Missouri River to a place called Crow Creek in southern Dakota Territory.

But before all of this could happen, the *Davenport* needed to stop just five miles downriver at Saint Paul to take on food, fuel, and other supplies during a half-hour layover. Approaching the city, crowded onto the boiler deck, the Dakota women and children watched as a crowd of citizens surged to the edge of the levee, gesturing and shouting. When the steamer pushed abreast of its dock—no thought seems to have been given to waiting until the situation could be defused—the crowd began to hurl large stones and other heavy objects up at the Indians, badly wounding several as they crowded away from the storm. A captain in command of forty soldiers from the Tenth Minnesota Regiment came to the railing and threatened to bring his men down the ramp with bayonets fixed, a warning that served to quell the riot. While the wounded Indians received whatever ministrations were available on board, their kin engaged in what one white observer called "prayer and singing."

Two days later a second steamboat arrived at Fort Snelling to collect the rest of the waiting Dakotas. But before the *Northerner* could take them aboard, it needed to deposit another human cargo along the same flat that held the Dakota enclosure. Six hundred Dakotas now looked upon a hundred or so black men from the southern reaches of the Mississippi, contraband slaves who were now free under the terms of the Emancipation Proclamation, brought north to be used as mule drivers for General Sibley's spring expedition to the Dakota Territory in search of Little Crow and the other escaped Dakotas. Captive Indians and free blacks exchanged stares and, according to one observer, entered into conversations that were not recorded by any reporter, diarist, or letter writer. Eventually the black men were brought up the steep incline to the fort to prepare for their spring work, after which the remaining Dakotas were loaded onto the steamboat for their journey out of Minnesota.

That same day, the *Saint Paul Pioneer* said a particularly rude good riddance to the final group of Dakota exiles: "The *Northerner* brought up a cargo of 125 niggers and 150 mules on Government account. It takes back some eight or nine hundred Indians. We doubt very much whether we benefit by the exchange. If we had our choice we would send both niggers and Indians to Massachusetts, and keep the mules here."

The day that the *Davenport* had slipped away from the vengeful crowd on the Saint Paul docks would be the first of twenty-four the Dakotas would spend aboard the grossly overcrowded ship. By the time they arrived at Fort Randall on the Missouri River on May 28, the remaining six hundred refugees had disembarked from the *Northerner* at Hannibal, Missouri, and taken an overland shortcut by train to meet them, sixty people to a car, bringing the total on board the *Davenport* to 1,300 and creating conditions that led to the deaths of at least one woman and several children during the last portion of their journey. As John P. Williamson described the scene, the "Indians were crowded like slaves on the boiler and hurricane decks of a single boat, and fed on musty hardtack and briny pork, which they had not half a chance to cook."

If any of the soldiers traveling aboard the *Davenport* knew enough about the Crow Creek reservation to describe it with any accuracy, the Dakotas' apprehensions would have only grown. The proposals for the final disposition of the innocent Dakota had included such far-flung locales as Devils Lake, Isle Royale in Lake Superior, and even the Dry

Tortugas off the coast of Florida, but in the end lame-duck interior secretary Caleb Smith, perhaps at the urging of Minnesota congressmen, had written a bill placing them near Fort Randall on the upper reaches of the Missouri River. That choice was made in December, but not until May, just a few days before the Dakota were scheduled to arrive, did Superintendent Clark W. Thompson visit the site, deciding on a spot hurriedly and hoping that it would be suitable. "It has good soil, good timber, and plenty of water," he wrote. "The only drawback I fear is the dry weather."

Thompson's choice was not suitable, much to the Dakotas' despair. Three years of extreme drought followed, and in a place where few crops would grow under good circumstances, food was impossible to produce. Isaac Heard, hardly one to profess sympathy for the Dakota, wrote that "it is a horrible region, filled with the petrified remains of the huge lizards and creeping things of the first days of time. The soil is miserable; rain rarely ever visits it. The game is scarce, and the alkaline waters of the streams and springs are almost certain death." The Missouri ran as low as it had in decades, putting Crow Creek beyond the reach of many traders and suppliers. What provisions did get to them—mostly meat and flour—were put into a barrel, mixed together, and ladled out. As no doctor lived at Crow Creek and no medicines were readily available, hundreds of Dakotas died within months of their arrival. Henry Whipple, Samuel Hinman, and Thomas S. and John P. Williamson wrote letter after letter to military and civilian authorities asking that the exiles be moved to a different reservation, but little attention was paid. The rest of the country remained focused on bigger, bloodier battles, and most ordinary Minnesotans, who might have had some reason to wonder where so many Dakotas had gone, simply forgot about them.

# Chapter Twenty

In June 1863, John Pope's punitive expeditions were launched, many months after Little Crow had assumed they would begin. In his caution, Pope was operating very much like his old nemesis George McClellan and nothing like the man who had introduced himself to the Army of the Potomac by crowing that "success and glory are in the advance, disaster and shame lurk in the rear." He could not shake the vision of Little Crow leading a massive, unified force out of Devils Lake and past Fort Abercrombie before advancing on Saint Paul, death and terror in his wake. Far from the action in Milwaukee, Pope was encouraged in this belief by Governor Ramsey, who insisted that the threat still posed by Little Crow was real, passing along for good measure a rumor that U.S. Senator Henry Rice was to replace Pope unless he could show some dramatic success over the summer.

All during the late winter and spring the reinforced line of federal forts in Minnesota and the surrounding states and territories had sent out soldiers on patrol, guarding against white looters and returning Dakota warriors. Now, according to John Pope's orders, two federal armies would execute a sweeping pincer movement: three thousand men under General Sibley would march across the middle of western Minnesota, cross the border, and make a beeline for Devils Lake, while a smaller force led by Alfred Sully, a veteran of Indian campaigns in the Far West, had already embarked by steamboat for Fort Pierre, on the Missouri River; from that point he would ride north through the Dakota Territory to meet up with Sibley sometime in late summer.

The idea was to capture, kill, or scatter the Dakota farther west, where their approach could be more easily seen and scouted. And indeed, the expeditions sent out to find and destroy Little Crow would end up killing more than a hundred Dakotas from every band in every division of the tribe, some in pitched battles, soldier against warrior, and others in situations of a less military nature. Rumor after rumor during the first months of 1863 placed Little Crow back in Minnesota, traveling with a great band of warriors and riding onto farmsteads bearing death and destruction, but the truth was much more modest. After recrossing the Red River of the North and reentering the state at the beginning of July, his small band split, one group determined to attack settlers and another to steal horses. Little Crow and his son joined neither party; instead, the two men headed for the Big Woods. One fifty-two-year-old man and his seventeen-year-old son were not a formidable war party, whatever Little Crow's prior exploits might suggest. Rather than bearing a great responsibility, he was suddenly given a new, rueful sort of freedom. His path from Devils Lake pointed straight at the Lower Agency and the last location of his own village, but his true motives remain forever obscure.

Late in the day on July 3, father and son stopped to pick raspberries on a farm just northwest of Hutchinson, where eleven months earlier Little Crow and his men had failed to dislodge soldiers from the Tenth Minnesota. Whether by coincidence or design, this put them within twenty-five miles of the site of the original killings in Acton, no more than one day's ride from the Lower Agency to the south and Fort Snelling to the east.

Some short time later, the sky, high and blue and still, filled with the snap of a rifle shot. Little Crow went to the ground, badly hurt and bleeding near his waist. He struggled to one knee and returned fire, seeing that he was dealing with one older man and one younger, a mirror image of his own traveling party. He fired several times and hit the older man, wounding him, but after another exchange of a few short bursts his younger opponent hit the mark, piercing Little Crow in his chest. Wowinape watched his father's killer vanish into the trees, but he had no time to spend in pursuit or, for that matter, in mourning.

Quickly he fulfilled his responsibilities as a son and a warrior, placing moccasins beside the body to aid in its long journey to the spirit world and wrapping the body in a blanket in accordance with Dakota custom. With no time to drag the body out of the field, and no knowledge of the terrain or of what other white men might be nearby, Wowinape fled, alone in the world.

A thousand miles to the east on the same afternoon, the last bullet of the third and last day of battle was fired just outside the once quiet Pennsylvania town of Gettysburg. In the First Minnesota's camp, the regiment counted losses that made their march over dead bodies in a cornfield at Antietam seem like a holiday. In one midafternoon action the day before, the Minnesotans had been ordered to charge forward off a long ridge to buy time so that a gaping hole in the Union line might be plugged. The remnants of eight companies, 262 soldiers in all, had run forward double-quick to meet the advancing edge of 1,600 Alabama men determined to plow them into the ground. The First Minnesota battled furiously before they finally broke, returning to find that their gambit had worked: a full regiment of infantry and several pieces of artillery now filled what five minutes earlier had been a hundred-yard-wide hole in the line. A quick count showed that only 47 Minnesotans had come through the action unscathed, while 215 had been wounded or killed, a casualty rate that eclipsed that sustained by any other Union unit in any single battle.

In an era when gallantry was the brightest coin of military honor, the First Minnesota became an instant legend. The following day, the fortunes of the Union took a final, fateful turn. Up and down the line atop Cemetery Ridge the bluecoats cheered and gasped as Pickett's Charge was repulsed, leaving Robert E. Lee no choice but to turn back toward Virginia and give up his hopes of forcing the North into negotiations for peace. Lincoln had waited more than two years for such a victory. Tomorrow was Independence Day. No one, from the soldiers of the First Minnesota to the president himself, had any inkling of how much fighting remained ahead, but all of them believed that the tide of war had finally turned.

> I am the son of Little Crow; my name is Wo-wi-nap-e; I am 18 years old; my father had two wives before he took my mother; the first one had one son, the second one a son and daughter;

the third wife was my mother. After taking my mother, he put away the first two; he had seven children by my mother, six are dead; I am the only one living now.

Until the "Statement of Wo-wi-nap-e, Captured July 28" appeared in the August 13, 1863, edition of the *Saint Paul Pioneer*, Little Crow's death had been part reality, part mystery, and part myth to most Minnesotans. Now it was stone-cold fact. For more than a month rumors of the killing of Little Crow had flown here and there throughout the state at the same time that Generals Sibley and Sully made their separate movements into the Dakota Territory. By the time Sibley arrived at his destination in late June, thousands of Dakota warriors, few of whom had been involved in the war of 1862, had already left, making their escape into the West. Pursuing white soldiers and Dakota warriors exchanged gunfire at Big Mound and Dead Buffalo Lake and Stony Lake, engagements that were less battles than delaying actions as the retreating Dakota bought time for their women and children to move across the Missouri River. Sibley was not willing to follow his quarry so far, especially since Sully had failed to link up with him by the appointed date, and so he returned home, where he discovered that Wowinape had been captured.

Now the reading populace of Minnesota had its first account of the final moments of Little Crow, along with Wowinape's solitary flight toward Canada, a translated "confession" that rendered as a blunt, staccato chronology what was in actuality a long and harrowing journey. Wowinape had known that he would share the fate of his father unless he soon found his kinsmen, and so he had headed back out to the Dakota Territory alone and on foot. He carried his father's rifle and his own, killing small game along the way and trying to stay out of sight. Reaching the Sheyenne River, some three hundred miles distant from where his father had fallen, he ran short of ammunition, and became ever weaker and hungrier during the final few days of his trip. He finally approached Devils Lake only to find all of his fellow Dakota gone and no trace of their camps; he was unaware that the advance edge of a white army was just a few days behind him. Slicing a single mismatched cartridge into slugs that would fit his rifle, he managed to shoot a wolf and eat it down to the bones, giving him enough energy to reach the water's edge, where he was eventually discovered by a party of Sibley's mixed-blood scouts.

Wowinape, son of Little Crow, at Fort Snelling Internment Camp, 1864

Another trial followed at Fort Abercrombie before another military commission to determine Wowinape's guilt of the crimes of "participating in the murders and massacres committed by the Sioux Indians upon the whites in Minnesota in the year 1862." A second charge of "attempt at murder and Horse Stealing" accused Little Crow's son simply of having the "intent and design" to do those things and "generally of outrages and depredations" on his return to the state. Wowinape's trial took two days—with a one-month break between day one and day two to move the commission from Fort Abercrombie to Fort Snelling—and included testimony from six witnesses, none of whom could establish anything beyond the defendant's complicity in a plan to steal a few horses. The final witness, in fact, was Nathan Lamson, father of Chauncey, the boy whose shot killed Little Crow, who told the most complete tale of Little Crow's death from the white point of view but added nothing to the case at hand, though the members of the commission did seem very interested in the question of whether Wowinape had returned Chauncey Lamson's fire.

In the end, it was another presentation of equivocal evidence, another guilty verdict, and another order that the prisoner was "to be hanged by the neck until dead," although only four of the six jurors approved the sentence. General Sibley set the place and date of execution—Fort Snelling, Friday, November 20, 1863, at noon—"subject," once again, "to the revision of the President of the United States." And once again another remarkable intervention took place, but this time it was not Lincoln and his Interior Department lawyers who slowed the rush to judgment. This new delay was the work of John Pope, of all people, who wrote to Judge Advocate General Holt from Milwaukee with his concerns that the military commission called by Sibley might have met in violation of the 65th Article of War, which Pope read to say that such a commission could not be ordered by the accuser of the prisoner.

The turnaround is startling, directly negating Pope's stance of one year earlier, and difficult to explain by any other evidence of conscience or outside intervention. And though no one inside or outside of Pope's chain of command made public comment on the lifted sentence, it raised many ticklish legal questions. As Sibley pointed out in an angry letter to Holt, "a precisely similar condition of things existed in 1862, when nearly four hundred Indian warriors, taken prisoner by the forces under my command, were tried and the greater number condemned to death by a Military Commission ordered by me upon charges and specifications preferred by myself." In other words, he was saying, Wowinape's trial was no different than those given the 303 originally sentenced to death or—most crucially in Sibley's argument—than those given the 38 eventually hanged. To deny the jurisdiction of the current commission, he argued, was to render the Christmas hangings illegitimate. But Wowinape did indeed receive his stay of execution, and thus did the basis of all of the previous year's legal maneuvering crumble into greater uncertainty, if quietly and with no publicity. The public didn't care if Little Crow's son did or did not dangle: unlike his father, Wowinape was a story, not a cause, and his reprieve caused little stir.

Wowinape was soon removed down the Mississippi River to a prison named Camp McClellan in Davenport, Iowa, where he was reunited with the men whose sentences had been placed in abeyance by Abraham Lincoln the year before, hundreds of his Mdewakanton kinsmen who were still awaiting news of their ultimate fate as their relatives began their ordeal at the Crow Creek reservation, six hundred miles to the northwest. Here, at Davenport, Little Crow's son heard tales of disease, starvation, and death told by his fellow captives, of the sights and sounds of the execution, and of the prisoners' steamboat journey past Fort Snelling in sight of their families gathered on the shore. Seven months after Lincoln's decision, no one could tell them why they were still prisoners, how long they would be prisoners, or when those questions might be answered.

John Pope's vision of a great pincer movement in the Dakota Territory driving the Dakota away forever did not go according to plan, but neither was he disappointed in the outcome. Generals Sibley and Sully were supposed to converge along the upper Missouri River, combining cavalry and infantry into one powerful army, but when Sibley arrived at the rendezvous point at the end of July 1863, he learned that Sully was still weeks away. His supplies already dangerously low, Sibley had turned around and headed back for Fort Abercrombie, where he found Wowinape a captive, still regaining strength after his long solo run for Devils Lake. On his way to the Missouri Sibley had driven thousands of Dakotas and Lakotas further west, killing many while losing only one of his soldiers, and in several letters back and forth with Pope both men pronounced themselves satisfied with the results.

As Sibley marched back to Minnesota, Sully and his smaller force of mounted men kept moving up the Missouri River, until they heard reports of Dakota and other tribes returning to hunt buffalo far up the James River to the west. Moving quickly, he made chase for three days, finally colliding with the Indians on September 3 at Whitestone Hill, near what is now the border between North and South Dakota. Bringing up his entire force, Sully loosed five hundred mounted men on a hastily packing Indian camp, pressing his soldiers to ride and shoot until darkness fell and two hundred Indians were dead, including many women and children. Sully then sent out detachments to destroy all of the goods and provisions his targets had left behind and marched the survivors overland to Crow Creek, where they joined their kin and told their story. Samuel J. Brown wrote to his father describing "the perfect massacre" and adding that Sully "ought [not] to brag of it at all, because it was, what no decent man would have done, he pitched into their camp and just slaughtered them, worse a great deal than what the Indians did in 1862."

With Pope pushing him forward and gold newly discovered in the northern reaches of the Dakota Territory, Sully went back out the next summer at the head of 2,200 better-trained and better-equipped soldiers with the aim of establishing a new and formidable federal presence in the Northwest. Ranging along the Missouri River almost all the way to its junction with the Yellowstone River near the present-day border of Montana, he was finally set upon in June 1864 by a large force of Indians who were determined to drive Sully back to Minnesota and confident they were better plains fighters than any collection of white men. Together, hundreds of warriors representing the Dakota, Yanktons, Yanktonais, Sans Arcs, Miniconjous, Blackfeet, and Hunkpapa rode out to meet Sully's men as their wives, children, and elders watched from a nearby prominence.

So began the Battle of Killdeer Mountain, which quickly evolved from a few stray gunshots into a cacophonous series of charges and flank movements on both sides. Sully's artillery flashed and his cavalry rode into the midst of his opponents, who found themselves staggering backward a few hundred yards at a time despite all their confident expectations. The battle was brisk, hard fought, and decisive: afterwards, a hundred or more Indian warriors lay dead, their companions scattered in the foothills to the west, and their supplies and foodstuffs in the hands of the whites, while Sully's forces had suffered only twelve casualties, two of them fatal.

Killdeer Mountain would have been an unmitigated disaster for the Indians had it not galvanized a small core of leaders into new ways of thinking about warfare and a new resolve not to let outsiders advance unchecked into their lands. "The Indians here have no fight with the whites," one warrior had shouted to Sully's advance scouts. "Why is it the whites come to fight with the Indians?"

The man who uttered those words would become the most famous warrior to emerge from the fighting at Killdeer Mountain and one of the most recognized figures of the nineteenth century. By the summer of 1864 the Hunkpapa warrior Sitting Bull was thirty-three and had already lived a remarkable life, one that in general outline was not so different from Little Crow's. His many feats of physical endurance and his dexterity in battle had earned him several eagle feathers before he left his teens, and in 1864 he had the unusual distinction of being the war chief of the Hunkpapa, one band of the numerous Lakota in the West, and being *wicasta wakan* at the same time, making him both a shaman and a great leader in battle. In the years following Killdeer Mountain, Sitting Bull became the best-known symbol of Indian resistance to white encroachment, refusing all treaty talk and showing no trust of white soldiers or politicians. But even in the battle's immediate aftermath he knew that he would need to learn to run and fight, run and fight, and resolved never to "make war after the manner of whites," as Little Crow would have put it.

While it is unlikely that Sitting Bull and Little Crow ever met, it is true that the Hunkpapa chief absorbed Little Crow's lessons as he watched Little Crow's people dispersed ever farther from their former homes, white soldiers behind them all the while. Land was all-important, not treaties or trade, and keeping the land was a matter of fighting fiercely and without compromise. For the next seventeen years, at least, he did what Little Crow had not done until forced to it in August 1862: abandoned his own history of accommodation and drawn a hard line in the dry ground.

On April 17, 1865, the day after Easter, the news came to Minnesota that Abraham Lincoln had been assassinated. In the flood of grief that filled the state, few commentators referred to the time thirty-two months earlier when the president's name had been anything but revered. By this time, almost all evidence of the Dakota villages had been removed from the Minnesota River Valley, where lands were now blanketed by the corn and wheat of white farmers. The American frontier had receded by many hundreds of miles, well into the Dakota Territory, and most Minnesotans no longer felt that they lived on the edge of anything. For the Dakota, on the other hand, an entire world had simply vanished.

The Dakota people had not vanished. Some still scraped along on the Crow Creek reservation, some had found their way west to live with the plains tribes, some remained in Canada, and some, even, were coming back into Minnesota under the protection of Henry Whipple, Thomas S. Williamson, and other clergy who sponsored Dakota villages complete with farms, churches, and schools. In 1866, Lincoln's successor, Andrew Johnson, finally pardoned the reprieved Dakota, as well as Wowinape and the others who had been added to the Davenport prison in the interim. Meanwhile, with each skirmish, pursuit, or pitched battle, the Indian wars of the Northwest took shape, making the Dakota Territory and the lands beyond into a bitterly contested ground full of subtle undulations, misleading vistas, and peculiar geographic features that the Indian warriors used to their full advantage.

An entire generation of warriors, many of them children or young men at the time of the Civil War, would learn year by year how to resist the American excursions, meeting with remarkable success for a time and bringing their leaders more lasting fame than anyone, white or Indian, involved in the Dakota War of 1862. Even Sitting Bull's celebrity would give way to that of Crazy Horse, the Oglala leader who would not allow himself to be photographed, who supposedly preferred mud and dirt to face paint, and who scored victory after victory in his own hit-and-run campaign against white forces.

In 1876, finally, Sitting Bull and Crazy Horse would team up to hand George Custer his infamous defeat. Little Big Horn was, in many ways, exactly Little Crow's dream, a confederation of Indians from many bands and tribes meeting and defeating white forces in heroic battle on Indian ground. He had not been the person to deliver that dream to his people, but the wars he helped to spark had forced the United States to spend many men and countless dollars in their prosecution. Not until 1890 did the vision dissipate with another massacre of Indians by whites, this time along Wounded Knee Creek. Little Crow never believed that whites could be driven off the land for good, but the historical renown of the Lakota, unmatched by any other Native American tribe, might have served him as a small sort of consolation.

The Dakota War left Little Crow dead in a raspberry patch; but its influence still echoes, even under cover of the great conflict that saw white Americans killing each other thousands at a time. Making the plains and prairie all Indian was a dream that Little Crow probably knew was impossible. But helping to give the Dakota a crucial role in the epic and ongoing story of Indian peoples was another matter.

# Chapter Twenty-one

In 1868, five years after Little Crow's death, a fashionable couple out for a night in the capital could go to the Saint Paul Opera House and pay one dollar apiece to view "The Panorama of the Indian Massacre of 1862 and the Black Hills," barkered as "The Great Moral Exhibition of the Age!" and "The Most Extraordinary Exhibition in the World!" and promising "War Dances, thrilling escapes, and landscape views." Ushered to their seats, they would have found the hall dark except for a fascinating apparatus, a screen six feet wide and a dozen feet high, designed with vertical rollers that held 222 feet of canvas on which three dozen images had been painted. As a man standing next to the device slowly turned an oversized crank, the story of the Dakota War paraded across the screen to the accompaniment of music.

The entertainment was new, sensational, and utterly captivating. Part of the point was the seeming reality of the panorama itself. "Ladies and gentlemen," the breathless narrator began, "the cause of the massacre, a portion of which we are now about to exhibit to your view, cannot be given. But a short account of the condition of the country will suffice to exhibit this tragic epoch in our country's history in its proper light." The war's causes weren't the point—no complex historical, political, racial, or moral questions would be asked of the audience—so what was this "proper light"? John Stevens, a sign painter by training, had moved beyond advertising and into the more lucrative realms of sensation and spectacle. His was not the only panorama traveling the country—the Civil War gave birth to hundreds—and like all of the others its brightly backlit images served many purposes: to titillate and awe, certainly, but also to confirm the public need to place the events of 1862 in the great sweep of the settlement of the West, joining the yeoman farmers of the Minnesota River Valley to the pressing imperatives of Manifest Destiny.

The mode of narration was epic and lurid: "Tumultuous horrors rent the midnight air, until the sad catalogue reached the fearful number of two thousand human victims from the gray haired sire to the helpless infant of a day, who lay mangled and dead on the bloody field. The dead were left to bury the dead; for the dead reigned there alone." Indeed, much of the exhibit consisted of a long catalogue of killings and maimings, scenes dripping with hatred for a people who now seemed long gone.

> The idea of executing three hundred Indian warriors aroused the sympathies of those far removed from these scenes of human butcheries, and the president was importuned by all unreasonable bounds for the release of these savages. The voice of the blood of innocence was crying from the ground. The bewailing of mothers bereft of their children was hushed in the louder cry of sympathy, and for the condemned the tide of sympathy rolled on, and the persistent applications to the president were successful, and in place of three hundred and three condemned by a military court, only forty were ordered to be executed.

Like Buffalo Bill's Wild West show many years later, Stevens's Sioux War panorama was a collective catharsis, a safe but thrilling coda to an unimaginably violent era. The success of the exhibition depended on the viewer's belief in a certain vision of history: playing to packed houses in Minnesota, Wisconsin, and Iowa, it put the settlers and soldiers of those states at the center of great events and gave them a status equal to those more famous locales on the national map. The first image of the panorama—a nine-square montage of Lincoln, his cabi-

*Panorama of the Indian Massacre of 1862 and the Black Hills,* scene 11, 1872

net, and, for good measure, Jefferson Davis—drove home the point: What had happened here was exciting. What had happened here was awful. And what had happened here mattered to everyone.

The portraits of the president and his advisers were juxtaposed with another panel featuring a similar collection of Indian faces: Little Crow, Cut Nose, Little Six, and other infamous leaders, including Chaska, whose history was now simplified to fit the needs of the narrative: "Shaska, one of the prominent actors in this fearful drama, was the murderer of George Gleason and the capturer of the Wakefield family." The rest of the show rolled by, image after image made of crude lines and garish hues: houses afire with Dakotas riding across the fields upon defenseless farmers; two white women being killed with a single bullet; and of course, the hanging, an image frozen just before the moment of the drop.

Imagine being in *that* audience, the show proposed, in order that viewers might marvel at being in *this* audience. The final image, "Minnesota Fruit," made clear the tale's happy outcome: three women in dresses attended a tree out of which grew not apples, but newborn white babies.

Stevens's panorama seemed to be many entertainments in one, looking to the past, present, and future with its mix of ages-old iconography and brand-new technology, but it was just one voice raised in an out-burst of postwar storytelling. While thousands of Dakota prisoners, exiles, and refugees sat around campfires and in lodges in a dozen dif-ferent far-flung places and retold the story in their own ways, unre-corded in print but remembered generation after generation, tens of thousands of whites turned to a set of ready-made popular genres to live and relive the final months of 1862, a hunger that would ebb and flow but never fully subside. Beginning within weeks of the execution, the citizens of Saint Paul, Milwaukee, and even Chicago were inun-dated with letters, pamphlets, songs, speeches, poems, photographs, drawings, dime novels, and popular histories. For an event that had slipped into the headlines under the cover of the American Civil War, the Dakota War of 1862—or Little Crow's War, or the Dakota Upris-ing, or the Minnesota Massacre, or the Dakota Conflict, depending on the era, author, and point of view—would come to have a dizzying number of chroniclers.

At the time that John Nicolay carried Lincoln's Annual Message to Congress, he had been penning two articles of his own, one on the affair with Hole in the Day for the January 1863 issue of *Harper's* and the other on the "Sioux War" one month later for the *Continental Monthly*. Nicolay had remained a frequent journalist after his move to Washington, D.C., often publishing anonymously, sometimes act-ing as a mouthpiece for Lincoln, and sometimes writing independent commentary. His article on Hole in the Day was even-handed, com-plimentary of the Ojibwe leader, and steeped in detail; it made good use of his immediate experience of the event. His article on the Dakota War—which was widely read and considered a key source—was a different animal: relying on thirdhand accounts and nebulous news-paper reports, Nicolay wrote in great brushstrokes of deepest purple, appealing to "hearts appalled by the gleam of the tomahawk and the scalping knife, as they descended in indiscriminate and remorseless slaughter."

Six months later *Harper's* published its own twenty-four-page account of the war, augmented by seventeen drawings from the pen of Minnesota soldier Albert Colgrave, many after photographs by fellow enlistee Adrian Ebell, who was also the author of the article. Most of the magazine's readers, including many in Minnesota, had little experience with Indian reservations and could not picture the drama's major players in their minds' eyes, so Colgrave's illustrations became their first and only look at the places and people involved: the Upper and Lower Agencies, the villages of traditional Indians and the farms of cut-hairs, the faces of Little Crow and William Marshall, the assault at New Ulm, the scenes at Camp Release and Camp Lincoln.

Closer to home, the *Mankato Weekly Record* made an unprecedented editorial decision to devote the entire front page of one February 1863 issue to a single engraved image. The often-imitated point of view was taken at an angle to the gallows, foreshortening the scene into a set of thick diagonal lines growing ever longer as they radiated outward from the scaffold: the condemned men, the double rows of foot soldiers, the single row of cavalry, and behind the cavalry masses of citizens spilling off the drawing's edge. In the center of the picture, an American flag rose high above the scene atop a needle of a pole. The Dakota themselves stood on the platform, blindfolded by their caps, their knees flexed in anticipation of the drop. In the lower left corner, a team and wagon waited to cart the dead bodies away.

Isaac Heard, Sibley's court reporter, used his access to the stories, testimony, and transcripts generated by over four hundred trials to help him write his *History of the Sioux War and Massacres of 1862 and 1863*, in which he affected an objective, reportorial tone that did nothing to mask his central purpose, which was to justify the conduct of the military commission. This was not as pro-white a stance as it might seem, as many of his readers would have concurred with Pope's original wish to execute the Indians as soon as they were captured, military commissions be damned. And Heard's account was at least based on firsthand experience and in-person testimony. The other major history of the conflict to appear in 1864 was written by an influential Saint Paul schoolteacher named Harriet Bishop, who pretended to offer a recitation of events but was far more concerned with placing the reader in the hearts and minds of the combatants, such as she viewed those hearts and minds. In Bishop's telling, the hearts of any Dakotas not baptized into the Christian faith were dark and only prone to becoming darker. In the end, *Dakota War Whoop* took so many liberties with dialogue, motivations, and thoughts to which Bishop was never privy that it was essentially a dime-store novel very thinly disguised as nonfiction.

No other genre of writing, however, approached the popularity of the captivity narrative. Local journalists and book printers beat the bushes in search of anyone with firsthand experience of the Dakota camps and a desire to talk, and over the next thirty-five years many dozens of such tales were published. Most cleaved to a set of standard elements—a trial by suffering, the deliverance by a just and merciful God—to produce an allegorical contest between primitivism and civilization. "The massacre was merely an expression and demonstration of the savagery and barbarism existing in every Sioux Indian," wrote one captive, painting the contrast between good and evil in the starkest possible terms. These were didactic works as much as narratives, taking the events of 1862 out of their chronological continuum in order that the future could now proceed without undue discussion of the past.

Exceptions did exist to this unquestioning view of the war, the first and most notable among them Sarah Wakefield's own memoir, *Six Weeks in the Sioux Tepees*. The book appeared in autumn of 1863, just months after Sarah wrote her final letters to Lincoln and Riggs, and some of it must have been written while she lived away from her husband in Red Wing before she returned to Shakopee. It is difficult to say today how wide the initial readership for *Six Weeks* was—few original editions still exist—but there was apparently enough interest in her story that she pondered its appeal in her home state of Rhode Island and offered "a liberal discount" for "local traveling agents" to sell the book around Minnesota and surrounding states. For such agents, the bet was a good one. Sarah was still notorious then, so much so that readers could experience a certain kind of thrill by buying or borrowing a copy to read about this woman who had, they'd heard, fallen in love with one of the redskins. But whatever prurient motives her readers might have, Sarah's purpose was not to titillate, to entertain, or even to educate. Her purpose was much more personal.

> I wish to say a few words in preface to my Narrative; First, that when I wrote it, it was not intended for perusal by the public eye. I wrote it for the especial benefit of my children, as they were so young at the time they were in captivity, that, in case of

my death, they would, by recourse to this, be enabled to recall to memory the particulars; and I trust all who may read it will bear in mind that I do not pretend to be a book-writer, and hence they will not expect to find much to please the mind's fancy. Secondly I have written a true statement of my captivity; what I suffered, and what I was spared from suffering, by a Friendly or Christian Indian, (whether such from policy or other motives, time will determine.) Thirdly, I do not publish a little work like this in the expectation of making money by it, but to vindicate myself, as I have been grievously abused by many, who are ignorant of the particulars of my captivity and release by the Indians.

Of the many narratives generated in the wake of the Dakota War of 1862, Sarah's is now the most widely studied, mainly because it upsets traditional expectations of the genre and paints her in a kind of progressive light too attractive to resist. Her attitudes toward faith and the Dakota people do seem liberal for her time, and her theology, however constructed, was unusual. But her motivation in writing the book was not theological. The flat contradiction between the first and third rationales set out in her preface mirrors the contradictions in her own person. If a certain amount of bald confession was necessary, it was only so that she could make an overarching point about what she had *not* done.

The book's frank opinion of the inadequacies of white military leadership and Sarah's sympathetic stance toward the Dakota would lead her fellow settlers to publicly brand her a "traitor" and "Indian lover." One year after the first edition of *Six Weeks* appeared, a German settler named Mary Schwandt, whose family had been decimated by the first round of attacks on the farms north of the Minnesota River, published a long narrative of her own in which she became one of the first to describe and criticize Sarah's conduct in print. Schwandt wrote that Sarah and another captive were "painted and decorated and dressed in full Indian costume, and seemed proud of it. They were usually in good spirits, laughing and joking, and appeared to enjoy their new life. The rest of us disliked their conduct, and would have but little to do with them."

In 1864, at about the same time Mary Schwandt's story appeared, Sarah issued an expanded and corrected second edition of her book.

In its preface, she complained about errors and omissions in the production of the first edition by her original printer, the Atlas Printing Company in Minneapolis, so now she worked through a hometown outfit, Argus Book and Job Printing in Shakopee, perhaps to keep a closer eye on the work or because she knew the printer personally and could trust him not to repeat the same kinds of mistakes. In any event, most of the book's typographical blemishes were remedied and eleven pages' worth of material added, as well as an image of Little Crow as a frontispiece. Sarah expanded the descriptions of her own suffering and further justified her seemingly "pro-Indian" or "anti-white" behavior, in every case citing either insanity or extenuating circumstances. She also more explicitly defended the Dakota of the peace party and more fully outlined Dakota motives for commencing the war, adding several examples of Chaska's constant protection and more completely describing the blameworthy or at least ambiguous behavior of other captive women.

The largest self-contained change to the second edition of *Six Weeks* appeared at the very end of the narrative, where Sarah added 1,400 new words. The new edition now contained the story of her husband's flight from the Upper Agency to the Big Woods and then back to Shakopee. The cursory reunion scene at Fort Ridgely she left untouched, still more focused on her children's good fortune at her husband's return than on her own. She capped her additions, and the second edition of her book, with the tale of one final postwar encounter with some of her Dakota protectors among a small band that had just returned to the state under the protection of Bishop Whipple and other clergy.

> A few days since a number of families passed through here, and as I saw them I ran with eagerness to see those old faces who were so kind to me while I was in captivity. I went down to the camp (for they stayed all night in Shakopee), and was rejoiced to be able to take them some food, and other little things which I knew would please them, and for this I have been blamed; but I could not help it. They were kind to me, and I will try and repay them, trusting that in God's own time I will be righted and my conduct understood, for with Him all things are plain. And now I will bid this subject farewell forever.

She kept her word, stepping off the stage and never reemerging as a figure of public attention. She bore two more children, Julia in 1866 and John two years later, but her marriage only worsened. Her husband drank ever more heavily, habituating several taverns for daily doses of beer and whiskey, and in February 1874 he died of an overdose of opium in their upstairs bedroom under circumstances that raised the possibility of suicide. Sarah was left with four children under seventeen and $5,000 in debt, an obligation that ate up nearly all of her assets and left her with no cushion as she struck out on her own.

By 1876 she had moved to Saint Paul, but there the documentary trail of her life nearly dries up. The few facts available indicate that she was able to buy a small plot of land and may have run a business. Her daughter Nellie, who had nursed at her breast throughout their six weeks of captivity, would graduate from Macalaster College and marry and divorce before she was thirty-five. Some records suggest that Sarah made a second marriage, but if so, it ended in divorce or a second widowhood, as she was unmarried on the date of her death, May 27, 1899.

Sarah was buried next to John in Shakopee. Her obituary—subtitled "She Was a Prisoner of the Sioux for Six Weeks During Their Outbreak"—listed the cause of death as "blood poisoning, resulting from other ailments," and called her an "old settler, having come to Minnesota in 1854." The notice contained no hint of controversy, no hint of her authorship of *Six Weeks in the Sioux Tepees*, no hint of trouble in her marriage to John, no hint of her husband's fate, and no hint of her connection to Chaska. Sarah had taken no part in the century-closing spate of nostalgia for frontier times, a boom in demand during the 1890s for lectures, new writings, revised editions, and interviews involving captives, Indians, soldiers, or anyone else able to provide purported eyewitness accounts of the great Dakota War almost forty years earlier. It may speak to weariness—or, more optimistically, to a personal peace—that Sarah Wakefield had been content to let the new surge of interest pass her by and keep on with the business of living.

John Pope's surprising intervention in the case of Wowinape and his support of pardons for the remaining Dakota prisoners turned out not to be aberrations. Following a brief stint as military governor overseeing the reconstruction of Atlanta, General Pope returned to the West in 1867 in order to take command of the federal government's war on the Apache, just one of many new Indian fronts now open in the wake of the Civil War. He soon became a leading proponent of a plan to shield Indian reservations from white encroachment by situating them behind existing federal forts and placing them under the administration of the Department of War and the United States Army, rather than the Interior Department and the Indian Bureau, which he viewed as a bastion of lazy and corrupt administrators.

Pope's plan can be read skeptically as an effort to increase his own military influence, or more generously as a genuine attempt to remove the graft and fraud so thoroughly enmeshed with the "Indian system." He called for doing away with annuities, for careful regulation of trade, and for a tight rein on traders stationed near the reservations. Pope's suggestions were, in fact, more radical and contentious than anything Henry Whipple ever proposed, as they would have essentially held the federal government responsible for any subsequent crimes or frauds perpetrated against the tribes. For this reason and many others, the plan was doomed from the start, and there is irony in the fact that Pope's efforts eventually earned him a label as a controversial "reformer" and "Indian lover," a role he grew to accept and even relish. It was an unfair label from both white and Indian points of view, however, as he never questioned the essential rightness of the concentration and acculturation policies begun so many decades before. He was in full agreement with William Tecumseh Sherman's statement that when it came to Indian affairs the army "gets the cuff from both sides," and had scant understanding of how much more accurate that statement was for the Indian tribes he sought to help.

Henry Benjamin Whipple's all-out efforts on behalf of Indians would last for another thirty-eight years until his death in 1901 at the age of seventy-nine. In 1863, with the Dakota all but driven out of Minnesota, Whipple took on the cause of the Ojibwe in the northern half of the state, sparking "one of the severest personal conflicts that I have had in my life" when the members of Lincoln's brain trust refused to listen to his accusations of fraud and double-dealing among the Indian agents assigned to the tribe. As Edwin Stanton wrote to Henry Halleck, "What does Bishop Whipple want? If he has come here to tell us of the corruption of our Indian system and the dishonesty of Indian agents, tell him that we know it. But the Government never reforms an evil until the people demand it. Tell him that when he reaches the heart of the American people, the Indians will be saved." This wasn't acceptable to Whipple, who, in one of the rare recorded instances of his frustration with specific individuals in power, told Commissioner Dole that "I came here as an honest man to put you in possession of facts to save another outbreak. Had I whistled against the north wind I should have done as much good." Though new treaties were soon signed with the Ojibwe, real reform seemed as far away as ever.

In 1865, Whipple made a pilgrimage to Palestine "simply as a Christian to join the crowd of loving hearts," and there he found in the hard, stark landscape of the Holy Land a ready analogy to the urban squalor of Chicago or the constricted space of Indian reservations. "It is plain that this is the land where Jesus found sermons for his untutored hearers in everything which their eyes saw," he wrote. "For Him everything held a sermon to lead bewildered men to find fellowship with God." Suffering a relapse of his lifelong bronchial condition on his return trip, he stopped in Paris, where he first heard of the assassination of President Lincoln. The only statement in his memoir about the news was brief: "No words can describe the feeling of sorrow which pervaded all classes, as if his death were a personal bereavement."

Speaking at New York's Cooper Union in 1866—standing on the same rostrum from which Lincoln had delivered his most famous campaign speech—Whipple spoke vehemently on the need for an Indian peace commission made of religious men and not politicians. Brought to the attention of Ulysses S. Grant, Whipple became a key consultant to the commission and one of the architects of the federal government's peace policy, working side by side and arguing frequently with Sherman, though not to the point that Whipple couldn't praise the general for "his singular uprightness of character and his devotion to his country." With military authorities and other clergy, Whipple also aided in the removal of the Dakota from the parched and deadly wasteland that was Crow Creek to a somewhat more hospitable location near Niobrara, Nebraska, along the South Dakota border, and he was instrumental in the safe return of Christian Indians to Minnesota, using a gift of land from the Dakota leader and scout Andrew Good Thunder to establish an Episcopal mission near the site of the old Birch Coulee battlefield.

In the 1870s and 1880s, Whipple became one of the leading international voices of the American Episcopal church, making mission trips to Alaska, Puerto Rico, Cuba, and Florida, where, for good measure, he caught a record tarpon in the Atlantic Ocean. In 1885 he was invited to preach on the subject of American Indians at Canterbury Cathedral, and during his long stay in London he befriended a host of luminaries, including Lord Tennyson, William Gladstone, John Greenleaf Whittier, and Henry Wadsworth Longfellow. Whipple also accepted an invitation for a private audience with Queen Victoria to discuss transoceanic relations between the British Anglican and American Episcopal churches and to speak to her of a lifetime of working on behalf of the Indians. Asked to contribute a preface to Helen Hunt Jackson's 1881 book *A Century of Dishonor: A Sketch of the United States Government's Dealings with Some of the Indian Tribes*—a widely read and impassioned catalogue of broken treaties, theft of Indian lands, and military malfeasance—Whipple wrote, "Nations, like individuals, reap exactly what they sow; they who sow robbery reap robbery. The seed-sowing of iniquity replies in a harvest of blood."

Whipple's industriousness on behalf of his Indian wards never flagged, but neither did his belief that the only solution was white customs and white religion, which led ultimately to his support for the Carlisle Indian Industrial School in Pennsylvania. The most visible manifestation of the peace policy's emphasis on "aggressive civilization" of the Indian, the Carlisle School took in and boarded Indian students, some as young as five, and forcibly separated them from everything that made them Indian: from their parents, their names, their languages, their clothing, their long hair, their medicine, and their customs of birth, marriage, and death. The goal was a complete erasure of self, society, and history, and some Indians complied, at least outwardly. Some who resisted, however, found themselves subject to beatings, hard labor, or confinement in a Dickensian misery mill that saw twice as many students drop out and run away as graduate in the latter part of the nineteenth century. No aspect of the Indian wars, however violent, was so painful to many Indians as this separation from culture, family, tribe, and lands.

In 1899, the Macmillan Company published Whipple's "reminiscences," *Lights and Shadows of a Long Episcopate*, and two years later the bishop died of heart failure at home in Faribault. Effusive tributes and reverential obituaries appeared in newspapers from New Ulm to Great Britain. His body was interred beneath the altar of the Cathedral of Our Merciful Savior in Faribault, after which forty Christian Dakotas sang "Asleep in Jesus." His legacy was massive and admirable, and in the final analysis Whipple earned his reputation as a friend of the Indian. But it was, in the end, a very complicated friendship.

As Wowinape, teenage son of Little Crow, had fled in one direction away from his father's body, so had Chauncey Lamson, killer of Little Crow, run in another. Returning later in the day with his brother, Lamson found signs that their wounded father had managed to crawl and then walk away. They also discovered that the Indian they'd killed was still in the raspberry patch, his body cold, his bare chest covered in dried blood, and two moccasins by his side. They hazarded no guesses as to the identity of their victim, but simply went to work with a large knife and removed the anonymous man's scalp, a trophy for which Lamson and sons would be later awarded the standard $25 bounty given for the murder of any Indian found free in the state.

Next, the Lamson brothers had carried the body into the middle of the Independence Day festivities in Hutchinson and dumped it in front of a store, where the ghoulish scene was made all the more so when an unidentified individual shouted out the astonishing news that this dead Indian was none other than the Dakota war chief Little Crow. For proof, he pointed out the badly deformed wrists. Some believed him, but most didn't, unwilling to accept that the body of such a notorious figure could be deposited so randomly in their midst. After some young boys tried to place firecrackers in the ears and mouth of the corpse, it was hurriedly taken away and buried in a gravel pit usually devoted to the bones and innards of slaughtered cattle. A few days later, a militia company led by Lieutenant James D. Farmer, who was among those convinced that he had indeed seen Little Crow's remains, dug out the body and removed its head with a sword, probably as an exaggerated act of "scalping." Stories of what happened next are contradictory, but eventually the skull made it into the possession of a local doctor, who placed it in a large cooking pot filled with a lime solution.

Three weeks after fleeing from his father's side, Wowinape was found near Devils Lake. Once he began to tell his story, all doubt was removed: Little Crow was dead. By the time this news reached Hutchinson, Colonel Farmer had the skull again. He kept it in his home for another thirteen years, until he gave it to Frank Powell, a doctor and collector of Indian memorabilia who would one day contribute much of his life's stash to Buffalo Bill Cody's Wild West Show.

Twenty years later, in 1896, when Powell decided he was finished with the trophy, he made a gift of it to the Minnesota Historical Society, then housed in the basement of the state capitol. There the skull was put on display next to Little Crow's scalp, which had gone through its own chain of possession, from Chauncey Lamson to a county sheriff named Bates and then to the state adjutant general, who had thrown it in the trash, where it was retrieved by a janitor and turned over to the state historical society for safekeeping. Wowinape's son Jesse spent forty-six of the last forty-seven years of his life trying to get the pieces of his grandfather's remains returned for proper burial, finally achieving his goal in 1970.

The remains presumed to be those of Cut Nose found no such champion until the twentieth century had come and nearly gone. One year after the Dakota War, William M. Mayo became examining surgeon for Minnesota's first district, meaning all of the state south of Saint Paul, a job that eventually led him to move his home and medical office to Rochester. He kept the skeleton he attributed to Cut Nose in a large iron rendering kettle, using the bones to explain various diagnoses to his patients and teaching his boys osteology by plucking various pieces out of the pot and asking for the correct identification. Eventually, the boys would put the skeleton on display in the front room of a new clinic bearing their name, a medical facility that would become one of the most famous and highly regarded in the world. In the 1930s the third generation of Mayos had the bones sent to the clinic's museum, where over the next fifty years institutional memory went soft and the whereabouts of Cut Nose became confused. Finally, in 1991, at the prodding of historians and Mdewakanton Dakota elders, a forensic examination of multiple remains kept by the Mayo Clinic's education division revealed the "high probability" that one of the skulls belonged to Cut Nose.

As for the fate of Chaska's scalp, John F. Meagher's search for George Gleason's kin never paid off. Eventually he had Chaska's hair fashioned into a watch chain that he would wear most of his adult life, until he sat down on the day after Christmas in 1887, twenty-five years to the day after the hangings, and wrote his own letter to the Minnesota Historical Society. Obviously reflecting on the momentous occasion and his life as a young man in Mankato—and probably aware of other Indian remains on display at the society—he offered his keepsake as a permanent donation. In his mind, it was time that his own needs took a back seat to those of history.

"I wore it until it was as you see about wore out," Meagher wrote. "And now I send it to you, thinking that some day it might be of interest with the other mementoes of those terrible times and that great hanging event."

# AFTERWORD

When news reached New Salem, Illinois, in March 1832 that the Sac Indian chief Black Hawk was crossing the Mississippi River, coming back into the state in defiance of a treaty signed during Thomas Jefferson's first administration, Abraham Lincoln was twenty-three and unemployed. Lincoln had set out three years earlier on his own as a flatboatman, riding down the Mississippi with a freedom he couldn't believe, freedom from the farming life he didn't want and the father he couldn't abide. In New Orleans, at the far end of his first journey, he'd witnessed a slave auction that left him with a lifelong revulsion for the customs and apparatus of human bondage. After his return upriver to New Salem, he had settled in as storekeeper, a position that gave him authority over two assistants and the prospect of owning his own establishment should the shipments of sugar, molasses, and other sought-after Southern commodities continue their northward flow.

New Salem was a rough, rowdy, alcohol-soaked town, and here Lincoln hit his stride. A figure of amusement and respect, he was known for his honesty in dealing with customers, for his prowess in wrestling matches and other contests of athletic skill, and for his vast cache of situational jokes full of shitting, farting, and drinking. All the while Lincoln set about a self-improvement program, studying deep into each night after his workday was over, cultivating his knowledge of grammar and history, reading Poe and Shakespeare, and nurturing a growing interest in the machinations of political races.

The habit gave him hope for the future and satisfied his intellectual needs in the present, but then the shop closed, thanks to a neglectful owner, and the company warehouse emptied for good. Lincoln needed something to do, and with Black Hawk crossing the river the state needed men. Sixty-seven residents of New Salem volunteered, and when Lincoln was elected captain of the rough-and-ready Fourth Illinois Regiment of Mounted Volunteers, he discovered that he liked the taste of electoral success. Going north, he and his men soon found themselves part of a horde of militia, over a thousand soldiers under the command of General Henry Atkinson, a veteran treaty negotiator with little experience in fighting Indians. Three tours of duty gave Lincoln several encounters with the scalped and decapitated bodies of soldiers and settlers, but no battle. Almost all of the New Salem men went home after the first tour, but Lincoln stayed on for two more; as he later wrote, "I was out of work, and there being no more danger of fighting, I could do nothing better." When, years later, he made a joke about fighting only mosquitoes, he was not far off. For six more weeks he rode around northern Illinois, running messages and listening for rumors of Black Hawk, until he too mustered out in mid-July. He walked most of the way home, as his horse had been stolen.

Had Lincoln left the service just a few weeks later, he might have taken part in the Battle of Bad Axe. For two days fresh recruits under General Atkinson fired on the remnants of the Sac and Fox as they retreated across the Mississippi River, killing more than a hundred men, women, and children who were attempting to swim or paddle canoes toward the western shore. Many of the white soldiers later spoke of their own actions with disgust: as one, coincidentally named John Wakefield, later wrote, "It was a horrid sight to witness little children, wounded and suffering the most excruciating pain, although they were of the savage enemy, and the common enemy of the country." Other militia wrote of coming across the bodies of Indian warriors and repaying their opponents by scalping them and cutting their skin into razor strops. By the time Lincoln was back in New Salem and launching his first run for the state legislature, seventy-five Indians had been taken prisoner, perhaps two hundred had been killed, and another two hundred were fleeing across Iowa and heading for their villages near the Cedar River.

It wasn't enough for the white commanders, however, to clear Illinois and Wisconsin of the last vestiges of Indian resistance. A series of councils now occurred between American generals and other Indian tribes already in the region, traditional enemies of the Sac and Fox, in order to finish off the fleeing enemy. Friendly Ho-Chunks from Wisconsin, kin of the small band living across the Mississippi River, were enlisted to chase Black Hawk, who had moved north to elude the militia forces massing along the river. And to follow the two hundred fleeing Sac and Fox across Iowa, white authorities turned to the Dakota.

Many weeks before the Battle of Bad Axe, two American commanders had traveled up the Mississippi to Wabasha's village to enlist as many Mdewakanton warriors as would agree to come. In the years before the first treaties governing the Minnesota Territory were signed, the Eastern Dakota, including Little Crow's father and grandfather, had fought the Sac and Fox to the east and south every bit as fiercely as they had fought the Ojibwe to the north. The enmities were centuries old, involving hunting rights to the very lands over which Lincoln had so recently ridden. What promises of payment or gifts of enticement were made to the Dakota are unknown, but the offer met with success, and several dozen of the most notable Mdewakanton warriors rode south. Two of them in particular catch our attention: Jack Frazer, the trader, scout, and hunter famous among whites in the region for his exploits in the West and notorious among the Dakota for his casual adherence to their spiritual and cultural traditions; and the future Little Crow, Taoyateduta, Frazer's boon companion, fellow entrepreneur, and partner in dissolute living.

Among Frazer's many regular hunting and trading partners, white and Indian, was the fur trader Henry Hastings Sibley. During the Dakota War, Frazer, spared by Little Crow, became a guard and defender at Fort Ridgely, ran messages, fought alongside white soldiers at Birch Coulee, and acted as a scout for the American forces. Following the Dakota War, Sibley collected his previous notes and observations of Iron Face, one of the many names by which Frazer was known, and published a short biography in a series of newspaper columns.

In chapter 13, "The Black Hawk War," Sibley told the story of how Frazer and Taoyateduta rode down to Prairie du Chien in southern Wisconsin after their councils with the American officers, at which point the older men in their party turned back, leaving nearly one hundred young warriors to act as scouts and sharpshooters for General Atkinson. During this period, beginning in June 1832 and lasting perhaps a month, Lincoln and Little Crow moved in proximity, one a popular frontiersman leading a company of white soldiers and the other a village chief's son in a party of Dakota warriors. Perhaps they rode through the same towns, along the same river trails, up to the same high bluffs overlooking the Mississippi, days or even hours apart. Perhaps they even crossed paths along a road or clearing and eyed each other curiously, white and Indian, two very different peoples fighting in the same war and on the same side for entirely different reasons.

After Bad Axe, wrote Sibley, Atkinson sent a messenger to the nearby Dakota, who arrived on the battlefield one day later and expressed their desire to follow the escaped Sac and Fox across the river and chase them across the prairie. Atkinson agreed, aware of everything his decision implied, but before he could deliver his message, Frazer and Taoyateduta had already crossed the Mississippi. For two days and nights one hundred Dakota warriors pursued the Sac and Fox across northeastern Iowa, closing in fast on two hundred exhausted women and children and warriors who thought they were heading for the asylum of their own lands.

At dawn on August 5, three days after the Battle of Bad Axe, Taoyateduta and the other warriors overtook the party and a battle ensued, one that quickly turned into a bloodbath. Sibley portrayed Frazer as the voice of mercy, a stay against madness who dashed about to save as many women and children as he could before he was made insensible from a wound. Of Taoyateduta's actions Sibley wrote nothing. But in the end, between 60 and 160 more Sac and Fox were dead on the prairie, old and young, men, women, and children. The Dakota men, nearly unscathed, returned to the Mississippi Valley and presented the Ho-Chunk agent with 22 prisoners and 68 scalps. By that time the Black Hawk War had been declared a success, the remaining militia disbanded, and the lands of the Sac and Fox declared forfeit.

Two massacres had taken place that week. One, conducted by white soldiers along the eastern bank of the Mississippi River, would soon be denounced by some of the very men who had shot at Indian women and children desperately trying to cross to the opposite shore. The second, along the eastern bank of the Cedar River, would earn little space in contemporary newspapers and none in American history textbooks. Abraham Lincoln, late of the Black Hawk War, would years later stand in the East Room of the White House and explain to a party of tribal chiefs how his "red brethren" were "disposed to fight and kill one another" in a way whites were not. The nearly constant employ of Indian tribes as valued mercenaries in American wars, from pre-Revolutionary times through the Civil War, seems to prove the depth of white belief in Lincoln's statement. Savagery was to be condemned, it seems, unless it could be turned to one's particular advantage.

Abraham Lincoln's yarns about his service in the Black Hawk War were designed to do little more than demonstrate his capacity to laugh at himself. When he told the story of his grandfather's death, however, his purposes were clearly more complex and the emotional currents much darker. If he'd grown up penniless, Indians were in part to blame. But there was also the matter of his uncle Mordecai, who inherited what Lincoln family money there was and left his younger brothers, Josiah and Thomas, to fend for themselves. Mordecai was the future president's savior, the man whose shot had saved Thomas from oblivion, and he was characterized by many observers as a remarkable raconteur in the Lincolnian mode, full of profane jokes and anecdotes. But he was also a haunted man, prone to especially dark moods his cousins called "the horrors," episodes of severe drink or depression when he would go silent, sitting in one place for hours with a grim visage or pacing the house with his fiddle in his hands.

It seems that Mordecai was full of hatreds he could not control. And most of all he hated Indians. William T. Clagett, who lived near Mordecai and his family during their short stay in Grayson County, Kentucky, told William Herndon of a time when "there came a few Indians through there and old Mordecai heard of them passing through mounted on his horse and took his rifle gun on his shoulder and followed on after the Indians and was gone two days when he returned he said he left one lying in a sink hole for the Indians had killed his father and he was determined to have satisfaction." It was not the only time that Abraham Lincoln's uncle had engaged in his own brand of faceless retribution. Augustus H. Chapman, who married one of Lincoln's many Hanks cousins, remembered that "young Mord Lincoln swore eternal vengeance on all Indians an oath which he faithful kept as he afterwards during times of profound peace with the Indians killed several of them in fact he invariably done so when he could without it being known that he was the person that done the deed."

This was solitary, cruel, indiscriminate violence—by another name, savagery—and it laid bare the taut, tangled knot at the heart of the unanswerable "Indian question." The pattern was so consistent as to seem inviolable: failures of law, failures of policy, and failures of justice created deep and lasting personal grievances on all sides that overwhelmed all attempts at systemic reform. Five months before violence erupted along the Minnesota River Valley, Henry Whipple wrote to Abraham Lincoln that "a nation which sowed robbery would reap a harvest of blood." Six weeks of war in the Northwest left hundreds dead and set off a chain reaction that would kill thousands more, white and Indian, most of whom could not begin to understand how they had become the targets of such all-consuming hatred. By the end of the nineteenth century, millions of words—legal, legislative, literary, journalistic, theological, and personal—would be devoted to the Dakota War and its aftermath. But in the end, it seems, "private revenge" spoke the loudest.

# ACKNOWLEDGMENTS

A great number of people have taken a professional or avocational interest in the U.S.-Dakota War in the 150 years since its conclusion. I thank all of them and want to highlight a few especially prominent members of the current dialogue, whose work has been vital to *38 Nooses:* Gary Clayton Anderson, Walt Bachman, Mary H. Bakeman, Clifford Canku, Waziyatawin Angela Wilson, Curtis Dahlin, Kirsten Delegard, Kathryn Zabelle Derounian-Stodola, Mark Diedrich, Rhoda R. Gilman, Lois Glewwe, Colette Hyman, Elden Lawrence, June Namias, Anton Treuer, David Treuer, Corinne L. Monjeau-Marz, Stephen Osman, John Peacock, Ed Red Owl, Florestine Renville, Virginia Driving Hawk Sneve, Gabrielle Tateyuskanskan, Gwen N. Westerman, Bruce White, Diane Wilson, Mary Lethert Wingerd, Alan R. Woolworth, and Carrie Reber Zeman.

Many researchers, historians, and park employees took time to speak with me over the past five years about the Dakota War and the stories surrounding it. Terri Dinesen, park manager of Upper Sioux Agency State Park, shared many resources and oriented me to the geography of the Upper Minnesota River Valley at the very beginning of my work; Thomas Sanders, manager of the Jeffers Petroglyphs site and former manager at the Lower Sioux Agency, took me on a most illuminating walk down to the flat place where the ferry once crossed the Minnesota River and shared his thoughtful perspective on the events there; Ted Alexander, chief historian at Antietam National Battlefield, opened his file on the First Minnesota Regiment and helped me make sense of the action near the Dunker Church on the morning of September 17, 1862,

# Acknowledgments

and the scene in the days following; Gabrielle Tateyuskanskan, a poet, artist, and educator, spoke with me on two occasions of the pitfalls of preconceived historical interpretation and the struggles of young men and women to find health and prosperity on modern-day reservations; Jim Moffet, president of the Historic First Minnesota Volunteer Infantry Regiment, proved a gracious host and a treasure trove of telling detail; James Percoco, a recent inductee of the National Teachers Hall of Fame, read an early draft of *38 Nooses* and provided important perspective on Abraham Lincoln; and Stephen Osman, retired senior historian at the Minnesota Historical Society and former director of Historic Fort Snelling, read an intermediate draft and saved me from several errors regarding the organization, protocols, and actions of military units during the Civil War.

Walt Bachman, independent historian, retired trial lawyer, and author of *Law v. Life: What Lawyers Are Afraid to Say About the Legal Profession,* met with me to discuss the historiography of the war and offered his thoughts on the military commission trials in a long string of back-and-forth e-mails. He also read an intermediate draft of *38 Nooses* and generously shared important documents culled from his own research, including two unpublished letters from John Pope to Henry Hastings Sibley that help to illuminate a previously foggy sequence of events as the trials got under way. Walt's legal acumen, his indefatigability as a researcher, and the well-earned clarity of his interpretations make him a uniquely stimulating correspondent.

Carrie Reber Zeman is an extraordinary independent scholar with X-ray vision that allows her to see unerringly through the current research to the next interesting set of questions. Her breadth and depth of knowledge on the historical sources and context of the Dakota War are, without exaggeration, unparalleled. Carrie's comments, questions, hints, and suggestions on two separate readings of my manuscript saved the final version from any number of slips; she also supplied drafts and working papers from her own research into the lives of many persons involved in the story, including Sarah Wakefield, Thomas Galbraith, and Henry Benjamin Whipple. And her lengthy introduction to the recently published edition of Mary Butler Renville's *A Thrilling Narrative of Indian Captivity: Dispatches from the Dakota War* (co-edited with Kathryn Zabelle Derounian-Stodola) is a model for anyone attaching scholarly apparatus to important primary texts.

All of those listed above and others have done vital work, some to acclaim and some without proper recognition. Thanks to them, and to everyone cited in my notes and bibliography, for so doggedly conducting their research and for so generously sharing their work and insights. I also thank the staffs at the Library of Congress, the National Archives, the Minnesota Historical Society, and at all of Minnesota's county historical societies, as well as the employees and historians at the many state and national parks connected to the events in *38 Nooses*. No one provided information, advice, wisdom, or opinions in bad faith, and any errors of fact or citation are entirely my responsibility.

As always, I recognize the writers, scholars, and researchers who surround me at George Mason University—students and faculty—for their encouragement, commitment, and passion. At William Morris, Suzanne Gluck shepherded the book with her usual enthusiasm and flair, while Eric Lupfer has my gratitude for his reassuring manner, his deep reservoir of genuine excitement, and his expert help shaping the threads of the narrative at the very start. This is my second book with Edward Kastenmeier at Pantheon/Vintage, following *Grand Avenues;* in both cases, thank goodness, his eye and pen provided not just valuable editorial assistance but an entire education in narrative writing. Other crucial support at Pantheon came from Ellen Feldman, Emily Giglierano, and Brian Barth. Susanna Sturgis's copyediting was invaluable, while Paul Gormont of Apertures, Inc. created the book's website and endpaper map with his customary feel for form and function. And once more I thank my friends and colleagues Dallas Hudgens, Wendi Kaufman, Robyn Wright, and Corrine Zappia Gormont for their considerable help, support, and encouragment.

Finally, I thank my family, beginning with my parents, Roger and Margaret, one a born Minnesotan and the other close enough. As tragic and troubling as the story of *38 Nooses* may be, it is our history, and worth the investigation. My wife, Cory, and my sons, Carter and Elliot, have been true friends and steady companions on this particularly complex and meandering journey. I trust that, in the end, all of the time was well spent.

Many of the institutions that foster knowledge and promote study of subjects such as the Dakota War are under debilitating financial stress.

## Acknowledgments

The cost in the present of supporting and encouraging such institutions is considerable; the cost in the future of failing to continue that support and encouragement will be incalculable. Accordingly, a portion of the advance for *38 Nooses* has been set aside as donations to the American Indian College Fund and the Minnesota Historical Society.

# A NOTE ON SOURCES

The Dakota War of 1862 is an inexhaustible tale, with deep roots and many branches. *38 Nooses* seeks to emphasize the small degrees of separation that existed between seemingly widely spaced actors: between Dakota Indians and whites, between individuals driving events and those swept up by events, between politicians in Washington, D.C., and settlers on the northwestern frontier, between battle-tested soldiers of the Civil War and civilian skirmishers in Minnesota. In my telling—as in any telling—certain moments and people are privileged and others are necessarily deemphasized or omitted. Those choices are not a judgment of value; rather, they are a by-product of the particular lenses I've used. Taken all together, the sources listed below are remarkable for their scope and detail, and those wishing to explore other parts of the story, or to revisit those narrated in *38 Nooses,* will find much to reward their curiosity.

A long list of academic scholars, independent historians, and other research-ers have devoted their attention to the themes, people, and events prominent in *38 Nooses.* Many of these people are thanked individually in the acknowledgments. But gratitude is also due to the thousands of people who created and maintain the primary sources on which the story depends, some of which are now available in impressive digital collections. In writing *38 Nooses* I made frequent use of the Cornell University Library's Making of America Collection (ebooks.library.cornell .edu/m/moawar/index.html), especially its searchable copy of *The War of the Rebellion: A Compilation of the Official Records of the Union and Confederate Armies,* as well as *The Collected Works of Abraham Lincoln* at the University of Michigan (quod .lib.umich.edu/l/lincoln) and the Abraham Lincoln Papers at the Library of Congress (lcweb2.loc.gov/ammem/alhtml/malhome.html). I also took advantage of the many indispensable online research databases available through the library system at George Mason University, including JSTOR, ProQuest Historical Newspapers, and Infotrac's 19th Century U.S. Newspapers. The two-volume compilation *Minnesota in the Civil and Indian Wars, 1861–1865,* recently reissued by the Minnesota Historical Society Press and available only in print, sometimes overlaps with *The*

# A Note on Sources

*War of the Rebellion,* but also includes many letters and other communications that are difficult to find elsewhere.

Offline, my most frequent destinations were the National Archives, the Newspaper and Current Periodical Reading Room at the Library of Congress, the libraries of the Washington Research Library Consortium, and the Manuscript and Newspaper Collections at the Minnesota Historical Society library. At these repositories I was able to access many important books, journals, personal papers, organizational records, and complete or nearly complete runs of the following newspapers, all of which are quoted in this book: from Minnesota, the *Faribault Republican, Mankato Independent, Mankato Record, Minneapolis Tribune, St. Cloud Democrat, St. Paul Pioneer, St. Paul Press, St. Paul Union,* and *Stillwater Messenger;* from New York, the *New York Daily News, New York Times,* and *New York Tribune;* from Washington, D.C., the *Congressional Globe, Daily Morning Chronicle,* and *National Intelligencer.*

Most of the white characters featured in *38 Nooses* left ample records of their lives. In addition to the forty-plus boxes of material in the Whipple Papers at the Manuscript Collections of the Minnesota Historical Society, Henry Benjamin Whipple left behind a memoir, *Lights and Shadows of a Long Episcopate,* and a detailed record of his journey to the South as a young adult, *Bishop Whipple's Southern Diary.* Sarah Wakefield's life is far better documented than that of most middle-class women of her place and era (at least during the years covered by this narrative), in the form of two editions of her captivity narrative, *Six Weeks in the Sioux Tepees,* and a small but revealing set of letters scattered in various libraries. (Three of these letters have been unearthed and examined in great detail by Kathryn Zabelle Derounian-Stodola in an article in the journal *Prospects: An Annual of American Cultural Studies;* that article forms the basis of parts of chapters 17 and 19.) Primary documents by and connected to Henry Hastings Sibley are found in the voluminous Sibley Papers in the Manuscript Collections of the Minnesota Historical Society. Documentary source material related to other characters is listed in the notes and bibliography.

The Dakota experience of the war and its aftermath has survived in parallel to the written historical record for 150 years, largely through oral histories told generation after generation. Those thoughts and actions of Dakotas written down in the years covered by *38 Nooses* were almost always recorded by white intermediaries in situations inviting a high degree of skepticism. I have privileged one text, *Through Dakota Eyes,* a collection of narratives from non-white perspectives carefully selected and accompanied by an excellent editorial apparatus by the preeminent Dakota War scholars Gary Clayton Anderson and Alan R. Woolworth. The many captivity narratives that emerged in the wake of the Dakota War may be unreliable taken one at a time, but they can be usefully used in concert. Isaac Heard's *History of the Sioux War* stands out among the contemporaneous histories written by whites for its use of firsthand accounts and trial-related testimony, though considerable adjustment needs to be made for Heard's own involvement in the events.

A superb collection of secondary sources forms the base of my interpretations of character. Most are listed here or in the bibliography, rather than chapter by chapter, as they suffuse every section of *38 Nooses.* Though Little Crow left behind few writings of his own, his very public stature and his lifelong interactions with white authorities created an unusually wide and deep documentary record of his life. Gary Clayton Anderson's *Little Crow* and *Kinsmen of Another Kind,* taken together, form a thorough panorama of the life and world of Little Crow. Mark Diedrich's more recent biography of Little Crow presents an extraordinarily detailed chronology that is difficult to piece together otherwise. Sarah Wakefield has had three accomplished scholars on her trail for several years now: June Namias, whose book *White Captives* reintroduced Wakefield to a wide academic audience; Kathryn Zabelle Derounian-Stodola, whose recent work on Wakefield's life and writings has masterfully placed them inside the frame of other captivity narratives from the Dakota War; and, again, Carrie Rebar Zeman, whose ongoing research promises a new perspective on Wakefield's life, especially before and after her six weeks as a captive of the Dakota. Henry Benjamin Whipple's life and work are ably laid out in Anne Beiser Allen, *And the Wilderness Shall Blossom,* and Andrew S. Brake, *Man in the Middle.*

The choices of secondary material related to Abraham Lincoln are nearly inexhaustible, and the degree of specialization impressive and greatly appreciated. Several such studies are listed in the bibliography. For my overall view of Lincoln's life and character, I quickly came to rely on Michael Burlingame's two-volume biography, *Abraham Lincoln: A Life,* published in 2008, when I was midway through my own project. No book brings the reader inside Lincoln's inner circle as well as Doris Kearns Goodwin's *Team of Rivals. Lincoln and the Indians,* by David A. Nichols, was the first book-length scholarly consideration of the subject and opened up a good number of intriguing lines of study and inquiry followed in *38 Nooses.* And Shelby Foote's three-volume *The Civil War: A Narrative* is still the most coherent and compulsively readable account of the war ever written.

If secondary sources related to Lincoln, his administration, and the Civil War have never been in short supply, a recent surge in scholarly attention to the history of Minnesota and the Dakota War couldn't have appeared at a more fortuitous time. Since 1872 the Minnesota Historical Society has published its own journal; that publication, now called *Minnesota History,* was recently joined by the independently produced *Minnesota's Heritage,* which focuses on the events and people of the Dakota War, often in great detail. In 2008 many of those responsible for *Minnesota's Heritage* combined with other scholars to publish *Trails of Tears: Minnesota's Dakota Indian Exile Begins,* a collection of studies and essays that examines the experiences of Dakotas brought to Mankato and Fort Snelling in the aftermath of the war. William Watts Folwell's four-volume *A History of Minnesota,* since 1961 the standard history of the state, has now been supplemented by Mary Lethert Wingerd's lively, readable, and lavishly illustrated *North Country,* which focuses on the history of the region up to the conclusion of the Dakota War.

In order to balance the need for careful documentation with space concerns, I have provided citations for all quoted material in the book. Secondary sources of special usefulness, when not listed above, have been listed under each chapter heading in the notes. I will list any postpublication emendations, additions, or reinterpretations at www.38nooses.com and www.scottwberg.com; I also welcome any

# A Note on Sources

queries or comments regarding source materials, which can be sent to scottwberg@
scottwberg.com. Finally, where spellings or translations are in dispute, I have tried
to make sensible and consistent choices. In some cases, punctuation or capitaliza-
tion in quoted material has been very lightly edited.

# NOTES

### INTRODUCTION

*Herndon's Informants* (Douglas L. Wilson and Rodney O. Davis, eds.) includes several different secondhand reports of the fatal encounter along Long Run. Colin G. Calloway, *The Shawnees and the War for America*, provides a short, authoritative introduction to that tribe's history and relationship to American settlers. Lowell H. Harrison and James C. Klotter, *A New History of Kentucky*, also provided important context.

   x   "the legend more strongly than all others": AL to Jesse Lincoln, April 1, 1854, *CW* 2:217.

   x   "Owing to my father being left": AL to Solomon Lincoln, March 6, 1848, *CW* 1:456.

   x   "By the early death of his father": AL, Autobiography Written for John L. Scripps, ca. June 1860, *CW* 4:61.

   x   "He regrets his want of education": Ibid., 4:62.

  XII  "a success which gave me more pleasure": AL to Jesse W. Fell, December 20, 1859, *CW* 3:512.

  XII  "It is quite certain": AL, Speech in the United States House of Representatives, July 27, 1848, *CW* 1:510.

### CHAPTER ONE

   4   "restless, unquiet disposition": Pond, *Dakota Life*, 9.

   7   "always seemed to say by their manner": Anderson and Woolworth, eds., *Through Dakota Eyes*, 24.

   9   "blackened his face": Gordon, *The Feast of the Virgins*, 342.

   9   "Taoyateduta is a coward!": Ibid., 343.

10  "The whites must be pretty hard up": Anderson and Woolworth, eds., *Through Dakota Eyes*, 26.

13  "sprang from his tepee": Gordon, *The Feast of the Virgins*, 343.

13  "Ta-o-ya-te-du-ta is not a coward": Ibid., 343–44.

15  "Soon the cry was 'Kill the whites'": Anderson and Woolworth, eds., *Through Dakota Eyes*, 36.

CHAPTER TWO

Henry David Thoreau's 1861 trip up the Minnesota River is discussed in detail in Robert L. Straker, "Thoreau's Journey to Minnesota," in the *New England Quarterly,* and in Corinne Hosfield Smith, "What a Difference a Year Can Make," in *Minnesota's Heritage.*

16  "Taking a final look": SW, *Six Weeks in the Sioux Tepees,* in Derounian-Stodola, ed., *Women's Indian Captivity Narratives,* 252.

19  "As I landed from the steamboat": Ibid., 242.

19  "A more beautiful sight": Ibid.

20  "the buffalo were said to be feeding": Thoreau, *Writings,* 11:390.

20  "were quite dissatisfied": Ibid.

21  "a curse to this country": Ross, *Recollections,* 139.

25  "Not a day passed": SW, *Six Weeks in the Sioux Tepees,* in Derounian-Stodola, ed., *Women's Indian Captivity Narratives,* 255.

25  "they often said he saved": Ibid., 256.

26  "driving down the hill": Ibid., 248.

27  "rapped violently": Ibid.

29  "We have waited a long time": Folwell, *A History of Minnesota,* 2:232.

29  "made great sport of me" and following: SW, *Six Weeks in the Sioux Tepees,* in Derounian-Stodola, ed., *Women's Indian Captivity Narratives,* 252–55.

CHAPTER THREE

32  "Now I will kill the dog": Heard, *History of the Sioux War,* 62.

36  "I kept up with him" and following: SW, *Six Weeks in the Sioux Tepees,* in Derounian-Stodola, ed., *Women's Indian Captivity Narratives,* 256–61.

CHAPTER FOUR

42  "I had never seen the Indians so restless": HBW, *Lights and Shadows,* 106.

42  "sad at heart": Ibid.

42  "We have in the party": HBW journal, MHS Manuscript Collections, Whipple Papers, Box 3.

43  "the defective teaching of Rome": Ibid.

43  "they stooped to the ground": Ibid.

43  "much disturbed": Ibid.

50  "the outlet for not only all northwestern": *St. Paul Press,* August 20, 1862.

52  "Everyone thought it was madness": HBW, *Lights and Shadows,* 18.

52  "So often the shadows were shifted": Ibid., 21.

52  "like a clap of thunder": HBW to unknown, July 21, 1859, MHS Manuscript Collections, Whipple Papers, Box 40.

52  "Society has not crystallized": HBW, *Lights and Shadows,* 203.

52  "one-roomed log huts": Ibid., 91.

53  "Many of the frontier settlers": Ibid.

53  "From my childhood": Ibid., 29–30.

53  "My habits of life are active": HBW to Rev. Bishop Whitehouse, Feb. 7, 1857, MHS Manuscript Collections, Whipple Papers, Box 40.

53  "gentle hand on my head": HBW, *Lights and Shadows,* 2.

53  "Nothing lingers longer in memory": Ibid., 149.

54  "planted a mission": Ibid., 61.

54  " 'enthusiastic tenderfoot' ": Ibid., 142.

54  "Good men": Ibid., 32.

54  AWFUL SACRILEGE: Ibid., 160.

54  "wandering Indians": Ibid., 33.

55  "perhaps": Ibid., 86.

55  "illicit intercourse between the sexes": Pond, *Dakota Life,* 122.

55  "White man go to war": HBW, *Lights and Shadows,* 65–66.

55  "Our Indian affairs were then at their worst": Ibid., 30.

56  "I know that it is a long way": Ibid., 61.

56  "American pagans whose degradation": HBW to James Buchanan, April 9, 1860, MHS Manuscript Collections, Whipple Papers, Box 2.

56  "The sad condition of the Indians": HBW, *Lights and Shadows,* 510.

57  "I have the honor to acknowledge": AL to HBW, March 27, 1862, *CW* 5:173.

57  "At once . . . sent a boy ringing a bell": HBW, *Lights and Shadows,* 122.

58  "filled with refugees": Ibid.

58  "The gratitude of some of the sufferers": Ibid.

CHAPTER FIVE

Francis Paul Prucha, *The Great Father,* and Paul VanDevelder, *Savages & Scoundrels,* together provide an excellent, readable overview of relations between the United States and Indian tribes during the country's first century.

59  "Well, boys, I am down to the raisins": Ward, *Abraham Lincoln,* 165.

60  "The Sioux Indians on our western border": Alexander Ramsey to Edwin M. Stanton, August 21, 1862, *OR* 1:13, 590.

60 "A most frightful insurrection": J. H. Baker to C. P. Walcott, August 21, 1862, *OR* 1:13, 590–91.

62 "to have a sweat of five or six days": Dahlgren, *Memoir,* 379.

63 "[A] great proportion of those who triumphed": *New York Tribune,* August 19, 1862.

63 "We ask you to consider": Ibid.

63 "the proper status of the negro in our civilization": Alexander H. Stephens, "Cornerstone Address, March 21, 1861," 45.

64 "the proper treatment of the original occupants": Ulysses S. Grant, *The Papers of Ulysses S. Grant, July 1, 1868–October 31, 1869,* 142.

65 "The utmost good faith" : Ordinance of 1787, 1 Stat. 50.

65 "to lay out the parts of the district": Ibid.

66 "what I have recommended to you": Washington, *Writings,* 958.

68 "domestic dependent nations": John Marshall, opinion in *Cherokee Nation v. State of Georgia.*

68 "have neither the intelligence": Message from the President of the United States, *House Executive Documents,* 23rd Congress, 1st Session, No. 1.

68 "truth at once in its neglected simplicity": *New York Daily News,* December 27, 1845.

69 "Away with all these cobweb tissues": Ibid.

CHAPTER SIX

73 "walking the floor": White, "Captivity Among the Sioux," 404.

73 "was determined to take back": Tarble, "The Story of My Capture," 33.

74 "in substance . . . his young men": Anderson and Woolworth, eds., *Through Dakota Eyes,* 131.

74 "We have begun, and must do": Taliaferro, "Auto-Biography of Maj. Lawrence Taliaferro," 247.

77 "Soldiers and young men": Heard, *History of the Sioux War,* 144.

77 "Hereafter . . . make war": Ibid.

78 "all night with their blankets": Anderson and Woolworth, eds., *Through Dakota Eyes,* 154.

78 "The young men were all anxious to go": Ibid.

79 "We paid no attention to the chiefs": Ibid.

79 "We will fix you, you devils!": Ibid., 138.

79 "might take a day or two": Ibid., 131.

80 "The object of the German Land Company for every German laborer": Berghold, *The Indians' Revenge,* 9.

80 "The natural beauty of the place": Ibid., 20.

81 "They learned that the Indians": Ibid., 27.

81 "What strange feelings overcame us": Ibid., 30.

83 "Their advance upon the sloping prairie": Charles E. Flandrau, *MICW* 2:204.

84 "The fighting from both sides": Ibid.

85 "week of tepee life": White, "Captivity Among the Sioux," 405.

86 "laid down": SW, *Six Weeks in the Sioux Tepees*, in Derounian-Stodola, ed., *Women's Indian Captivity Narratives*, 271.

86 "My father could not have done differently": Ibid.

86 "I dared not contradict it": Ibid.


CHAPTER SEVEN

Anton Treuer, *The Assassination of Hole in the Day* and *Ojibwe in Minnesota* (with David Treuer), helped me to portray the Ojibwe world and the council between William P. Dole and Hole in the Day. Harlan Hoyt Horner, *Lincoln and Greeley*, is the definitive study of the relationship between the president and the nation's most influential newspaper editor.

90 "occasionally found it convenient": Helen Nicolay, *Lincoln's Secretary*, 151.

90 "sour and crusty": Burlingame, ed., *With Lincoln*, xix.

90 "scrupulous, polite, calm, obliging": Ibid., xviii.

91 "a fair French and German scholar": Ibid.

91 "show where Minnesota is": Neill, *History of Minnesota*, 5.

91 "Grand scenery, leaping waters": Ibid., 27.

91 "Like all ignorant and barbarous people": Ibid., 54.

91 "entertained no sentimental illusions": Helen Nicolay, *Lincoln's Secretary*, 155.

92 "If in the wild woods": John Hay to JN, August 11, 1862, *At Lincoln's Side*, 24.

93 "seemed to him 'primitive'": Helen Nicolay, *Lincoln's Secretary*, 152.

94 "[t]he whole border at once took alarm": JN, *Lincoln's Secretary Goes West*, 32.

94 "at break-neck speed": Ibid., 33.

95 "The Indian war is still progressing": Alexander Ramsey and William P. Dole to Edwin M. Stanton, August 25, 1862, *OR* 1:13, 596.

96 "With the concurrence of Commissioner Dole": Alexander Ramsey to AL, August 26, 1862, *OR* 1:13, 597.

96 "We are in the midst of a most terrible": Morton Wilkinson, William P. Dole, and JN to AL, *OR* 1:13, 599.

96 "The Indian war grows more extensive": JN to Edwin M. Stanton, *OR* 1:13, 599–600.

97 "Yours received": AL to Alexander Ramsey, August 27, 1862, *OR* 1:13, 599.

98 "If there be in [Greeley's 'Prayer'] any statements" and following: *New York Tribune*, August 25, 1862.

99 "expelled most of those Indians" and following: Ibid.

100 "Indians, from Minnesota to Pike's Peak": James Craig to Edwin M. Stanton, August 23, 1862, *OR* 1:13, 592.

100 "satisfied rebel agents have been at work": James Craig to Halleck, August 25, 10, *OR* 1:13, 596.

100 "that some vicious influence is at work": James Craig to James G. Blunt, August 28, 1862, *OR* 1:13, 608.

# Notes

100   "The hostilities are so extensive": Caleb B. Smith to HWH, Aug. 28, 1862, NARA RG 48, Letters Sent, Interior Department, Roll 4, M606.

100   "national war": Alexander Ramsey to AL, September 6, 1862, ALPLC online.

100   "editors in the vicinity": *Scientific American*, September 6, 1862, 147.


### CHAPTER EIGHT

102   "confusion of Babel": SW, *Six Weeks in the Sioux Tepees,* in Derounian-Stodola, ed., *Women's Indian Captivity Narratives,* 277.

102   "I wish it was within my power": Ibid., 276.

102   "He was stripped of his clothing": Ibid., 278.

103   "These houses are large and strong": Renville, "A Sioux Narrative of the Outbreak in 1862," 599.

103   "she took a wrong course with the Indians": SW, *Six Weeks in the Sioux Tepees,* in Derounian-Stodola, ed., *Women's Indian Captivity Narratives,* 283.

103   "If that is so": Ibid.

105   "take up arms against them": Anderson and Woolworth, eds., *Through Dakota Eyes,* 170.

105   "I want to speak now to you": Ibid., 196.

106   "should not be released": Renville, "A Sioux Narrative of the Outbreak in 1862," 602.

107   "the leader of those who made war": Ibid., 603.

107   "Over the earth I come": Anderson and Woolworth, eds., *Through Dakota Eyes,* 197.

113   "If Little Crow has any proposition": Heard, *History of the Sioux War,* 147.

113   "We made a treaty with the government": Ibid.

114   "I want to know from you": Ibid., 156–57.

115   "I wish no more war": Sharon, *Viola,* 322.

115   "I tell you we must fight": Heard, *History of the Sioux War,* 158–59.

115   "You have murdered many of our people": HHS to LC, September 8, 1862, MHS Manuscript Collections, Sibley Papers.

115   "I have not come into this upper country": HHS to unnamed, September 13, 1862, *OR* 1:13, 632.

117   "the muss with Hole-in-the-Day": Helen Nicolay, *Lincoln's Secretary,* 153.

118   "kill all the whites": JN, *Lincoln's Secretary Goes West,* 68.

118   "Where is your scalp?": John Hay to JN, Aug. 27, 1862, *At Lincoln's Side,* 25.

118   "They came on in irregular, straggling groups": JN, *Lincoln's Secretary Goes West,* 35.

119   "blown to hell": Treuer, *The Assassination of Hole in the Day,* 137.

119   "gave them a short nice speech": Ibid., 138.

119   "a deadly and desperate melee": JN, *Lincoln's Secretary Goes West,* 40.

119   "merely an hour's preliminary": Ibid., 40–41.

120   "My scalp is yet safe": JN to John Hay, September 12, 1862, *With Lincoln,* 88.

120  "felt almost ready to hang himself": Bates, note to Meditation on the Divine Will, September 2, 1862, *CW* 5:404.

122  "Let us understand each other": JP, July 14, 1862, *OR* 1:12, 473–74.

122  "The Indian hostilities that have recently broken forth": Edwin M. Stanton to JP, September 6, 1862, *OR* 1:13, 617.

CHAPTER NINE

Ernest Furgurson, *Freedom Rising,* is an engaging and detailed portrait of Washington, D.C., during the Civil War. Ronald C. White, Jr., *Mr. Lincoln's Greatest Speech,* provides essential background for the "Meditation on the Divine Will" and Lincoln's visit with the delegation of "Chicago Christians."

125  "An order from General R.E. Lee": McClellan to Halleck, September 13, 1862, *OR* 19:2, 281–82.

125  "destroy the rebel army, if possible": AL to McClellan, September 16, 1862, *CW* 5:426.

126  "a long series of years": John Ross to AL, September 16, 1862, ALPLC online.

126  "great mass of the Cherokee People": Ibid.

127  "What good would a proclamation": AL, "Reply to a Memorial Presented by Chicago Christians of All Denominations," *CW* 5:420.

127  "I hope it will not be irreverent": Ibid.

127  "God cannot be *for*": AL, "Meditation on the Divine Will," *CW* 5:404.

128  "Every kind of labour is performed": HBW, *Southern Diary,* 14.

128  "the efforts of abolitionists at the North": Ibid., 31.

128  "When will the cupidity and cruelty": Ibid., 21.

129  "wonder of wonders": Ibid., 167–68.

129  "tall, thoughtful-faced": HBW, *Lights and Shadows,* 34.

129  "Mr. Whipple of New York": Ibid.

130  "From the beginning of the Civil War": Ibid., 102.

130  "intimately from boyhood": Ibid., 100.

130  "the instrument of no political faction": HWH to HBW, November 29, 1861, MHS Manuscript Collections, Whipple Papers, Box 2.

131  "little more . . . than a first-rate clerk": Burlingame and Ettlinger, eds., *Inside Lincoln's White House,* 183.

131  "going on a tour of pleasure": HBW to William T. Dana, February 23, 1861, MHS Manuscript Collections, Whipple Papers, Box 39.

131  "a strong conservative element": HBW to John Whipple, March 4, 1861, MHS Manuscript Collections, Whipple Papers, Box 39.

132  "the splendid carpet is in threads": HBW, *Southern Diary,* 166.

132  "a public shame": Ibid., 167.

132  "seemed to diminish in size": Helen Nicolay, *Lincoln's Secretary,* 88.

133  "a great Christian nation": HBW, *Lights and Shadows,* 511.

133 "an account of the outbreak": Ibid., 136.

133 "He was deeply moved": Ibid.

133 "Bishop . . . a man thought that monkeys": Ibid.

133 "Give Bishop Whipple any information": Ibid., 137.

134 "waiting for heavy fog to rise": AL to Andrew G. Curtin, September 16, 1862, *CW* 5:427.

CHAPTER TEN

Four books in particular helped me to understand and portray Antietam, both the battle and its aftermath: James M. McPherson, *Crossroads of Freedom;* Stephen W. Sears, *Landscape Turned Red;* Kathleen A. Ernst, *Too Afraid to Cry;* and Ezra A. Carman, *The Maryland Campaign of September 1862* (Joseph Pierro, ed.). James A. Wright, *No More Gallant a Deed* (Steven Keillor, ed.), and Richard Moe, *The Last Full Measure,* together provide a detailed look inside the First Minnesota Regiment.

135 "some military officer of high rank": Edwin M. Stanton to JP, September 6, 1862, *OR* 1:13, 617.

136 "The examination of a portion of this Territory": JP, "The Report of an Exploration of the Territory of Minnesota," in Senate Executive Documents, 31st Congress, 1st Session, Doc. 42.

136 "I can only attribute to ignorance": Ibid.

136 "as yet entirely ignorant": Ibid.

137 "From all indications and information": JP to HWH, September 16, 1862, *OR* 1:13, 642.

137 "have also begun to rob and murder": Ibid.

137 "Time is everything here": Ibid.

138 "Our victory was complete": George B. McClellan to HWH, September 19, 1862, ALPLC online.

139 "Houses (some of them)": Wright, *No More Gallant a Deed,* 203.

140 "It beggars description": HBW to E. G. Gear, November 5, 1862, MHS Manuscript Collections, Whipple Papers, Box 40.

140 "The slain of higher condition": Oliver Wendell Holmes, *Atlantic Monthly,* December 1862, 743–44.

140 "There was a hushed stillness": HBW to E. G. Gear, November 5, 1862, MHS Manuscript Collections, Whipple Papers, Box 40.

140 "one of the most solemn services": HBW, *Lights and Shadows,* 96.

140 "expression of loving confidence": Ibid.

144 "When it was found that Lee": Carman, *Maryland Campaign,* 369.

144 "pierced by the balls of half a score of battle fields": HBW, Sermon, 1863, MHS Manuscript Collections, Whipple Papers, Sermons and Addresses, P823, Box 3.

144 "I could not help but thank them": Ibid.

145 "Will you do me the favor": HBW, *Lights and Shadows,* 97.

146 "The pestilence is the work of innumerable particles": Brake, *Man in the Middle*, 48.

146 "wicked neglect and robbery": Ibid., 50.

146 "fostered a system": Ibid.

146 "inequity and fraud of an Indian system": Ibid.

147 "able to ask an engineer": HBW, *Lights and Shadows*, 19.

147 "You do not know": Ibid., 97.

147 "If it were not for wearying you": Ibid., 98–99.

148 "the great act of the age": Hannibal Hamlin to AL, September 25, 1862, ALPLC online.

CHAPTER ELEVEN

153 "howling wilderness": Monjeau-Marz, *The Dakota Indian Internment*, 20.

153 "the Indians made much sport": SW, *Six Weeks in the Sioux Tepees*, in Derounian-Stodola, ed., *Women's Indian Captivity Narratives*, 291.

154 "I tried to urge Chaska not to go": Ibid., 292.

154 "as sweet as the chimes": McClure, "The Story of Nancy McClure," 454.

154 "When you bring up the prisoners": HHS to unnamed, September 23, 1862, *OR* 1:13, 664.

154 "I have not come to make war": HHS to Ma-za-ka-tame, Toopee, and Wa-ke-nan-nan-te, September 24, 1862, *OR* 1:13, 667.

155 "advise your bands not to mix": HHS to Ta-Tanka-Nazin, September 24, 1862, *OR* 1:13, 667.

155 "bearing wounded": McClure, "The Story of Nancy McClure," 454.

155 "Any one that has heard one squaw": SW, *Six Weeks in the Sioux Tepees*, in Derounian-Stodola, ed., *Women's Indian Captivity Narratives*, 292.

156 "Seven hundred picked warriors": Anderson and Woolworth, eds., *Through Dakota Eyes*, 223.

156 "I told them it was very foolish": SW, *Six Weeks in the Sioux Tepees*, in Derounian-Stodola, ed., *Women's Indian Captivity Narratives*, 293.

156 "You are going back": Ibid.

156 "cried over James and begged me": Ibid., 293–94.

157 "Yes, cousin, we are most safe now": Anderson and Woolworth, eds., *Through Dakota Eyes*, 253.

157 "Little Crow called all his warriors together": Ibid., 223.

157 "simply laughed at Little Crow's bombastic talk": Ibid.

158 "like a man": HHS to Little Crow, September 8, 1862, MHS Manuscript Collections, Sibley Papers.

158 "Sibley would like to put the rope around my neck": Anderson and Woolworth, eds., *Through Dakota Eyes*, 253.

160 "He said he felt as if they would kill": SW, *Six Weeks in the Sioux Tepees*, in Derounian-Stodola, ed., *Women's Indian Captivity Narratives*, 295.

160 "If I am killed": Ibid.

160  "every man and woman in the camp": Anderson and Woolworth, eds., *Through Dakota Eyes*, 224.

160  "I felt feelings of anger": SW, *Six Weeks in the Sioux Tepees*, in Derounian-Stodola, ed., *Women's Indian Captivity Narratives*, 297.

161  "The Indians became much alarmed": Ibid.

161  "good woman . . . talk good to your white people": Ibid., 298.

162  "repeatedly told us": *Morton Enterprise*, January 29, 1909.

162  "assurance that they would not have dared": HHS to JP, September 27, 1862, *MICW* 2:255.

162  "After I was introduced to Sibley": SW, *Six Weeks in the Sioux Tepees*, in Derounian-Stodola, ed., *Women's Indian Captivity Narratives*, 298.

162  "I was a vast deal more comfortable": Ibid., 299.

163  "News of the great event of the war": *St. Paul Daily Press*, September 26, 1862.

163  "the Sioux Indians of Minnesota": *Executive Documents of the State of Minnesota for the Year 1862*, 12.

CHAPTER TWELVE

Carol Chomsky, "The United States–Dakota War Trials," in the *Stanford Law Review*, is the longest and most rigorous published analysis to date of the formation of the military commission and the subsequent trials. Walt Bachman's manuscript-in-progress, a biography of Joseph Godfrey, overturns much of the conventional understanding regarding the pace and legal procedures of the trials, as well as the role of John Pope, and has served as an important source here. David Glazier, "Kangaroo Court or Competent Tribunal? Judging the 21st Century Military Commission," in the *Virginia Law Review*, includes a well-documented look at the earliest uses of military commissions in American wars.

164  "long conversation with one of the officers": SW, *Six Weeks in the Sioux Tepees*, in Derounian-Stodola, ed., *Women's Indian Captivity Narratives*, 300.

164  "thought it very strange": Ibid., 301.

165  "pale and frightened": Ibid.

165  "the white men were not doing as they promised": Ibid.

165  "No . . . I am not a coward": Ibid.

165  "seven of the black devils": Ibid.

165  "had become so infatuated": HHS to Sarah Sibley, September 27, 1862, Sibley Papers, MHS Manuscript Collections, P6202, Box 1.

165  "threatens that if *her* Indian": HHS to Sarah Sibley, September 28, 1862, Sibley Papers, MHS Manuscript Collections, P6202, Box 1.

165  "If found guilty": HHS to JP, September 28, 1862, OR 1:13, 686–87.

166  "a stretch of my authority": HHS to Charles E. Flandrau, September 28, 1862, OR 1:13, 687–88.

166  "try summarily the mulatto": Heard, *History of the Sioux War*, 251.

167  "that the innocent": Riggs, *Mary and I*, 207.

168 "In this that the said" and following: We-chank-wash-to-don-pee trial, MHS Manuscript Collections, P1423.

170 "The horrible massacres of women and children": JP to HHS, September 28, 1862, *OR* 1:13, 685–86.

171 "Colonel Henry H. Sibley is made a brigadier-general": HWH to JP, September 29, 1862, *OR* 1:13, 688.

171 "There is my father!": SW, *Six Weeks in the Sioux Tepees,* in Derounian-Stodola, ed., *Women's Indian Captivity Narratives,* 307–8.

172 "You have already made much trouble": Anderson, *Little Crow,* 168.

174 "incarnate demon": Diedrich, *Little Crow and the Dakota War,* 237.

CHAPTER THIRTEEN

Edwin G. Burrows and Mike Wallace, *Gotham,* and Ernest A. McKay, *The Civil War and New York City,* paint a vivid picture of Civil War–era New York.

175 "most unhappy contest": *New York Times,* October 2, 1862.

175 "subdued by pride": Ibid.

176 "meeting of the colored people of Brooklyn": *New York Times,* October 3, 1862.

176 "prevailing sentiment was against": Ibid.

177 "the Secretary called for delegates": Ibid.

177 "petitioning the Almighty": *New York Times,* October 4, 1862.

177 "the South has ignored the Prayer-Book": Ibid.

177 "irritating action": *New York Times,* October 5, 1862.

177 "his entire theme": *New York Times,* October 6, 1862.

177 "First, the American Indian": Ibid.

178 "the actual starving to death": Ibid.

178 "a valuable, eloquent and powerful discourse": Ibid.

178 "If our Government should send": *New York Times,* October 2, 1862.

178 "Are *the Indians* of the West part and parcel": Ibid.

179 "in advance two of their principal men": HHS to unnamed, October 3, 1862, *OR* 1:13, 709.

179 "The greater part of the men": HHS to JP, October 5, 1862, *OR* 1:13, 711–12.

179 "I have given them no assurances": Ibid.

180 "all the men necessary": JP to HHS, September 17, 1862, *OR* 1:13, 648–49.

180 "destroying crops and everything else": Ibid.

180 "embarrass the command": HHS to JP, September 19, 1862, *OR* 1:13, 650–51.

181 "I would not have been displeased": Ibid., *OR* 1:13, 651–52.

182 "I have received no dispatches": NARA RG 393, Part 1, Dept. of NW, Headquarters, Entry 3436.

182 "I think still that the Indians": Ibid.

182 "disarm, and send down to Fort Snelling": Ibid.

182 "The whole of the Indians": JP to HHS, October 10, 1862, Letters Received by the Office of the Adjutant General, Manuscript Collections, MHS, M166.

183 "I would tell the men to step inside": Anderson and Woolworth, eds., *Through Dakota Eyes*, 226.

183 "the poor women's wailings": HHS to Sarah Sibley, October 17, 1862, Sibley Papers, MHS Manuscript Collections, P6202, Box 1.

184 "the orders were very strict": Connolly, *A Thrilling Narrative*, 144.

184 "At a given signal": *Minneapolis Tribune*, July 15, 1923.

184 "It was promised that the Indians": Ibid.

CHAPTER FOURTEEN

*Trails of Tears* (Mary H. Bakeman and Antona M. Richardson, eds.) is a welcome collection of studies that shed new light on the experiences of the condemned men and the Dakota families on their enforced eastward journeys from Camp Release.

185 "I am sure you know that what I undertake": JP to Edwin P. Stanton, September 22, 1862, *OR* 1:13, 658.

185 "make some order defining the extent": Edwin P. Stanton to HWH, September 23, 1862, *OR* 1:13, 658–59.

186 "You do not seem to be aware": JP to HWH, September 23, 1862, *OR* 1:13, 663–64.

186 "yet to be found and dealt with": HHS to JP, October 17, 1862, *OR* 1:13, 744–46.

186 "You have no idea of the wide": JP to HWH, September 23, 1862, *OR* 1:13, 663–64.

187 "The Sioux war may be considered at an end": JP to HWH, October 9, 1862, *OR* 1:13, 722.

187 "The Sioux war is at an end": JP to HWH, October 10, 1862, *OR* 1:13, 724.

188 "no fear of the results": JP to HWH, October 14, 1862, *OR* 1:13, 737.

188 "There is strong testimony": JP to HWH, October 13, 1862, *OR* 1:13, 733.

188 "any sentence of death": *Barnes Federal Code*, 449.

189 "the judgment of every court-martial": Ibid., 558.

189 "I was disgusted with the tone and opinions": Welles, *Diary*, 171.

189 "to say that he desires you to employ": Edwin P. Stanton to JP, October 14, 1862, *OR* 1:13, 737.

189 "the President directs that no executions": JP to HHS, NARA RG 94, Adj. Gen., M619, Roll 483.

190 "To hate rebellion, so uncaused": *New York Times*, October 18, 1862.

190 "knocked down": *St. Cloud Democrat*, October 23, 1862.

192 "fired in the battles": Heard, *History of the Sioux War*, 269.

193 "I am for shooting down": Osman, "Sibley's Army in November 1862," 22.

193 "400 have been tried in less time": Monjeau-Marz, *The Dakota Indian Internment*, 28–29.

194 "I find the greatest difficulty": HHS to Sarah Sibley, October 22, 1862, Sibley Papers, MHS Manuscript Collections, P6202, Box 1.

195 "I would risk my life": *St. Paul Press,* November 8, 1862.

195 "When this outrage broke out": *St. Paul Pioneer,* November 7, 1862.

196 "As I am told you intend": Charles Roos to HHS, Sibley Papers, MHS Manuscript Collections, P6202, Box 3.

196 "all conceivable weapons": *Minneapolis Tribune,* August 5, 1923.

197 "the first I knew": Amos Watson, undated, Dakota Conflict Collection, MHS Manuscript Collections, M582, reel 3.

197 "the presence of the women and children": HHS to JP, November 11, 1862, Ramsey Papers, MHS Manuscript Collections, Box 3.

197 "utmost endeavor to prevent the attack": Frederick Brandt to HHS, Ramsey Papers, MHS Manuscript Collections, Box 3.

197 "Your dispatch giving the names": AL to JP, November 10, 1862, *CW* 5:493.

198 "anxious to not act with so much clemency": AL to Senate, December 11, 1862, *CW* 5:551.

198 "I hope the execution of every Sioux Indian": Alexander Ramsey to AL, November 10, 1862, *OR* 1:13, 787.

199 "We found the streets crowded": Anderson and Woolworth, eds., *Through Dakota Eyes,* 227.

199 "quietly laid away": Ibid.

200 "There was something about it so weird": Thomas Rice Stewart, *Memoirs, 1905, 1929,* MHS Manuscript Collections, P1519.

CHAPTER FIFTEEN

201 "a paper latch-key": Helen Nicolay, *Lincoln's Secretary,* 88.

202 "The Indian tribes upon our frontiers": AL, Annual Message to Congress, *CW* 5:518.

202 "In the month of August last": Ibid., 525.

203 "In giving freedom to the slave": Ibid., 537.

203 "The causes of the Indian hostilities": Message from the President of the United States, *House Executive Documents,* 37th Congress, 3rd Session, No. 1.

204 "the efforts of secession agents": Ibid.

204 "It is . . . almost invariably true": Ibid.

204 "Three hundred Indians have been sentenced to death": AL to Holt, December 1, 1862, *CW* 5:537–38.

205 "I do not understand the precise form": Joseph Holt to AL, December 1, 1862, ALPLC online.

207 "I desire to represent to you": JP to AL, November 11, 1862, *OR* 1:13, 788.

207 "I will do the best I can": Ibid.

207 "In the name of a thousand murdered victims": *Stillwater Messenger,* November 12, 1862.

208 "bustling little woman": *Minnesota History,* 22:2, 176.

208 "The Indian and the Slaveholder": Hoffert, *Jane Grey Swisshelm,* 154.

# Notes

209 "who attempts to screen these monsters": *St. Cloud Democrat,* October 2, 1862.

209 "a Sioux has just as much right to life": *St. Cloud Democrat,* October 16, 1862.

209 "It rests upon the people": *St. Cloud Democrat,* November 13, 1862.

209 "We leave them really without any government": HBW to Alexander Ramsey, November 8, 1862, MHS Manuscript Collections, Whipple Papers, Box 40.

210 "We cannot hang men by hundreds": HBW to Henry Rice, November 12, 1862, MHS Manuscript Collections, Whipple Papers, Box 40.

210 "When I know that they opened the throbbing womb": Henry Rice to HBW, November 19, 1862, MHS Manuscript Collections, Whipple Papers, Box 3.

211 "Who is guilty of the causes": *Faribault Central Republican,* December 3, 1862.

211 "a sacred trust": Ibid.

211 "While we execute justice": Ibid.

212 "With all my heart I thank you": HBW to AL, December 4, 1862, MHS Manuscript Collections, Whipple Papers, Box 40.

212 "This Indian system is a sink of inequity": HBW to HWH, December 4, 1862, MHS Manuscript Collections, Whipple Papers, Box 40.

213 "an extensive secret organization": Stephen Miller to HHS, November 16, 1862, NARA RG 393, Letters Received, Part 3, Entry 346.

213 "a matter of deep regret" and "was very busy exciting the citizens": Ibid.

213 "a firm and almost universal determination": Stephen Miller to HHS, November 22, 1862, NARA RG 393, Letters Received, Part 3, Entry 346.

214 "Who comes there?": *St. Peter Herald,* April 13, 1906.

215 "Much as I should deplore": HHS to Alexander Ramsey, December 6, 1862, NARA, RG 393, Letters and Telegrams Sent, Part 3, Entry 343.

215 "Death, indeed, is the least atonement": *St. Paul Press* and *St. Paul Pioneer,* December 7, 1862.

216 "cavalry battalion in front": *St. Paul Union,* December 10, 1862.

216 "if he resists unless forbidden": Stephen Miller to Rollin Olin, December 6, 1862, NARA RG 393, Unentered Letter, Part 1, Entry 3449.

216 "best citizens of this town": Stephen Miller to Rollin Olin, December 5, NARA RG 393, Letters Received, Part 3, Entry 346.

216 "Hemp on the throat of them": *Mankato Record,* December 13, 1862.

217 "The Members of Congress from Minnesota": Welles, *Diary,* December 4, 1862.

218 "Resolved, That the President be requested" and following: *Congressional Globe,* December 5, 1862, 13.

219 "Ordered that of the Indians and Half-breeds": AL to HHS, December 6, 1862, MHS Manuscript Collections, Neill and Family Papers, Reserve 92, Box 1.

221 "If there is a worse place than hell": Burlingame, *Abraham Lincoln: A Life,* 2:446.

221 "What has God put me in this place for?" Ibid.

221 "awful arithmetic": Stoddard, *Inside the White House,* 101.

221 "No man on Earth": Rice, *Reminiscences,* 450.

222 "If a man had more than one life": Lamon, *Recollections,* 87.

CHAPTER SIXTEEN

225 "serve well for future occasions": *St. Paul Press,* December 28, 1862.

226 "had the President been less squeamish": Ibid.

226 "in a place where it would be of service": *Mankato Independent,* January 2, 1863.

226 "the slash of a sword": Ibid.

227 "the sale, tender, gift or use": *Mankato Record,* December 26, 1862.

228 "Tell these thirty-nine condemned men" : *St. Paul Press,* December 28, 1862.

229 "very coolly": Ibid.

229 "privileged to designate" and following: *Mankato Record,* December 26, 1862.

232 "The doomed men wished it to be known": *St. Paul Press,* December 28, 1862.

232 "All at once": Ibid.

233 "Chains and cords": Ibid.

233 "crowding and jostling each other": Ibid.

234 "convicted of shooting": *Mankato Record,* December 26, 1862.

234 "felt it was all right with him": SW, *Six Weeks in the Sioux Tepees,* in Derounian-Stodola, ed., *Women's Indian Captivity Narratives,* 308.

235 "go East, try to counteract" : Swisshelm, *Half a Century,* 233–34.

235 "Eastern people . . . endorsed the massacre": Ibid.

237 "I could not afford": Alexander Ramsey, Diary, November 23, 1864, MHS Manuscript Collections, Ramsey Papers, Roll 39.

238 "everything went off quietly": HHS to AL, December 27, 1862, ALPLC online.

238 "our Indian matters look well": Morton S. Wilkinson to Alexander Ramsey, December 26, 1862, MHS Manuscript Collections, Ramsey Papers, Roll 13.

239 "I was perfectly charmed": Clapesattle, *The Doctors Mayo,* 38.

241 "sure that all who were executed": John F. Meagher to MHS, December 26, 1887, MHS Manuscript Collections, M582, Reel 1.

241 "Among those resurrected was Chaska Don": Ibid.


CHAPTER SEVENTEEN

Corinne L. Monjeau-Marz, *The Dakota Indian Internment at Fort Snelling, 1862–1864,* collects a range of essential source material related to the camp at Fort Snelling.

243 "a beautiful sheet of water": Chaffin, *Pathfinder,* 72.

245 "now on the Missouri River": James S. Williams, W. A. Burleigh, and W. Jayne to AL, December 24, 1862, *OR* 1:22, 867.

246 "with streets, alleys, and public square": Bishop, *Dakota War Whoop,* 243.

246 "a low flat place": *Report of the American Board of Commissioners for Foreign Missions.*

246 "We had no land, no homes": Anderson and Woolworth, eds., *Through Dakota Eyes,* 234.

# Notes

247 "Papooses are running about": Cooke, *A Badger Boy*, 24.

247 "lifting up the little doors and looking in": Monjeau-Marz, *The Dakota Indian Internment*, 43.

247 "Nearly all of them were alike": Cooke, *A Badger Boy*, 25.

249 "They would like to have some place": John P. Williamson to Thomas S. Williamson, November 17, 1862, in Monjeau-Marz, *The Dakota Indian Internment*, 38.

249 "an Indian squaw": *St. Paul Pioneer*, November 19, 1862.

249 "The truth of the matter": *St. Paul Union*, November 22, 1862.

249 "Since the Dakota camp has been placed": *St. Paul Press*, December 11, 1862.

250 "the crying hardly ever stops": Stephen R. Riggs to Selah B. Treat, 1863, in Monjeau-Marz, *The Dakota Indian Internment*, 60.

250 "The ever-present query was": John P. Williamson, quoted in Riggs, *Mary and I*, 217.

251 "were subdued, and felt very sore": HBW, *Lights and Shadows*, 133.

251 "some white roughs from St. Paul": Ibid.

251 "Those who live much with the Indians": Ibid.

251 "sure that our friendship": HBW to HHS, March 7, 1863, MHS Manuscript Collections, Whipple Papers, Box 40.

252 "There were no such flags": HHS to HBW, March 11, 1863, MHS Manuscript Collections, Whipple Papers, Box 3.

252 "Then came along Mr. Gleason and Mrs. Wakefield": *Mankato Record*, December 26, 1862.

252 "I understand that Chaska's mother": SW to Stephen R. Riggs, March 22, 1863, in Derounian-Stodola, "Many Persons Say I Am a 'Mono Maniac,'" 18.

253 "I would be pleased to learn": Ibid.

253 "I will introduce myself" and following: SW to AL, March 23, 1863, ALPLC online.

CHAPTER EIGHTEEN

257 "The two races cannot live together": *Daily Morning Chronicle*, January 2, 1863.

258 "the information in his possession": *Congressional Globe*, December 5, 1862, 13.

258 "radical moving cause" and "That there was any *direct* interference": Thomas Galbraith in *House Executive Documents*, 37th Congress, 3rd Session, no. 68, 29.

259 "tampering with the Indians": Thomas Galbraith in *House Executive Documents*, 38th Congress, 1st Session, no. 58, 8.

259 "As to the real cause" and "unscrupulous and designing persons": John P. Usher in *House Executive Documents*, 37th Congress, 3rd Session, no. 68, 2.

259 "the most ample arrangements": Ibid.

259 "general and cordial co-operation with him": Ibid.

260 "From all the inquiry and examination": Ibid.

260 "I cannot but regret": Ibid.

262 "the hard and cruel lines" and following: *Daily Morning Chronicle*, March 28, 1863.


### CHAPTER NINETEEN

267 "a black coat with velvet collar": *St. Paul Press*, June 23, 1863.

267 "heavy price on his head . . . thin and cadaverous": *St. Paul Pioneer*, June 1863.

267 "the folds of the red flag": Hargrave, *Red River*, 291.

268 "After we have fought for you": Meyer, *History of the Santee Sioux*, 30.

268 "endeavor to bring their grievances": Alexander Grant Dallas to HHS, June 3, 1863, *Annual Reports of the Department of the Interior*, 456.

269 "look for him": *St. Paul Press*, June 25, 1862.

269 "I have determined if I can procure": SW to Stephen R. Riggs, April 9, 1863, in Derounian-Stodola, "Many Persons Say I Am a 'Mono Maniac,'" 19–20.

270 "I could willingly devote": Ibid.

270 "Did Jesus Christ come into this world" and following: SW to Stephen R. Riggs, April 25, 1863, in Derounian-Stodola, "Many Persons Say I Am a 'Mono Maniac,'" 20–22.

273 "As the boat moved off": *Davenport Democrat*, April 27, 1863.

273 "This assurance calmed them somewhat": Ibid.

274 "prayer and singing": Bishop, *Dakota War Whoop*, 276.

275 "The *Northerner* brought up a cargo": *St. Paul Pioneer*, May 6, 1863.

275 "Indians were crowded like slaves": Meyer, *History of the Santee Sioux*, 146.

276 "It has good soil": Clark W. Thompson to William P. Dole, June 1, 1863, *Annual Reports of the Secretary of the Interior*, 424–25.

276 "it is a horrible region": Heard, *History of the Sioux War*, 295.


### CHAPTER TWENTY

277 "success and glory are in the advance": JP, July 14, 1862, *OR* 1:12, 473–74.

279 "I am the son of Little Crow": *St. Paul Pioneer*, August 13, 1863.

281 "participating in the murders and massacres committed": Wowinape trial transcript, MHS Manuscript Collections, P1423.

282 "subject . . . to the revision of the President": Ibid.

282 "a precisely similar condition": HHS to Holt, December 7, 1863, Sioux War Trials, MHS Manuscript Collections, P1423.

283 "the perfect massacre": Carley, *The Dakota War*, 91.

284 "The Indians here have no fight": Utley, *The Lance and the Shield*, 59.

# Notes

Kathryn Zabelle Derounian-Stodola, *The War in Words,* provides unique and invaluable context for and analysis of a wide range of captivity narratives.

287 "Ladies and gentlemen" and following: Bell, "The Sioux War Panorama."

290 "hearts appalled by the gleam": Helen Nicolay, *Lincoln's Secretary Goes West,* 45.

292 "The massacre was merely an expression and demonstration": Tarble, "The Story of My Capture," 12.

292 "a liberal discount": Namias, *White Captives,* 238.

292 "I wish to say a few words in preface": SW, *Six Weeks in the Sioux Tepees,* in Derounian-Stodola, ed., *Women's Indian Captivity Narratives,* 241.

293 "painted and decorated and dressed in full Indian costume": Schwandt, "The Story of Mary Schwandt," 473.

294 "A few days since": SW, *Six Weeks in the Sioux Tepees,* in Derounian-Stodola, ed., *Women's Indian Captivity Narratives,* 313.

295 "blood poisoning": *St. Paul Pioneer Press,* May 29, 1899.

296 "gets the cuff from both sides": Hutton, *Phil Sheridan and His Army,* 195.

296 "one of the severest personal conflicts": HBW, *Lights and Shadows,* 145.

296 "What does Bishop Whipple want?": Ibid., 144.

297 "I came here as an honest man": Ibid.

297 "simply as a Christian": Ibid., 235.

297 "No words can describe": Ibid., 238–39.

297 "his singular uprightness of character": Ibid., 310.

298 "Nations, like individuals": Jackson, *A Century of Dishonor,* v.

301 "I wore it until it was as you see": John F. Meagher to MHS, December 26, 1887, MHS Manuscript Collections, M582, Reel 1.

Kerry A. Trask, *Black Hawk,* devotes several chapters to the Black Hawk War and includes memorable descriptions of the Battle of Bad Axe and the pursuit of fleeing Sac and Fox by a detachment of young Dakota warriors.

304 "I was out of work": Herndon and Weik, *Herndon's Lincoln,* 73.

304 "It was a horrid sight": John A. Wakefield, *History of the Black Hawk War,* 133.

307 "there came a few Indians": Wilson and Davis, eds., *Herndon's Informants,* 220.

307 "young Mord Lincoln swore": Ibid., 96.

308 "a nation which sowed robbery": HBW, *Lights and Shadows,* 105.

# SELECTED BIBLIOGRAPHY

House Executive Documents, 23rd Congress, 1st Session, No. 1, Message of the President of the United States to the Two Houses of Congress.

House Executive Documents, 37th Congress, 3rd Session, No. 1, Message of the President of the United States to the Two Houses of Congress, including Report of the Secretary of the Interior and Report of the Commissioner of Indian Affairs.

House Executive Documents, 37th Congress, 3rd Session, No. 68, Message from the President of the United States in Answer to Resolution of the House of the 18th December Last, Respecting the Cause of the Recent Outbreaks of the Indian Tribes in the Northwest.

House Executive Documents, 38th Congress, 1st Session, No. 1, Message of the President of the United States, and Accompanying Documents, to the Two Houses of Congress, including Report of the Secretary of the Interior and Report of the Commissioner of Indian Affairs.

House Executive Documents, 38th Congress, 1st Session, No. 58, Letter from the Secretary of the Interior, Transmitting Report of Commissioners on Claims Presented for Injuries and Depredations by the Sioux Indians, in Minnesota, in 1862.

Senate Executive Documents, 31st Congress, 1st Session, No. 42, Report of the Secretary of War, Communicating the Report of an Exploration of the Territory of Minnesota, by Brevet Captain Pope.


Allen, Anne Beiser. *And the Wilderness Shall Blossom: Henry Benjamin Whipple, Churchman, Educator, Advocate for the Indians.* Afton, Minn.: Afton Historical Society Press, 2008.

Anderson, Gary Clayton. *Kinsmen of Another Kind: Dakota-White Relations in the Upper Mississippi Valley, 1650–1862.* St. Paul: Minnesota Historical Society Press, 1997.

———. *Little Crow: Spokesman for the Sioux.* St. Paul: Minnesota Historical Society Press, 1986.

# Selected Bibliography

Anderson, Gary Clayton, and Alan R. Woolworth, eds. *Through Dakota Eyes: Narrative Accounts of the Minnesota Indian War of 1862*. St. Paul: Minnesota Historical Society Press, 1988.

Aron, Stephen. *How the West Was Lost: The Transformation of Kentucky from Daniel Boone to Henry Clay*. Baltimore: Johns Hopkins University Press, 1996.

Atkins, Annette. *Creating Minnesota: A History from the Inside Out*. St. Paul: Minnesota Historical Society Press, 2007.

Bachman, Walt. "Colonel Miller's War." In *Trails of Tears: Minnesota's Dakota Indian Exile Begins*, ed. Mary Hawker Bakeman and Antona M. Richardson. Roseville, Minn.: Prairie Echoes Press (Park Genealogical Books), 2008.

Bakeman, Mary H., and Alan R. Woolworth. "The Family Caravan." In *Trails of Tears: Minnesota's Dakota Indian Exile Begins*, ed. Mary Hawker Bakeman and Antona M. Richardson. Roseville, Minn.: Prairie Echoes Press (Park Genealogical Books), 2008.

Bakeman, Mary Hawker, and Antona M. Richardson, eds. *Trails of Tears: Minnesota's Dakota Indian Exile Begins*. Roseville, Minn.: Prairie Echoes Press (Park Genealogical Books), 2008.

Barnes, Uriah, Henry Craig Jones, and Ira E. Robinson, eds. *Barnes' Federal Code: Containing All Federal Statutes of General and Public Nature Now in Force*. Charleston, W.Va.: Virginia Law Book Company, 1919.

Bell, John. "The Sioux War Panorama and American Mythic History." *Theatre Journal* 48, no. 3 (October 1996): 279–99.

Berghold, Alexander. *The Indians' Revenge, or Days of Horror: Some Appalling Events in the History of the Sioux*. Edited by Don Heinrich Tolzmann. Roseville, Minn.: Edinborough Press, 2007.

Berkhofer, Jr., Robert F. *The White Man's Indian: Images of the American Indian from Columbus to the Present*. New York: Vintage Books, 1978.

Bond, J. W. *Minnesota and Its Resources*. New York: Redfield, 1853.

Boutin, Loren Dean. *Cut Nose Who Stands on a Cloud*. St. Cloud, Minn.: North Star Press of St. Cloud, 2006.

Brake, Andrew S. *Man in the Middle: The Reform and Influence of Henry Benjamin Whipple, the First Episcopal Bishop of Minnesota*. Lanham, Md.: University Press of America, 2005.

Brands, H. W. *Andrew Jackson: His Life and Times*. New York: Anchor Books, 2003.

Bray, Edmund C. "Surveying the Seasons on the Minnesota Prairies." *Minnesota History* 48, no. 2 (Summer 1982): 72–82.

Brown, Samuel J. "In Captivity: The Experience, Privations and Dangers of Sam'l J. Brown, and Others, While Prisoners of the Hostile Sioux, during the Massacre and War of 1862." In *The Garland Library of Narratives of North American Indian Captivities*, ed. Wilcomb E. Washburn. Vol. 76. New York: Garland Publishing Co., 1900.

Brunson, A. "Missionary Intelligence." *Christian Advocate and Journal*, July 21, 1837.

Bryant, Charles S., and Abel B. Murch. *A History of the Great Massacre by the Sioux Indians, in Minnesota, Including the Personal Narratives of Many Who Escaped*. Cincinnati: Rickey & Carroll, Publishers, 1864.

Buck, S. "Radiograms of Minnesota History: Lincoln and Minnesota." *Minnesota History* 6, no. 4 (December 1925): 355–61.

Burlingame, Michael. *Abraham Lincoln: A Life.* 2 vols. Baltimore: Johns Hopkins University Press, 2008.

Burrows, Edwin G., and Mike Wallace. *Gotham: A History of New York City to 1898.* New York: Oxford University Press, 1999.

Butler, Diana Hochstedt. *Standing Against the Whirlwind: Evangelical Episcopalians in Nineteenth-Century America.* New York: Oxford University Press, 1995.

Calloway, Colin G. *The American Revolution in Indian Country: Crisis and Diversity in Native American Communities.* Cambridge Studies in North American Indian History. Cambridge: Cambridge University Press, 1995.

———. *The Shawnees and the War for America.* Penguin Library of American Indian History. New York: Viking, 2007.

Carley, Kenneth. *The Dakota War of 1862: Minnesota's Other Civil War.* 2nd ed. St. Paul: Minnesota Historical Society Press, 1976.

———. "The Second Minnesota in the West." *Minnesota History* 38, no. 6 (June 1963): 258–73.

———. "The Sioux Campaign of 1862: Sibley's Letters to His Wife." *Minnesota History* 38, no. 3 (September 1962): 99–114.

Carman, Ezra A. *The Maryland Campaign of September 1862: Ezra A. Carman's Definitive Study of the Union and Confederate Armies at Antietam.* Edited by Joseph Pierro. New York: Routledge, 2008.

Caruso, John Anthony. *The Appalachian Frontier: America's First Surge Westward.* Appalachian Echoes. Knoxville: University of Tennessee Press, 2003.

Castiglia, Christopher. *Bound and Determined: Captivity, Culture-Crossing, and White Womanhood from Mary Rowlandson to Patty Hearst.* Chicago: University of Chicago Press, 1996.

"The Causes of the Minnesota Massacre." *Continental Monthly* 6, no. 2 (August 1864): 174–89.

Chaffin, Tom. *Pathfinder: John Charles Frémont and the Course of American Empire.* New York: Hill and Wang, 2002.

*Cherokee Nation v. State of Georgia.* 30 U.S. 1 (1831).

Chomsky, Carol. "The United States–Dakota War Trials: A Study in Military Injustice." *Stanford Law Review* 43, no. 1 (November 1990): 13–98.

Clapesattle, Helen. *The Doctors Mayo.* Minneapolis: University of Minnesota Press, 1941.

Confer, Clarissa W. *The Cherokee Nation in the Civil War.* Norman: University of Oklahoma Press, 2007.

Connolly, A. P. *A Thrilling Narrative of the Minnesota Massacre and the Sioux War of 1862–1863.* Chicago: A. P. Connolly, 1896.

Cooke, Chauncey H. *A Badger Boy in Blue: The Civil War Letters of Chauncey H. Cooke.* Detroit: Wayne State University Press, 2007.

Cook-Lynn, Elizabeth. "The Lewis and Clark Story, the Captive Narrative, and the Pitfalls of Indian History." *Wicazo Sa Review* 19, no. 1 (Spring 2004): 21–33.

# Selected Bibliography

Cox, Hank H. *Lincoln and the Sioux Uprising of 1862.* Nashville: Cumberland House, 2005.

Cozzens, Peter. *General John Pope: A Life for the Nation.* Urbana: University of Illinois Press, 2000.

Dahlgren, Madeleine Vinton. *Memoir of John A. Dahlgren, Rear-Admiral United States Navy.* Boston: J. R. Osgood, 1882.

Dahlin, Curtis A. "Outside the Barricades: The August 23, 1862, Battle for New Ulm." *Minnesota's Heritage,* no. 2 (July 2010): 24–39.

Davis, Jane S. "Two Sioux War Orders: A Mystery Unraveled." *Minnesota History* 41, no. 3 (Fall 1968): 117–25.

Deloria, Ella. *Speaking of Indians.* Lincoln: University of Nebraska Press, 1998.

Derounian-Stodola, Kathryn Zabelle. " 'Many Persons Say I Am a "Mono Maniac' ": Three Letters from Dakota Conflict Captive Sarah F. Wakefield to Missionary Stephen R. Riggs." *Prospects: An Annual of American Cultural Studies* 29 (2005): 1–24.

———. *The War in Words: Reading the Dakota Conflict through the Captivity Literature.* Lincoln: University of Nebraska Press, 2009.

Derounian-Stodola, Kathryn Zabelle, ed. *Women's Indian Captivity Narratives.* New York: Penguin Books, 1998.

Diedrich, Mark. "Chief Hole-in-the-Day and the 1862 Chippewa Disturbance: A Reappraisal." *Minnesota History* 50, no. 6 (Spring 1987): 193–203.

———. *Little Crow and the Dakota War.* Rochester, Minn.: Coyote Books, 2006.

Donald, David Herbert. *Lincoln.* New York: Simon & Schuster, 1995.

El-Hai, Jack. "The Knights of Blue Earth County." *Minnesota Monthly,* September 2006.

Elias, Peter Douglas. *The Dakota of the Canadian Northwest: Lessons for Survival.* Manitoba Studies in Native History. Winnipeg: University of Manitoba Press, 1988.

Ellis, Richard N. *General Pope and U.S. Indian Policy.* Albuquerque: University of New Mexico Press, 1970.

———. "The Humanitarian Generals." *Western Historical Quarterly* 3, no. 2 (April 1972): 169–78.

———. "Political Pressures and Army Policies on the Northern Plains, 1862–1865." *Minnesota History* 42, no. 2 (Summer 1970): 42–53.

Ernst, Kathleen A. *Too Afraid to Cry: Maryland Civilians in the Antietam Campaign.* Mechanicsburg, Pa.: Stackpole Books, 2007.

*Executive Documents of the State of Minnesota for the Year 1862.* St. Paul, Minn.: Wm. R. Marshall, State Printer, 1863.

Faust, Drew Gilpin. *This Republic of Suffering: Death and the American Civil War.* Vintage Civil War Library. New York: Vintage Books, 2008.

Fitzharris, Joseph C. "Field Officer Courts and U.S. Civil War Military Justice." *Journal of Military History* 68, no. 1 (January 2004): 47–72.

Folwell, William Watts. *A History of Minnesota.* 4 vols. 2nd ed. St. Paul: Minnesota Historical Society Press, 1961.

Foote, Shelby. *The Civil War: A Narrative.* 3 vols. New York: Random House, 1958.

Furgurson, Ernest. *Freedom Rising: Washington in the Civil War*. New York: Alfred A. Knopf, 2004.

Furness, Marion Ramsey. "Childhood Recollections of Old St. Paul." *Minnesota History* 29, no. 2 (June 1948): 114–29.

Gibson, Arrell Morgan. "Native Americans and the Civil War." *American Indian Quarterly* 9, no. 4 (Autumn 1985): 385–410.

Gilman, Rhoda R. *Henry Hastings Sibley: Divided Heart*. St. Paul: Minnesota Historical Society Press, 2004.

———. "Last Days of the Upper Mississippi Fur Trade." *Minnesota History* 42, no. 4 (Winter 1970): 122–40.

Gilman, Rhoda R., Carolyn Gilman, and Deborah M. Stultz. *The Red River Trails, 1820–1870: Oxcart Routes Between St. Paul and the Selkirk Settlement*. St. Paul: Minnesota Historical Society Press, 1979.

Glazier, David. "Kangaroo Court or Competent Tribunal?: Judging the 21st Century Military Commission." *Virginia Law Review* 89, no. 8 (December 2003): 2005–93.

Glewwe, Lois A. "The Journey of the Prisoners." In *Trails of Tears: Minnesota's Dakota Indian Exile Begins*, ed. Mary Hawker Bakeman and Antona M. Richardson. Roseville, Minn.: Prairie Echoes Press (Park Genealogical Books), 2008.

Gluek, Jr., Alvin C. "The Sioux Uprising: A Problem in International Relations." *Minnesota History* 34, no. 8 (Winter 1955): 317–24.

Goodwin, Doris Kearns. *Team of Rivals: The Political Genius of Abraham Lincoln*. New York: Simon & Schuster, 2005.

Gordon, Hanford Lennox. *The Feast of the Virgins and Other Poems*. Chicago: Laird & Lee, Publishers, 1891.

Guelzo, Allen C. *Lincoln's Emancipation Proclamation: The End of Slavery in America*. New York: Simon & Schuster, 2004.

Hargrave, Joseph James. *Red River*. Montreal: Joseph James Hargrave, 1871.

Harrison, Lowell H., and James C. Klotter. *A New History of Kentucky*. Lexington: University Press of Kentucky, 1997.

Hart, John Fraser, and Susy Svatek Ziegler. *Landscapes of Minnesota: A Geography*. St. Paul: Minnesota Historical Society Press, 2008.

Hay, John. *At Lincoln's Side: John Hay's Civil War Correspondence and Selected Writings*. Edited by Michael Burlingame. Carbondale: Southern Illinois University Press, 2000.

———. *Inside Lincoln's White House: The Complete Civil War Diary of John Hay*. Edited by Michael Burlingame and John R. T. Ettlinger. Carbondale: Southern Illinois University Press, 1997.

———. *Lincoln's Journalist: John Hay's Anonymous Writings for the Press, 1860–1864*. Edited by Michael Burlingame. Carbondale: Southern Illinois University Press, 1998.

Heard, Isaac V. D. *History of the Sioux War and Massacres of 1862 and 1863*. New York: Harper & Brothers, Publishers, 1863.

Henig, Gerald S. "A Neglected Cause of the Sioux Uprising." *Minnesota History* 45, no. 3 (Fall 1976): 107–10.

# Selected Bibliography

Herndon, William H., and Jesse W. Weik. *Herndon's Lincoln*. Edited by Douglas L. Wilson and Rodney O. Davis. Knox College Lincoln Studies Center. Champaign: University of Illinois Press, 2006.

Hoffert, Sylvia D. *Jane Grey Swisshelm: An Unconventional Life, 1815–1884*. Chapel Hill: University of North Carolina Press, 2004.

Holzer, Harold. *Lincoln at Cooper Union: The Speech That Made Abraham Lincoln President*. New York: Simon & Schuster, 2004.

Horner, Harlan Hoyt. *Lincoln and Greeley*. [Champaign-Urbana:] University of Illinois Press, 1953.

Huggan, Nancy. "Mrs. Huggan the Minnesota Captive." In *The Garland Library of Narratives of North American Indian Captivities*. Vol. 86. New York: Garland Publishing Co., 1894.

Hutton, Paul Andrew. *Phil Sheridan and His Army*. Lincoln: University of Nebraska Press, 1985.

"The Indian Massacres and War of 1862." *Harper's New Monthly Magazine*, June 1863.

Isch, John. "You Had to Be There: Panoramas of the Dakota War." *Minnesota's Heritage*, no. 3 (January 2011): 4–23.

Jackson, Helen Hunt. *A Century of Dishonor: A Sketch of the United States Government's Dealings with Some of the Indian Tribes*. New York: Harper & Brothers, Publishers, 1881.

Jones, Robert Huhn. *The Civil War in the Northwest: Nebraska, Wisconsin, Iowa, Minnesota, and the Dakotas*. Norman: University of Oklahoma Press, 1960.

Kaplan, Anne R., and Marilyn Ziebarth, eds. *Making Minnesota Territory: 1849–1858*. St. Paul: Minnesota Historical Society Press, 1999.

Karstad, Ruby G. "The 'New York Tribune' and the Minnesota Frontier." *Minnesota History* 17, no. 4 (December 1936): 411–20.

Klement, Frank. "The Abolition Movement in Minnesota." *Minnesota History* 32, no. 1 (March 1951): 15–33.

Klingman, William K. *Abraham Lincoln and the Road to Emancipation, 1861–1865*. New York: Viking, 2001.

Lamon, Ward Hill. *Recollections of Abraham Lincoln, 1847–1865*. Edited by Dorothy Lamon. Chicago: A. C. McClurg and Company, 1895.

Landes, Ruth. "Dakota Warfare." *Southwestern Journal of Anthropology* 15, no. 1 (Spring 1959): 43–52.

Lass, William E. "The Birth of Minnesota." *Minnesota History* 55, no. 6 (Summer 1997): 267–79.

———. "The Eden of the West." *Minnesota History* 56, no. 4 (Winter 1998–99): 202–14.

———. *Minnesota: A History*. 2nd ed. New York: W. W. Norton, 1998.

———. "The Removal from Minnesota of the Sioux and Winnebago Indians." *Minnesota History* 38, no. 8 (December 1963): 353–64.

Leonhart, Rudolph. *Memories of New Ulm: My Experiences During the Indian Uprising in Minnesota, 1862*. Edited by Don Heinrich Tolzmann. Roseville, Minn.: Edinborough Press, 2005.

"Lincoln's Sioux War Order." *Minnesota History* 33, no. 2 (Summer 1952): 77–79.

Mardock, Robert Winston. *The Reformers and the American Indian*. Columbia: University of Missouri Press, 1971.

Marszalek, John F. *Commander of All Lincoln's Armies: A Life of General Henry W. Halleck*. Cambridge, Mass.: Belknap Press of Harvard University Press, 2004.

Marvel, William. *Lincoln's Darkest Year: The War in 1862*. Boston: Houghton Mifflin Company, 2008.

Mayo, Charles W. *Mayo: The Story of My Family and My Career*. Garden City, N.Y.: Doubleday, 1968.

McClure, Nancy. "The Story of Nancy McClure." *Collections of the Minnesota Historical Society* 6 (1894): 438–60.

McConkey, Harriet E. Bishop. *Dakota War Whoop: Indian Massacres and War in Minnesota*. Edited by Dale L. Morgan. Chicago: Lakeside Press, R.R. Donnelley & Sons, 1965.

McKay, Ernest A. *The Civil War and New York City*. Syracuse, N.Y.: Syracuse University Press, 1990.

McPherson, James M. *Crossroads of Freedom: Antietam, the Battle That Changed the Course of the Civil War*. Oxford: Oxford University Press, 2002.

Meyer, Roy W. "The Candian Sioux: Refugees from Minnesota." *Minnesota History* 41, no. 1 (Spring 1968): 13–28.

———. *History of the Santee Sioux*. Lincoln: University of Nebraska Press, 1967.

*Minnesota in the Civil and Indian Wars: 1861–1865*. 2 vols. St. Paul: Minnesota Historical Society Press, 2005.

Moe, Richard. *The Last Full Measure: The Life and Death of the First Minnesota Volunteers*. New York: Avon Books, 1993.

Monjeau-Marz, Corinne L. "Alexander Ramsey's Words of War: Opening the Special Session of the Legislature, September 9, 1862." *Minnesota's Heritage*, no. 1 (January 2010): 62–81.

———. *The Dakota Indian Internment at Fort Snelling, 1862–1864*. St. Paul, Minn.: Prairie Smoke Press, 2005.

Morgan, Robert. *Boone: A Biography*. Chapel Hill, N.C.: Algonquin Books of Chapel Hill, 2007.

Namias, June. *White Captives: Gender and Ethnicity on the American Frontier*. Chapel Hill: University of North Carolina Press, 1993.

Neill, Edward Duffield. *The History of Minnesota: From the Earliest French Explorations to the Present Time*. 1st ed. Philadelphia: J. B. Lippincott & Co., 1858.

Newcombe, Barbara T. "'A Portion of the American People': The Sioux Sign a Treaty in Washington in 1858." *Minnesota History* 45, no. 3 (Fall 1976): 82–96.

Newson, Mary J. "Memories of Fort Snelling in Civil War Days." *Minnesota History* 15, no. 4 (December 1934): 395–404.

Nichols, David A. *Lincoln and the Indians: Civil War Policy & Politics*. Urbana: University of Illinois Press, 2000.

———. "The Other Civil War: Lincoln and the Indians." *Minnesota History* 44, no. 1 (Spring 1974): 2–15.

Nicolay, Helen. *Lincoln's Secretary: A Biography of John G. Nicolay*. Westport, Conn.: Greenwood Press, 1949.

# Selected Bibliography

Nicolay, John G. "Hole-in-the-Day." *Harper's New Monthly Magazine*, January 1863.

———. *Lincoln's Secretary Goes West: Two Reports by John G. Nicolay on Frontier Indian Troubles 1862.* Edited by Theodore C. Blegen. La Crosse, Wisc.: Sumac Press, 1965.

———. "The Sioux War." *The Continental Monthly,* February 1863.

———. *With Lincoln in the White House: Letters, Memoranda, and Other Writings of John G. Nicolay, 1860–1865.* Edited by Michael Burlingame. Carbondale: Southern Illinois University Press, 2000.

Oneroad, Amos E., and Alanson B. Skinner. *Being Dakota: Tales and Traditions of the Sisseton and Wahpeton.* St. Paul: Minnesota Historical Society Press, 2003.

Osman, Stephen E. "Audacity, Skill, and Firepower: The Third Minnesota's Skirmishers at the Battle of Wood Lake." *Minnesota's Heritage,* no. 3 (January 2011): 24–38.

———. "Sibley's Army in November 1862." In *Trails of Tears: Minnesota's Dakota Indian Exile Begins,* ed. Mary Hawker Bakeman and Antona M. Richardson. Roseville, Minn.: Prairie Echoes Press (Park Genealogical Books), 2008.

Ostler, Jeffrey. *The Plains Sioux and U.S. Colonialism from Lewis and Clark to Wounded Knee.* Cambridge Studies in North American Indian History. Cambridge: Cambridge University Press, 2004.

Owens, Robert M. *Mr. Jefferson's Hammer: William Henry Harrison and the Origins of American Indian Policy.* Norman: University of Oklahoma Press, 2007.

Palmer, Jessica Dawn. *The Dakota Peoples: A History of the Dakota, Lakota, and Nakota through 1863.* Jefferson, N.C.: McFarland & Company, 2008.

Peacock, Thomas D., and Donald R. Day. "Nations Within a Nation: The Dakota and Ojibwe of Minnesota." *Daedalus* 129, no. 3 (Summer 2000): 137–59.

Pearce, Roy Harvey. "The Metaphysics of Indian-Hating." *Ethnohistory* 4, no. 1 (Winter 1957): 27–40.

Peterson, William J. "The Early History of Steamboating on the Minnesota River." *Minnesota History* 11, no. 2 (June 1930): 123–44.

Pond, Samuel W. *Dakota Life in the Upper Midwest.* St. Paul: Minnesota Historical Society Press, 1986.

———. *Two Volunteer Missionaries Among the Dakotas: Or the Story of the Labors of Samuel W. and Gideon H. Pond.* Chicago: Congregational Sunday-School and Publishing Society, 1893.

Pope, John. *The Military Memoirs of John Pope.* Edited by Peter Cozzens and Robert I. Girardi. Civil War America. Chapel Hill: University of North Carolina Press, 1998.

Prescott, Philander. *The Recollections of Philander Prescott, Frontiersman of the Old Northwest: 1819–1862.* Edited by Donald Dean Parker. Lincoln: University of Nebraska Press, 1966.

Prucha, Francis Paul. *American Indian Treaties: The History of a Political Anomaly.* Berkeley: University of California Press, 1994.

———. "Fort Ripley: The Post and the Military Reservation." *Minnesota History* 28, no. 3 (September 1947): 205–24.

———. *The Great Father: The United States Government and the American Indians.* 2 vols. Lincoln: University of Nebraska Press, 1984.

———. "Minnesota's Attitude Toward the Southern Case for Secession." *Minnesota History* 24, no. 4 (December 1943): 307–17.

Relf, Frances H. "Removal of the Sioux Indians from Minnesota." *Minnesota History* 2, no. 6 (May 1918): 420–25.

Renville, Gabriel. "A Sioux Narrative of the Outbreak in 1862, and of Sibley's Expedition in 1863." *Collections of the Minnesota Historical Society* 10, part 2 (February 1905): 595–618.

Renville, Mary Butler. *A Thrilling Narrative of Indian Captivity.* Minneapolis: Atlas Company's Book and Job Printing Office, 1863.

———. *A Thrilling Narrative of Indian Captivity: Dispatches from the Dakota War.* Edited by Kathryn Zabelle Derounian-Stodola and Carrie Reber Zeman. Lincoln: University of Nebraska Press, 2012.

*Report of the American Board of Commissioners for Foreign Missions.* Vols. 52–54. Boston: Press of T. R. Marvin & Son, 1861.

Rice, Allen Thorndike, ed. *Reminiscences of Abraham Lincoln by Distinguished Men of His Time.* Edinburgh: William Blackwood and Sons, 1886.

Richardson, Elmo R., and Alan W. Farley. *John Palmer Usher: Lincoln's Secretary of the Interior.* Lawrence: University of Kansas Press, 1960.

Riggs, Stephen R. *Mary and I: Forty Years with the Sioux.* Boston: Congregational Sunday-School and Publishing Society, 1880.

Rogin, Michael Paul. *Fathers and Children: Andrew Jackson and the Subjugation of the American Indian.* New York: Alfred A. Knopf, 1975.

Ross, Alexander Milton. *Recollections and Experiences of an Abolitionist, from 1855 to 1865.* Toronto: Roswell and Hutchinson, 1875.

Russo, Priscilla Ann. "The Time to Speak Is Over: The Onset of the Sioux Uprising." *Minnesota History* 45, no. 3 (Fall 1976): 97–106.

Satterlee, Marion P. *Outbreak and Massacre by the Dakota Indians in Minnesota in 1862.* Edited by Don Heinrich Tolzmann. Westminster, Md.: Heritage Books, 2009.

Schultz, Duane. *Over the Earth I Come: The Great Sioux Uprising of 1862.* New York: St. Martin's Press, 1992.

Schwandt, Mary. "The Story of Mary Schwandt." *Collections of the Minnesota Historical Society* 6 (1894): 460–74.

Sears, Stephen W. *Landscape Turned Red: The Battle of Antietam.* New York: Houghton Mifflin, 2003.

Sibley, Henry Hastings. *Iron Face: The Adventures of Jack Frazer, Frontier Warrior, Scout, and Hunter.* Edited by Theodore C. Blegen and Sarah A. Davidson. Chicago: The Caxton Club, 1950.

———. "Sketches of Indian Warfare." *Spirit of the Times,* March 11, 1848.

Silver, Peter. *Our Savage Neighbors: How Indian War Transformed Early America.* New York: W. W. Norton, 2008.

"Sketches on the Upper Mississippi." *Harper's New Monthly Magazine,* July 1853.

# Selected Bibliography

Smith, Corinne Hosfield. "What a Difference a Year Can Make: Henry David Thoreau and the Grand Pleasure Excursion of 1861." *Minnesota's Heritage*, no. 4 (July 2011): 76–89.

Stephens, Alexander H. "Cornerstone Address, March 21, 1861." In *The Rebellion Record: A Diary of American Events with Documents, Narratives, Illustrative Incidents, Poetry, etc.* Edited by Frank Moore. New York: Putnam, 1862.

Stoddard, William O. *Inside the White House in War Times: Memoirs and Reports of Lincoln's Secretary.* Edited by Michael Burlingame. Lincoln, Nebr.: Bison Books, 2000.

Straker, Robert L. "Thoreau's Journey to Minnesota." *New England Quarterly* 14, no. 3 (September 1941): 549–55.

Swisshelm, Jane Grey. *Half a Century.* 3rd ed. Chicago: Jansen, McClurg & Company, 1880.

Taliaferro, Lawrence. "Auto-Biography of Maj. Lawrence Taliaferro." *Collections of the Minnesota Historical Society* 6 (1894): 189–255.

Tarble, Helen M. "The Story of My Capture and Escape During the Minnesota Indian Massacre, with Historical Notes, Descriptions of Pioneer Life, and Sketches and Incidents of the Great Outbreak of the Sioux or Dakota Indians as I Saw Them." In *The Garland Library of Narratives of North American Indian Captivities.* Vol. 105. New York: Garland Publishing Co., 1904.

Thoreau, Henry David. *The Writings of Henry David Thoreau.* Vol. 11. Boston: Houghton, Mifflin & Co., 1894.

Tinker, George E. *Missionary Conquest: The Gospel and Native American Cultural Genocide.* Minneapolis: Fortress Press, 1993.

Trask, Kerry A. *Black Hawk: The Battle for the Heart of America.* New York: Henry Holt, 2006.

Trenerry, Walter N. "The Shooting of Little Crow: Heroism or Murder?" *Minnesota History* 38, no. 3 (September 1962): 150–53.

Treuer, Anton. *The Assassination of Hole in the Day.* St. Paul, Minn.: Borealis Books, 2011.

———. *Ojibwe in Minnesota.* The People of Minnesota. St. Paul: Minnesota Historical Society Press, 2010.

Treuer, Anton, and David Treuer. "A Day in the Life of Ojibwe." *Minnesota History* 56, no. 4 (Winter 1998–99): 172–74.

Tyler, Alice Felt. "William Pfaender and the Founding of New Ulm." *Minnesota History* 30, no. 1 (March 1949): 24–35.

"The Upper Mississippi." *Harper's New Monthly Magazine*, March 1858.

Utley, Robert M. *The Indian Frontier of the American West, 1864–1890.* Histories of the American Frontier. Albuquerque: University of New Mexico Press, 1984.

———. *The Lance and the Shield: The Life and Times of Sitting Bull.* New York: Henry Holt, 1993.

VanDevelder, Paul. *Savages and Scoundrels: The Untold Story of America's Road to Empire Through Indian Territory.* New Haven, Conn.: Yale University Press, 2009.

Wakefield, John A. *Wakefield's History of the Black Hawk War*. Madison, Wisc.: Roger Hunt, 1976.

Wakefield, Sarah F. *Six Weeks in the Sioux Tepees*. Guilford, Conn.: Globe Pequot Press, 2002.

Wallace, Anthony F. C. *Jefferson and the Indians: The Tragic Fate of the First Americans*. Cambridge, Mass.: Belknap Press of Harvard University Press, 1999.

Ward, William Hayes, ed. *Abraham Lincoln: Tributes from His Associates, Reminiscences of Soldiers, Statesmen, and Citizens*. New York: Thomas Y. Crowell and Company, 1895.

Washington, George. *George Washington: A Collection*. Edited by William B. Allen. Indianapolis, Ind.: Liberty Fund, 1988.

———. *Writings*. Edited by John H. Rhodehamel. Vol. 91. Library of America, 1997.

Welles, Gideon. *Diary of Gideon Welles, Secretary of the Navy Under Lincoln and Johnson*. Edited by Howard K. Beale. Vol. 1. New York: W. W. Norton, 1960.

Wheeler, Tom. *Mr. Lincoln's T-Mails: How Abraham Lincoln Used the Telegraph to Win the Civil War*. New York: HarperCollins, 2008.

Whipple, Henry Benjamin. *Bishop Whipple's Southern Diary: 1843–44*. Edited by Lester B. Shippee. Minneapolis: University of Minnesota Press, 1937.

———. *Lights and Shadows of a Long Episcopate: Being Reminiscences and Recollections of the Right Reverend Henry Benjamin Whipple, Bishop of Minnesota*. New York: Macmillan Company, 1899.

———. "My Life Among the Indians." *North American Review* 150, no. 401 (April 1890): 432–40.

White, Richard. *The Middle Ground: Indians, Empires, and Republics in the Great Lakes Region, 1650–1815*. Cambridge Studies in North American Indian History. Cambridge: Cambridge University Press, 1991.

———. "The Winning of the West: The Expansion of the Western Sioux in the Eighteenth and Nineteenth Centuries." *Journal of American History* 65, no. 2 (September 1978): 319–43.

White, Ronald C., Jr. *Lincoln's Greatest Speech: The Second Inaugural*. New York: Simon & Schuster, 2002.

White, Urania. "Captivity Among the Sioux, August 18 to September 26, 1862." In *The Garland Library of Narratives of North American Indian Captivities*, edited by Wilcomb E. Washburn. Vol. 104. New York: Garland Publishing Co., 1901.

Wills, Jocelyn. *Boosters, Hustlers, and Speculators: Entrepreneurial Culture and the Rise of Minneapolis and St. Paul, 1849–1883*. St. Paul: Minnesota Historical Society Press, 2005.

Wilson, Angela Cavender. "A Day in the Life of Maza Okiye Win." *Minnesota History* 56, no. 4 (Winter 1998–99): 200–201.

Wilson, Douglas L., and Rodney O. Davis, eds. *Herndon's Informants: Letters, Interviews, and Statements About Abraham Lincoln*. Chicago: University of Illinois Press, 1998.

Wilson, James. *The Earth Shall Weep: A History of Native America*. New York: Grove Press, 1998.

# Selected Bibliography

Wilson, Waziyatawin Angela. "Decolonizing the 1862 Death Marches." *American Indian Quarterly* 28, no. 1–2 (Winter–Spring 2004): 185–215.

———. "A Journey of Healing and Awakening." *American Indian Quarterly* 28, no. 1–2 (Winter–Spring 2004): 258–82.

———. "Manip Hena Owas'in Wicunkiksuyapi (We Remember All Those Who Walked)." *American Indian Quarterly* 28, no. 1–2 (Winter–Spring 2004): 151–69.

Wingerd, Mary Lethert. *North Country: The Making of Minnesota*. Minneapolis: University of Minnesota Press, 2010.

Woolworth, Alan R. "Adrian J. Ebell, Photographer and Journalist of the Dakota War of 1862." *Minnesota History* 54, no. 2 (Summer 1994): 87–92.

Wooster, Robert. *The Military & United States Indian Policy: 1865–1903*. Lincoln: University of Nebraska Press, 1988.

Wright, James A. *No More Gallant a Deed: A Civil War Memoir of the First Minnesota Volunteers*. Edited by Steven J. Keillor. St. Paul: Minnesota Historical Society Press, 2001.

Zeman, Carrie R. "Through the Heart of New Ulm." In *Trails of Tears: Minnesota's Dakota Indian Exile Begins*, ed. Mary Hawker Bakeman and Antona M. Richardson. Roseville, Minn.: Prairie Echoes Press (Park Genealogical Books), 2008.

# INDEX

Page numbers in *italic* refer to illustrations.

# Index

# Index

# Index

# Index

# Index

# Index

# Index

Born and raised in the Twin Cities, Scott W. Berg holds a BA in architecture from the University of Minnesota, an MA from Miami University of Ohio, and an MFA in creative writing from George Mason University, where he now teaches nonfiction writing and literature. Since 1999, he has been a regular contributor to *The Washington Post*.